SOPHOCLEAN TRAGEDY

BOWRA, C. M. CECIL MAURICE
1898-1971

SOPHOCLEAN TRAGEDY

SOPHOCLEAN TRAGEDY

BY

C. M. BOWRA

Warden of Wadham College

OXFORD
AT THE CLARENDON PRESS

Oxford University Press, Ely House, London W. 1

GLASGOW   NEW YORK   TORONTO   MELBOURNE   WELLINGTON
CAPE TOWN   SALISBURY   IBADAN   NAIROBI   LUSAKA   ADDIS ABABA
BOMBAY   CALCUTTA   MADRAS   KARACHI   LAHORE   DACCA
KUALA LUMPUR   HONG KONG   TOKYO

FIRST PUBLISHED 1944
REPRINTED LITHOGRAPHICALLY IN GREAT BRITAIN
AT THE UNIVERSITY PRESS, OXFORD
FROM CORRECTED SHEETS OF THE FIRST EDITION
1945, 1947, 1952, 1960, 1964, 1967

PREFACE

IN this book I have attempted to show the importance and place of certain ideas in the seven plays of Sophocles and through them to estimate what the plays really mean and what Sophoclean tragedy really is. I am aware that in such an undertaking I may be criticized from two points of view. Some will think that much of what I say is obvious and not worth saying. To them I can only answer that I am delighted that they should agree with my opinions; for in the study of Sophocles agreement is by no means so common as it ought to be. Others may equally feel that I have laid too much emphasis on Sophocles' ideas and paid too little attention to the poetry and the dramatic interest. If I have done this, I have done it deliberately, because I think that it ought to be done and that the formative thought of Sophocles has too long been neglected, as his style and dramatic effects have not. In trying to elucidate the meaning of ideas in the plays I have naturally been forced to discuss Greek opinions on various matters, and some of this may seem laboured or even irrelevant. I hope that it is not. We too often assume that the Greeks thought just as we do, and it is of primary importance to find out where they would agree or disagree with us, even though we may have to examine trite or commonplace questions. In writing such a book I am greatly indebted to many who have edited Sophoclean plays or have written about them. Every page will show how much I owe to the great editions of R. C. Jebb and A. C. Pearson. In different ways I have learned much from the work of J. T. Sheppard, M. Pohlenz, K. Reinhardt, and T. B. L. Webster. But I have not encumbered my text or notes with controversy or references to contemporary literature, partly because I am already so indebted to the Clarendon Press for printing my book in times like these that I have thought it right to relieve the printers of some labour, partly because I feel that the study of Sophocles has been obscured by controversy and that what is now most needed is a return to his text and a careful study of it. At the suggestion of the Delegates of the Clarendon Press I have kept Greek quotations for the notes and put translations in the text, in the hope that those who have little or no Greek but wish to know about Sophocles may be able to read my book without continual frustration. In the chapters on *King Oedipus* and *Electra* Dr. J. T. Sheppard has generously allowed me to use his published versions, and to him and to the Syndics of the Cambridge University Press I am most grateful for this privilege.

I had intended to dedicate this book to a friend and colleague and to ask him to accept it as a small token of the great gratitude which I feel for all the help and encouragement that he has given me for over twenty years. But the conditions of publication in wartime forbid dedications, and I must content myself with writing the words

TO

J. D. DENNISTON

C. M. B.

CONTENTS

I.	The Nature of the Subject	1
II.	Ajax	16
III.	Antigone	63
IV.	The Women of Trachis	116
V.	King Oedipus	162
VI.	Electra	212
VII.	Philoctetes	261
VIII.	Oedipus at Colonus	307
IX.	Some Conclusions	356
	Index	382

I

THE NATURE OF THE SUBJECT

IN the study of Greek literature we try to recreate for ourselves an experience, to recapture through scholarship something of what it meant to those for whom it was written. For such a task linguistic learning is an indispensable means, but hardly less indispensable is an understanding of the times and circumstances in which the poet worked, of the intellectual background against which he formed his ideas and of which he was, consciously or unconsciously, bound to take notice. This historical approach to classical studies is of comparatively recent birth. It was hardly known to men of the Renaissance or of the Age of Reason. For them antiquity was something to be admired and copied and used, but not, in the scholar's sense, to be understood. It was almost beyond inquiry, a model and an inspiration. It provided a liberating and enlivening force, a contrast beyond reckoning with other traditions, a magical and enthralling material which was somehow outside ordinary life. The modern world is not allowed to see antiquity like this. It is bound to relate it to history, to ask what the ancient writers really meant, how they worked, what was their attitude to their age and what was its effect on them. The change of approach is particularly clear in the study of Greek poetry. The works which provided Racine and Milton with models that were beyond criticism and seemed hardly to have been written by ordinary men have been swept into the net of history, explained by their historical circumstances, and given a place in their own age. In this something has undeniably been lost, the belief in a radiant world of almost Olympian beings who were not subject to the complexities and limitations of ordinary life. We can no longer isolate the works of Greek poetry in a sphere of pure and timeless art. But for this loss there are great compensations. The more carefully the Greek achievement is examined, the richer it is found to be. The view of life which it yields to study gives more material for thought than was found in the old remote ideal. Even for those who love poetry without wishing to know too much about its origins, the historical method has its uses. It helps us to follow the poet's thought more carefully than if we read him simply in the light of our own prepossessions, and in the end it rewards us with something immeasurably rich and individual. Since a Greek poet could not

but write for his own times, we gain a far more intimate understanding of him if we know what his contemporaries were likely
to have thought and felt about such matters as he treated.

The historical method, which has been busy with Homer and
with Euripides, has tended to neglect Sophocles. For this there are
reasons. Sophocles presents no such technical problems as confront
us in the unfamiliar methods of epic composition and does not adorn
his poetry with the contemporary manners and mannerisms which
delighted the audiences of Euripides and still provide thought for
scholars. He lacks, too, those references to events of his own time
which may be detected in Pindar; for even the most subtle in-
genuity can hardly persuade us that his Oedipus is modelled on
Pericles or his Philoctetes on Alcibiades. Moreover, Sophocles
suffers from being a better artist than Euripides. His sense of the
stage and the quality of his poetry still make his plays so compelling
that we may not care what they really mean; we may be content
to enjoy the splendour of the words and the excitement of the
situations. There is a conviction, hardly warranted but undeniably
lively, that Sophocles transcended his time and was a pure artist,
a dramatist who made his plays from the unchanging elements in
human life and needs no reference to his own age for explanation.
Whatever the reasons may be, the results are undeniable. There
is uncertainty about almost every play of Sophocles, not merely
about matters of language and text but about the whole meaning
of an episode or even of a play. The *Antigone* and *Electra* have
been explained in entirely different ways; the structure of the
Ajax and *Women of Trachis* has been severely criticized; there is no
agreement about questions so fundamental as the fall of Oedipus,
the moral issue in the *Philoctetes*, the plan of *Oedipus at Colonus*.
Yet all these, and many similar matters, force themselves on the
mind, and it is impossible to understand Sophocles without finding
an answer to them. It is at least a tenable hypothesis that we
shall be better qualified to face these difficulties if we try to find
what in general would be thought about them in Athens of the
fifth century and what evidence can be found in Sophocles' work
for his own approach to them.

To understand the background of Sophoclean tragedy we
must first know something about the intellectual atmosphere of
his age. He wrote for a public, and any conviction that he held,
any view that he advanced, any feeling that he had about a
dramatic character or situation, would mean far more to men
of the fifth century than it would to us. For them issues which

now seem remote and unreal were actual and vivid. Their reactions to them would be instantaneous. They would understand naturally what the poet meant. Above all, they would catch his hints and suggestions, and know if he intended to surprise them with a paradox or to expose some familiar way of thought. We cannot hope to revive in ourselves this ready reaction, to catch instinctively all that the poet meant. We must try laboriously to discover what effect in general his plays would make. In this it is not enough to follow our own reactions and emotions. The differences between us and the Athenians are too great for us to see dramatic events as they saw them. Their views on religion and ethics were not ours; they were interested in many matters which have ceased to have meaning for us. Above all, they expected from tragedy something different from what we, with Shakespeare in our bones, expect from it. If we are to understand Sophocles as he ought to be understood, we must try to see him with the eyes and mind of the fifth century. It is an unattainable ideal, but any progress that can be made towards it well repays the effort.

At the outset it is obvious that it is almost impossible to attribute any complete or coherent body of thought to an Athenian audience of the fifth century. The Athens of Cimon or Pericles or Cleon was notoriously a place where very different opinions could be held on most matters. Its thought cannot even be divided into such obvious sections as conservative and advanced, obscurantist and enlightened. In the general historical scheme we may attach such labels to individuals, but no clear lines of this kind seem to cut across the structure of Athenian intellectual life. Efforts to isolate even a body of 'aristocratic' thought are not very convincing. The philosophy of life which we find in the works attributed to Theognis has something in common with that of Pindar, but the differences are as great as the similarities, and neither Theognis nor Pindar was an Athenian. The Athenians whose opinions we know, the Old Oligarch, Thucydides, Socrates, Xenophon, present a tantalizing variety, and even when they agree, as they do in their distrust of extreme democracy, we do not know how representative they are and suspect that they speak for a minority. When Sophocles wrote for an Athenian audience he knew that he was addressing a very varied body of opinion, that his views might appeal to some men and alienate others. The most that we can hope is to suggest to what kind of person this or that element in his plays would appeal, what effect it would have. The task is of great difficulty, but not beyond attempting.

Despite the large variety of Athenian opinions there were at least some points on which there was substantial agreement. First, Attic law was based on certain principles and embodied certain beliefs. These might be disputed by some people, but the law existed and was familiar. If Sophocles touches, as he sometimes does, on matters relevant to the law, we know at least what the orthodox opinion would be. Secondly, though the religion of his age had no sacred book and no fixed body of doctrine, it too embodied a number of views about the relations of man with the gods, views which are known equally from those who accepted them, like Pindar, and from those who doubted them, like Euripides. If Sophocles deals with a religious matter, we have some inkling what the conventional view of it would be. Thirdly, after his death the philosophers Plato and Aristotle were much concerned to create theories of ethics. Their theories were largely their own and show their predilections, but the material which they use, the opinions on conduct which they record or criticize, are often traditional and represent what was believed by many. If Sophocles makes use of such beliefs, we may assume that he deals with something that everyone understood. Fourthly, certain authors of his time have so revealed themselves in their works that we know what they thought on several important matters. In Herodotus, Thucydides, and Xenophon, hardly less in Aeschylus and Euripides, are stores of information on subjects with which Sophocles dealt. Their opinions cannot be classified, but we can at least surmise what they would feel about a person or an event in Sophoclean tragedy. These different sources are of course inadequate to provide any complete survey of Athenian thought. Perhaps no evidence, however abundant, could do that. But we can at least mark tendencies and positions, and make for ourselves a picture of the varied intellectual scene in which Sophocles worked and to which he addressed himself.

This is not the only factor in the problem. There is also the question of Sophocles' own opinions. He shaped his material in his own way, gave it his own colour, and touched it with his own views. In examining his work we must find what his point of view was, what effect he intended to make, what opinions he supported or denied, what conclusion, if any, he wished to be drawn. No poet, however impersonal, can fail to make an individual impression, to excite emotions, even thoughts. Though Sophocles, like Shakespeare, says nothing about himself and seldom reveals his own opinions, his plays show by his handling of themes and characters his special approach to his material. We do not know what he thought of his subjects in his ordinary life, but we ought to know what he thought about them in his work. If we can find what impression he intended to make, we should also be able to find what is the special nature of his tragic art. We need not assume that he had a theory comparable to Aristotle's or Hegel's, but he had a practice which reveals itself in what he wrote. We should be able to see what principles inform this practice, what in effect he thought that tragedy was. Such an inquiry must proceed through the works themselves, and only after analysis of them can general conclusions be formed.

To recognize a poet's manner and characteristics is not the same as to know what he means. If we speak of his 'meaning', we usually assume that he follows a kind of abstract scheme and presents in a highly individualized form a subject which can be expressed in more general and abstract terms. The presumption is not always warranted. It may stress one factor at the expense of another or fail to take notice of what is really important. It may be risky to search for any such formula in Sophocles, and if we do search for it, we must remember that it is after all only a formula. Nor in the rich and complex world of his creation need there necessarily be any abstract theme. His plays might be confined to the fortunes of individuals and gain our interest without any reference to more general considerations. But in Greek poetry, much more than in modern, such considerations suggest themselves and may have been present to some degree in the mind of the author. It is true that they are of no importance in Homer, but in Greek lyric poetry they force themselves on our notice. When Pindar tells a story, it is nearly always to illustrate a general truth. This may sometimes seem to be neglected in the brilliance of the telling, but the poet is often emphatic that his story gives a special example of a universal truth. Even when he does not stress this purpose, we assume that it exists. In *Olympian I*, for instance, the contrasted characters and destinies of Tantalus and his son Pelops are surely intended to show the difference between a bad and a good king; Hieron, to whom the poem is addressed, has it in his power to follow the one or the other. It is true that lyric poetry is no sure guide to tragedy and that we must not expect tragedy to use its plots in this illustrative way. Yet the example of Aeschylus shows that it could. He is less obviously didactic than Pindar, but his massive trilogies are built on an architectural plan, on an idea which permeates the whole and can be abstracted from the particular presentation. In his choral songs he explains tne universal type of which his particular story is an example. In effect he does with tragedy what Pindar does with lyrical narrative, though he does not speak in the first person and his dramatic action is far more individualized. If Aeschylus does this, we may well ask if Sophocles does not also do it.

The answer seems to be that Sophocles does something that is not the same but of the same kind. He gives much less guidance and explanation than Aeschylus, and in consequence the meaning of his plays has been disputed. But the mere fact that it is disputed suggests that it exists. And this seems to be right. Not only have Sophocles' tragedies a subject in the sense of a complex dramatic issue, but this subject is typical of a whole class of situations. Something of the kind was in Aristotle's mind when he said: 'Poetry tells rather of universal things, history of particular.'[1] He saw in tragedy events which seemed to follow a kind of law and were illustrative of other similar events. His words do not apply with the same force to most modern drama, even at the highest level. The universal truths in Shakespeare or Racine are more in countless small points than in the main designs, which are so complex that any attempt to reduce them to abstractions seems doomed to mutilate their essential nature. Yet in Sophocles we seem to search for such formulae and even to need them for a proper understanding of his plays. When we find them, they increase our pleasure. No doubt this is partly because Sophocles lived and worked in a remote world which requires considerable mental adjustment if we are to appreciate it properly. But that is not the whole truth. There is something in his art which is typical or, as Aristotle would say, universal. His drama seems to follow patterns, and at the end of a play we have formed an idea of what its pattern is, of what the play 'means' or is 'about'. This is not simply an emotional effect, a balance of thrills and sensations. Events are presented in so sharp outline that much of the pleasure is intellectual. We believe that we are learning something important about life and that each play shows an example of a certain kind of destiny. It is therefore legitimate to ask what is the real meaning of his plays, what general truths are embodied in his particular presentations, and what, if any, was his own opinion about them.

It would have been perfectly possible and proper for Sophocles to tell his audience directly what he expected them to think, to

---

[1] *Poet.* 1451 b 7 ἡ μὲν γὰρ ποίησις μᾶλλον τὰ καθόλου, ἡ δ᾽ ἱστορία τὰ καθ᾽ ἕκαστον λέγει.

provide a comment on his tragic events, and to draw an explicit conclusion on any problem that they may raise. Aeschylus had done this. In most of his plays the Chorus acts as his own mouthpiece and gives in superb and noble commentary the universal truths set out in the particular action. Euripides was no less personal. He adorned his plays with maxims and reflections which are undoubtedly his own and do not always bear much relevance to the context or to the characters who utter them. Sophocles uses neither method. His Chorus is not his own voice, except at rare intervals and in doubtful cases. It is usually an actor like the other actors, subject to error and to partial or limited understanding. It passes judgements and philosophizes, but most of its conclusions are no more valid for a final view of the play than are those of any other character. Sophocles even uses the Chorus to propound theories which look convincing at the time but are proved later to be wrong. If he uses it for his own views, it is not always clear that he is doing so. Nor does he resemble Euripides in making his characters pass general reflections which are obviously his own. No personage of his speaks so surprisingly as the Euripidean Electra who on seeing the body of Aegisthus soliloquizes on the folly of unequal marriages, the insecurity of wealth, and the vanity of personal beauty.[1] These are the poet's own ideas, interesting perhaps for their own sake, but inappropriate to the situation and to the speaker. Such oddities do not occur in Sophocles. He is eminently quotable; he even abounds in sentences which may be detached from their context and quoted as maxims, but in their context these belong to the character who speaks them and concern his situation. They cannot be assumed to throw any light on what the poet himself thinks.

If this method of self-revelation is excluded no less than that through the Chorus, we might well wonder if after all Sophocles really gives any lead to his audience on what to think about his plays, whether he was not content, like Shakespeare, to arouse the emotions and no more. But in reading or seeing a play of Sophocles much more than our emotions is involved. We inevitably find that there is an issue on which we are almost forced to take sides or at least to recognize a difference and a conflict of opinions. The conflicts which he dramatizes are not merely clashes of temperament or personality or interest. The characters seem to stand for principles, to represent points of view, to be typical of various human destinies. As we watch their sensational

[1] Eur. *El*. 914-51.

careers, we are not only moved by their individual fortunes but driven to ask what general issues are at stake, and even at times to pass moral judgements. The human scene which Sophocles presents is like life in that it evokes thoughts of right and wrong, like and dislike. In the *Ajax* he actually presents a debate on a concrete issue and so weights the scales that we are forced to take the side of Teucer. He excites many and various feelings, but among them are approval and disapproval. He is more casuistical, if the word may be allowed, than Shakespeare, who, though he presents extreme forms of evil and shows how horrible they are, does not call on us to judge between competing causes or to decide on which side right lies. This Sophocles sometimes does. The *Antigone* turns on a moral problem—shall the dead traitor Polynices be buried? We are bound to face the problem if we are to understand the play in the right spirit. It is not enough simply to follow the drama and to be moved by the pity and other emotions which it awakes. Sooner or later we must make up our minds whether Antigone is right to act as she does and whether Sophocles thought so. Of course not all his subjects are so ethical. In the dark emotions aroused by *King Oedipus* approval and disapproval have a very small place. But just as in life a complex situation may force us to take sides and to pass judgements, so in Sophoclean tragedy the conflicts make the same demand. And when this happens, we are particularly likely to be led astray by modern notions. The Greeks had strong feelings, but these did not always work in the same way or in the same field as our own.

It is one thing to dramatize a conflict, another to explain it or to pass judgement on those who are involved in it. *King Lear* raises dark questions about the justice of the gods, but Shakespeare does not answer them. The uncertainty in which he leaves us is part of his tragic effect. We may well ask if Sophocles does not do the same. There is no reason why he should not, and many have claimed that he does, or that, if he does pass a judgement or give an explanation, too much attention need not be paid to it. It is certainly true that in *King Oedipus* and the *Women of Trachis* the tragic horror overwhelms and outweighs other emotions, and that we are less interested to know why such things happen than appalled that they do. Even in more casuistical plays like *Ajax* and *Philoctetes* the first interest is in the human destinies and in the effect that they have on us. Sophocles is primarily a dramatist, and his first effect is dramatic. But since such catastrophes as he depicts may well stir us to ask questions of a far-reaching character, it would not be inartistic if he were to give answers or hints of answers to them. In effect he does. In his quiet way he guides us to conclusions, makes us takes sides and pass judgements, shows his own point of view and the idea which has shaped a play. His method is more subtle than that of Aeschylus or Euripides. In many cases he leaves us quite uncertain, and his first appeal is always to the emotions that tragedy arouses. But since the themes of his plays are examples of some conflict in human life, we ask what principles they involve and what universal aspects they present. Not to relate these events to a wider scheme is to destroy much of their significance. In reading the plays one of our first duties is to see what they mean not only in themselves but in relation to a scheme of life. They imply backgrounds, metaphysical or religious or ethical, which are essential to them and certainly part of the poet's design.

In his own way Sophocles gives hints and even directions. The first and most obvious kind is the small song which the Chorus sing at the end of the *Ajax*, *Antigone*, *Women of Trachis*, *Electra*, and *Oedipus at Colonus*, and in it pass in brief review what has happened. However partial or misguided the Chorus may have been during the play, at the end they speak with authority and point out some important conclusion. In *King Oedipus* a like conclusion is spoken in trochaic verse, and in *Philoctetes* three lines from the Chorus indicate the joy and relief proper to the occasion. These summaries are mere summaries. They do not always look very impressive, though there is more in them than is obvious at first sight. The most detailed and emphatic is that of the *Antigone*, and it looks as if Sophocles were determined to set beyond dispute that his play is concerned with Creon's punishment for pride. The task of these final words is not to pass judgement on everything that has happened but to strike a note, to give a tone, of relief or acceptance or understanding or joy, and so to put the dramatic events in their right perspective. They leave no doubt what we should feel when the play is over, what our general impression ought to be. If they advance a concrete proposition, as they do in the *Antigone* and *Women of Trachis*, that is because events may have confused us and a merely general sentiment is not enough. In any case, the last words of a play are final so far as they go. In them the poet gives a lead which we must take when we review the play in retrospect. If we have followed him carefully, they may not be necessary, but they help the unwary or the misled, and they are indispensable to any understanding of the poet's intention.

This kind of final song is not to be found in the existing final plays of Aeschylus' trilogies. The *Oresteia* ends with a great hymn of exultant joy which is far removed from the dark events of the *Agamemnon* and *Libation-bearers*. It looks not backward but forward, proclaims the great future which awaits Athens, and does not dwell on its causes. The *Seven against Thebes*[1] and the *Persians*, which is not the last play of a trilogy but seems to be an independent unity, both end with a kind of lament, the one by Antigone and Ismene for their fallen brother, the other by Xerxes for his own perished glory. These songs are part of the dramatic action; they do not review it or stand outside it; they show what the catastrophe means to some of the characters caught in it. There was no need for Aeschylus to use Sophocles' method of a final summary; for he explains events as they happen and reserves his last words for an emotional or imaginative effect. The method of Euripides shows some variety, but little resemblance to that of Sophocles. In five of his plays, *Alcestis*, *Medea*, *Andromache*, *Helen*, and *Bacchants*, he uses with one small variation an identical form of words and proclaims the unexpected and manifold things that may come from the gods. Such an epilogue conveys very little about what has preceded it, and it is noteworthy that it is used equally for plays with happy and with unhappy endings. It is little more than a conventional pious statement and tells next to nothing of what the poet really thinks about his play. More commonly the last words of a Euripidean play indicate a mood of acceptance and suggest some kind of action suitable to it. The close of the *Trojan Women* or the *Hecuba* stresses the resignation and exhaustion after tragic events, but the poet provides no comment on them. Only in the *Ion* and the *Phoenician Women*, if indeed the end is his, does Euripides pass something like a judgement, and for both trochaic verse is used. The first proclaims that the good prosper and the wicked do not, the second, spoken by Oedipus, that men must endure whatever the gods send. Neither is entirely satisfactory. The slick moralizing of the *Ion* has hardly been borne out by the events of the play, and there is much more in the destiny of the House of Laius than the conclusion given. On the whole it looks as if Euripides did not choose to explain his main purpose in this way. His conclusions convey a mood, but little more. Sophocles' method is his own. He uses it because he needs it to sum up his performance and leave no room for serious uncertainty about his main intention.

[1] This assumes that the *Seven against Thebes* ends at 1004 and that what follows is the work of a later hand.

In two plays, the *Ajax* and *Philoctetes*, Sophocles uses a special device to show us what to think. He presents a divine being on the stage who speaks with authority and cannot be gainsaid. Athene explains why Ajax is humiliated with madness, Heracles why Philoctetes must go to Troy. Their word, so far as it goes, is final. After hearing them we may be certain that Ajax is rightly humiliated and that Philoctetes has been wrong in refusing to go to Troy. With such divine epiphanies we are familiar in Aeschylus. Hermes in the *Prometheus Bound* and Athene and Apollo in the *Eumenides* speak with authority and explain much of importance. Apollo expounds why Orestes should not be punished by the Furies, Hermes why Prometheus shall suffer for his pride. In the lost *Daughters of Danaus* Aphrodite seems to have justified Hypermnestra because she alone of fifty sisters accepted her lover instead of killing him. When the gods give such a lead, it enables us to judge correctly what happens. Sophocles uses his deities rather differently. His Athene appears at the beginning of the *Ajax* and explains the situation as it then is; much more follows that is outside her scope. Heracles appears right at the end of the *Philoctetes*, and until then the situation is clouded and permits of varying judgements. Even when he does appear, he does not explain everything. He merely tells Philoctetes to go to Troy. No doubt in some lost plays Sophocles used deities for a more Aeschylean purpose. In the *Triptolemus* the speech of Demeter to Triptolemus seems to have given instructions about a journey which was of fundamental importance to the play. But the *Triptolemus* was produced in 468 B.C., and Sophocles was no doubt still under the influence of Aeschylus, perhaps even of Prometheus' prophecy to Io in the *Prometheus Bound*. The interventions of gods in the plays of Sophocles are subordinated to the action and limited in their scope. They tell us something of importance, but not everything.

In at least two plays Sophocles uses a third and different means to guide his audience. In Odysseus in the *Ajax* and in Theseus in *Oedipus at Colonus* he makes a human being the medium of his own opinions, or rather the representative of justice and right. Since they are human beings, they are liable to error and need instruction, as Athene gives it to Odysseus and Oedipus to Theseus. But, once instructed, they know what is right, and their comments are right. They are handicapped by being involved in the dramatic events and by not knowing all the facts, but, so far as their knowledge allows, they act in a way that the poet clearly approves. When Odysseus draws a lesson on the need for modesty from Ajax' fall or champions his burial against the Atridae, we cannot doubt that he shows where right lies and what we ought to think. When Theseus accepts the polluted Oedipus without qualm, we know that he too is right. Sophocles uses these characters as if he wished to save us from being misled about important points in the plays' action. He makes it clear that Ajax is rightly punished and rightly buried, and that Oedipus ought to be received at Athens despite the doubts of the Chorus. But such characters fulfil only a limited function. They help one to understand some of the play but not the whole. They guide us through part of it, and their opinion must be heard, but they are not the final authority and they do not cover the whole issue.

These three means, final song, divinities on the stage, and impartial human characters, help to guide us through the plays and to see events in their right light. But they do not disclose everything that the poet felt or tell us all that we wish to know or confirm all that we feel when the plays are acted. They are subsidiary to something else which is harder to define and yet more important, the way in which the plays force us to strong feelings and even to definite opinions and judgements about the characters and events. In the *Antigone*, for instance, we are made to feel that in the last resort Antigone is right to do as she does. Her nobility moves us, and her defence is far more touching and convincing than Creon's accusations. In due course we find that our feelings are justified. The gods punish Creon, and the Chorus at the end condemn him. But long before these revelations we are sure of our feelings and condemn Creon as we admire Antigone. Again, in the *Philoctetes*, where the issues are far more tangled and obscure, our feeling that Neoptolemus is wrong to do what Odysseus tells him and right to disobey him even in the face of what seems to be a divine plan are justified in the end, but we do not wait for the end to believe it. These feelings are forced on us not by what the characters say in their own defence but by what they are and by what they do. We react to them not merely with our intellects but with our hearts and consciences. We feel that it is unjust for Antigone to be treated as she is, that Neoptolemus is right not to tell lies, no matter for how important an end. In different ways this is true of all the plays. In each there are characters who appeal more to us than others and seem to have right on their side. We cannot always prove it during the play, but at the end we see that our feelings are justified.

It may seem rash to speak of right and wrong in a tragedy.

There are forms of tragic suffering where such distinctions do not exist, where all that matters is the suffering of human beings. There are others, like Racine's *Britannicus*, which display great forces of evil at work but allow no clear distinction between right and wrong. Agrippine is indeed Nero's victim, but she is no virtuous woman and her troubles are the fruit of her own past crimes. The situation is different in Shakespeare. When Desdemona is ruined through the machinations of Iago or Macbeth driven to murder by his wife, we may distinguish between good and evil and feel as much hostility for the wicked as pity for their victims. But in the onrush of overwhelming emotions which he awakes we hardly wait to assess the balance of right and wrong, at least while we read or see the tragedy. Sophocles is not like this. The tragic emotions are as great as in Shakespeare; the excitement of the action is hardly less great. But in all the excitement and horror there is an element which is absent from Shakespeare. The tragic events are such that we inevitably try to explain them to ourselves and to find out how the poet explains them.

The reason of this is that while the conflict in Shakespeare is between men and men, in Sophocles it arises in the last analysis between men and gods. It is the gods who make Ajax mad, who ordain his hideous end for Heracles, who punish Creon, who arrange the whole career of Oedipus, who send Orestes to kill his mother, who decide that Philoctetes shall take Troy, who turn the old Oedipus into a daemonic being. When they are at work, the whole setting is different from Shakespeare's. It is in some sense theological, and if the gods act in this or that way, we ask why they do and what it means. We can hardly do otherwise, and Sophocles demands such questions from us; for he has his answers to them. To understand his tragic pattern we must understand his theology. It is a product of his age, and we know something about it. The difficulty is to find his own treatment of accepted doctrines in his presentation of particular issues. The chief evidence is what happens. When the gods intervene or display their will through oracles or prophets, we know what they mean and what their part is. In every play this happens. Some of the machinery may mean little or nothing to us. It is, for instance, hard to attach great importance to oracles. But, whatever Sophocles may have thought about them in ordinary life, and there is a good possibility that he believed in them, in his plays they account for a great deal, and that is all that concerns us. The plays are nearly all that we have of his and certainly all that matters. They show that Sophocles built his tragic conflicts on the relations of men with the gods, and therefore we must know what these relations are and mean.

Because of this, issues of right and wrong are more emphatic in Sophocles than in Shakespeare. If the gods force a fate on men, we ask not only why they do it but if they are right and if their victims deserve it. The question may not always be relevant, but we cannot but ask it, and Sophocles evidently intended that we should. Thus in his treatment of Oedipus, though he does not allow that Oedipus' hideous misfortunes are in any sense deserved, he knows that some will think that they are and has his answer for them. In the *Ajax* and *Antigone* the fall of Ajax and Creon follows a traditional scheme and is by Greek standards deserved. In the *Electra* and *Philoctetes* the issue is much less clear. Until the action is quite advanced we may wonder whether Electra is really right to desire vengeance on her mother or whether the gods' plan to bring Philoctetes to Troy is really right, but in the end we see that what the gods approve is right and must be accepted. This interest in rights and wrongs is an essential part of the play's effect on us. Because our moral emotions are aroused, we are more excited about what happens. The conflict between right and wrong, its obscurities and its excitements, is fundamental to Sophoclean tragedy.

This interest touches more than the mere structure of a play or its main theme. The chief characters sometimes argue and disagree on right and wrong as they do not in Shakespeare. The burial of Polynices is a matter for bitter disagreement not only between Antigone and Creon but between Antigone and Ismene; Deianira's attempt to win back Heracles by magic is viewed differently by the Chorus, by Hyllus, and by Heracles; Odysseus and Neoptolemus do not see eye to eye about the uses of deceit for political ends; the old Oedipus argues fiercely with Creon about his alleged crimes. In these controversies passions are aroused and are undeniably dramatic, but the issue has to be settled and is a matter of morals. In Euripides debates on such points are no less common. Jason and Medea, Dionysus and Pentheus, represent opposite causes and apply rhetoric and sophistry to them. But in Sophocles the subjects of dispute seem simpler and more fundamental. The interest is less in the give and take of debate than in the importance of what is at stake. Euripides may not always care which side we support; Sophocles clearly cares a great deal and, though he is always dramatic, he leads us to a decision.

With him actual argument counts less than it does with Euripides. His debates and disputes appeal first to the conscience and to the heart. He wishes to convince us in all our being, to carry us with him in a full and imaginative understanding of what is at stake.

It may then be said that there is in all Sophocles' plays an element of ethical discussion, of casuistry, which pervades the atmosphere and gives meaning to the tragic events. As his art developed, these issues became more complex and more subtle. In the early plays they are quite simply and directly presented, but in the later plays, notably in the *Electra* and *Philoctetes*, they are so complex that much of the excitement lies in finding out what they are. The protagonists in a struggle no longer stand on opposite sides of right and wrong but seem to present such a struggle in themselves. As he grew older, Sophocles did not abate his love of an ethical issue but brought it closer to the complexities of human nature. But in all the plays the dramatic material demands close considerations of right and wrong. They are forced on us, and we cannot neglect them. This does not mean that Sophocles is didactic or instructional in any narrow or derogatory sense, that he uses his characters simply to illustrate moral truths. He is always a dramatist, and the ethical issues are subordinated to human interests. But just as it is impossible to understand human life without considering moral issues and even passing moral judgements, so in Sophoclean tragedy much of the interest turns on such issues. Sophocles is as much concerned with men's souls as with their fortunes.

It is perhaps in this that his peculiar difficulty lies. In the scheme of every play there is a moral or religious problem, an issue to which there must be a right answer but on which more than one opinion is tenable. This issue is presented in a very personal and concrete form, with all the richness that great art can give. As in life we may be deceived and form wrong opinions about matters of great moment, so in his plays Sophocles shows how deceptive many issues are, presents different views of them, and looks at them from more than one angle. As the drama develops, the nature of the problem becomes clearer, and eventually we know what it is. It follows that in examining his work we must find what these problems are and how they are presented. If we can do this, we have made a considerable advance in the study of his work and art.

II
AJAX

THE chief character of the *Ajax* had already a long history when Sophocles wrote a play about him. His story would be familiar to an Athenian audience. Without any great knowledge of its details everyone would know that Ajax was a pre-eminent hero who had killed himself in circumstances both humiliating and horrible. His prowess was nobly celebrated by Homer, who in the *Iliad* made him the greatest Achaean after Achilles[1] and drew him with loving care as stalwart in battle, gigantic and beautiful, a match for Hector, the peer of Ares, the bulwark of the Achaeans, aptly symbolized by his tower-like shield made of seven bulls'-hides. Such a hero was well qualified for the high status which he held at Athens. There he had a cult,[2] a ceremony in which he was believed to take part,[3] and a tribe named after him.[4] The illustrious clans of the Eurysacidae and the Philaidae claimed descent from him, and the common respect for him is shown in the Attic Drinking-song, which follows Homer is making him second only to Achilles in valour.[5] In Salamis he had his feast of the Aiantea,[6] and showed his love for the island and for Athens by coming to the help of the fleet in the battle against the Persians in 480 B.C.[7] He was no less important at Aegina, where he was revered as an Aeacid, portrayed on the pediment of Aphaia's temple, and introduced by Pindar as a type of heroic excellence into poems written for Aeginetans.[8] Ajax' prowess was recognized, and he was held in high honour because of it.

On the other hand, this great being had come to a dark, even a shameful, end. Deprived of the arms of Achilles, he had become mad, tried to kill the Achaean chieftains and then, in humiliation, killed himself. This story had grown in the post-Homeric epic, notably in the *Aethiopis* and *Little Iliad*. But in some form it was known to Homer,[9] whose Ajax was suited to it by his obstinate simple character[10] and by the sudden fury of which he was capable.[11] Where Homer gave a hint, other poets completed a portrait. In the *Sack of Troy* Ajax seems to have gone mad, and Machaon marked his Eyes that flamed as the lightning and wits weighed down with a burden.[12]

---

[1] *Il.* ii. 768–9.   [2] Paus. i. 35. 3.   [3] Schol. Pind. *Nem.* ii. 19.   [4] Hdt. v. 66.
[5] No. 15, Diehl.   [6] Hesych. s.v. Αἰάντεια.   [7] Hdt. viii. 121.
[8] *Nem.* iv. 48, vii. 26, viii. 27; *Isthm.* vi. 26.   [9] *Od.* xi. 543–7.   [10] *Il.* xi. 558–62.
[11] Ib. vii. 212.   [12] Fr. 5, 8 Allen ὄμματά τ᾿ ἀστράπτοντα βαρυνόμενόν τε νόημα.

Tradition agreed that Ajax had an ugly quarrel with Odysseus about the arms of Achilles, failed to win them, and killed himself. Some, certainly the author of the *Little Iliad*, went farther and associated this failure with a murderous plot against his fellows.[1] For the heroic age and for the epic poets this story, painful and tragic as it undoubtedly was, need not necessarily detract from Ajax' essential greatness. In the heroic view of life disasters of this kind are almost inevitable to greatness, the price that a man pays for being more eminent than his fellows. They may excite compassion, but there is no need to condemn them. In the fifth century it was different. While the greatness of Ajax was still recognized, his end needed explanation. A civically minded age could not lightly accept as a hero a man who had tried to kill his leaders in a great enterprise. The career of Ajax suggested a real problem: how could a man who wished to kill his leaders be held in high esteem as a type of noble manhood? The Greeks set a high value on loyalty between soldiers, and Ajax had been desperately disloyal. Sophocles accepted the story much as the *Little Iliad* had left it. He had therefore to adapt it to his own times, to show the paradox of Ajax' life and death, the contrast between his undoubted prowess and his painful, perhaps dishonourable, end.

That this paradox was realized in the fifth century is clear from Pindar's references to Ajax. He was familiar with the story as the *Little Iliad* told it and undeniably exercised by it. He found a characteristically bold solution. In *Nemean* vii he deplores that Homer, by whom he probably means the poet of the *Little Iliad*, has given more than his deserts to Odysseus, and complains that the human herd is blind:

> For if it could see the truth,
> Never from wrath over armour would mighty Ajax
> Have driven a smooth sword through his breast.[2]

In his view the death of Ajax was due to men's inability to discern true merit; the judges preferred Odysseus, and Ajax killed himself. In *Nemean* viii he goes farther and suggests foul play on the part Odysseus:

> The greatest reward belongs to a glancing lie.
> In hidden ballot the Danaans honoured Odysseus,

---

[1] Procl. *Chrest.* p. 106, 22 Allen; Apollod. *Ep.* v. 6.

[2] *Nem.* vii. 24–6

εἰ γὰρ ἦν
ἒ τὰν ἀλάθειαν ἰδέμεν, οὔ κεν ὅπλων χολωθεὶς
ὁ καρτερὸς Αἴας ἔπαξε διὰ φρενῶν
λευρὸν ξίφος.

                    And Ajax, robbed of the golden armour,
                    Wrestled with death.[1]

Pindar elaborates what this foul play was; it was slander which
consorts with lies and attacks true worth. This was one way out of
the difficulty. Nothing is said about Ajax' madness or murderous
intention. He is simply the victim of envy and slander, his death
their result. Pindar, we must assume, thought it right that Ajax,
robbed of his honour, should kill himself. To save Ajax' character
Pindar sacrifices that of Odysseus, and the result was no doubt
satisfactory to the Aeginetans, who held Ajax in great honour.

Sophocles' play follows quite different lines. It accepts the story
as it was known from the epic, dramatizes it in tragic form, and
gives to it an intellectual structure which helps to explain and
justify the end of Ajax. Its design includes not only the madness
and death of Ajax but the rehabilitation of his character after
death. It shows both why he falls and why he is rightly honoured.
The combination and contrast of the two themes explain the
structure of the play. Sophocles boldly makes it fall into two
unequal halves. The first gives the events from Ajax' slaughter of
the cattle to his death and the discovery of his body, the second
the debate about his burial and its successful conclusion. Although
this arrangement may not appeal to modern taste and has been
criticized by standards which would have meant nothing to
Sophocles,[2] it is both artistically satisfactory and intellectually
necessary. The play moves from the horror and shame of Ajax'
madness to the climax of his death, and then in the second part
anxiety and pity for Ajax are prolonged in such a way that his
final justification comes with an enhanced emphasis. Some such
means as this was required to show both the depth of his fall and
the difficulties which must be overcome before his name is
rehabilitated. To have closed simply with the death would have
left him unjustified, even dishonoured, and his honour was of deep
concern to Athenians. Intellectually the division is no less justifiable. Ajax is a great man who has committed grave offences
against gods and men. It would be unjust simply to dwell on the
offences, to leave the whole question of his worth out of the play or to
confine it to a few lines at the end. The play is built on the combination of two themes, of heavy wrongdoing and of ultimate nobility.

[1] *Nem.* viii. 25–7   μέγιστον Δ' αἰόλῳ ψεύδει γέρας ἀντέταται·
                    κρυφίαισι γὰρ ἐν ψάφοις 'Οδυσσῆ Δαναοὶ θεράπευσαν·
                    χρυσέων Δ' Αἴας στερηθεὶς ὅπλων φόνῳ πάλαισεν.

[2] An early offender is the Scholiast on 1123 μετὰ γὰρ τὴν ἀναίρεσιν ἐπεκτεῖναι
τὸ Δρᾶμα θελήσας ἐψυχρεύσατο καὶ ἔλυσε τὸ τραγικὸν πάθος.

The two are weighed against each other, and in the end the nobility
is seen to outweigh the faults. In each part Sophocles emphasizes
something fundamental to it. The first begins after Ajax' intended
assault on the Achaean chieftains and the slaughter of the cattle
that full attention may be drawn to his humiliation and suffering.
Through this we see what his fall means, the part that Athene
plays in it, the brutality in Ajax himself which causes it, the misery
which his realization of it brings to him, the recrudescence of the
madness in his self-destruction. The full tragic process wins pity
and sympathy for Ajax. His murderous impulses gradually cease to
count against him, for they fall on his own head. In the second
part the angry hatred and the devoted loyalty which Ajax still
arouses after death show that he is not like other men, that his
virtues outweigh his faults, and that he deserves the high regard in
which he has been held. Through both parts Ajax is so presented
that the audience take a peculiarly personal interest in him and his
fate. He illustrates important rules which govern men in relation
to the gods, but his is an individual destiny and appeals as such.

Since the *Ajax* deals with the destiny of an individual and its action
turns on his character and worth, Ajax' nobility must be beyond
dispute. Sophocles secures this. His Ajax is undeniably a real
person. Both in the confidence of madness and the humiliation of
sanity we know the principles that control his being, or rather, we
think that we know them, so clearly is he imprinted on our memories after hearing the play. But this simple effect hides considerable
subtlety of delineation. It was no easy task to create a character
who was both a heroic being from a legendary past and a man whom
the fifth century could understand from its own experience and by
its own standards. Sophocles' Ajax is not Homer's, and the differences between the two show how the later poet adapted this heroic
figure to his own civically minded age, which lacked Homer's
admiration for unfettered individuals and had its own notions of
what a great man ought to be. Of course there are Homeric traits
in the Sophoclean Ajax, but they are simple and almost inevitable
to any presentation of him. He is a great warrior who knows
that he is as good as his father (439); he prays that his son
may be as good as himself (551); Teucer relates his deeds of
prowess (1272–88), and both the defence of the ships and the
single combat with Hector are based, not very closely, on the *Iliad*.[1]

[1] In *Il.* xiv. 409 ff. Ajax repulses the Trojans when they cross the Achaean wall, but
it is before any ship is set on fire. When Protesilaus' ship is set on fire (*Il.* xv. 705)
Ajax is driven back, and Patroclus finally beats back the enemy.

But on the whole, Ajax' soldierly prowess is merged in a wider, more essential greatness. His outstanding qualities are conveyed by what he himself says and does on the stage and by what others, notably the Chorus, Tecmessa, and Teucer, feel about him. The picture that emerges is complex and more intimate than Homer's. Sophocles has changed his hero to suit the ideals and experience of imperial Athens. Instead of copying the epic model he has recreated a heroic type and given it a new significance. What this is we can best see if we try to see Ajax against the background of the fifth century.

To the Chorus, who are sailors from his own island of Salamis, Ajax is the great commander, the vulture among other birds (168–71). They do not criticize him but accept all that he says, his decision that a man of honour should die if he is disgraced (481–2), his announcement that he is going to kill himself (624–34). They are alert on his behalf when the Messenger brings menacing news (813–4), full of shame when his dead body is found, and guiltily conscious that they might have prevented his death (909–14). They foresee the exultation of Odysseus (955–60); they stress the duty of immediate burial (1041), and know that their master will have everlasting fame (1166). They are loyal followers whose life is absorbed in their leader. Their unstinted and unshaken trust in Ajax shows him to be a man who can command and keep devotion. Through their eyes we see him not as the Homeric hero of single combats but as the ideal commander who looks after his men and secures their safety. Homer's heroes are not remarkable for their capacity to command or to win the devotion of their nameless followers. They are of course 'leaders of men' and 'shepherds of the people', but this aspect of their activity receives little attention in comparison with their individual prowess. The emphasis on the power to command and on the trust which a leader should inspire is characteristically Athenian and bears the mark of the Periclean age. For while Aeschylus' Eteocles preaches the virtue of obedience to a general,[1] he does not stress the parallel virtue of being able to win men's trust. But Ajax' men honour him not because they are compelled but because they trust and admire him. They remind us rather of the way in which Pericles claims that in Athens pre-eminence is allowed to individuals because of personal excellence,—'a man is less honoured for his social position in the state than for his merit'[2]. Ajax almost rules over willing subjects as Euripides' Menelaus claims to do:

---

[1] *Sept.* 224–5.   [2] Thuc. ii. 37. 1.

No tyrant who commands by violence,
But ruler of the willing youth of Greece.[1]

He resembles the general whom Xenophon's Socrates praises in
that he sees that his men are safe and well looked after and is
trusted by them because they believe him to be the best.[2]   Ajax
leads by virtue of his own excellence. The Athenian audience,
used to war and appreciative of the qualities that make for success
in it, would see a great commander in him.

Tecmessa sees Ajax differently; for she is more dependent on
him, more intimately involved in his life. She sees that he is a
strange, rather formidable being,

Terrible, mighty, with strength untamed,[3]

and that he must not be crossed, hardly even counselled. His
sorrows are hers, and she says pathetically that what is a single
burden to him is a double burden to her (271–6); she suffers both
for herself and for him. She seems to expect no tender words from
him and accepts his rough ways without complaint (529 ff.). Even
when she makes her last request to him, it is extremely guarded
and moderate (591–5). Her feelings for him are revealed in
her appeal to him not to kill himself and desert her (484–524).
Nowhere does Sophocles show greater skill in adapting an epic
theme to his own time and thought. For behind this speech we
can hear the famous words of Homer's Andromache to Hector.[4]
The main themes are the same: the proud home from which the
woman comes, the slavery that waits her and her child if the man
dies, the taunts that they will suffer, the misery that will fall on his
old father and mother. Like Andromache, Tecmessa lives entirely
in her husband. For Andromache Hector is everything:

Hector, remember that you are my father and gracious mother,
You are my brother, and you are my strong partner in wedlock.[5]

and so is Ajax to Tecmessa:

Without you then what fatherland were mine?
What wealth? On you alone my safety rests.[6]

Yet between the two appeals there is a great difference. Despite

---

[1] Eur. *Hel.* 395–6   τύραννος οὐδὲν πρὸς βίαν στρατηλατῶν,
        ἑκοῦσι δ' ἄρξας Ἑλλάδος νεανίαις.
Cf. *El.* 1082, *Or.* 1167–8.
[2] *Mem.* iii. 3, 9.   [3] 205 ὁ Δεινὸς μέγας ὠμοκρατής.
[4] *Il.* vi. 407–39.
[5] Ib. 429–30 Ἕκτορ, ἀτὰρ σύ μοί ἐσσι πατὴρ καὶ πότνια μήτηρ
        ἠδὲ κασίγνητος σὺ δέ μοι θαλερὸς παρακοίτης.
[6] 518–19   τίς δῆτ' ἐμοὶ γένοιτ' ἂν ἀντὶ σοῦ πατρίς;
        τίς πλοῦτος; ἐν σοὶ πᾶσ' ἔγωγε σώζομαι.

her dependence on Hector, Andromache speaks to him with the
freedom that the heroic age allowed between wives and husbands.
But Tecmessa, though she speaks with courage, has yet to give
reasons for speaking at all, to explain how grave the results of Ajax'
death will be, to appeal to any gratitude that he may feel for her.
She is not a wife, like Andromache, but a captive concubine. Her
inferior status and the restrictions which Athens and the fifth
century imposed on women prevent her from using the same
intimate frankness. She cannot even address Ajax so openly as the
captive Briseis laments the dead Patroclus.[1] In comparison with
Andromache Tecmessa is at a disadvantage. She is a concubine,
and the Periclean age had begun to have doubts about the liberties
allowed to her kind. And she is a woman who conforms to the
Athenian theory that she must keep her place. She is completely
dependent on Ajax. She has no family, no friends among the
Achaean chieftains, no protection except from Ajax. Her complete dependence on him shows both her pathos and his power to
win affection and trust.

An even more marked contrast between Homer and Sophocles
may be seen in the different answers which the two men make to
these appeals. Hector admits the horrors that lie ahead and makes
no attempt to mitigate them, but even in speaking of them he
somehow comforts Andromache by showing how well he understands her anxieties. This is not Ajax' way. After her speech and
the Chorus's commendation if it, he simply says:

> She shall win my approval verily,
> If she has heart to do what I command.[2]

and Tecmessa answers dutifully and without complaint:

> Dear Ajax, in all things will I obey.[3]

He seems to give her no assurance, no comfort, to pay little
attention to her. Yet in fact he has been moved by her, as he himself admits later; she has really softened his resolve to kill himself
(651–2). Of this at the moment he says nothing. His present
concern is to enforce his will on her, to keep her in her place. When
he has made a decision, he will not listen to questions or arguments
from her:

> Question me not. 'Tis best to be discreet.[4]

---

[1] *Il.* xix. 287–300.
[2] 527–8   καὶ κάρτ' ἐπαίνου τεύξεται πρὸς γοῦν ἐμοῦ,
                 ἐὰν μόνον τὸ ταχθὲν εὖ τολμᾷ τέλειν.
[3] 529   ἀλλ', ὦ φίλ' Αἶας, πάντ' ἔγωγε πείσομαι.
[4] 586   μὴ κρῖνε, μὴ 'ξέταζε· σωφρονεῖν καλόν.

When she persists, he is harsh and even cruel. He tells her that she
vexes him (589) and talks too much (592), that she will make no
impression on him:

> You seem to be a fool,
> If now you think that you can school my mood.[1]

Yet he has shown glimmerings of tenderness when he praises her
for keeping their child away when his fury was raging (536), and
when the little boy is brought to him Ajax shows all the pride, love,
and hope that a father may in his son. For a moment his absorp-
tion in his troubles is broken as he wishes Eurysaces to continue in
the happiness of childhood:

> Till then be fed on gentle airs, and cherish
> Your tender life, and be your mother's joy.[2]

Ajax understands what the child means to Tecmessa. We must
not accuse him of hardness of heart. In this scene he is still a prey
to great humiliation and anxiety. His first thought is for himself
and his honour. But the distance which he keeps between himself
and Tecmessa is probably not temporary or due merely to his
present state. It is a kind of style, of manners, what is expected
from a great man of action to his concubine.

One small point illustrates Ajax' behaviour towards Tecmessa
and its Athenian character. She tells how, when the fury first
came on him, he answered her questions with a stock form of
words:

> Woman, silence is women's ornament.[3]

Of course he is going mad, and we cannot press what he says as
being always characteristic of him. But Tecmessa understands
him at once and obeys him as if she were used to this kind of
treatment. He seems to hold a view of womanhood which was
held in theory at Athens even if it was not always translated
into fact. Aristotle[4] quotes Ajax' words without comment as if
they were generally accepted as true. Literature supports him.
When Eteocles sacrifices before battle he says to the Theban
woman who leads the Chorus:

> Yours to be silent and remain indoors.[5]

---

[1] 594–5   μῶρά μοι Δοκεῖς φρονεῖν,
                    εἰ τοὐμὸν·ῆθος ἄρτι παιΔεύειν νοεῖς.

[2] 558–9   τέως Δὲ κούφοις πνεύμασιν βόσκου, νέαν
                    ψυχὴν ἀτάλλων, μητρὶ τῇΔε χαρμονήν.

[3] 293   γύναι, γυναιξὶ κόσμον ἡ σιγὴ φέρει.

[4] Pol. 1260 a 30.

[5] Aesch. Sept. 232 σὸν Δ' αὖ τὸ σιγᾶν καὶ μένειν εἴσω Δόμων.

Macaria in the *Sons of Heracles* apologizes for interfering in public affairs:

> For women to be silent and discreet
> Is best, and to stay quiet in the house.[1]

Nor did the sentiment belong only to the ideal world of high poetry. The wise Democritus said that 'fewness of words is an ornament to a woman',[2] and Aristophanes' Lysistrata complains that when she asked her husband about the political situation in the Peloponnesian War he used to tell her to be silent.[3] The Athenians seem to have felt that in public matters like war and politics women had no place and should keep silence while men talked. Xenophon expresses much the same notion when he says that a man's place is out of doors and a woman's indoors.[4] In practice there must have been many exceptions to the theory, and few of Sophocles' heroines display Tecmessa's humility. But that is because they have some of the spacious independence which belongs to women of the heroic age and because they are usually in situations which forbid retirement. The ordinary Athenian woman was expected not to interfere in her husband's affairs but to keep to her house.[5] Ajax expects Tecmessa to observe this kind of modesty and subservience. He lives for war and great affairs. Such matters are not her concern. This does not mean that he feels no tenderness for her; it means that he is slow to show it and that he takes his important decisions alone. That is why, when he seems determined to kill himself, he orders her and her child to go away (578 ff.). Even here he feels for her despite his brusque words. He wishes her away because

> Women are too fond of tears,[6]

and he seems to fear that her anxieties may undermine his resolution. His subsequent orders, harsh though they sound (592 ff.), still show that he has some consideration for her, but he feels that he must not display it. His whole relation to her is real and convincing. Tecmessa feels no grievance about it. She is utterly devoted to him, and his death is an annihilating blow to her:

> I am lost, destroyed, utterly broken, friends.[7]

---

[1] Eur. *Heracl.* 476–7

> γυναικὶ γὰρ σιγή τε καὶ τὸ σωφρονεῖν
> κάλλιστον, εἴσω θ' ἥσυχον μένειν δόμων.

[2] Fr. 274 κόσμος ὀλιγομυθίη γυναικί.   [3] *Lys.* 514–15.   [4] *Oecon.* 7. 30.

[5] For a different view of the whole question cf. A. W. Gomme, *Essays in Greek History and Literature*, pp. 89–115. But cf. Lys. iii. 6, Isae. iii. 14. 3, Thuc. ii. 45. 2, Eur. *Phoen.* 92–5.

[6] 580 κάρτα τοι φιλοίκτιστον γυνή.

[7] 896 ᾤχωκ', ὄλωλα, διαπεπόρθημαι, φίλοι.

Her whole life has been absorbed in him, and that shows his importance.

The third person who helps to show Ajax' character is his half-brother Teucer. The two are never together on the stage, but after Ajax' death Teucer champions his cause and tells his revilers what he thinks about him. He too feels the death of Ajax as an appalling personal loss (1001). He fears that many sorrows now await him (1005), that Telamon will blame him for what has happened (1008-20), that he is helpless against his enemies (1021-2). He is too fond of Ajax to believe that he ever acted wrongly and brushes aside the accusation, justified though it is by facts, that Ajax wished to kill the Atridae (1127). He recalls his valorous deeds (1277-88), and so loyal is he to his half-brother's memory that he will not allow even the chivalrous Odysseus to take part in the burial because he and Ajax have been enemies (1393-7). Teucer shows the loyalty which Ajax arouses in a friend. Unlike the Homeric heroes, he is not concerned about his own name and fame; what matters to him is Ajax. Of course the epic had its classic examples of devoted loyalty like Achilles and Patroclus, but its sense of individual honour prevented it from setting so high a value on such relations as the fifth century did. The essence of such loyalty was to share a man's fortunes both good and bad, to support him with complete truth and faithfulness. Theognis appeals often enough to this feeling, and similar sentiments are to be found in the Attic Drinking-songs. Xenophon reports as a commonplace that 'a clear and good friend is the best of all possessions".[1] Teucer would appeal to Athenians by his devotion to Ajax and seem the ideal comrade. Their relation is almost that which Aristotle praised as 'the perfect friendship of men who are good and alike in virtue".[2] Such friendship is based on a resemblance between the participants, and Teucer resembles Ajax in his simplicity and directness, his distrust of superior officers, his warlike tastes, his outbursts of hot temper. That is why he neither allows nor understands criticism of Ajax and believes that everything Ajax has done is right.

So from three points of view, through the followers, the wife, and the friend, we see Ajax as commander, husband, and comrade. The personality that emerges is different from Homer's with his portentous strength and occasional hebetude; it is that of a great man with a power to command, able to win affection and loyalty, but somewhat remote and self-absorbed, except perhaps to one

[1] *Mem.* ii. 4. 1.   [2] *Nic. Eth.* 1156 b 6.

intimate companion. Despite this remoteness Ajax is fundamentally human, liked and loved as well as admired and obeyed.
Indeed his remoteness contributes to the impression of 'strength
and majesty which he makes. He is one of those superior beings
who find it difficult to enter into equal relations with others. The
Athenians of the fifth century liked to think that a man should be
easy and approachable, but none the less they had some regard for
those who from some innate superiority kept themselves apart.
The intellectualization of this feeling can be seen in Aristotle's
account of the 'great-souled' man whose aim is honour and who
is defined as 'thinking himself worthy of great things, being
worthy of them'.[1] He may never have existed or may owe much
to Aristotle's own fancy and predilections, but he shows that a
Greek could respect so superior and remote a being. Ajax is unlike him in many ways, but in his high regard for honour and his
high estimate of his own qualities he shows a resemblance. His
aim in life is well illustrated by Heraclitus' words that 'the best
choose one thing before everything, undying glory among men',[2]
and by his contrast of the 'best' with the crowd who are glutted like
beasts. Ajax is one of the 'best' in this sense. He lives for honour,
is never quite forgetful of his own worth, and even in the first
discovery of his shame emphasizes his own greatness:

> See'st thou me, the bold, the brave of heart,
> Me who never shrank in combat with the foe?[3]

To this theme he returns in his speech to Tecmessa (441–4) and to
his son (551). It is this which makes so bitter his feeling that he is
dishonoured (439). He knows that he is a great man who deserves
great honours, but he has been robbed of them. He lives for glory,
and that makes him distant to those about him.

When so great a man as Ajax falls, there may be some explanation of it. Pindar explained it by the failure of others to appreciate
him: they were victims of envy. Sophocles too employed this idea,
but in a different way. The Chorus know that Odysseus hates
Ajax and spreads stories against him (148 ff.), and their explanation is simple:

> 'Tis against the strong that jealousy creeps.[4]

Ajax is a superior being and excites envy. This is of course

---

[1] *Nic. Eth.* 1123 b 2.
[2] Fr. 29 αἱρεῦνται ἓν ἀντὶ ἁπάντων οἱ ἄριστοι, κλέος ἀέναον θνητῶν.
[3] 364–5 ὁρᾷς τὸν θρασύν, τὸν εὐκάρδιον,
τὸν ἐν δαΐοις ἄτρεστον μάχαις.
[4] 157 πρὸς γὰρ τὸν ἔχονθ' ὁ φθόνος ἕρπει.

dangerous, but not necessarily to his discredit. Envy was almost inevitable to greatness, as Pindar shows when he tells Hieron:

> To be envied is better than pitied.[1]

This belief helped the great to feel that such envy as they excited was a tribute to their success. No doubt this was hardly consistent with real modesty, but it stood for something. The mere fact that Ajax excites envy is not against him. But Sophocles sees more in the situation than Pindar did. Ajax excites envy not so much because he is great as because he is proud. It must be for this reason that Odysseus hates him (1347) and is sure that his hatred is good. Odysseus is such a pattern of virtue in the play that we cannot dismiss his hatred of Ajax as an accident. It arises, as he says, after the award of arms (1336–7), and we must assume that it is due to Ajax' arrogant behaviour. With the Atridae it is different. They hate Ajax because they are jealous of him. In fact Ajax excites envy for good and for bad reasons, and both are connected with his character.

It is a commonplace of Shakespearean criticism that the great tragic characters, Hamlet, Othello, Lear, Macbeth, come to disaster through some flaw in otherwise noble natures. Something of the same kind may be seen in Ajax. Sophocles has taken pains to show his pre-eminent qualities and to display how these come to disaster through his pride. It is this for which Athene punishes him, this which turns into mad wrath and leads him to do what he does. Athene says that he wished to kill the Atridae

> In heavy wrath about Achilles' arms.[2]

This wrath is strong in the appalling scene when he thinks that he is scourging Odysseus (105–13) and still strong when he recovers sanity and wishes to kill his enemies:

> Would that the most crafty one,
> The hateful dissembler I might kill,
> And the two kings, partners in rule—
> At last myself to perish![3]

He still hates them so much that he refuses to die fighting in case

---

[1] *Pyth.* i. 85 κρέσσων οἰκτιρμοῦ φθόνος. Cf. Hdt. iii. 52. 5, Aesch. *Ag.* 939, Eur. fr. 814, Plat. *Menex.* 242 a.

[2] 41   χόλῳ βαρυνθεὶς τῶν Ἀχιλλείων ὅπλων.

[3] 388–91   πῶς ἂν τὸν αἱμυλώτατον
                   ἐχθρὸν ἄλημα, τούς τε Ἀτσ-
                   σάρχας ὀλέσσας βασιλῆς,
                   τέλος θάνοιμι καὐτός;

that brings glory to them (466–9). He has as yet no regrets for what he has done, but complains that he has let his enemies slip:

> Unfortunate, from my hands
> I have let slip those men accursed.[1]

All through this he is moved by a violent desire for revenge on those who have humiliated him. His wrath is more likely to excite pity than condemnation; he seems to be not really master of himself. Yet this wrath is closely connected with his pride and essential to his tragedy.

Greek morality had no objection to anger as such and held that in certain circumstances it was even right. Aristotle thought that to endure insults to oneself or one's friends was slavish.[2] No doubt he reproduced what most Greeks felt. Homer's heroes are angry when they are affronted, and their natural impulse is to demand the punishment of the affronter.[3] There were exceptions, like Pittacus[4] and Socrates,[5] who advised forgiveness or submission to evil, but they did not affect popular opinion. In the sixth and fifth centuries anger was thought proper to a manly character, and a Theognidean poem shows what freedom was allowed to the expression of it in respectable circles.[6] Many would feel sympathy for Ajax in his wrath against Odysseus and the Atridae. They had certainly humiliated him, and he naturally claimed revenge. Yet the action of the play shows that Ajax' anger is disastrous. Through it he is brought to misery and death.

Ajax' anger makes him wish to kill his generals. It is frustrated by Athene, who turns his fury on to the cattle. She condemns his action and treats it as if it were a kind of pride (127–33). She even says that in it he is base. To connect anger and pride in this way was unusual in Greek psychology. The philosophic Aristotle[7] and the political Demosthenes[8] distinguish between the two. Ajax' case is of a special kind. In his wrath over his injuries he makes his intolerable and arrogant attempt to kill the generals. It is his angry pride which annoys men and brings on him the condemnation of the gods. His besetting fault is a kind of contemptuous fury in which he both despises and hates those who get in his way. For this Athene punishes him. He knows that the gods even abhor him for it and feels that he is cut off from them, that he is an outcast from both gods and men:

[1] 372–3   ὦ δύσμορος, ὃς χεροῖν
                      μεθῆκα τοὺς ἀλάστορας.

[2] Nic. Eth. 1126 a 8.   [3] Il. iii. 351, Od. viii. 166 ff.
[4] Diog. Laert. i. 75, cf. Hdt. iii. 53. 4.   [5] Plat. Gorg. 527 c.
[6] Theogn. 341–50.   [7] Nic. Eth. 1149 b 20.   [8] xxi. 41.

Neither on the race of gods
Nor men of a day may I look upon
To claim a kindness from them.[1]

From this it is but a small step to thinking that the gods hate him:

And now what must I do, who by the gods
Am manifestly hated?[2]

In this mood he feels that he has severed relations with the gods and is no longer concerned with them. When Tecmessa fears that he purposes something ill and asks him what it is, he answers with brutal frankness:

You vex me overmuch. Do you not know
I owe no further duty to the gods?[3]

Anger and pride have robbed him of the modesty which all men should observe. No wonder that the Chorus see that something is gravely wrong: Not with his inbred thoughts
Dwells he assured, but a stranger outside them.[4]

Ajax, even in his humiliation, is full of pride, and this pride is closely connected with the revengeful anger which moved him before his madness and is still strong in him. From the beginning of the play we see how this trait affects Ajax and is fraught with dangers for him.

Ajax' pride shows itself both with men and with gods. Menelaus complains that it is difficult to control subordinate officers when they are so unruly as Ajax:

Nor can a host be providently ruled
Without the shield of fear and reverence.[5]

He suggests that Ajax is arrogant and irreverent. So when he speaks of Athene turning his fury from the Atridae to the flocks, he calls the fury 'pride': But now a god
Has turned his pride to fall on sheep and herds.[6]

[1] 398–400
οὔτε γὰρ θεῶν γένος
οὔθ' ἀμερίων ἔτ' ἄξιος
βλέπειν τιν' εἰς ὄνασιν ἀνθρώπων.

[2] 457–8
καὶ νῦν τί χρὴ δρᾶν; ὅστις ἐμφανῶς θεοῖς
ἐχθαίρομαι.

[3] 589–90
ἄγαν γε λυπεῖς. οὐ κάτοισθ' ἐγὼ θεοῖς
ὡς οὐδὲν ἀρκεῖν εἴμ' ὀφειλέτης ἔτι;

[4] 639–40
οὐκέτι συντρόφοις
ὀργαῖς ἔμπεδος, ἀλλ' ἐκτὸς ὁμιλεῖ.

[5] 1075–6
οὔτ' ἂν στρατός γε σωφρόνως ἄρχοιτ' ἔτι
μηδὲν φόβου πρόβλημα μηδ' αἰδοῦς ἔχων.

[6] 1060–1
νῦν δ' ἐνήλλαξεν θεὸς
τὴν τοῦδ' ὕβριν πρὸς μῆλα καὶ ποίμνας πεσεῖν.

Later he calls Ajax 'fiery and insolent'.[1] Menelaus is of course a
hostile witness, but that does not mean that his opinion is worthless. From a human 'standpoint and towards other men Ajax is
undeniably proud. His pride makes him treat his superiors in a
way that they resent even after his death. It is the first cause of
their refusal to bury him. But this arrogance towards men is not
primarily what concerns the gods. They are bound to resent the
pride that he shows towards them. It is this which leads to his
madness, humiliation, and death.

This point is made with such emphasis that we are forced to take
notice of it. Calchas, who is an impeccable witness, gives, as the Messenger reports, two cases in which Ajax has shown arrogance to the
gods. The first was when he told his father that he could win glory
without divine help (767-9), the second when he told Athene to help
the other Achaeans since the line would never break where he stood
(770-7). If the first was spoken 'boastfully and foolishly',[2] the second
is 'a dire and blasphemous word'.[3] Calchas sums the matter up:

> For gross unprofitable bodies fall,
> Struck down with great calamities from heaven,
> (So spake the seer), when one of human birth
> Imagines thoughts too high for man's estate.[4]

This is traditional doctrine. The gods punish those who show
arrogance towards them. The imagery, too, is familiar. The
proud man is seen as a great overgrown body. So Herodotus makes
Artabanus warn Xerxes that 'God loves to lop all things that grow
grossly'.[5] Ajax' size is almost a symbol of the excess which the
gods resent. So at least his enemies think. Menelaus makes the
point clearly enough:

> For though a man be grown to mighty bulk,
> Let him beware lest some small chance destroy him.[6]

Agamemnon repeats it:
> 'Tis not the big
> Broad-shoulder'd men who are the most secure.[7]

---

[1] 1088 αἴθων ὑβριστής.

[2] 766 ὑψικόμπως κἀφρόνως.   [3] 773 Δεινὸν ἄρρητόν τ' ἔπος.

[4] 758-61   τὰ γὰρ περισσὰ κἀνόνητα σώματα
              πίπτειν βαρείαις πρὸς θεῶν Δυσπραξίαις
              ἔφασχ' ὁ μάντις, ὅστις ἀνθρώπων φύσιν
              βλαστὼν ἔπειτα μὴ κατ' ἄνθρωπον φρονῇ.

[5] Hdt. vii. 10 φιλέει δ' ὁ θεὸς τὰ ὑπερέχοντα πάντα κολούειν.

[6] 1077-8   ἀλλ' ἄνδρα χρή, κἂν σῶμα γεννήσῃ μέγα,
              Δοκεῖν πεσεῖν ἂν κἂν ἀπὸ σμικροῦ κακοῦ.

[7] 1250-1   οὐ γὰρ οἱ πλατεῖς
              οὐδ' εὐρύνωτοι φῶτες ἀσφαλέστατοι.

They are of course perverting the doctrine. It is not because he is strong that the gods strike Ajax, but because he is proud. His pride is seen as an object which must be reduced. To this point Sophocles gives an emphatic place just before Ajax' death, when both his offences are said to be what does not befit a man (761,777). Ajax has forgotten the rule that men must attempt only what is human,[1] and tried to treat the gods as equals. Sophocles underlines Ajax' pride and the fact that it is directed against the gods. His verdict is similar to that of some lines by Euripides:

> But as our body is of mortal breed,
> It is not fitting to indulge a temper
> Immortal, if a man knows modesty.[2]

Ajax thinks himself the peer of the gods, and this delusion is part of his high temper. For it the gods punish him.

If a man is proud, he may fall into a blind infatuation of soul and commit impious or criminal acts. This process is as old as Hesiod, who makes it the text of a lesson to Perses,[3] and in various shapes it is repeated by Solon, Theognis, Aeschylus, Pindar, and Herodotus. There is no matter for surprise at its appearance in Sophocles. He uses it of Ajax whose arrogant character breeds an infatuation that leads to his fall. Odysseus, a fair-minded observer, comments on Ajax' illusion of triumph as he stands among the slaughtered cattle and thinks they are the bodies of his enemies:

> He is yoked to an evil doom,[4]

and the Chorus, loyal though they are to their master, say to him when they see him amid the sinister and pathetic wreckage:

> Keep silence from bad words. Nor adding ill
> To ill make sorrow greater than your doom.[5]

This doom is the fury which began with Ajax' desire to kill his enemies, but it survives in the madness which makes him kill the cattle. The transition from pride to this is entirely natural, an increase of violence and fury in the soul of Ajax, which continues even after it has spent its main force. One fury turns into another; the illusions of injured pride become the illusions of real madness.

---

[1] Pind. *Isthm.* v. 16, Soph. fr. 346, Eur. *Alc.* 799.

[2] Fr. 799   ὥσπερ δὲ θνητὸν καὶ τὸ σῶμ' ἡμῶν ἔφυ,
             οὕτω προσήκει μηδὲ τὴν ὀργὴν ἔχειν
             ἀθάνατον ὅστις σωφρονεῖν ἐπίσταται.

[3] *Op.* 214–16.

[4] 123   ἄτῃ συγκατέζευκται κακῇ.

[5] 362–3   εὔφημα φώνει· μὴ κακὸν κακῷ διδοὺς
             ἄκος πλέον τὸ πῆμα τῆς ἄτης τίθει.

Sophocles has made the process true to human nature. Ajax'
tragedy arises out of his peculiar temper, his pride which needs no
help and brooks no rivals. Sophocles shows the horror of this doom
in its naked brutality, especially in the heart-rending scene when
Ajax comes out of his tent with a bloody scourge in his hand and
refuses Athene's request to spare the animal which he insanely
believes to be Odysseus:

> Athene, in all else I bid thee hail,
> But he shall have this and no other doom.[1]

This shows the nature and degree of Ajax' infatuation. It is a
madness which has grown out of his pride and anger until it sub-
dues his whole being and makes him live among phantoms in an
insane, illusory world. The bitter, shameful process is the result of
his arrogance towards the gods.

Athene punishes Ajax for his pride. It has been directly aimed
at her. It is her help that he has refused or derided, and she is
right to teach him a lesson. Her action would seem perfectly just
and real to any ordinary Athenian. It was no mere fancy drawn
from the Homeric world, though there are good precedents for it
there.[2] In the fifth century many believed that if the gods were
insulted, they were angry and exacted vengeance. Pindar draws
the moral more than once, for Tantalus, Ixion, and Bellerophon.[3]
In his account of Coronis he makes the message plain:

> It is not light, the anger of god's children.[4]

When Sophocles applied it to Ajax, it is possible that he had in
mind the sad example of Aeschylus' Capaneus who is no less great
in size and unbridled in speech:

> Another giant this, greater than he
> I spoke of, and his boasts too proud for man.[5]

Just as Capaneus is punished, so will Ajax be. Nor is such an event
unusual even in Sophocles. In early plays, in *Niobe*, *Thamyris*, and
Locrian Ajax, he seems to have dramatized cases of presumption

---

[1] 112-13   χαίρειν, 'Αθάνα, τἄλλ' ἐγώ σ' ἐφίεμαι·
                 κεῖνος Δὲ τείσει τήνΔε κοὐκ ἄλλην Δίκην.

[2] *Il.* ii. 594 ff., ix. 533 ff.; *Od.* i. 19 ff., viii. 224.

[3] *Ol.* i. 55 ff., *Pyth.* ii. 20 ff., *Isthm.* vii. 42.

[4] *Pyth.* iii. 11-12   χόλος Δ' οὐκ ἀλίθιος
                                γίνεται παίΔων Διός.

[5] *Sept.* 424-5   γίγας ὅΔ' ἄλλος τοῦ πάρος λελεγμένου
                        μείζων, ὁ κόμπος Δ' οὐ κατ' ἄνθρωπον φρονεῖ.

which incurred divine anger and met with hideous punishment.
So, too, with Ajax. When Calchas says of him:

> By such words did he win the goddess's
> Pitiless wrath, with thoughts too high for man[1]

the theological position is clear: Athene will punish Ajax because
she is angry with him for insulting her.

The manner of punishment, however, is unusual. Ajax is not
smitten directly by Athene nor by some natural power at her
disposal. She pursues a more original and more humane method.
When Ajax purposes to kill the Achaean leaders, she makes
him mad and turns his wrath against the cattle and sheep
(51 ff.). No doubt she is partly moved by a desire to save her
friend Odysseus and her favoured Achaeans. But her action is
more complex than that. She punishes Ajax through his own
chief fault, his pride and angry temper. In his fury he wishes to kill
his enemies; his fury turns to madness and becomes the means to
his humiliation. Not Odysseus but Ajax suffers. It was an old
belief that the gods first make mad those men whom they intend
to destroy:

> Whenever god plans evil for a man,
> He first destroys the wits with which he plots.[2]

But whereas such madness might lead a man to work his own
undoing by hateful acts, Ajax' madness saves him from doing
what he intends and through this helps to make him conscious of his
humiliation. He is chastised through his madness, and the chastise-
ment is hard for him to bear. Yet Athene is not so severe as we
might expect. She does not wish merely for her pride to be
satisfied by the spectacle of Ajax' fall; she wishes him to learn
wisdom by the experience and to instruct others by his example.
She might well have treated him like the Locrian Ajax. But
perhaps from respect for his great qualities (119–20) she is content
to humble him. To do this she works through his greatest fault,
his anger which is akin to madness. She tries to cure this by
showing to what it brings him.

With remarkable boldness Sophocles presents the wrath of
Athene on the stage. She appears with Odysseus, who presents a
complete contrast to her. The man appeals to modern feelings by

---

[1] 776–7   τοιοῖσΔέ τοι λόγοισιν ἀστεργῆ θεᾶς
ἐκτήσατ' ὀργήν, οὐ κατ' ἄνθρωπον φρονῶν.

[2] Tr. ad. fr. 455   ὅταν Δ' ὁ Δαίμων ἀνΔρὶ πορσύνη κακά,
τὸν νοῦν ἔβλαψε πρῶτον ᾧ βουλεύεται.

his moderation and chivalry; the goddess seems to exult brutally in the helpless humiliation of her victim. She begins by congratulating Odysseus on his unrelenting pursuit of his enemies (1–2). Such a sentiment was common enough and need occasion no surprise in the national protectress of Athens and conqueror of the Giants. Then she calls on Odysseus to look on Ajax in his madness. She feels that he will enjoy the spectacle:

> Is it not sweetest mockery to mock foes?[1]

When Odysseus shows qualms which do him credit, she almost taunts him with cowardice:

> Are you afraid of a madman, face to face?[2]

When the mad Ajax comes out of his tent she plays with him in what seems a sinister, merciless spirit, taking what he says at its face-value, making no effort to bring him back to his senses and feeling no kind of compassion for him. Then, when he goes back into his tent, she changes her tone and explains to Odysseus:

> You see, Odysseus, how great is the gods' strength?
> Who could be found more prudent than this man,
> More fit for action when occasion called?[3]

We see the actual punishment, the spirit in which Athene conducts it, the importance which she attaches to it, the blind brutal fury of Ajax which is none the less inexcusable because it has been expended on animals. We see, too, the irresistible power of the gods, the helplessness and bestiality of the man who has resisted it. The sharp painful contrast, set in the very forefront of the play, shows the vast gap that divides men from the gods. And this exhibition contains a lesson—that men must be modest before the gods if they wish to avoid such a punishment. Ajax' madness is a warning against boastfulness and presumption:

> Look therefore upon on this and never say
> Yourself presumptuous words against the gods,
> Nor swell with arrogance, though you surpass
> Others in weight of hand or wealth's great store.
> A day can lay all mortal actions low

---

[1] 79   οὔκουν γέλως ἥδιστος εἰς ἐχθροὺς γελᾶν;

[2] 81   μεμηνότ' ἄνδρα περιφανῶς ὀκνεῖς ἰδεῖν;

[3] 118–20   ὁρᾷς, 'Οδυσσεῦ, τὴν θεῶν ἰσχὺν ὅση;
                  τούτου τίς ἄν σοι τἀνδρὸς ἢ προνούστερος
                  ἢ δρᾶν ἀμείνων ηὑρέθη τὰ καίρια;

Or raise them up again. But the gods love
The modest-hearted and detest the base.[1]

With this emphatic enunciation of traditional morality Athene
disappears. It is clear that Ajax' punishment comes from the gods,
is fully deserved, and intended for his good.

Yet though Athene's punishment of Ajax is orthodox, its
manner is undeniably surprising. We do not expect divine wrath
to be displayed so candidly, and we cannot but feel that Athene
finds her triumph sweet. Her wrath looks like malicious pleasure in
Ajax' fall. The angry gods of Pindar are not said to take pleasure
in the fall of their victims; even in the destruction of the worthless
Suitors Homer's Athene raises no cry of triumph. In his *Niobe*
Sophocles had made Apollo kill the children on the stage,[2] but so
fearful a vengeance can hardly have been an occasion for divine
joy. It is true of course that Athene is playful with Odysseus
and that this playfulness may owe something to the *Odyssey*.
Odysseus was traditionally her favourite, and she treats him with
an easy intimacy which contains irony and humour. But that
does not explain her joy in taunting Ajax. The nearest parallel to
such divine behaviour on the Attic stage is in Euripides' *Bacchants*,
where Dionysus finds pleasure in mocking the helpless deluded
Pentheus and lures him to an awful doom. Sophocles' Athene is
less merciless than this. She wishes to give a lesson as well as to
exact a punishment. But the similarity exists. We can understand
why Dionysus acts as he does. He is a power of nature, potent to
exalt and to humble, beyond good and evil, hardly a true Olympian. But Athene is an authentic Olympian, the goddess of Athens.
We hardly expect her to behave in so emphatically human, even
feminine, a way. The explanation is that the Greeks regarded
their gods as embodiments of power. When they come into conflict
with men this power is displayed. It is this of which men must
beware. Athene shows the power of the gods to do their will when
they are outraged, and her pleasure in her victim's humiliation is
the triumphant joy of a conqueror over an enemy who has acted
wrongly and been punished for it.

---

[1] 127–33   τοιαῦτα τοίνυν εἰσορῶν ὑπέρκοπον
μηδέν ποτ' εἴπῃς αὐτὸς εἰς θεοὺς ἔπος
μηδ' ὄγκον ἄρῃ μηδέν', εἴ τινος πλέον
ἢ χειρὶ βρίθεις ἢ μακροῦ πλούτου βάθει.
ὡς ἡμέρα κλίνει τε κἀνάγει πάλιν
ἅπαντα τἀνθρώπεια· τοὺς δὲ σώφρονας
θεοὶ φιλοῦσι καὶ στυγοῦσι τοὺς κακούς.

[2] Fr. 442. The attribution of the fragment to Sophocles is not quite certain.

Athene, however, tempers her justice with a mercy that is rare in insulted divinities. Though Ajax has twice derided her, her anger against him is limited in time. He has been humiliated, and she does not wish to push her advantage too far. Her wrath lasts only for a single day:

> He shall be hunted on this day alone
> By great Athene's wrath[1]

and even on this day all will be well for Ajax if he keeps to his tent (753–5). Instead of killing him Athene will humble him and give him a chance to escape death. It is unusual in a god to allow this measure of mercy, and we may suspect that it is an invention of Sophocles. But whether it is or not, Sophocles must have had his reason for introducing it, and this may be surmised. The short duration of Athene's wrath and Ajax' chance of escaping it mean that she is willing to treat him lightly, presumably because of his great qualities and the services that he has done for the Achaean cause which she supports. The goddess recognizes his great merits while she punishes his faults. Moreover, this device has its uses for the drama. It has a symbolical or psychological truth. If Ajax had stayed in the tent, the presence of Tecmessa, his son, and his faithful followers might well have softened his heart against killing himself. It is only when he goes out alóne with the accursed sword that once belonged to Hector that these ties fail to hold him and he falls back into his old mood of angry resentment and self-destructive despair. Ajax' psychology agrees with the divine plan. The goddess's will works as much through him as on him.

Just as the presence of Athene draws attention to the nature of Ajax' presumption before the gods, so the presence of Odysseus shows how an ordinary, modest man sees the situation. He finds no pleasure in the humiliation of his enemy. Once he knows the truth he is content with what he hears and has no wish to see the horrors that delight Athene. He says that he is afraid of Ajax mad though he would not be of him sane (82), consents to see him only because Athene desires it, and reverently accepts her promise that Ajax shall not see him in return:

> All things can happen when a god contrives.[2]

Then towards the end of the scene he anticipates what Athene is going to say. Seeing the pitiful plight of Ajax he thinks of

---

[1] 756–7   ἐλᾷ γὰρ αὐτὸν τῇδε θἠμέρᾳ μόνῃ
                Αἴας Ἀθάνας μῆνις.

[2] 86   γένοιτο μέντἂν πᾶν θεοῦ τεχνωμένου.

his own human condition:

> I see that we are nothing else but phantoms,
> All we who live, or unsubstantial shades.[1]

Even in this short space the contrast between Odysseus and Ajax is complete. Ajax is the superior being, full of strength and pride, Odysseus the modest man who humbles himself before the gods and keeps to the Mean. It is he, and not the Chorus, who provides the role of impartial critic on what happens. The man whom Pindar regarded as the villain of the piece is presented as a faultless character. Both here and after Ajax' death it is his decency and his wisdom which win our support. Though he has hated Ajax, as by Greek standards he may, he is scrupulously fair to him in his anguish and after his death.

The hatred of Ajax and Odysseus and their rivalry for the arms of Achilles belonged to tradition. Odysseus almost had to have a part in the play. But Sophocles was bold to give him this particular part. His serious, modest, compassionate Odysseus bears little resemblance to the gay, enterprising, reckless hero of Homer and still less to the cold-blooded Odysseus of Euripides. In this change Sophocles is doubly justified. First, Odysseus is the friend of Athene. So Homer had depicted him; so no doubt the *Little Iliad* accounted for Athene's support of him in the award of arms. But Sophocles' Odysseus does not treat Athene as Homer's does. The badinage, the playful trickery, the comradeship in deception and revenge, the real similarity of character, have disappeared; Odysseus is strictly, severely respectful. Sophocles may have felt it irreverent for a man to treat a goddesss as Homer's Odysseus treats Athene. It was in any case out of character in one who was to be a model of reverence and propriety. So the relation between man and goddess leaves the world of epic fancy and is brought nearer to the facts of religious experience as the fifth century understood them. The goddess may be triumphant, wilful, and playful, but the man must none the less treat her with profound respect. Secondly, Sophocles uses Odysseus as a foil to Ajax, and contrasts the sanity and modesty of the one with the pride and madness of the other. This contrast is vital to the play's design. In Ajax we see pride and its result, in Odysseus modesty and the good ends to which it leads. This is not to say that Sophocles preferred Odysseus to Ajax or thought him really superior. He displays in him a way of life which is best suited to men and most likely to lead to happiness.

[1] 125–6   ὁρῶ γὰρ ἡμᾶς οὐδὲν ὄντας ἄλλο πλὴν
                 εἴδωλ' ὅσοιπερ ζῶμεν ἢ κούφην σκιάν.

Ajax is governed by different principles. He aims at something more dangerous and more difficult; his superior gifts contain the seeds of his undoing. Humanly speaking, he is grander and nobler than Odysseus. But his great virtues are matched by great faults. The conflict in his nature is contrasted with the harmony in that of Odysseus.

The end of the prologue comes so emphatically and with so clear a message from man and goddess that we cannot but accept it as given *ex cathedra* by the poet. What follows supplements this lesson, but where it stands, it is final on what has happened. It is Sophocles' verdict on Ajax' collapse and madness. It shows that Athene is right to punish him and that men should learn modesty from cases like his. It is therefore important to see what Sophocles means, especially in the words which he gives to Odysseus. This is not the only place where he speaks in this way about the nothingness of man. In the *Antigone* the Messenger says that Creon's life after his disasters is not worth the shadow of smoke. A line from the *Locrian Ajax*, where another eminent hero was punished for presumption towards the gods, must have conveyed a similar conclusion:

> Man is a breath, a shade, and nothing more.[1]

Such misfortune forces the conviction that man is nothing but a phantom or a shadow or a breath, utterly unsubstantial and transitory. Disaster takes away from a man his sense of strength and life, his feeling that he is free to choose his way and to exert his will. He should always be conscious of this and know that before the gods he is as nothing. The right doctrine is that of the Sophoclean character who says:

> O miserable and mortal race of men!
> For we are naught but semblances of shadows,
> Walking, a useless burden to the earth.[2]

The imagery has more in it than a mere sense of emptiness and futility. It belongs to a consistent view of human life as dependent on the gods for everything that matters. A shadow depends on light, a phantom implies something real of which it is a copy. Behind human appearances exists the reality of the gods. It is this which the images suggest. Its strength gives light to men in joy and power. It is the reality of which human life is at the best but a reflection or a copy. For Pindar human life is a shadow in a dream

---

[1] Fr. 13   ἄνθρωπός ἐστι πνεῦμα καὶ σκιὰ μόνον. Cf. Eur. *Med.* 1224.
[2] Fr. 945   ὦ θνητὸν ἀνΔρῶν καὶ ταλαίπωρον γένος,
                         ὡς οὐΔέν ἐσμεν πλὴν σκιαῖς ἐοικότες,
                         βάρος περισσὸν γῆς ἀναστρωφώμενοι.

until the god-given glory illumines it, and then all is sweet.[1] But
without this divine sustenance and support the thoughts and
activities of men are nothing but a phantasmagoria. So when
Ajax cuts himself off from the gods, his life is empty and unreal and
has no meaning. By setting himself up against them and coming
into conflict with them he shows the pitiful weakness of man in his
own state. If men wish to enjoy fullness of living, they must attend
to the gods and respect them. For the moment the divine light and
strength have been taken from Ajax, but the play is at its beginning,
and before its close something will be given back to him. His
honour will be established, his name survive, his friends champion
him. Against the background of angry gods and transitory unsubstantial men Sophocles builds up something more secure and
more abiding.

The gods have displayed their power, but the lesson which
Odysseus sees at once is not yet apparent to Ajax. It is some time
before he works the evil out of his system. When he first recovers
his sanity, the emotions that dominate him are resentment, anger,
humiliation, desire for revenge, desire for death. He still cherishes
his hatred for the Atridae and for Odysseus. He regrets that they
have slipped through his hands (372-3); he prays that he may be
allowed to kill them (387-91); he says nothing of having offended
the gods; he shows no signs of a chastened disposition. His words
pain Tecmessa, who feels that they are not true to his real
character and says what most would approve:

> Ah woe is me, that a good man should say
> Such things as he would not have dared before.[2]

In his apparent disregard of Tecmessa's appeal Ajax still seems to
be angry, and we can understand why the Chorus refer to his
grievous affliction (643). But he does not stay in this self-absorbed,
self-pitying mood. The lesson of the gods, the human appeal of
Tecmessa, have their effect on him. Sophocles does not show the
phases or process of the change, but simply the result in Ajax after it
has taken place. The great speech which he makes at 646-92 shows
that he has recovered himself, got rid of his evil passions and
illusions, learned the lesson which the gods have taught him. This
speech has been variously interpreted. Some have even claimed that
Ajax is lying and that the whole speech is a deliberate imposture
intended to put the Chorus off their guard while he goes away to

[1] *Pyth.* viii. 95-7.
[2] 410-11   ὦ δυστάλαινα, τοιάδ' ἄνδρα χρήσιμον
                φωνεῖν, ἃ πρόσθεν οὗτος οὐκ ἔτλη ποτ' ἄν.

kill himself. But this view is surely untenable. First, it is at variance with Ajax' character, which is nothing if not direct and outspoken, and it is impossible that if he were lying he would speak so tenderly of his wife and child:

> From pity I cannot leave
> Her widowed with her foes, my boy an orphan.[1]

We cannot suspect imposture in these words. Secondly, if the speech is a deception, Ajax dies without having made his peace with god and man, without having learned the lesson that Odysseus has so emphatically stated, without having rid himself of his devasting anger and pride. Surely Sophocles would not send this great being to his death in an unchastened, unrepentant spirit, hated by the gods and hating them in return. In fact the only argument for this view is that later Ajax acts against the decision which he here announces and kills himself after all. For this change of purpose there are, as we shall see, special reasons. For the moment we must take his words to mean what they say and accept them as a true account of what he now thinks. Their poetry is too genuine, their emotion too strong for them to be a calculated piece of deceit. On the stage their effect can only be that Ajax is telling the truth. There is no evidence that as he develops his speech he introduces into it a hidden purpose inconsistent with the beginning. In his later plays Sophocles made a powerful use of deliberate falsehood, but the glittering lies of the Paedagogus in the *Electra* have nothing in common with this moving, profound, simple speech. Their circumstantial details, their confident heartless air, their absence of any human appeal, are quite alien to the authentic poetry of this self-revelation.

The speech unveils Ajax' mind at the moment. Tecmessa's appeal has softened him and brought him at last to his senses, though his pride makes him a little ashamed that this should be so (650 ff.). What he most desires now is to make peace with gods and men. The gods come first. He must purify himself of his pollution and hide the sword which is the instrument of his sorrow. When he says:

> But I will seek the water and the shore
> And meadows, there to wash my stains away
> And so escape the goddess's heavy wrath[2]

---

[1] 652–3   οἰκτίρω δέ νιν
χήραν παρ' ἐχθροῖς παῖδά τ' ὀρφανὸν λιπεῖν.

[2] 654–6   ἀλλ' εἶμι πρός τε λουτρὰ καὶ παρακτίους
λειμῶνας, ὡς ἂν λύμαθ' ἁγνίσας ἐμὰ
μῆνιν βαρεῖαν ἐξαλύξωμαι θεᾶς.

he means just what he says, that he is polluted with bloodshed and must wash away the pollution. He feels, like Iphigeneia, that

> The sea can wash away all human ills.[1]

His sword must be buried because it has been an instrument of destruction. It is accursed, and its burial in the earth will bind the curse to the earth. So Jason buries the sword with which he killed Apsyrtus.[2] As his purification will rid Ajax of pollution, so the burial of the sword will free him from future danger. He feels that it is accursed because an enemy gave it to him, and that he will be better without it (661–5).

The first resolution is followed by a second, to make peace with men:

> Therefore henceforth I'll study to obey
> The gods and reverence the sons of Atreus.[3]

The Atridae are Ajax' commanders and should be obeyed. The complaint raised later by Menelaus that Ajax has been a disloyal subordinate (1075–6) has in the past had some justification, but now Ajax decides to remove any grounds for it. He feels the respect which is due to princes and commanders,[4] and abjures his old independence. He is even prepared to make friends of his former enemies:

> I have learned of late
> That we should only hate our foes so much
> As we shall love them later.[5]

The words echo a saying of Bias of Priene, 'like as if you would afterwards hate, and hate as if you would afterwards like',[6] but their effect is not quite the same. The old piece of worldly wisdom becomes a means to convey that Ajax accepts life as it is with all its uncertainties and changes. It shows his newly found modesty.

This change of heart in Ajax is splendidly compared by him to changes in physical nature. Just as winter yields to summer, night to day, storm to calm, so he too will yield. The superb images do more than give fire and force to his sincerity. They show that he accepts the belief that the universe, animate and inanimate, has a

---

[1] Eur. *I. T.* 1193   θάλασσα κλύζει πάντα τἀνθρώπων κακά.

[2] Ap. Rhod. iv. 696.

[3] 666–7   τοιγὰρ τὸ λοιπὸν εἰσόμεσθα μὲν θεοῖς
εἴκειν, μαθησόμεσθα δ' Ἀτρείδας σέβειν.

[4] *Il.* x. 238, xv. 129; Aesch. *Pers.* 699; Xen. *Cyr.* viii. 7. 22; *Hell.* v. 3. 22.

[5] 678–9   ἐπίσταμαι γὰρ ἀρτίως ὅτι
ὅ τ' ἐχθρὸς ἡμῖν ἐς τοσόνδ' ἐχθαρτέος
ὡς καὶ φιλήσων αὖθις.

[6] Arist. *Rhet.* 1389 b 24.

controlling harmony to which he, who has recently proclaimed his severance from the gods, must conform. In giving him these words Sophocles transposes a thought from natural science. Diogenes of Apollonia, who no doubt followed what others said before him, argued that the measure to be found in nature is an argument for a directing intelligence; 'for it would not be possible for things to be divided in this way without intelligence, so that it keeps the measures of everything, of winter and summer, of night and day, or rains and winds and calms'.[1] Sophocles has this or something like it in his mind. Again he may be compared with Euripides, whose Jocasta in the *Phoenician Women* pleads with her sons to divide their inheritance equally because in nature, notably in light and darkness, there is a directing equality:

> For measures and allotted posts to men
> Equality gives, in due proportion set;
> And equal in the year's course is the path
> Of sunlight and the night's unseeing eye,
> And neither feels resentment in defeat.[2]

Her plea is ingenious and apposite. She too advocates the submission of private aims to a universal order. But somehow her words lack the power and distinction of Sophocles. The abstract Equality has not the same appeal as the unnamed and unmentioned order which Ajax invokes. His acceptance of the harmony in the universe and his decision to shape his life in accordance with it rise from his own spiritual needs. He has been in conflict with the gods, with other men, with himself. In modesty and self-denial he finds his solution for the conflicts and agonies which have beset him.

In this speech Ajax shows true modesty. He has himself learned the lesson which Odysseus learned from the sight of him in his madness. And with this the whole episode of his mad wrath might end. The gods have had their way; Ajax is healed of his grave fault; he has made amends. The Chorus, who are deeply concerned about his fate, are overjoyed, and their words show how they understand him and think that he has done what is right before the gods:

[1] Fr. 3 οὐ γὰρ ἂν οἶόν τε ἦν οὕτω δέδασθαι ἄνευ νοήσιος, ὥστε πάντων μέτρα ἔχειν, χειμῶνός τε καὶ θέρους καὶ νυκτὸς καὶ ἡμέρας καὶ ὑετῶν καὶ ἀνέμων καὶ εὐδιῶν.

[2] *Phoen.* 541–5   καὶ γὰρ μέτρ' ἀνθρώποισι καὶ μέρη σταθμῶν
                      Ἰσότης ἔταξε κἀριθμὸν διώρισε,
                      νυκτός τ' ἀφεγγὲς βλέφαρον ἡλίου τε φῶς
                      ἴσον βαδίζει τὸν ἐνιαύσιον κύκλον,
                      κοὐδέτερον αὐτῶν φθόνον ἔχει νικώμενον.

All rites due to the gods he now
Rightly performs with loyal worship.[1]

No wonder that they call on gods of joy and comfort and welcome
the prospect of better days now that Ajax has abandoned his anger
and time has done its work of healing (714–18). Their happiness
is soon turned to despair. Ajax leaves them, but when he next
appears the scene has changed to a deserted place on the sea-shore.
Ajax is alone, and to our appalled surprise he has decided to kill
himself. He does not even announce his decision; he simply tells
how he is going to effect it and takes his last farewell of earth and
sun. He has changed his mind and gives no reason for it. His words
take no account of what has passed and look forward to the accomplishment of his new, deadly resolve. Sophocles evidently intended
this change to come with the shock of a great surprise, to make us
feel that some powerful influence has been at work on Ajax and
made him forget or abandon his former resolutions. This revolution of purpose might be attributed to an immature or imperfect
technique in the poet; it might be argued that for some reason
Sophocles could not or would not dramatize the stages through
which Ajax passes. But this would be wrong. Sophocles has
reasons for presenting the change in so abrupt and surprising a
way. In the interval between Ajax' departure from his tent and
his appearance on the sea-shore the Messenger arrives and explains
Athene's intentions about him. She is angry for only one day, and
if Ajax stays in his tent, he will be safe. Calchas has told Teucer
what should be done:

> By every means
> Throughout this day that now shines over us
> Keep Ajax in his tent, nor let him out,
> If you would wish to see him still alive.[2]

But Ajax has left his tent, and therefore the goddess's anger is
powerful against him. That follows inevitably. Naturally Tecmessa and the Chorus feel a grave anxiety that at this moment
Ajax should have gone out. So, when he next appears, he is preparing to kill himself.

Ajax' decision is intelligible only on the supposition that he is

---

[1] 711–13
                    θεῶν
    Δ' αὖ πάνθυτα θέσμι' ἐξ-
    ήνυσ' εὐνομίᾳ σέβων μεγίστᾳ.

[2] 752–5
                  παντοίᾳ τέχνῃ
    εἷρξαι κατ' ἦμαρ τοὐμφανὲς τὸ νῦν τόδε
    Αἴανθ' ὑπὸ σκηναῖσι μηΔ' ἀφέντ' ἐᾶν,
    εἰ ζῶντ' ἐκεῖνον εἰσιΔεῖν θέλοι ποτέ.

not master of himself but the victim of superior forces and powers.
Naturally he does not understand this and cannot say anything
about it. We must base our conclusions on the way in which he
speaks and acts. And they are inevitable. In this speech Ajax has
returned to some of the passions which beset him in his madness
and in the dark hours after his recovery. The quieter thoughts of
his sanity, the humbleness, the desire for friends, the reverence,
have disappeared. Once again he is full of hatred, not merely
for the Atridae and Odysseus but for the whole Achaean army
(835–44). He says nothing now of Tecmessa or his child, nothing
of the miseries which await them, though lately he was conscious
of these. He is his old angry, revengeful, self-absorbed self. He is in
a fury akin to madness, and we may assume that since Athene's
anger is on him as it was when he was mad, it is again the cause of
his fury. Once again the goddess's will works on him through his
own actions. He thinks that he acts of his own choice but he is
really the victim of her curse. From her comes the unreasonable
impulse to self-destruction. For this tragic reversal Sophocles has
prepared the audience not only by the Messenger's words but by
· the tragic irony at the close of Ajax' earlier speech:

> But I shall go there where I have to go.
> Do what I say, and you will find perhaps
> That I, who am now unfortunate, am saved.[1]

Then he believed that he was going to the right place for purification and for the salvation of his wounded spirit, but he spoke
more truly than he knew. He goes where he must go, but it is to
his death. The audience will have seen the irony and suspected
that the words portend evil. In that case they will not be absolutely taken aback when Ajax appears determined to kill
himself.

Sophocles uses a special means to indicate the fatality of Ajax'
death. Too little attention has been paid to the theme of Hector's
sword which Ajax owns and with which he kills himself. Yet great
prominence is given to it, and we see why. The sword is the gift of
an enemy and therefore accursed. It could bring no good:

> Nothing is good that comes from an enemy.[2]

It is a fitting instrument for Ajax' doom. At each point in his

---

[1] 690–2   ἐγὼ γὰρ εἶμ' ἐκεῖσ' ὅποι πορευτέον·
                 ὑμεῖς δ' ἃ φράζω δρᾶτε, καὶ τάχ' ἄν μ' ἴσως
                 πύθοισθε, κεἰ νῦν δυστυχῶ, σεσωμένον.

[2] 'Menander', Sent. 166 ἐχθροῦ παρ' ἀνδρὸς οὐδέν ἐστι χρήσιμον.

downfall something is said of it. After killing the cattle with it he
is seen
                Leaping across the plain with reeking sword.[1]

Therefore when he is sane, he wishes to rid himself of it and to bury
it in the earth; for it has brought him misfortune:

> For from the time my hand accepted it,
> A gift from Hector, my worst enemy,
> No good thing has come to me from the Greeks.[2]

When the fury returns, his thoughts are again on the sword, but not
now as of something hateful but as the means to the death which he
desires. He speaks almost with affection of its new edge sharpened
on the whetstone (820). He hopes that it will give him a quick
death (815–16); he calls it 'most friendly' (822). With this sword
he kills himself; his body is found pierced with it (899). No wonder
that Teucer bursts into denunciation of the deadly weapon:

> Surely some vengeful Fury forged this sword.[3]

He is quite right. The sword is the means by which Athene makes
Ajax kill himself, her instrument of vengeance. Teucer almost sees
this when he concludes:

> Yes, I would say that this, and everything
> At every time, the gods contrive for men.[4]

Ajax' own words about the sword:

> Foes' gifts are no gifts, and they bring no good[5]

have proved to be right. Once he has gone out with it in his hand,
he is lost. For Athene's power is on him, and he carries the means
of his own destruction. The Byzantine poet, Leontius Scholasticus,
understood the situation when, in his epigram on the interchange
of gifts between Ajax and Hector, he said:

> The sword killed Ajax in madness.[6]

That is why when Ajax appears on the sea-shore he has changed
his mind and resolved to kill himself.

This death, which is so great a loss to Tecmessa and Teucer and

---

[1] 30   πηδῶντα πεδία σὺν νεορράντῳ ξίφει.
[2] 661–3   ἐγὼ γὰρ ἐξ οὗ χειρὶ τοῦτ' ἐδεξάμην
                  παρ' Ἕκτορος δώρημα δυσμενεστάτου,
                  οὔπω τι κεδνὸν ἔσχον Ἀργείων πάρα.
[3] 1034   ἆρ' οὐκ Ἐρινὺς τοῦτ' ἐχάλκευσε ξίφος;
[4] 1036–7   ἐγὼ μὲν οὖν καὶ ταῦτα καὶ τὰ πάντ' ἀεὶ
                  φάσκοιμ' ἂν ἀνθρώποισι μηχανᾶν θεούς.
[5] 665   ἐχθρῶν ἄδωρα δῶρα κοὐκ ὀνήσιμα.
[6] Anth. Pal. vii. 152. 5 τὸ ξίφος εἶλ' Αἴαντα μεμηνότα.

even to the Achaeans, is after all what Ajax himself desired (479–80) until he yielded to Tecmessa's entreaty. It is for him the best solution for his shame. Tecmessa knows this when after it she says:

> Bitter his death to me if joy to them,
> But to his own content.[1]

So when Athene's curse works again on Ajax, it is really what he would desire. We may wonder why Sophocles resorted to this means, but perhaps there is an answer. The Greeks held various views about suicide. While most would in general condemn it, there were some who allowed it if the circumstances were especially hard. Euripides makes a Chorus say:

> If a man's woes are more than he can bear,
> He may take leave of life, and none shall blame him.[2]

and Plato admits that a man may kill himself 'if he falls into a disgrace from which there is no escape and which makes life impossible'.[3] By such rules Ajax would be justified in killing himself. But there were others who did not allow these exceptions. The Pythagoreans thought that suicide was to desert one's post,[4] and Aristotle condemned it because it did harm to a city.[5] Sophocles must have known of this difference of opinion, and perhaps he gave this end to Ajax because the strictest moralist could not blame it. Since he acts in a madness sent by the gods, Ajax is not responsible for his action. In any case the death is what he really desired, the solution for his shame and his troubles.

With Ajax' death the wrath of Athene is satisfied. We hear no more of it. Ajax has paid his debt in full. In so much as he recovered his sanity and moderation in his earlier speech and is not his own master at the end, he is beyond blame and cavil. The gods can demand no more of him. Tecmessa understands the situation. She knows that this is what he desired, though he shrank from it, and that his death concerns the gods:

> What he longed to have
> He has achieved, the death that he desired.

---

[1] 966–7 ἐμοὶ πικρὸς τέθνηκεν ἢ κείνοις γλυκύς,
αὐτῷ δὲ τερπνός.
[2] *Hec.* 1107–8 συγγνώσθ' ὅταν τις κρείσσον' ἢ φέρειν κακὰ
πάθῃ, ταλαίνης ἐξαπαλλάξαι ζόης.
[3] *Laws* ix. 873 c αἰσχύνης τινὸς ἀπόρου καὶ ἀβίου μεταλαχών.
[4] Plat. *Phaed.* 62 b, Ath. iv. 157 c.
[5] *Nic. Eth.* 1138 a 13.

Why should they then deride him? 'Tis the gods
Must answer for his death, not those men, no.[1]

The gods have given him through their own means an end for
his troubles. He is at peace with them. But there remains the
question of his relations with men. His madness arose from his
hatred of his fellows; he cannot die and leave that account un-
settled. The Atridae and Odysseus know nothing of his change of
heart, his hard-won modesty. They must still regard him as a
deadly enemy whose murderous purposes have been frustrated
only by divine intervention. They can hardly be blamed if they
continue to execrate him after death. But this discord is unendurable if Ajax is really a great man, who, apart from one great
fault, deserves honour and respect. He must be justified in the
eyes of men as in the sight of the gods; he cannot be left under the
imputation of treachery and intended murder. His worth must be
properly assessed, his virtues weighed against his faults. His weakness has been shown fully; it is time that his strength received its
proper valuation.

Sophocles deals with this unresolved discord in a struggle, or
series of struggles, in which the chief characters dispute Ajax'
right to burial. He takes a hint from the *Little Iliad*, which said
that in his wrath Agamemnon refused to allow the body to be
burned but ordered it to be buried in a coffin.[2] The natural
meaning of this is that Agamemnon refused to allow what was in
heroic times the normal rite of cremation and insisted on the
humbler rite of burial because he was still angry with Ajax. On
the other hand, Philostratus says that Calchas insisted on burial
because 'suicides may not lawfully receive cremation'.[3] It looks as
if different reasons were given for the decision, though of course
Philostratus may be trying to explain the story in a modern way.
Anyhow there was a tradition that Ajax' body was not treated
like the bodies of other men in the heroic age. Sophocles alters the
details. He accepts the tradition that Ajax was denied the proper
rites, but states the issue in a new way and gives a new point to it.
We can guess his reasons. In his time burial was the normal way to
dispose of the dead, and to bury a man instead of cremating him
was no dishonour. So he remodelled the episode and made the

---

[1] 967–70   ὧν γὰρ ἠράσθη τυχεῖν,
ἐκτήσαθ' αὐτῷ, θάνατον ὅνπερ ἤθελεν.
τί δῆτα τοῦδ' ἐπεγγελῶεν ἂν κάτα;
θεοῖς τέθνηκεν οὗτος, οὐ κείνοισιν, οὔ.

[2] Fr. 3 Allen.   [3] *Her.* 13. 7.

issue not between burial and cremation but between burial and refusal of it. This would mean something to his time and helped him to present a particular point about Ajax which concerned him.

Before he dies Ajax is afraid that he may be denied burial and prays to Zeus:

> And let no enemy espy me first
> And I be cast a prey to dogs and birds.[1]

His fear is justified; for soon after his death Menelaus appears and tells Teucer not to complete the rites but to leave the body as it is (1048), and adds:

> But cast out somewhere on the yellow sands
> It shall be food for birds that haunt the sea.[2]

For this Menelaus has reasons: Ajax has plotted the death of the Achaean leaders (1052-6). We know what he means. In heroic times it might sometimes be the practice to refuse burial to an enemy as Achilles refused it to Hector,[3] but in the fifth century decency demanded that enemies should be buried like friends In the Persian Wars both sides observed this rule, and so well approved was it that when Lysander failed to bury the Athenian dead at Aegospotami, it was an indelible blot on his name.[4] But what was proper for enemies was not necessarily proper for traitors who died fighting or plotting against their own land. Such were commonly condemned to be buried outside its frontiers. Cases in point are Aristodemus in the Second Messenian War,[5] Archeptolemus and Antiphon,[6] and the Athenian generals at Arginusae.[7] Ajax, in somewhat different circumstances, was also guilty of treachery. He has attempted to kill the Achaean generals when they are engaged in a great war on foreign soil. It might therefore be held that he should suffer in an advanced degree a traitor's fate and be forbidden even such rites as custom allowed to them. The Atridae think that since he has escaped their vengeance by death, he shall be pursued after death by the only means available. If he is refused burial, his ghost will wander uneasily apart from the other dead; his body will be mangled by birds of prey. With nothing else will his enemies be satisfied.

Menelaus thinks that Ajax is a traitor, and Agamemnon shares

---

[1] 829-30   καὶ μὴ πρὸς ἐχθρῶν του κατοπτευθεὶς πάρος
ῥιφθῶ κυσὶν πρόβλητος οἰωνοῖς θ' ἕλωρ.

[2] 1064-5   ἀλλ' ἀμφὶ χλωρὰν ψάμαθον ἐκβεβλημένος
ὄρνισι φορβὴ παραλίοις γενήσεται.

[3] Il. xxiii. 34.   [4] Paus. ix. 32. 7.   [5] Paus. iv. 22. 7.

[6] Plut. Vit. X Or, 834 b.   [7] Xen. Hell. i. 7. 22.

his view. That they are not entirely unjustified may be seen from the Chorus, who anticipate some such accusation. When they first discover what Ajax has done, they are afraid of the doom that the Atridae will impose upon them:

> I am afraid
> Of death by stoning,
> Of sharing my master's ruin.[1]

When Teucer comes to the Achaean army, he is taunted with his kinship to Ajax and told:

> Nothing
> Shall save you. Stoned and mangled you shall die.[2]

Stoning was not a common punishment, and Sophocles has not chosen it for its horror but because it was used for traitors. The Chorus see that they will be accused of aiding Ajax in treachery, and such an accusation is practically thrown at Teucer. In this Sophocles no doubt draws on his own times. The Persian Wars provided examples of traitors who were stoned to death, such as Lycidas, who voted for the proposal of Mardonius before Plataea, and the Mytilenean tyrant Coes for his Persian sympathies.[3] The threat of stoning shows what the Achaeans think of Ajax' murderous attempt on their leaders. Ajax escapes such an end by killing himself, but the charge against him stands and has to be settled.

This issue occupies the second part of the play—shall Ajax be denied burial? His offence was indisputably grave and would in the judgement of some deserve the punishment decreed for it. The question is whether his virtues outweigh his faults, not whether he is innocent or guilty. It is tempting to think that Sophocles chose this issue because in his own time he had known burial refused to a great man because he was believed and judged to be a traitor. There is little enough similarity between the characters and careers of Ajax and Themistocles, and it would be rash to think that the conception of the one owed anything to the life of the other. Yet on this point their destinies were similar. Themistocles had saved the Athenians at Salamis, yet later he was condemned for

---

[1] 253–5   πεφόβημαι
                λιθόλευστον Ἄρη
                ξυναλγεῖν μετὰ τοῦδε τυπείς.

[2] 727–8   ὡς οὐκ ἀρκέσοι
            τὸ μὴ οὐ πέτροισι πᾶς καταξανθεὶς θανεῖν.

[3] Hdt. ix. 5; v. 38, 1. The whole question is discussed by A. C. Pearson, C. Q. xvi (1922), pp. 124–37, who also quotes Thuc. v. 60, Dem. xix. 99, Aristoph. Ach. 184, 236, 285.

treachery,[1] and, when he died, burial in his own land was refused to him, 'for it was against the law to bury an outlaw for treason'.[2] None the less his body was brought secretly to Athens and buried there by his relatives. Whether his fate suggested to Sophocles his treatment of Ajax or not, we may be fairly confident that an Athenian audience would be acquainted with the difficulty of burying a man who had been judged to be a traitor, and would not find the debates about Ajax' burial in the least unreal.

The controversy falls into three sections: first between Teucer and Menelaus, second between Teucer and Agamemnon, third between Agamemnon and Odysseus. In all three the body of Ajax lies on the stage, recalls his greatness in life, and raises doubts about the rightness of refusing him burial. In the second and third stages the pathos and insistent claims of the dead body are reinforced by the child Eurysaces and Tecmessa, who kneel in silence by it and suggest that the dead man is waiting to be justi-fied and restored to honour. Those who complain that the play falls into two separate parts tend to forget the presence of the body. It shows that the problem of Ajax is not yet solved, and explains why he is still a centre of fierce controversy. Moreover, though he is dead, he has in Teucer an advocate who bears considerable resemblance to him in his tendency to anger, his impatience with authority, his contempt for meanness and pretension. In fact when Teucer taunts Agamemnon with doubtful lineage (1295–7) he does what in Aeschylus' *Award of Arms* Ajax seems to have done to Odysseus.[3] The mantle of Ajax has fallen on Teucer, and through him we hear the dead man's case stated as he himself might have done. A debate of this kind is no calm discussion of principles or exchange of views. It is a series of conflicts fought out by men with strong feelings, a complex process by which right emerges with strain and difficulty through wrong judgements, prejudice, and anger.

To present three scenes of discussion, no matter how heated, on a single subject might well seem undramatic and inartistic, and so perhaps it would be if Sophocles had not given a pattern and a shape to the whole sequence. Each colloquy engages interest and attention in a different way. In the first it is soon clear that between Teucer and Menelaus no agreement is possible. For though Teucer may be in the right on his main contention that Ajax should be buried, he argues in a wrong spirit and is incapable of persuading Menelaus to give in. The argument ends inevitably

[1] Plut. *Them.* 23.   [2] Thuc. i. 138. 6.   [3] Aesch. fr. 175

in a deadlock; for the issue is not properly posed or understood. In
the second colloquy Teucer answers Agamemnon with real force
and some sense. His points tell, and he gets the better of the
interchange. But Agamemnon is as hard to persuade as Menelaus
and seems unlikely to listen to what Teucer has to say. But the
case for Ajax has been well put, and a definite advance has been
made for his cause. In the third colloquy, as Odysseus reasons
with Agamemnon, passion gradually yields to sense and hatred to
decency. The fierce atmosphere which clouded the earlier discus-
sions makes way for a calmer air in which arguments can be
understood and appeals to principle appreciated. At last a
solution is found. So through the three scenes reason and decency
gradually fight their way out from enveloping passions and
triumph over them. In the first neither side shows any moderation, in the second Teucer shows some signs of it and Agamemnon none, in the third Agamemnon gives in to the reasonableness
of Odysseus. Ajax' burial, which is demanded by considerations of honour and decency, can only be secured when modesty
defeats hatred and prejudice. The fight is hard but won at last.

In his debate with Teucer Menelaus has something of a case. It
is that Ajax disobeyed his superior officers (1071-90) and plotted
their death (1053-60). Because of this he has been a greater
enemy than the Trojans to his own side (1054). Therefore he is a
traitor and must not be buried. The facts are correct enough, but
do not justify the conclusion drawn from them. We may doubt if
Sophocles would have thought it right in any circumstances to
refuse burial even to a traitor, or would have approved of any
attempt to harry an enemy after death. He would probably have
accepted the authority of Homer's Odysseus:

It is unholy to boast and rejoice over men who have fallen.[1]

and regarded any display of triumph over Ajax as wrong. Still, not
everyone would agree with him, and Menelaus' case must be
answered. Teucer might have countered him by showing that
Ajax is not a traitor, or that, even if he is, there is no reason to
leave him unburied. He does indeed deny that Ajax can be
accused of insubordination, for he came as a willing ally (1093-
1117), but he says nothing to dispose of the charge of treachery and
attempted murder. Yet his defence, intellectually inadequate as it
is, may well have had an emotional appeal for an Athenian
audience. When he says:

[1] *Od.* xxii. 412 οὐχ ὁσίη κταμένοισιν ἐπ' ἀνδράσιν εὐχετάασθαι.

> How are you his commander? Have you right
> To rule the men whom he brought from his home?
> You came as king of Sparta, not of us.[1]

he appeals to that distrust of Spartan methods which lay in many an Athenian breast. When Athens, at Cimon's instigation, sent volunteers to crush the Messenian rebels, they were ignominiously sent back. The incident rankled, and many would remember with what churlishness the Spartans treated those who tried to help them. Menelaus, like a typical Spartan, wishes to bully his allies, and Teucer would win support by challenging him on this point.

A similarly Spartan tone may be detected in Menelaus' notion of military discipline. He thinks that government and command are based on fear:

> But he in whom are fear and reverence,
> Be sure, will prosper in security.[2]

His doctrine is that of the Spartan king Archidamus who in addressing his troops lays great emphasis on the virtue of fear in soldiers, and claims that through it a small army has often defeated a greater too confident army, and that in warlike preparations fear is a great asset.[3] In his speech at Sparta before the declaration of war he lays no less an emphasis on order and discipline. He claims that the Spartans are wise in that they are too self-controlled to break the laws.[4] It was a common defence of autocracy and distasteful to Athenian democrats. Their own leader claimed that Athens stood for the opposite principle. In the Funeral Speech Pericles says that Athens trusts her citizens to act and think without constant recourse to authority.[5] While Spartans valued good discipline, Athenians valued good morale. The antithesis was familiar, and when Menelaus claims support for his Spartan belief in discipline and Teucer replies that he has no right to apply this to free allies, we can imagine what an Athenian audience would feel. Teucer may not argue on the main issue, but what he says secures sympathy and respect for his cause.

What really counts against Menelaus is the temper in which he speaks. He argues ably enough, but it is clear that he is actuated

---

[1] 1100–2 ποῦ σὺ στρατηγεῖς τοῦδε; ποῦ δέ σοι λεὼν
     ἔξεστ' ἀνάσσειν ὧν ὅδ' ἡγεῖτ' οἰκόθεν;
     Σπάρτης ἀνάσσων ἦλθες, οὐχ ἡμῶν κρατῶν.

[2] 1079–80 Δέος γὰρ ᾧ πρόσεστιν αἰσχύνη θ' ὁμοῦ,
     σωτηρίαν ἔχοντα τόνδ' ἐπίστασο.

[3] Thuc. ii. 11, 4–5. [4] Id. i. 84.3. [5] Id. ii. 39. 4; 40. 3.

by an ugly arrogance. His true motives slip out when he says:

> Fortune goes round in turns. This man was hot
> And arrogant once. 'Tis mine now to be proud.[1]

His words betray him. The pride which he claims as his right is that which the gods punish.[2] The audience must see that he speaks from arrogance and that he must be viewed with suspicion. The Chorus mark this when they say to him:

> Menelaus, do not, laying down wise rules,
> Yourself then offer outrage to the dead.[3]

Menelaus, who might have put forward a persuasive case, spoils it by revealing his corrupt motives. He is himself no better than he alleges Ajax to have been. His treatment of Teucer is more than discourteous. He enters with a peremptory command not to bury Ajax and shows no consideration for Teucer's feelings. His contempt comes out in one significant point, his claim to despise Teucer for being a bowman:

> It seems the archer has no little pride.[4]

His charge comes ultimately from the epic where Diomedes upbraids Paris:

> Archer, reviler, renowned with the bow.[5]

and of course in the heroic world where the archer avoided that hand-to-hand fighting which brought the greatest honour, there was a sting in the gibe. But in the fifth century the significance was different. It cannot be an accident that another character, even more disagreeable than Menelaus, Lycus in Euripides' *Heracles*, should also cast scorn on archers:

> Arrows are no test of a man's brave heart,
> But whoso stands and sees with steady gaze
> The spear's swift furrow as he keeps his ranks.[6]

In Athens the value of archers had been proved in war. At

---

[1] 1087–8   ἕρπει παραλλὰξ ταῦτα· πρόσθεν οὗτος ἦν
             αἴθων ὑβριστής, νῦν δ' ἐγὼ μέγ' αὖ φρονῶ.

[2] Hdt. vii. 10, Eur. *Hipp.* 6.

[3] 1091–2   Μενέλαε, μὴ γνώμας ὑποστήσας σοφὰς
             εἶτ' αὐτὸς ἐν θανοῦσιν ὑβριστὴς γένῃ.

[4] 1120   ὁ τοξότης ἔοικεν οὐ σμικρὸν φρονεῖν.

[5] *Il.* xi. 385   τοξότα, λωβητήρ, κέρᾳ ἀγλαέ.

[6] *Her.* 162–4   ἀνδρὸς δ' ἔλεγχος οὐχὶ τόξ' εὐψυχίας,
              ἀλλ' ὃς μένων βλέπει τε κἀντιδέρκεται
              δορὸς ταχεῖαν ἄλοκα τάξιν ἐμβεβώς.

Salamis they did good work on the Athenian ships,[1] and later the
experienced Xenophon saw their use.[2] On the other hand, the
Spartans, with their belief in heavily armed infantry, seem to have
despised them, and no doubt admirers of Sparta at Athens felt
that there was something degrading in being an archer. It is
this suggestion that Teucer answers:

> 'Tis no degrading craft that I possess.[3]

In this too he appeals to Athenian sentiment against Spartan
self-satisfaction and contempt for others.

   Menelaus does little to win sympathy for his demand, but
Teucer too spoils his case by his presentation of it. The only
telling point that he makes is when he denies that Ajax was insub-
ordinate. He appeals by his sturdy independence and by his
loyalty to Ajax, but he fails to reach any agreement with Menelaus
partly because he loses his temper and matches his opponent's
arrogance with his own anger. In such circumstances no result is
possible. The Chorus, who know that Teucer has a good cause to
plead, deplore his conduct of it:

> I like not such a tongue in evil times;
> For harshness rankles, be it ne'er so just.[4]

Teucer's anger may be justified, but it is dangerous and leads to
trouble. It illustrates a maxim of Theognis:

> Whose mind is ruled by wrath, always in trouble,
> Is he, Cyrnus, and in great distress.[5]

He is almost an example of Aristotle's 'hot-tempered' man, who
'retaliates openly owing to quickness of temper', and shows the
truth of the words that 'such men are most troublesome to themselves'.[6] He does no good to Ajax or to himself.

   Naturally the conclusion is a deadlock, and Sophocles marks it
in a remarkable way. At the end of the dispute each tells the
other a little fable. These are of approximately the same length
and constructed on similar lines. Menelaus says that Teucer
reminds him of a bold-spoken man at sea who is afraid when the

---

[1] Plut. *Them.* 14.   [2] *Anab.* iii. 4. 15.
[3] 1121   οὐ γὰρ βάναυσον τὴν τέχνην ἐκτησάμην.
[4] 1118–19   οὐδ' αὖ τοιαύτην γλῶσσαν ἐν κακοῖς φιλῶ·
                   τὰ σκληρὰ γάρ τοι, κἂν ὑπέρδικ' ᾖ, δάκνει.
[5] Theogn. 631–2   ᾧ τινι μὴ θυμοῦ κρείσσων νόος, αἰὲν ἐν ἄταις,
                    Κύρνε, καὶ ἐν μεγάλαις κεῖται ἀμηχανίαις.
Cf. Eur. *Med.* 446–7.
[6] *Nic. Eth.* 1126 a 16.

storm comes, Teucer that Menelaus reminds him of one who triumphs in a neighbour's woes and is warned that he himself will come to harm. The Scholiast, surprised at the appearance of such matter, says 'such a thing belongs rather to comedy, not to tragedy', and it is true that the best parallel to such an interchange comes from Aristophanes' *Lysistrata*.[1] It is a primitive device that comes from the literature of abuse. But here it serves a special purpose. It shows that both Teucer and Menelaus have by their methods of dispute passed beyond reasonable limits and reached a hopeless position. The Chorus see this and know that worse is in store (1163). Desperately they urge that Ajax' tomb should be promptly raised, but the atmosphere is dark with gloom. All the hopes of burial seem small despite Teucer's determination to secure it (1184). In this mood of hopelessness the Chorus lament their home-sickness and hatred of war. Their song emphasizes the grimness of the situation.

The second contest, between Teucer and Agamemnon, may not lead to any practical solution, but it clears the situation in two ways. The debate turns on two questions, and in each Teucer gets the better of it both in the points that he makes and in the spirit in which he makes them. The first is his own station, his right to argue with his generals about Ajax' burial. The second is the vital question of Ajax' real worth. Both are relevant to the situation. For since Teucer is Ajax' advocate, he must speak with authority if he is to convince anyone, and since what really justifies respect for Ajax is his prowess, there must be no doubt about it. Naturally both points excite passion and even abuse. Arguments *ad hominem* are still not absent. But this time it is clear that Teucer is on good ground, and we need not deplore his fierce temper; for it does not disturb his presentation of the facts. Instead of the sharp interchange of stichomythia, the debate is conducted in formal speeches. The issues are becoming clearer, and though there is no result, we are ready for the intervention of Odysseus, when it comes, to stop further wrangling.

Agamemnon attacks Teucer on personal grounds and tells him that he should not presume to stand up to his superiors since he is the son of a captive concubine (1226 ff.). Teucer answers by saying that this may be true but he stood by Ajax' side in his great doings, and gives tit for tat by pointing out that Agamemnon's own ancestry carries a singular burden of crime (1291-4) and that his birth is worse than Teucer's since he is the son of Aerope and a

[1] *Lys.* 781-96, 805-20.

paramour (1295-7). It is hard to see how exactly this should be taken. The story was fairly well known and was made the subject of Euripides' *Cretan Women* in 438 B.C. It is not clear whether Sophocles expects us to accept it or not. What matters is that while Teucer is the son of an honest concubine, Agamemnon has the stigma of a tainted stock. He has no right to criticize Teucer's free speech. Teucer appeals to the feeling, not uncommon among the Greeks, that the son of a concubine might have a nobler character than the son of the legitimate wife. Sophocles made the point in his *Aleadae*:

> *A.* No bastard has so true-born power as he.
> *B.* All that is good is true-born in its breed.[1]

The idea was favoured by Euripides[2] and was no doubt familiar to many. In basing his claim to speak on nobility and not on birth Teucer appeals to Athenian democratic sentiment. He almost anticipates the Euripidean view that

> For me good birth lies in good character.[3]

No doubt the average member of the audience, intolerant of aristocratic pretensions, would feel that there was truth in his words and rally to him.

Agamemnon fails no less signally when he tries to belittle the achievements of Ajax. His only point is that Ajax was no better than himself:

> What was this man whose praise you vaunt so loud?
> Where went he, or where stood, where stood not I?
> Was he the only man among the Greeks?[4]

Teucer easily answers this with a general appeal to gratitude and good feeling:

> Alas, how quickly gratitude to the dead
> Fades and is caught in treachery to them.[5]

and follows with an account of two occasions when Ajax' courage was beyond dispute and rendered great services to the Achaeans. The difference between the two disputants is clear and much in

---

[1] Fr. 87   A. ὅδ', εἰ νόθος τις, γνησίοις ἴσον σθένει.
                  B. ἅπαν τὸ χρηστὸν γνησίαν ἔχει φύσιν.
[2] *Andr.* 638, frs. 141, 168, 377.
[3] Fr. 336   ὁ μὲν γὰρ ἐσθλὸς εὐγενὴς ἔμοιγ' ἀνήρ.
[4] 1236-8   ποίου κέκραγας ἀνδρὸς ὧδ' ὑπέρφρονα;
                  ποῖ βάντος ἢ ποῦ στάντος, οὗπερ οὐκ ἐγώ;
                  οὐκ ἄρ' Ἀχαίοις ἄνδρες εἰσὶ πλὴν ὅδε;
[5] 1266-7   φεῦ· τοῦ θανόντος ὡς ταχεῖά τις βροτοῖς
                  χάρις διαρρεῖ καὶ προδοῦσ' ἁλίσκεται;

Teucer's favour. For while he speaks in loyalty and truth, Agamemnon speaks as the envious man who is pained at all good fortune to others.[1] He is jealous of Ajax' prowess and reputation. Therefore his words fail to convince. The Greeks knew that the envious often fail in their aims:

> Another man, with envious looks,
> Tosses in the dark an empty thought
> Which falls to the ground.[2]

So Agamemnon fails. Even his argument that military promotion should go to merit sounds as hollow as his other words. When Teucer has finished his answer we know where the right is and feel that it has begun to be fairly stated. The Chorus are a little anxious before he begins (1264–5), but despite his indignation he wins all sympathies.

The arrival of Odysseus starts the third round of the contest. It is different from the other two in that it is conducted in a friendly spirit. For Odysseus and Agamemnon are friends and fellows in command, and Odysseus has suffered as much from Ajax as the Atridae have. Agamemnon cannot question his right to speak, and has to listen to him. As at the beginning of the play, so at the end Odysseus is the embodiment of sanity and decency. He has been the enemy of Ajax, but none the less he insists on burial. His enmity for the man when alive was permissible. The two were rivals, and in such rivalry hatred might well have a place. But to maltreat the dead is another matter; Odysseus admits freely that he has been Ajax' enemy (1336, 1347, 1355, 1357), but he has no hesitation in pressing for his burial. He claims that it is wrong to leave the body unburied, and begs Agamemnon:

> And let not violence so subdue your will
> To hatred that you trample on the right.[3]

A little later he explains:

> Outrage would not be done to this dead man,
> But to the gods' laws. 'Tis not right to harm
> A brave man dead, not even though you hate him.[4]

[1] Aristot. *Nic. Eth.* 1108 b 4.

[2] Pind. *Nem.* iv. 39–41 φθονερὰ Δ’ ἄλλος ἀνήρ βλέπων
γνώμαν κενεὰν σκότω κυλίνΔει
χαμαὶ πετοῖσαν.

[3] 1334–5 μηΔ’ ἡ βία σε μηΔαμῶς νικησάτω
τοσόνΔε μισεῖν ὥστε τὴν Δίκην πατεῖν.

[4] 1343–5 οὐ γάρ τι τοῦτον, ἀλλὰ τοὺς θεῶν νόμους
φθείροις ἄν· ἄνΔρα Δ’ οὐ Δίκαιον, εἰ θάνοι,
βλάπτειν τὸν ἐσθλόν, οὐΔ’ ἐὰν μισῶν κυρῇς.

It is not right and it is against the laws of the gods to leave a body unburied; moreover, human feelings are outraged when the body is of so noble a man as Ajax. Odysseus' position may not sound so rigorous or so uncompromising as Antigone's, but it is based on the same principle. Like her he appeals to the gods' laws and justice. It is the spirit in which Aethra begs Theseus to bury the dead:

> First, son, I bid you look to holy things,
> Lest from dishonouring the gods you fall.[1]

Against such a divine ordinance there is no real argument. Odysseus knows this and does not try to find reasons for it. He tells Agamemnon that he acts from violence. Against this he sets his own calm modesty, the peace of mind which is the best weapon against any violent temper.[2] He strengthens his case by stressing the nobility of Ajax, though he has no need to do so. But this too serves a purpose. If Odysseus praises Ajax' noble qualities, Agamemnon may come to see them and to rid himself of anger and contempt.

Odysseus' speech does not immediately convince Agamemnon, and a dialogue follows in which points are made and answered. In the close debate Odysseus tries to counter a series of objections from Agamemnon: that we should trample on an enemy (1348), that it is hard for a king to observe piety (1350), that Ajax does not deserve decent treatment (1354, 1356), that permission for burial will be taken as a sign of weakness (1362), that Agamemnon will not take the responsibility for what happens (1368). In this interchange the king's obduracy gradually weakens until he is concerned only with the conduct of the burial. But though he weakens and eventually gives in, Agamemnon shows a consistent point of view. With Teucer his reasons of state look like personal vanity; with Odysseus they carry weight because they are advanced with candour and seriousness. He is faced with a hard problem, the submission of his own will and authority to the gods. He naturally thinks that what he wishes is for the good of the state, and he is asked to override this for another, different good. An earlier generation would have seen no problem in this. That the state could override the laws of the gods was not an idea that existed for Homer or Hesiod. But in the fifth century that state had developed an importance of its own and made claims which challenged the claims of the gods. In the eyes of some its laws

[1] Eur. *Supp.* 301–2 ἐγὼ δέ σ', ὦ παῖ, πρῶτα μὲν τὰ τῶν θεῶν
σκοπεῖν κελεύω μὴ σφαλῇς ἀτιμάσας.
[2] Pind. *Pyth.* viii. 15.

were more important than those of Olympus. The quarrel about
the burial of Ajax, which began on a purely personal level, has
reached a point at which it involves a dispute of the greatest
importance. The issue was known to the audience, but they
would hardly be of one mind about it. Sophocles, true child of the
established religion, takes his stand firmly on the side of the gods.

The conflict between politics and religion, between the claims
of authority and deeply rooted feelings of obligation, was dramatized by Aeschylus in his *Prometheus Bound*. Whatever solution he
found to the struggle between the newly established potentate Zeus
and his old benefactor Prometheus, we may feel sure that not all
the right was on the side of Prometheus. Power, as represented by
Zeus, can hardly have been altogether in the wrong. Later in the
century the conflict between the two kinds of claim was matter for
grave thought with Thucydides, who in the Melian Dialogue
displayed to what conclusions attachment to the State's interests
might lead. In a world where one city wished to dominate
others and was ready to use any means for the purpose, it was
perhaps idle to speak of justice. So at least the Athenians argue—
'of the gods we believe, and of men we know, that by a necessary
law of their nature they rule wherever they can'.[1] This is only
another form of Thrasymachus' doctrine that justice is 'the interest
of the stronger'.[2] Even when the claim was not presented so boldly
or so crudely as this, there was often a presumption that the state's
interests were paramount, needed no excuse, and brooked no
opposition. So the Syracusan Hermocrates regards the desire to
rule others as perfectly natural,[3] and the Athenian envoys at Sparta
say that it has always been the case that the lesser is dominated by
the more powerful.[4] In such examples reasons of state and power
are all that count for cities as for individuals. With these advocates
of authority Agamemnon has much in common, though he is
particularly concerned with his own sovereignty. Yet he gives in,
not indeed to argument but to reasons of the heart. He feels that
since he is a friend of Odysseus, he must grant him this favour:

> And yet in spite of everything, know this
> That I would grant you a greater privilege;
> But this man, be he there or here, shall be
> Most hateful to me. Do then what you please.[5]

[1] Thuc. v. 105. 2.   [2] Plat. *Rep.* i. 338 c.   [3] Thuc. iv. 61. 5.   [4] Id. i. 76. 2.

[5] 1370–3   ἀλλ' εὖ γε μέντοι τοῦτ' ἐπίστασ', ὡς ἐγὼ
σοὶ μὲν νέμοιμ' ἂν τῆσδε καὶ μείζω χάριν·
οὗτος δὲ κἀκεῖ κἀνθάδ' ὢν ἐμοιγ' ὁμῶς
ἔχθιστος ἔσται· σοὶ δὲ δρᾶν ἔξεσθ' ἃ χρῇς.

He still nurses his hatred for Ajax, but his pride and obstinacy have been undermined on the question of refusing burial. No wonder that the Chorus praise Odysseus for his skilful handling of the situation (1374–5). Yet it is not skill that has won the day but the quiet moderation of Odysseus which has impressed Agamemnon and made him feel that he cannot refuse such a request to so noble a man who is also his friend. The claims of position and authority are countered by honest decency and reason. Against these Agamemnon cannot maintain his resistance.

Once Agamemnon yields and goes away, there is little to be done. The atmosphere is calm, but not full of forgiveness. Just as Ajax died cursing the Atridae, so at the end of the play Teucer calls another curse down on them:

> May therefore the high Father on Olympus,
> The mindful Fury, and fulfilling Right,
> Destroy these vile men vilely, just as they
> Sought wrongly to cast out this man in shame.[1]

As Ajax' faithful friend and advocate, Teucer shares his hatred for the Atridae, and would not be thought the worse for it. Yet we may be surprised that Sophocles sees fit to insert this note of discord into his otherwise peaceful conclusion. The reason must surely be that he thought it wrong of the Atridae to refuse burial and not truly right to grant it without seeing its absolute obligation or understanding the true worth of Ajax. He seems to have wished to prevent his audience from feeling that after all the Atridae behaved well. Right is against them, and Teucer's curse shows this. It is part of Ajax' rehabilitation, of his triumph over his enemies. We might also find some insensitiveness in Teucer's refusal to allow Odysseus to take part in the funeral; for after all he has made it possible. Here the dead man's feelings are the cause. Teucer has qualms about refusing and recognizes his debt to Odysseus (1381–5), but he does not wish to do anything that might cause displeasure to Ajax (1395). His feeling is easy to understand when we remember how Homer makes the Ghost of Ajax refuse to speak to Odysseus because of his anger about the arms of Achilles.[2] To the Greeks with their vivid belief that a dead man could be conscious and resentful in the tomb Teucer's action would seem a prudent precaution.

---

[1] 1389–92   τοιγάρ σφ' 'Ολύμπου τοῦΔ' ὁ πρεσβεύων πατὴρ
μνήμων τ' 'Ερινὺς καὶ τελεσφόρος Δίκη
κακοὺς κακῶς φθείρειαν, ὥσπερ ἤθελον
τὸν ἀνδρὰ λώβαις ἐκβαλεῖν ἀναξίως.

[2] *Od.* xi. 543.

When all is ready for burning Ajax' body, the Chorus sing their last words of epilogue:

> To men who have seen much knowledge will come
> But before they see, no one has the sight
> To divine what destiny waits him.[1]

Such epilogues are common, and we do not expect too much from them. They create an effect, an atmosphere. They do not review all that has happened or say what must be thought on the chief events. This epilogue draws a general lesson: the future is unforeseen to everyone. Ajax, who seemed to be the victim of an appalling humiliation, is in the end vindicated and honoured. So Sophocles sums up the reversal of fortune in his play. For him this is a proof of the ignorance in which man lives, and, implicitly, of the power of the gods. He drew a similar conclusion in his *Tereus*, which seems to have passed through even more hideous catastrophes to amends and consolation:

> Men of mortal race must think mortal thoughts,
> Knowing this full well, that there is none
> But Zeus to dispose of what is to come
> In the way that it must be accomplished.[2]

Here he emphasizes man's uncertainty before the gods who do as they choose with him. In this condition all that man can do is to admit that he knows nothing and conduct himself modestly. So too the *Ajax* ends in a humble confession of ignorance, just as it began with the lesson which Odysseus learns from Athene. Both in humiliation and in success man must admit his powerlessness. This lesson should bring peace of mind. After the agonies of Ajax' fall and the anxieties of his rehabilitation, the conclusion is in modesty and peace. Men see and learn, but before they see, they are in utter ignorance.

This, however, is only a conclusion. The particular lesson, if it can so be called, is more complex. A difficult issue has been presented in a particular case. How can a man like Ajax, who has been guilty of pride against the gods, be worthy of honour? The

---

[1] 1418–20   ἦ πολλὰ βροτοῖς ἔστιν ἰδοῦσιν
γνῶναι· πρὶν ἰδεῖν δ' οὐδεὶς μάντις
τῶν μελλόντων, ὅ τι πράξει.

[2] Fr. 590   θνητὴν δὲ φύσιν χρὴ θνητὰ φρονεῖν,
τοῦτο κατειδότας, ὡς οὐκ ἔστιν
πλὴν Διὸς οὐδεὶς τῶν μελλόντων
ταμίας ὅ τι χρὴ τετελέσθαι.

answer is twofold, though the two parts are closely connected. Ajax has paid for his pride, and once he has paid for it it becomes clear that his virtues outweigh his faults. The method is quite different from Pindar's excusing of Ajax from all blame. It faces a real problem, that of a great man who is marred by a great fault. In the last resort we must weigh the weakness against the strength, and in Ajax the strength wins. That is why in the last scenes his nobility is so stressed, why Odysseus calls him 'mighty' (1319), second only to Achilles (1340–1), 'noble' (1345), 'illustrious' (1355), possessed of prowess (1357), why for Teucer he belongs to the company of 'best men' (1380) and is surpassed by no man (1415–16). Ajax is a 'good man' not in the later sense which the Platonic Socrates gives to it[1] but in the sense in which Pindar applied it to Achilles[2] and to Aeacus.[3] Even Athene has admitted his gifts in counsel and action (119–20). Nor is there any serious doubt about them. Ajax, despite his faults, deserves high honour by all human standards. In no other play is Sophocles so emphatic about his conclusion or so traditional in his thought. For the virtue which he here displays and honours belongs to an ancient school of manners. The new intellectual movements of the fifth century had not shaken his reverence for the ideal of the 'man four-square' whom an earlier generation had admired and praised.

[1] Plat. *Gorg.* 515 c ff.   [2] *Isthm.* viii. 37.   [3] *Nem.* viii. 8.

III

ANTIGONE

AT some date about 441 B.C. Sophocles produced his *Antigone*, and tradition records that its success led to his election as general. As the colleague of Pericles he commanded in the expedition against Samos in 440. The poet of the *Antigone* was a prominent figure in Athenian public life at a time when Pericles had entered on his fifteen successive years of generalship and that personal control of the Athenian democracy which so impressed Thucydides.[1] It was a time of high hopes and vaulting ambitions, of imperial aims and foreign conquest. We might therefore expect the Athenian people to have elected Sophocles to military office because he had glorified their achievements or celebrated some peculiarly national characteristic. But the *Antigone* does nothing of the kind. It has no word about Athens, no political propaganda, no contemporary allusions, no appeal to patriotism. It is concerned with what might be called a political issue, but this is seen from an exalted detachment as an incident in the relations between god and man. Such overt conclusion as Sophocles draws is that we must avoid irreverence and proud words. The *Antigone* cannot have owed its first success to any ephemeral or topical attractiveness in its subject. It deals with a theme that in its narrowest aspects means little to us, but it raises broader issues which still have such vitality that it has been claimed to deal with matters so universal as the conflict of family and state, of individual and government, of human and divine laws. All these may with some justice be found in it. But the actual play concerns individual destinies. It is only through an understanding of these that we can see what wider conclusions may be drawn. The characters may be examples or symbols or types of human destiny, but they must first be understood as the dramatist presents them.

The *Antigone* presents a conflict between a man and a woman, between Creon and Antigone, on a precise issue: should the dead traitor Polynices be forbidden burial or not? In the *Ajax* a similar issue is raised between the Atridae and Teucer about Ajax, but, though important, it is not the central issue of the play. For while Ajax' treachery is a fault in an otherwise noble character, and has some excuse in the treatment that he has received, no attempt is

[1] ii. 65. 8–9.

made to praise or to condone Polynices. In him Sophocles takes an indubitable traitor who has little to recommend him. As the first song of the Chorus shows, he has tried to destroy his own city, and his death in battle is an occasion for rejoicing. But despite this, his burial is a paramount duty, above all in his sister's eyes. About it she and Creon disagree so finally that both come to disaster. It is the source of the tragic element in the *Antigone* as it is not in the *Ajax*. It is presented in a much starker form. Whether Polynices shall be buried or not is a matter of ultimate principle. It does not matter whether he is a traitor or not, whether he is a good or a bad man. We may well wonder why Sophocles was so attracted by this question, why he treated it subordinately in one play and devoted most of another to it. All we can say is that he recognized burial as a sacred duty to which no exceptions were allowed. In the *Antigone* he took a test case and showed what it meant. But once he had made this the central theme of his play, he evoked wider issues until the *Antigone* seems to touch on fundamental problems of human life. The advance from the original subject is natural, even inevitable. The burial of Polynices is demanded by the gods and refused by a man. Antigone, who supports the divine ordinance, has her own reasons and her own characteristics just as Creon, who opposes her, has his. Each represents a point of view, and each is a human being. Each claims the support of high principles, and the play is reasonably regarded as depicting the clash of these.

Unlike the *Ajax*, the *Antigone* is not based on a familiar and popular story. Antigone is not mentioned by Homer or, so far as we know, by the lyric poets. It is therefore difficult to assess how much the audience would know or what it would feel about her when Sophocles produced his play. It is true that the extant version of Aeschylus' *Seven against Thebes* ends with a scene in which Antigone proposes to bury Polynices despite the contrary orders of the Theban government (1026 ff.), but since the scene is spurious and even based on Sophocles, it tells nothing about the early history of the legend. In fact the legend seems less likely to come from books than from local tradition. We may assume that in all its versions Antigone tried to bury her brother in defiance of authority, but beyond this little is known. What matters is that the relative obscurity of his story left Sophocles free to refashion it in his own way, to build a clear and straightforward play without too much regard for established details. His aim seems to have been to confine the conflict to the two main characters. What is in essence a conflict of principle becomes a personal conflict, with all that that implies, between Creon and Antigone. Moreover, this construction leaves Antigone to act almost alone. Her courage and her decision are brought into high relief. Her only possible helper is her sister Ismene, who shrinks from giving help when asked for it and thereby shows the unique quality of Antigone's devotion. The subsidiary characters serve mainly to mark intermediate stages between the opposite standpoints of Creon and Antigone. They may try to find a point of agreement or of compromise, but they fail, and their failure shows how absolute the conflict is. The play is rightly called *Antigone*; for she is the most important figure in it; but, so far as composition is concerned, it deals with Creon even more than with her. His personality pervades the whole and holds it together after she has left the stage. It is wrong to say that the play falls into two separate parts. Its subject is the conflict between Creon and Antigone, and it does not end until this reaches its final stage with Creon's humiliation.

Modern critics who do not share Sophocles' conviction about the paramount duty of burying the dead and who attach more importance than he did to the claims of political authority have tended to underestimate the way in which he justifies Antigone against Creon. To their support they have called in the great name of Hegel, who was fascinated by the play and advanced remarkable views on it.[1] His remarks have been taken out of their context, and he has been made responsible for the opinion that Sophocles dramatized a conflict not between right and wrong but between right and right, that Antigone and Creon are equally justified in their actions and that the tragedy arises out of this irreconcilable conflict. Hegel's own words lend some support to this view: 'In the view of eternal justice both were wrong, because they were one-sided; but at the same time both were right.' But if we look at Hegel's observations in their own place, we find that this summary hardly conveys his full meaning. He was thinking of something much vaster than the play, of the whole logic of history which is here symbolized in a concrete example. In this the conflict of opposites ends by producing a synthesis which is itself right. The conclusion is what matters, and that is different from saying that both sides in the conflict are themselves right. The tragic conclusion is, so to speak, a lesson of history, a fact which cannot be denied, real and therefore right, but the conflict which

---

[1] *Philosophie der Religion*, xvi, 1. 133, *Aesthetik*, ii. 2, Absch. i. Cf. A. C. Bradley, *Oxford Lectures on Poetry*, pp. 69–92.

precedes it cannot be judged in isolation and neither side in it is right or wrong except in a relative sense. Hegel used the *Antigone* to illustrate his view of tragedy and his view of existence. He drew his own conclusions about the actions portrayed in it, as he was fully entitled to do. But his views are not those of Sophocles, and he should not be thought to maintain that Creon and Antigone were equally right in the eyes of their creator.

Sophocles leaves no doubt what conclusion should be drawn from the *Antigone*. He closes with a moral on the lips of the Chorus which tells the audience what to think:

> Wisdom has first place in happiness,
> And to fail not in reverence to the gods.
> The big words of the arrogant
> Lay big stripes on the boasters' backs.
> They pay the price
> And learn in old age to be wise.[1]

This can refer to no one but Creon, whose lack of wisdom has brought him to misery, who has shown irreverence to the gods in refusing burial to Polynices, been chastened for his proud words, and learned wisdom in his old age. To this lesson the preceding action in which Creon has lost son and wife and happiness has already made its effective contribution. We may be sure that the Chorus speak for the poet. It is as silent about Antigone as it is emphatic about Creon. There is no hint that she has in any way acted wrongly or that her death should be regarded as a righteous punishment. Of course the final words do not sum up everything important in the play, but we may reasonably assume that they pass judgement on its salient events as they appear in retrospect when the action is finished. There is no real problem about the ethical intention of the *Antigone*. It shows the fall of a proud man, and its lesson is that the gods punish pride and irreverence. But what matters much more than the actual conclusion is the means by which it is reached, the presentation of the different parties in the conflict, the view that we take of each, the feelings that are forced on us. The interest and power of the *Antigone* lie in the tangled issues which are unravelled in it.

A conclusion so clear as this is only worth reaching if it has been

---

[1] 1348–53
πολλῷ τὸ φρονεῖν εὐδαιμονίας
πρῶτον ὑπάρχει· χρὴ δὲ τά γ᾽ εἰς θεοὺς
μηδὲν ἀσεπτεῖν· μεγάλοι δὲ λόγοι
μεγάλας πληγὰς τῶν ὑπεραύχων
ἀποτείσαντες
γήρᾳ τὸ φρονεῖν ἐδίδαξαν.

preceded by a drama in which the issues are violent and complex. The rights and wrongs of the case must not throughout be so obvious as they are at the end; the audience must feel that the issue is difficult, that there is much to be said on both sides, that the ways of the gods are hard to discern. Without this the play will fail in dramatic and human interest. And Sophocles has taken great care to show the issues in their full difficulty before he provides a solution for them. He makes the two protagonists appear in such a light that at intervals we doubt if all the right is really with Antigone and all the wrong with Creon. To Creon, who defies the divine ordinance of burial, he gives arguments and sentiments which sound convincing enough when they are put forward, and many must feel that he has some good reason to act as he does. On the other hand Antigone, who fearlessly vindicates the laws of the gods, is by no means a gentle womanly creature who suffers martyrdom for the right. She may be right, but there are moments when we qualify our approval of her, when she seems proud and forbidding in her determination to do her duty and to do it alone. For these variations in our feelings Sophocles is responsible. He makes us find some right in Creon, some wrong in Antigone, even if we are misled about both. He built his play on a contrast not between obvious wrong and obvious right but between the real arrogance of Creon and the apparent arrogance of Antigone. The first deceives by its fine persuasive sentiments; the second works through Antigone's refusal to offer concessions or to consider any point of view but her own. This contrast runs through much of the play, accounts for misunderstandings of what takes place in it, provides false clues and suggests wrong conclusions, and adds greatly to the intensity of the drama. When a play is written round a moral issue, that issue must be a real problem about which more than one view is tenable until all the relevant facts are known. So the *Antigone* dramatizes a conflict which was familiar to the Periclean age, would excite divergent judgements and feelings, and make some support Antigone, some Creon, until the end makes all clear.

The complexity of the issues and the skilfulness of their presentation may first be seen in Creon, who is longer on the stage than any other character and by his fate illustrates the final moral. Since the tradition was comparatively unfamiliar, the audience would not know at the start that he is wrong. Sophocles, after letting us hear from Antigone that Creon has forbidden the burial of Polynices, is free to produce him in an ambiguous light, to make him

persuasive, and to give him the appearances of nobility. Antigone
has ironically called him 'the good Creon' (31), but when he first
appears, he seems to deserve the adjective. He begins with a series
of general maxims about himself and his position, about government and patriotism, which are in themselves innocent enough, the
approved utterance of public men. Their general acceptability
is proved by the way in which Demosthenes quotes 175–90
against Aeschines and blames him for not having remembered them
in his political life.[1] Their substance would seem no less worthy to
an Athenian of the fifth century. When Creon says that a man
should have no friend dearer than his city (182–3), and that this is
an element in her safety (188 ff.), he says much what Euripides
said in his *Erechtheus* and the patriotic politician Lycurgus approved
so strongly:

> My country, would that all who dwell in you
> Would love you just as I do. Easy then
> Would our lives be, and you would suffer nought.[2]

When Creon goes on to say of his country

> She only keeps us safe, and when she fares
> Safe, in our voyage we can make true friends.[3]

his words have a Periclean ring, a similarity to the proud statement
of the Funeral Speech, 'I am of opinion that national greatness
is more for the advantage of private citizens than any individual well-being coupled with public humiliation.'[4] The verbal
echoes between this and Creon's words may be accidental, and
there is no need to assume that either Pericles or Sophocles copied
the other. Such ideas were in the air and met with common
approval. The similarity merely shows that Creon's maxims are in
themselves impeccable. They are the legitimate commonplaces of
a patriot and would be accepted as such. They help to create a
good impression of him at his first appearance.

It would be unjust to Pericles to claim that Creon's inaugural
address is really like the Funeral Speech. It bears a superficial

---

[1] xix. 247.

[2] Fr. 360. 53–5 ὦ πατρίς, εἴθε πάντες οἱ ναίουσί σε
οὕτω φιλοῖεν ὡς ἐγώ· καὶ ῥᾳδίως
οἰκοῖμεν ἄν σε, κοὐδὲν ἄν πάσχοις κακόν.

[3] 189–90 ἥδ' ἐστὶν ἡ σῴζουσα καὶ ταύτης ἔπι
πλέοντες ὀρθῆς τοὺς φίλους ποιούμεθα.

[4] Thuc. ii. 60. 2 ἐγὼ γὰρ ἡγοῦμαι πόλιν πλείω ξύμπασαν ὀρθουμένην ὠφελεῖν
τοὺς ἰδιώτας ἢ καθ' ἕκαστον τῶν πολιτῶν εὐπραγοῦσαν, ἀθρόαν δὲ σφαλλομένην

resemblance in its insistence on the superiority of the city to its citizens, but what counts is the difference of spirit. Pericles speaks with moving and obvious devotion; Creon, we feel, does not hold his views with much conviction. The maxims flow too easily to carry much weight. Creon advances them with such glibness that we soon suspect him of trying to make a good impression or wonder if he does not deceive himself. And Sophocles surely intended us to be a little wary. To the sharp-witted he gives a hint when he makes Creon say:

> It is impossible to know a man
> In soul and spirit and in mind, until
> He is proved versed in rule and law-giving.[1]

Creon asserts that no man can be known until he has been tried in office; in the meanwhile he will state his principles. It sounds correct enough, but there is a lurking irony in it. For it is an expansion of the sage Bias' words, 'Rule will show the man', which Aristotle quotes to show the difference between virtue in private and in public matters.[2] Creon may be a good man in private life, but he has not yet been tested in public. Sophocles hints that he will be tested, and we wonder what the result will be. Creon pretends to be modest, but we doubt if he is, for he has a high notion of what kingship means to him and of his own capacity for it. An Athenian audience, quick to detect the first approaches of pride, might well begin to suspect it in him. The words which he uses of himself in apparent modesty may, we fear, prove the opposite of what he wishes to convey; he will show his true nature as soon as he begins to exercise power.

Misgivings about Creon deepen as he develops his theories and applies them to the special case of refusing burial to Polynices. The transition from principle to practice comes so easily that we may fail to mark it:

> Now in accord with this I have proclaimed. . .[3]

The refusal of burial, it seems, is the logical consequence of a belief that his city demands a man's highest loyalty. This conclusion comes all the more easily since Polynices is undoubtedly a traitor. Moreover, since he is dead, the only possible punishment for him

---

[1] 175–7   ἀμήχανον δὲ παντὸς ἀνδρὸς ἐκμαθεῖν
      ψυχήν τε καὶ φρόνημα καὶ γνώμην, πρὶν ἂν
      ἀρχαῖς τε καὶ νόμοισιν ἐντριβὴς φανῇ.

[2] *Nic. Eth.* 1130 a 1   ἀρχὴ ἀνδρὰ δείξει.

[3] 192   καὶ νῦν ἀδελφὰ τῶνδε κηρύξας ἔχω . . .

must be inflicted on his corpse and spirit. If his body is devoured
by birds of prey and his spirit shut out from such consolations as
the grave offers, he will suffer, and this should deter others from
following his example. The refusal of burial to Polynices is different
from refusing it to a foreign foe and should not be illustrated by
the discussion in Euripides' *Suppliant Women* about the burial of the
Argive dead. The ordinary way to treat Polynices would be to
allow him burial outside the boundaries of his own land. This
Creon does not mention. He has either not thought of it or
thought of it and rejected it. His edict is that the body must be
left unburied where it is (29, 105). [He proposes to punish the dead
man after death, and in this he follows not custom but his own
theories. Such a punishment is unusual but it is not unique. For
Plato, another theorist, ordains that the slayer of kinsmen—and
such Polynices was—shall be cast out of the land unburied.[1] When
he prescribes the same punishment for the impious and for robbers
of temples and parricides,[2] he may be called in to support Creon's
decision; for Polynices has tried to destroy his country's temples
and has taken arms against his own kin. [Creon's position is
unusual, but it can be defended. It has a certain logic, and the
audience would see that he treats treason very seriously and
wishes to punish it with utmost severity.] The Chorus accept his
decision without criticism but also without approval. They do not
deny that, if he chooses, Creon can act like this:

> Power is yours to use what law you will
> Both for the dead and all of us who live.[3]

The words, perhaps, suggest some doubt and uneasiness. The
Chorus seem to feel that the edict is not right, but they are not
prepared to say so. For the moment the audience may almost be
deceived into believing that in this special case an exception is
allowed to the universal duty of burial, or at least that Creon is
entitled to do what he thinks fit in the matter.

Creon is wrong. The gods allow no exception to their rule.
The sequel will show this, and no doubt it is already clear to
keener consciences. But if Creon is wrong, what is the flaw in his
reasoning? what fault leads him to this false conclusion? From a
Greek point of view Creon errs because he assumes that reasons of
state justify him in denying their due to the gods. He neglects the

---

[1] *Laws* ix. 873 c.   [2] *Ib.* x. 909 c, xii. 960 b.
[3] 213–14
        νόμῳ δὲ χρῆσθαι παντί, τοῦτ᾽ ἔνεστί σοι
        καὶ τῶν θανόντων χὠπόσοι ζῶμεν πέρι.

distinction between what is due to them and what is due to men, between what is holy and what is merely just. It is fundamentally wrong to sacrifice the first to the second or what seems to be it, to think that human necessities or rules can ever override divine obligations. A characteristic example of such an error is Pentheus in Euripides' *Bacchants*, who persecutes the new religion of Dionysus with quite honourable motives and persuades himself that its adherents are bad citizens, drunken and lascivious. He may have a kind of justice on his side, but he violates 'Holiness, Queen of the gods'[1] on whom the Bacchants call for vengeance. So Creon also acts on what he believes to be excellent reasons. If the State were really all that mattered, he would act rightly. But above it are the gods, and when he sacrifices their claims to its, he acts unholily. His logic is at fault because he fails to take account of the gods.

Creon feels no doubts, no qualms. He is sure that he is right. When the news comes that rites have been paid to Polynices' body and the Chorus suggest that this may be prompted by heaven, he dismisses the suggestion impatiently:

> You say what is not to be endured, who say
> That the gods care at all for this dead man.[2]

It is firmly fixed in his mind that Polynices came to burn the temples of Thebes. He said this before (199 ff.) and he says it again (285–6). He sums up with a clinching rhetorical question:

> Do you see the gods honouring evil men?[3]

At first sight he again seems to be on good ground. The notion that the gods punish the wicked was deeply rooted in Greek belief. But such punishment has nothing to do with Creon. In so far as he refuses burial, he is himself wicked in the eyes of the gods. His delusions lead him into impiety, a special kind of pride, just as Pentheus for similar reasons refuses to recognize the divinity of Dionysus and is equally guilty of impious pride.[4] In both cases this pride blinds its victims. They fail to see what their divine duty is and have specious excuses for avoiding it. They may be convinced by these excuses, but that does not make them valid. Both in effect claim to know more than the gods. At the best this was useless,[5] but it could be much worse. It was well known that

---

[1] *Bacch.* 370   Ὁσία πότνα θεῶν
[2] 282–3   λέγεις γὰρ οὐκ ἀνεκτά, Δαίμονας λέγων
          πρόνοιαν ἴσχειν τοῦδε τοῦ νεκροῦ πέρι.
[3] 288   ἢ τοὺς κακοὺς τιμῶντας εἰσορᾷς θεούς;
[4] Eur. *Bacch.* 375, 1297.   [5] Hom. Hymn iv. 548.

no man could really know the mind of the gods,[1] and that those who thought themselves wiser than the gods were impiously proud and suffered from an infatuation of soul. The impeccable Euripidean Theseus puts the truth succinctly:

> But wisdom seeks to be more powerful
> Than God. With empty vanity in our hearts
> We think us wiser than divinity.[2]

It was particularly presumptuous to think that one could override the gods in their own special sphere of what was due to them from men. They had laid down rules which must be obeyed without question or exception. Creon is no more an unbeliever than Pentheus is, but in holy matters he too suffers from a deluding pride, and that makes him irreverent.

Nor is Creon's fault merely intellectual. It is more a fault of character. Indeed he is so presented that before long the audience would begin to see in him some qualities of the typical, traditional tyrant, such as Athenians normally loathed. Despite his expressed desire that all should speak their minds to him (180–1), he blusters and threatens when the Chorus ventures a very guarded statement, and virtually accuses them of corruption. Tyrants were known to dislike criticism and not to get it.[3] So Creon dismisses the suggestion of the Chorus that the burial is the work of the gods by saying that they will make him angry (280). His temper clouds his judgement, as it was well known to do, and it is of course a tyrannical trait. A tyrant, like Herodotus' Cyaxares, is quick to wrath.[4] He is also suspicious,[5] and Creon is particularly suspicious of corrupt motives. He has his own theory of civic disobedience— it is prompted by love of money. He warns the Chorus:

> But through their hopes
> Has love of profit often ruined men.[6]

and develops the theme when he hears of the burial:

> These men, I know it well, have led them on
> With bribery to do what they have done.[7]

---

[1] Hes. *Op.* 483–4, Solon fr. 17.
[2] Eur. *Supp.* 216–18 ἀλλ' ἡ φρόνησις τοῦ θεοῦ μεῖζον σθένειν
ζητεῖ, τὸ γαῦρον δ' ἐν φρεσὶν κεκτημένοι
δοκοῦμεν εἶναι δαιμόνων σοφώτεροι.
[3] Isocr. ii. 15 c.   [4] Hdt. i. 73. 4.   [5] Dio Chrys. *Or.* ii. 75.
[6] 221–2   ἀλλ' ὑπ' ἐλπίδων
ἄνδρας τὸ κέρδος πολλάκις διώλεσεν.
[7] 293–4   ἐκ τῶνδε τούτους ἐξεπίσταμαι καλῶς
παρηγμένους μισθοῖσιν εἰργάσθαι τάδε.

This is the language of the politician, as we know it from contro-
versialists like Theognis[1] and Aristophanes.[2] In making Creon
speak like this Sophocles indulges his irony. Creon shows himself
to be a tyrant, and tyrants often based their power on other men's
love of money.[3] Creon applies to others what might well be applied
to him. It is part of the illusion in which he moves, and it shows
the tyrant at work in him. As Aristotle says, 'it is characteristic of
a tyrant to distrust his friends'.[4] Creon is true to type.

So though Creon professes admirable sentiments, he shows traits
of tyrannical arrogance. These have led him to his wrong judgement in refusing burial to Polynices. As the plot develops, Creon's
faults also develop. He becomes more tyrannical, more unreasonable, more convinced that he is right and that everyone else is
wrong. The play gives a rich study of such a man. Creon keeps
up the air of being a patriot and a disinterested statesman. He is
not openly brutal like Lycus in Euripides' *Heracles*. He seems even
to show some vestiges of humour in his dealings with the simple
and homely Guard. But as he is faced with graver issues, his faults
become clearer. When he knows that Antigone has disobeyed his
edict, he does not attempt any real answer to her defence. He
remains convinced that his treatment of Polynices is right, and
does little more than reiterate his earlier arguments. He counters
Antigone with maxims about the dangers of obstinacy which might
sound well enough in themselves but are no adequate answer to
her (473–8). Nor do they hide his tyrannical streak. He may be
all for order, but the order which he demands is little less than
servitude. His true temper slips out when he says of Antigone:

> There is no place
> For pride in one who is his neighbours' slave.[5]

The word 'slave' comes ill from a close kinsman to one whose
father has recently been king, and would awake uneasy feelings
in the average Athenian. It would remind him that tyrants regarded their subjects as slaves, as Asiatic monarchs commonly do
in Herodotus or as Plato speaks of a city ruled by tyrants as a
slave-city.[6] Creon's feelings towards Antigone are ultimately similar to those of the odious Lycus towards the family of Heracles:

---

[1] 46, 50.   [2] *Thesm.* 360.   [3] Theogn. 823, Soph. fr. 88.   [4] *Pol.* 1313 b 30.
[5] 478–9   οὐ γὰρ ἐκπέλει
        φρονεῖν μέγ' ὅστις ΔοῦΛός ἐστι τῶν πέλας.
[6] *Rep.* ix. 577 d   Δούλη καὶ τυραννουμένη πόλις.

You shall not forget
That you are slaves to serve my tyranny.[1]

Creon shows that he regards others, even his own kin, with the
contempt that an Asiatic monarch or a Greek tyrant has for his
subjects.

Even with his own son, Haemon, Creon's tyrannical temper
breaks through the airs of the father who claims to desire nothing
but his son's welfare. Here he starts, so far as the audience is
concerned, with a great initial advantage. The Greeks demanded
a high degree of respect from children to parents. It was one of
the three fundamental duties of men as Aeschylus knew them:

To reverence those that bare us,
Third is this written in the rules
Of Justice, greatly honoured.[2]

The same voice echoes from Pindar, who attributes to Chiron the
lesson that a man should honour Zeus first and then his parents,[3]
to Plato, who says that no child should ever utter an unbecoming
word to his parents.[4] So when Creon greets Haemon with what
might seem to be an undue sense of paternal dignity:

For so, my son, should be your spirit's law,
To stand in all behind your father's will.[5]

his claims are perfectly proper. When Haemon loses his temper
with his father, defies and even abuses him, he is a bad son,
worthy of strong condemnation. The Chorus try to excuse him
on the ground that love for Antigone has led him astray, but their
words to Eros,
                    The hearts of the just in injustice
                    You drag aside to their bane,[6]

explain more than they excuse. When finally Haemon goes off
in a towering rage, he is, by conventional standards, deeply in
the wrong. In the whole controversy the scales are heavily
weighted for Creon. Yet even here his justifiable sternness is shot
through with something less reputable.

[1] Eur. *Her.* 251–2   μεμνήσεσθε Δὲ
                    Δοῦλοι γεγῶτες τῆς ἐμῆς τυραννίδος.

[2] *Supp.* 707–9   τὸ γὰρ τεκόντων σέβας
                    τρίτον, τόδ' ἐν θεσμίοις
                    Δίκας γέγραπται μεγιστοτίμου.

[3] *Pyth.* vi. 23–7.·   [4] *Laws* iv. 717 d.

[5] 639–40   οὕτω γάρ, ὦ παῖ, χρὴ Διὰ στέρνων ἔχειν
                    γνώμης πατρῴας πάντ' ὄπισθεν ἑστάναι.

[6] 791–2   σὺ καὶ Δικαίων ἀδίκους
                    φρένας παρασπᾷς ἐπὶ λώβᾳ.

Even before he breaks out in anger against Haemon Creon speaks of the obedience that he expects from others:

> Whomso the city raise, we must obey
> In small things, right things, and their opposites.[1]

The last two words need not mean very much, but they suggest that Creon demands an absolute, unquestioning obedience and does not care if it is right or wrong. The audience, suspicious already of him, might well detect another tyrannical trait. His formula has a singularly autocratic ring. It is similar to another line:

Slave, you must obey your masters both in right things and in wrong,[2]

and we remember how an Aeschylean Chorus, subjected to the tyranny of Aegisthus and Clytaemnestra, say that they must despite themselves approve of things 'right and not right'.[3] But what is only a hint at first in Creon comes out nakedly when his temper is aroused and his self-control shaken. When he bases his demand for absolute authority on the claim that the city belongs to him:

> Does not the master own the commonwealth?[4]

he touches on a matter familiar to all Athenians. This is the old claim of tyrants which Athenian democracy denied in practice and in theory. The claim of Pericles that the government belonged not to the few but to the many,[5] the proud line of Aeschylus that the Athenians were the slaves and subjects of no man,[6] the statement of the Euripidean Theseus:

> No single man
> Is ruler of our city. It is free.[7]

are all variations on the theme that the city belongs to the whole body of citizens. Creon claims to be its owner and can only excite suspicion. Some of the audience might even agree with Aristotle that absolute monarchy is against nature,[8] and many would recall dark stories of tyrants like Hippias and Periander.

---

[1] 666–7   ἀλλ' ὃν πόλις στήσειε, τοῦδε χρὴ κλύειν
καὶ σμικρὰ καὶ δίκαια καὶ τἀναντία.

[2] Tr. Adesp. 436   δοῦλε, δεσποτῶν ἄκουε καὶ δίκαια κἄδικα.

[3] Aesch. Cho. 78 δίκαια καὶ μὴ δίκαια.

[4] 738   οὐ τοῦ κρατοῦντος ἡ πόλις νομίζεται;

[5] Thuc. ii. 37. 1.   [6] Pers. 242.

[7] Supp. 404–5   οὐ γὰρ ἄρχεται
ἑνὸς πρὸς ἀνδρός, ἀλλ' ἐλευθέρα πόλις.

[8] Pol. 1287 a 12.

The temper which Creon shows to Haemon is confirmed by his actions. In his anger he is not content to punish Antigone alone but decides that her sister shall share her fate (478–92). Ismene is innocent, and Creon has no real reason to think that she is guilty except that he has seen her distraught in the house (492). He simply assumes that she is Antigone's confederate. The suspicious element in him is reaching dangerous proportions. Even when Antigone declares in his hearing that Ismene has taken no part in the burial of Polynices (578–81), he takes no notice but orders her arrest and death. This headstrong decision arises out of his anger. He illustrates the truth of Aristotle's argument that a democracy is preferable to a tyranny[1] because 'when the individual is mastered by anger or some other passion of the kind, his judgement must necessarily be spoilt'. Creon is mastered by anger and has lost his judgement, his sense of fact and of justice. His fine sentiments about the safety of the State take the form of punishing the innocent. An Athenian audience would see the tyrant in him and know him for what he is.

No less sinister and revealing are Creon's feelings about Antigone. His original decision that anyone who disobeyed his order should be stoned (35–6) had at least the excuse that stoning was a common punishment for treason and that the burial of a traitor might be construed as aiding and abetting treason. But when Creon finds that it is Antigone who has disobeyed his edict, he feels particular resentment that it is a woman who has flouted him. To this grievance he recurs (484, 678, 740, 746). In itself this might arouse some sympathy. It is what in a different world stirs the Magistrate in Aristophanes' *Lysistrata*:

No, no. Never shall women conquer us![2]

But Creon is not justified in overriding the duties owed to his kin and in deciding to shed their blood. The Greeks attached a special sanctity to the bonds of the family. Antigone and Ismene, as Creon admits, share his hearth and are the special wards of Zeus of the Household (487). To break this bond was a grave matter. Plato must be following ancient belief when he says that he who honours his kindred and those who share his gods may expect the gods to prosper his seed.[3] He indicates that this is a very special and sacred relation. It may explain why before long

[1] *Pol.* 1286 a 32.
[2] *Lys.* 450–1   ἀτὰρ οὐ γυναικῶν οὐδέποτ' ἔσθ' ἡττητέα
                            ἡμῖν.
[3] *Laws* v. 729 c.

Creon's own seed is lost with his son's death; the punishment is appropriate to one who has broken the ties of family. In deciding to kill Antigone Creon acts against the gods even though he is consistent with his own policy. This drives him to a terrible act. When he asserts that he will carry out his design against a close kinswoman

> Be she my sister's child or closer still
> Than all who worship Zeus within my house[1]

he shows the fury that drives him on.

Creon is a tyrant, his fault the deluding pride of a man who has enough power to indulge himself. He is well described in Herodotus' account of the tyrant as one who 'sated with arrogance, does many shameless things'.[2] In fact, if we apply Herodotus' test to him, it shows him up—'For if the best of all men were established in this power, you would put him outside the customary opinions.'[3] That is Creon's trouble, and Haemon warns him of it:

> If any man thinks he alone is wise,
> Or that in speech or mind he has no peer,
> These, when laid open, are found empty souls.[4]

The Greeks were keenly sensitive to the dangers of being unlike other men. 'Theognis' recognized the situation in social life:

> If one believes his neighbour to know nothing,
> And that he himself has many arts,
> He is a fool. His noble mind is ruined.
> For we all alike know various things.[5]

The defence of variety and tolerance could be applied equally to public and political life. Creon tries to be different from other men, to keep himself apart, to follow his own ideas, to indulge his own fancies. He runs a grave danger and does what no man should. Like Herodotus' typical tyrant, he 'breaks the laws of the land' in forbidding burial to Polynices and 'puts men to death without trial' in his summary condemnation of Ismene. Gradually his true character emerges, and at the end of the scene with Haemon his faults are plain. By then even those who have been

---

[1] 486-7 ἀλλ' εἴτ' ἀδελφῆς εἴθ' ὁμαιμονεστέρα
τοῦ παντὸς ἡμῖν Ζηνὸς ἑρκείου κυρεῖ . . .

[2] iii. 80. 4.   [3] iii. 80. 3.

[4] 707-9 ὅστις γὰρ αὐτὸς ἢ φρονεῖν μόνος δοκεῖ,
ἢ γλῶσσαν, ἣν οὐκ ἄλλος, ἢ ψυχὴν ἔχειν,
οὗτοι διαπτυχθέντες ὤφθησαν κενοί.

[5] 221-4 ὅστις τοι δοκέει τὸν πλησίον ἴδμεναι οὐδέν,
ἀλλ' αὐτὸς μοῦνος ποικίλα δήνε' ἔχειν.
κεῖνός γ' ἄφρων ἐστί, νόου βεβλαμμένος ἐσθλοῦ.
ἴσως γὰρ πάντες ποικίλ' ἐπιστάμεθα.

deceived by his fine words or impressed by his 'realistic' reasons of state must see that something is wrong in him.

The analysis of Creon's character and behaviour shows that for a Greek audience he was by no means an abstraction. He is a type familiar to them in life and in literature. His interest is not in the least that he represents the State and its claims but that he is a human being put in a special position and assailed by the faults which such an isolation almost inevitably awakes and fosters. His misfortune is that he is not good or strong enough to resist the temptations which beset a man in his place. He gives in to them and becomes the familiar type of tyrant. In presenting the complexities of such a case Sophocles shows much subtlety. He shows a conflict in which it is not at first clear which side is really right. Therefore he makes Creon persuasive and impressive, and often puts a real or apparent right on his side. By this means the issue of Polynices' burial is not seen as a clear-cut issue of right and wrong but as something which involves diverse, even confused, feelings. Gradually we are led to see where the right lies, but not before we have seen the other side and perhaps been impressed by it. This is the way in which a serious problem is often presented in life, and it is right that it should so be presented in art. For what counts is its human interest, the views that are held of it, the emotions and illusions which prompt and foster them, the complexity of it in actual fact. Therefore the issue is best presented in an individual man. Creon is a human being who is moved by ordinary emotions. To the Greeks they were perhaps more familiar than to us, but they belong to mankind. Sophocles does not suggest, and certainly did not believe, that all men in power were like Creon. His Creon is not a criticism of kingship. It is a case of an individual destiny, not, however, too individual to be rare. Creon illustrates the special dangers of power to a man of his kind. It is too much for him, and ruins his character. In presenting him in this light Sophocles follows the tradition of many Greek thinkers, of Solon and Theognis, even of Pindar. When such a man as Creon is in power and follows his proud whims, the chances are that something wrong will be done. He is of the kind to enforce his will in the wrong way and to cause disaster.

To Creon Antigone presents an exact contrast. Creon may seem to be right but is wrong; Antigone is right but often seems to be wrong. Creon begins by seeming to be an ordinary, decent man and is slowly revealed to be a tyrant; Antigone begins with unwomanly strength and an air of arrogance, but ends as a creature of deep affections and noble courage. Sophocles is not afraid to take risks with her or to make her for the moment remarkably far from Greek ideals of womanhood; so confident is she that she is right, so determined to do her duty, and to despise anyone who does not go the whole way with her. In fact by giving this bold uncompromising part to a woman Sophocles may well have shocked conventional minds. Even Aristotle distinguishes a woman's courage from a man's,[1] and seems to have said that it was unsuitable for a woman in a tragedy to be brave.[2] He may have been prejudiced, but his prejudice was not unique; and on her first appearance Antigone would certainly excite some distrust because she is a woman who sets out to do something bold and dangerous. This feeling would grow when the audience saw that she is determined to break the law. The Athenians prided themselves on being a law-abiding people,[3] and if the *Crito* represents what Socrates believed, there was at least some opinion that laws should never be disobeyed, because disobedience to them at one point undermined their whole authority, and because they protect a man's country, which is even more holy than his family.[4] Xenophon claims that Socrates regarded 'lawful' and 'just' as synonymous, and in that case any breach of the laws was morally wrong.[5] Such a belief was not necessarily common, but we can hardly doubt that many would think it wrong in any circumstances to break the law, and would condemn Antigone because she proposes to do so.[6]

Sophocles makes full allowance for hostile feelings of this kind and even indulges them. He sees that a woman who breaks the laws can only be justified if she has a very good case indeed and that she may reasonably be criticized from various points of view. His method is to present the opposition against which Antigone contends. He begins with Ismene, who is a typical woman, the sister of Antigone, who can speak to her with frankness and has the same obligation to their unburied brother. She pleads for a quiet life after the dire misfortunes of their family, and wishes to take no risks. She has her argument, that woman cannot fight against men and must give in to the stronger:

> For to do things
> Beyond our scope—there is no sense in that.[7]

---

[1] *Pol.* 1260 a 22. [2] *Poet.* 1454 a 20. [3] Thuc. ii. 37. 3.
[4] 50 b, 51 b. [5] *Mem.* iv. iv. 18. [6] Cf. ' Andoc.' *In Alc.* 19.
[7] 67–8
　　　　　　　　τὸ γὰρ
περισσὰ πράσσειν οὐκ ἔχει νοῦν οὐδένα.

She says that Antigone is in love with the impossible (90), and

It is not right to hunt the impossible.[1]

She seems to speak with the authority of established morality and
recalls what happens to women who aspire above their station as
Pindar's Coronis did when 'she was after what was not there'[2] and
came to a ghastly end. In her passive acceptance of evil Ismene
might illustrate Aristotle's view that the courage of a woman is
shown in submission.[3] On this point Socrates would have disagreed
with him,[4] but he would none the less have disapproved of Antigone
for breaking the law. Through Ismene we are led to think of Antigone as a proud and reckless creature until we see that Ismene
herself does not advocate a true modesty and that Antigone is not
guilty of pride. Ismene is moved not by principles but by timidity.
She dares not join Antigone in so great a risk. In fact she feels
qualms and has some guilt about her refusal. She knows that
the dead will not be pleased with her:

> Therefore I beg of those below the earth
> For pardon in that I am forced in this,
> And shall obey authority.[5]

Though she says, and may believe, that Antigone is mad (98),
Ismene both admires and loves her. She accepts her reproofs
without resentment or defence, and we are left with the impression
that she would herself act in the same way if she had the courage.
She does not convict Antigone of irreverent pride for the good
reason that Antigone is innocent of it. At the risk of her life she
does the gods' will and, whatever human judgement may think,
before the gods she is innocent.

　　Though at first Ismene refuses to help her sister, when Antigone
is arrested she takes her side and says boldly and untruthfully:

> I did the deed, if she allows my claim,
> And share and take the burden of the guilt.[6]

Antigone will not accept her as a partner and again seems forbidding and unfriendly. She has no word of praise for Ismene's
action, courageous and loyal though it is. The burial of Polynices

---

[1] 92　　　　　　ἀρχὴν δὲ θηρᾶν οὐ πρέπει τἀμήχανα.

[2] *Pyth.* iii. 20　　　ἤρατο τῶν ἀπεόντων.

[3] *Pol.* 1260 a 23.　　　　[4] *Meno* 72 a–73 c.

[5] 65–7　　　　ἐγὼ μὲν οὖν αἰτοῦσα τοὺς ὑπὸ χθονὸς
　　　　　　　ξύγγνοιαν ἴσχειν, ὡς βιάζομαι τάδε,
　　　　　　　τοῖς ἐν τέλει βεβῶσι πείσομαι.

[6] 536–7　　　δέδρακα τοὔργον, εἴπερ ἥδ' ὁμορροθεῖ,
　　　　　　　καὶ ξυμμετίσχω καὶ φέρω τῆς αἰτίας.

is her own affair, and she will die for it (547). To Ismene she says

> Look to yourself; I grudge not your escape.[1]

She gives no sign of sisterly love or gratitude. Seeing that Ismene is her only close relative in the world, Antigone is remarkably cold to her. And yet in this too she is right. The original conception of burying Polynices was hers, and hers its execution. It is not enough that Ismene, who refused to act with her, should now wish to share her punishment and claim:

> But now our fault is equal, yours and mine.[2]

Antigone is concerned with a strict duty; Ismene has shirked this and deserves neither the glory nor the suffering that belong to it. Antigone is harsh to her simply because she has shirked. If she seems to lack sisterly feelings, it is because she has them in abundance and lavishes them on her dead brother who needs them, not on her sister who does not. In her single-minded devotion to her task she has no place for compromise.

More surprisingly, Antigone herself sometimes leads us to think that she condemns her own action or at least acts wilfully in a position where contending duties give no clear lead. She speaks of her decision as if it were legally or morally wrong, even though the gods command it. When she says

> My crime has been most holy,[3]

the splendid paradox seems to glorify her deed as a crime demanded by the gods. Her words even suggest that at the gods' bidding she has done something repellent or revolting. She means nothing of the kind. She uses bold defiant language to express her contempt for those who think her action wrong. It is ironical, almost a quotation from critics and enemies. Again, when she says

> But let me and this folly that is mine
> Suffer this dreadful thing,[4]

her reference to her folly does not in the least convey what she really thinks or what the audience will think when they know the facts and see them in the right perspective. She speaks of her action as if it were criminally foolish, but of any such folly she is quite innocent. She speaks in irony because in their ignorance men

---

[1] 553   σῶσον σεαυτήν· οὐ φθονῶ σ' ὑπεκφυγεῖν.
[2] 558   καὶ μὴν ἴση νῷν ἐστιν ἡ 'ξαμαρτία.
[3] 74   ὅσια πανουργήσασα.
[4] 95–6   ἀλλ' ἔα με καὶ τὴν ἐξ ἐμοῦ δυσβουλίαν
             παθεῖν τὸ δεινὸν τοῦτο.

think her guilty. Later, in the presence of death, she says of herself:

> My piety is called impiety.[1]

Whatever her action is, it is not that. Yet she has earned a name for it. She refers especially to the Chorus who have failed to understand her and thought her guilty of pride. She speaks now more in bitterness than in irony, but the two are closely related, and we can see how Antigone, convinced though she is that she is right, knows that others will not see things in her way, and cannot help using words such as they might use in disapproval.

No less effective is the way in which Sophocles makes Antigone rather remote and forbidding. In the first scene with Ismene she has no sympathy for her sister once she finds that she will not help to bury their brother. She knows no compromise, accepts no excuses. Because Ismene will not help, they are enemies (86–7, 93–4). She dismisses Ismene's genuine fear for her with a curt command to look after herself (83). When Ismene urges the need for secrecy, Antigone tells her to blazon the news abroad (86). Her sense of duty seems to have dried up all human feelings except love for her brother. The same hardness appears when Ismene wishes to share her guilt and is dismissed from any responsibility in it. Yet this hardness is built on a real tenderness even for Ismene. In the first words of the play when Antigone addresses her sister:

> Ismene, mine own sister, one with me,[2]

we see what her usual feelings are. And in her last words to her hatred has died away:

> Be of good cheer; you live. But long ago
> My life has died to give help to the dead.[3]

Antigone thinks that Ismene has failed in her duty, but here she makes a concession and admits that there is a difference between herself and her sister which cannot be overcome and leads them on different ways. She is absorbed in the dead, but Ismene continues the ordinary life of the living. Antigone is intent on doing what is right. This may make her act harshly, but she is not harsh by nature.

Antigone takes upon herself to defy the law or what is at least

---

[1] 924   τὴν δυσσέβειαν εὐσεβοῦσ' ἐκτησάμην.

[2] 1   ὦ κοινὸν αὐτάδελφον Ἰσμήνης κάρα.

[3] 559–60   θάρσει· σὺ μὲν ζῇς· ἡ δ' ἐμὴ ψυχὴ πάλαι
              τέθνηκεν, ὥστε τοῖς θανοῦσιν ὠφελεῖν.

elieved to be the law. The decision is momentous and would undoubtedly create strong prejudice against her in many of the audience. The Greeks, whose political liberties were intimately associated with the existence of laws, prided themselves upon them, with reason. It was the possession of laws that distinguished Greece from barbarian countries.[1] Euripides' Bacchants say that no knowledge or practice should override the laws,[2] and his Tyndareos says that it is characteristically Hellenic

> Not to desire to be above the laws.[3]

Athenian orators stress the same point, as when Aeschines says that we must go not before but after the laws,[4] or Demosthenes considers it typical of the base Meidias that he thinks his own power more important than them.[5] The respect for law was not confined to Athens. It was deeply ingrained in the Spartan discipline, and their King Archidamus approved of the system which inculcated it.[6] Antigone, in defiance of all this established sentiment, sets herself above Creon's law and claims to know better what is right. This is dangerous in anyone, and especially dangerous in a woman. At the outset of the play Antigone shows her contempt and hardly even troubles to explain it. It is not till she is confronted with Creon that she gives her reasons. In the interval she may well be suspected by a law-loving audience and condemned, if not for pride, at least for folly. Her determination to defy the laws requires considerable excuse. Sophocles was fully conscious of this. He knew how grave a step Antigone takes and what will be thought of it. Only when the strength of the opposition has been revealed do we see how right Antigone is.

The qualms and misgivings that an ordinary man might feel about Antigone are dramatized in the Chorus. They are Theban elders whose natural instinct is to support the established power of Creon. In their first song they tell of their relief at the defeat and departure of the invaders. After such a strain they want nothing but peace and quiet, to forget the war (150-1). They are naturally averse to anyone who, like Antigone, seems likely to cause new troubles. But they have a certain decency and sense of honour, and are in fact typical citizens. They admit Creon's power to make what rules he pleases, but they do not say that they approve, and they claim that they are too old to see that his edict is carried out

[1] Eur. *Med.* 536-7.   [2] *Bacch.* 881-2.
[3] *Or.* 487   καὶ τῶν νόμων γε μὴ πρότερον εἶναι θέλειν.
[4] iii. 23.   [5] xxi. 66.   [6] Thuc. i. 84. 3.

(216). They are uneasy about the refusal of burial to Polynice
but not prepared to do anything about it. Still, when they hear o
the first rites done to him, they are pleased and suggest that it ma
be the work of the gods (278). As Creon's tyrannical tempe
grows, they still offer little suggestions, say that Haemon ha
spoken well (724-5), and plead with success for the life of Ismen
(770). They are perhaps not quite easy in their minds abou
what has happened. They accept Creon's edict for the sake o
peace and quiet, but they are not convinced that it is right. Fo
a time their desire for peace triumphs, and they condemn Antigon
who disturbs it. Their position is hardly reasoned, but it i
perfectly intelligible.

The Chorus are able to consider the nature of Antigone'
action without knowing that it is she who has committed i
Their first judgement is therefore impartial in so far as it is im
personal. In the song, 332-75, they give their general views o
what the Guard has just reported and bring the burial of Poly
nices into its universal relations as they see them. This famou
song on man is so often taken out of its context that its specia
dramatic relevance is obscured. It is not a hymn of praise t
man's power, but something more complex and more closely re
lated to the play. Behind it we may detect a song from Aeschylu
Libation-Bearers which begins, as this does, by stressing the strange
ness of life:

> Many strange dreads and griefs
> Are the earth's fosterlings,[1]

and goes on to tell of bold and criminal deeds attempted b
women. The Chorus of the *Antigone* seem to follow this in a moo
of surprise that anyone should dare to do what Antigone has jus
done in breaking Creon's edict. This action prompts them t
consider man's strange paradoxical nature, which is composed o
opposites and capable of great evil as of great good. In thei
shock and amazement they try to relate what has happened t
what is almost a philosophy of history, to explain their disapprova
by general principles, and at the same time to justify these princi
ples. Their doctrine owes something to Protagoras. It is that th
undeniable progress of man, his success in many spheres, his con
quest of physical nature, and his establishment of an ordere
society, are maintained and secured by the existence of law
Protagoras, according to Plato, described the advance of mankin

---

[1] *Cho.* 585-6   πολλὰ μὲν γᾶ τρέφει
                        δεινὰ δειμάτων ἄχη.

n such terms, and at the end of his myth tells how Zeus sends
Hermes to give men justice and decency, and orders him, 'And
give a law from me, to kill as a disease in the city the man who
cannot partake of decency and justice.'[1] The root of this theory is
that men are sustained and improved by law, and civilization
rests on respect for it, because law brings with it the moral virtues.
It is a noble and impressive theory, and the Chorus hold it. It
is the climax and point of their song. The first three parts are
concerned with the greatness of human achievements, but they
are only a preliminary to the fourth part, which explains how laws
and the respect for them make this achievement possible.

The essence of the song is its emphatic conclusion:

> With cunning beyond belief
> In subtle inventions of art
> He goes his way now to evil, now to good.
> When he keeps the laws of the land
> And the gods' rule he has sworn to hold,
> High is his city. No city has he
> Who in rash effrontery
> Makes wrongdoing his fellow.[2]

From the variety of man's achievements the Chorus advance to
the conclusion that he is capable of both evil and good, and that
if he keeps the laws, all is well with him and his city, but if not,
the city and he are ruined. The doctrine is plain. It is what
Pericles, Protagoras, and Socrates believed about the laws—that
they hold a city together, and that if they are broken, the individual is ruined no less than the city. Man is 'strange' because he
has in himself such possibilities for good and for bad, for order
and for destruction. The only real safeguard against his vagaries
is the rule of laws which are, as Protagoras said, sanctioned by
divine approval. If a man keeps them, the city stands; if he
breaks them, he destroys its structure. The chief danger is presumptuous boldness, which was well known to be capable of
destroying a city.[3] After its great preliminaries and praise of man
the song ends on a note of anxiety, a prayer that lawlessness may

---

[1] Plat. *Prot.* 322 c–d.
[2] 365–71	σοφόν τι τὸ μαχανόεν
	τέχνας ὑπὲρ ἐλπίδ' ἔχων
	τότε μὲν κακόν, ἄλλοτ' ἐπ' ἐσθλὸν ἕρπει·
	νόμους περαίνων χθονὸς
	θεῶν τ' ἔνορκον Δίκαν·
	ὑψίπολις· ἄπολις ὅτῳ τὸ μὴ καλὸν
	ξύνεστι τόλμας χάριν.
[3] Hdt. i. 96. 3, Eur. *I.A.* 1090 ff.

not prevail. The Chorus, anxious at all costs to keep order, are
frightened by the menace of anarchy which the burial of Polynices
seems to indicate.

This theory must have a particular reference and be concerned
with something that has happened in the play. It cannot refer to
Creon. He may have broken the laws of the gods, but these are
not in question, and he certainly has not broken the laws of the
land, which are. The Chorus refer to the yet unidentified person
who, despite a legal order, has buried Polynices. They take their
stand with Creon and, as they believe, with law and order. In
fact they even echo his sentiments. When they say that obedience
to the laws exalts a city (370), they repeat what he has said about
the place of discipline in the State (191); their attack on rash boldness repeats his disapproval of those who are enemies of the city
(187 ff.). In effect they condemn Antigone, though they do not
know that she is the culprit. Nor is this surprising. The Chorus
desire quiet. They will have nothing to do with law-breakers:

> May he never share my hearth,
> Never think thoughts of mine,
> Who does this.[1]

Their feelings are quite understandable. Their song would appeal
to a large number who felt that it was in any circumstances wrong
to break the laws and that anyone who did so was presumptuous
and wicked. The song expresses in advance a strong disapproval
of Antigone and gives reasons for it.

The Chorus do not change their minds when they know who
the criminal is. Despite their amazement that Antigone should
have acted like this, they say

> What is this? Is it you who have disobeyed
> The laws of the king and are dragged hither,
> Arrested in folly?[2]

The emphatic mention of the laws after the importance given to
them in the preceding song shows that the Chorus are still thinking on the same lines; Antigone has broken the laws, and the only
explanation is that she has acted in senseless folly. To this view
they hold with some obstinacy. Even when Antigone has made

---

[1] 373–5   μήτ' ἐμοὶ παρέστιος
                    γένοιτο μήτ' ἴσον φρονῶν
                    ὃς τάδ' ἔρδοι.

[2] 381–3   τί ποτ'; οὐ δή που σέ γ' ἀπιστοῦσαν
                    τοῖς βασιλείοισιν ἄγουσι νόμοις
                    καὶ ἐν ἀφροσύνῃ καθελόντες;

her great defence to Creon and shown that she does not recognize
any validity in his so-called laws, the Chorus are not moved but
comment:

> The father's cruel temper in the child
> Shows, and she knows not how to yield to trouble.[1]

They see in her a pride closely akin to folly. Creon agrees with
them and proceeds to dilate on the dangers of obstinacy. In what
follows they take no part except to express surprise at Creon's
decision that Haemon shall not marry Antigone (574) and unwilling resignation when she is condemned to death (576). In
effect they think that her action is wrong but that she is more
foolish than wicked, and that she is punished with undue severity.
They do not appreciate her real motives or the importance of what
she has done.

In their next song, 582–625, the Chorus again expound their
views of Antigone. If their earlier song was inspired by civic respect for law, this is inspired by considerations of moral theology.
Protagoras gives place to Aeschylus. The song is an exposition in
the Aeschylean manner of the hereditary evils of the House of
Labdacus. In his *Seven against Thebes* Aeschylus had explained the
misfortunes of Oedipus and his children by the belief that the gods
punish the descendants of Laius to the third generation because he
disobeyed an oracle.[2] Sophocles may well have had his play in
mind, since his Chorus, like that of Aeschylus, compare the successive waves of the curse to a stormy sea[3] and see the human actors
as victims of madness.[4] Four times the Chorus refer to 'doom'
(584, 614, 624, 625), and it provides the main theme of their song.
The gods have sent destruction on the family, and it is still potent
(593–7). The Chorus believe that it is now at work on Antigone:

> Now over the last stock
> A light had been shed in Oedipus' house.
> But it is brought down
> By the bloody dust of the nether gods,
> Folly of words, and the heart's fury.[5]

---

[1] 471–2   Δηλοῖ τὸ γοῦν λῆμ' ὠμὸν ἐξ ὠμοῦ πατρὸς
           τῆς παιδός· εἴκειν Δ' οὐκ ἐπίσταται κακοῖς.

[2] *Sept.* 742–5.   [3] 586–93, *Sept.* 758–61.   [4] 603, *Sept.* 756.

[5] 599–603   νῦν γὰρ ἐσχάτας ὑπὲρ
         ῥίζας ἐτέτατο φάος ἐν Οἰδίπου Δόμοις·
         κατ' αὖ νιν φοινία θεῶν τῶν
         νερτέρων ἀμᾷ κόνις,
         λόγου τ' ἄνοια καὶ φρενῶν 'Ερινύς.

Antigone is the last of the house of Oedipus. All seemed well with her until the handful of blood-stained dust which she threw on Polynices became the instrument of her destruction. Her fault is a kind of madness, an hereditary fury that works in her heart and drives her on as it drove on her father and grandfather before her.

The Chorus say about Antigone what Aeschylus might have said. To some of the audience this might seem the right view. It does not make her guilty of more than rash action and bold speech; it explains her conduct and its punishment by the wrath of the gods against her family and so excuses her from any grave guilt herself. For those who felt it unjust that Antigone should suffer as she does, such an explanation might contain comfort. At least her suffering is not seen as a monstrous act of injustice. We learn later that this is not the poet's own view, but for the moment the Chorus produce a theory which is reasonably tenable. It was as old as Hesiod,[1] had been popularized by Solon[2] and by Aeschylus and was held even by Herodotus[3] and Euripides.[4] It sounds convincing. Actually it seems never to have been held by Sophocles, who found other and different explanations of human suffering. Yet the power which he gives to its presentation shows that he understood its appeal to many hearts. It was one way of looking at a difficult moral problem, but it was not the right way. Antigone does not act in folly and blindness of soul but from a clear knowledge of the divine will. Such is human ignorance that it may mistake this for an almost criminal infatuation.

From their special account of Antigone's doom the Chorus advance to more general considerations, especially to a noble address to Zeus, whose power no man can control:

> To thy power, o Zeus,
> What human trespass can fix bounds?[5]

Against the illusions of men they set the everlasting, unsleeping strength of Zeus, and give as an example one of his laws:

> In what shall be and is to come,
> In what was before, this law
> Shall hold: nothing that grows too vast
> Comes to men's life without a curse.[6]

---

[1] Op. 240.   [2] Fr. 1. 25 ff.   [3] i. 91, vii. 137.   [4] Hipp. 830-1.

[5] 604-5
τεάν, Ζεῦ, Δύναμιν τίς ἀνδρῶν ὑπερβασία κατάσχοι;

[6] 611-14
τό τ' ἔπειτα καὶ τὸ μέλλον
καὶ τὸ πρὶν ἐπαρκέσει
νόμος ὅδ'· οὐδὲν ἕρπει
θνατῶν βιότῳ πάμπολύ γ' ἐκτὸς ἄτας.

Their meaning is clear. This is their answer to Antigone's claim
that she is simply carrying out the gods' command. Against the
laws which she invokes they set up another, the divine rule that
men are victims of a doom or curse which makes them think right
what is wrong (621–3). They try to convict her by her own
methods, to turn the tables on her. She is made to appear the
victim of an illusion that she knows what the gods' will really is.
Once again Sophocles contrasts her with Creon, who is really
the victim of such an illusion. The Chorus too are wrong, and
they show it when against Antigone's alleged foolishness they set
up their own pretended wisdom (620).

The Chorus explain and condemn Antigone's action. They persist in their view even when she appears for the last time on her
way to her living tomb. When they say to her,

> To uttermost effrontery
> You went, and with your steps you struck
> On Justice's high throne, my child:
> You are paying for your father's trespass,[1]

they are still thinking in Aeschylean terms. They assume that
Antigone is guilty of criminal boldness and has attacked that
Justice which is embodied in the laws. They now see her as a
lawless spirit who attacks holy things and is doomed to disaster.
The notion is familiar[2] and needs little explanation. Then, a little
later, they seem to have changed their ground and to be on the
point of making some concession:

> All reverence should be revered,
> But power, to whomso power belongs,
> Must never be transgressed in aught.
> Your self-willed temper has destroyed you.[3]

They admit after all that the honour in which she holds her dead
brother is a kind of reverence, but they try to compromise and to
set against this the indubitable fact that authority will not brook
disobedience. They seem to think that Antigone's error lies in

[1] 853–6   προβᾶσ' ἐπ' ἔσχατον θράσους
             ὑψηλὸν ἐς Δίκας βάθρον
             προσέπαισας, ὦ τεκνον, ποδοῖν·
             πατρῷον Δ' ἐκτίνεις τιν' ἄθλον.

[2] Aesch. Ag. 381–4; Eur. fr. 362, 29–31; Tr. ad. fr. 418.

[3] 872–5   σέβειν μὲν εὐσέβειά τις,
             κράτος Δ', ὅτῳ κράτος μέλει,
             παραβατὸν οὐδαμᾷ πέλει·
             σὲ Δ' αὐτόγνωτος ὤλεσ' ὀργά.

being one-sided, that she does not fully understand the true meaning of reverence and of what should be revered. They still think
that her high temper has ruined her. To the last fatal moment
the Chorus maintain their position with eloquence and power.
For this the poet must have had a good reason. Surely it is that
he felt the paradox of Antigone's action, knew the great honour
in which the laws of men are normally and rightly held, and yet
knew that she was right to resist them. To show the forces against
which she contends and the opposition that any action like hers is
bound to meet he makes the Chorus condemn her on grounds
which are at least specious and would appeal to many in his
audience.

By these different means, by Ismene, by certain ambiguities in
Antigone's own language, and by the open disapproval of the
Chorus, Sophocles leads us to think that perhaps Antigone is not
entirely or truly in the right. At the end, after the gods have revealed their will and exacted their punishment from Creon, we
know how little these counterclaims are worth, but at the moment
they make their effect. Dramatically this method makes Antigone's justification all the greater, but it is not merely dramatic.
The conflicting feelings which she arouses show that an action like
hers is not easily undertaken or immediately understood. There
is an apparent conflict of duties, and to understand the rightness
of her choice we must understand the difficulties which attend it.
It is all part of Sophocles' method in displaying a contrast between
Creon's real arrogance and the apparent arrogance of Antigone.
Yet though he shows the opposition to Antigone in all its force, it
is always countered by Antigone herself, by her essential nobility
and purity of motive which assert themselves even when she is
least conciliatory. Antigone is not merely right; she appeals for
her own sake. If she has some forbidding qualities, they are after
all only the natural result of her situation and her unflinching
determination to do her duty. Nor is nobility her only appeal.
She is a human being, moved by deep affection and capable of
true love. And she is young, a girl on the verge of womanhood,
not yet married, with a girl's directness and refusal to compromise.
She is no embodiment of abstract devotion to duty, no martyr
for martyrdom's sake, but a girl of strong character and strong
feelings. Her motives are fundamentally simple, but are displayed
now in one light, now in another, as her circumstances or her
needs vary.

Almost from the beginning there is an apparent uncertainty in

Antigone's motives. She thinks it good to die and to be with her
brother:

> Doing this, 'tis good to die;
> Belov'd I shall abide with him I love.[1]

She finds comfort in the thought that her death will be noble
(96–7). She tells Creon that her life is misery and that she
counts death a gain:

> For whoso lives in many miseries
> As I do, how is death no gain to him?[2]

The argument in each case looks different. She first wishes to die
that she may join her brother, then to win glory, then to be rid of
the world's misery. Yet after all these different reasons arise out
of a single deep emotion, her love for her brother and her desire
to do the right thing by him at no matter what cost. In death she
will be with him, and such a death will both be glorious and bring
relief from the misery of living without him. The unity of her
motives may be seen from a comparison with Euripides' Macaria
in the *Sons of Heracles*. She too offers to die for her brothers, and
her reasons are that she deplores her unhappiness, wishes for glory,
and would gladly give up her life.[3] But her words, touching as
they are, do not show such a love for her brothers as Antigone has
for Polynices. She seems to be moved more by principle than by
affection. Antigone unites love and principle in a dominating
desire to do what is right. Her affection shines out in her first
mention of her brother's name:

> Dead Polynices who died miserably.[4]

It appears again in her feeling that to leave him unburied is both
cruelty (29–30) and treachery (46), in the way that she calls him
'dearest of men' (81), in her desire to please him (89). She has
lost a brother whom she loves, and when she hears that burial has
been forbidden to him, her deepest affections are outraged. So
when later she says that her spirit has long been dead, she means
that she is so absorbed in him that life no longer means anything
to her.

To understand more clearly what Antigone feels, we must see

[1] 72–3
> καλόν μοι τοῦτο ποιούσῃ θανεῖν·
> φίλη μετ' αὐτοῦ κείσομαι φίλου μέτα.

[2] 463–4
> ὅστις γὰρ ἐν πολλοῖσιν ὡς ἐγὼ κακοῖς
> ζῇ, πῶς ὅδ' οὐχὶ κατθανὼν κέρδος φέρει;

[3] *Heracl.* 523 ff.

[4] 26
> τὸν δ' ἀθλίως θανόντα Πολυνείκους νέκυν.

what is meant when Creon refuses burial to Polynices. The punishment is extreme and fearful. The spirit of the unburied dead was
thought to wander uneasily and to be deprived even of such small
satisfactions as the dead might find. When Achilles leaves Patroclus unburied, his Ghost appears and begs for burial at once, for
till then he must be shut off from the other dead and wander alone
in the Gates of Hades.[1] That is why the Ghost of Elpenor tells
Odysseus that he must bury him if he does not wish to incur the
wrath of the gods.[2] Even to be neglected in the grave was a serious
matter, and the good normally pray for children to bury them.[3]
It meant that somehow after death the affection of this world sur-
vived. The thought that he might not be buried would bring a
chill to the bravest heart.[4] Antigone knows and feels all this. In
her mind the sufferings of Polynices' spirit are closely related to
those of his outraged body. There is real horror in her description of what Creon's edict means:

> Leave him unwept, unburied, for the birds
> To watch and feed on at their own sweet will.[5]

This is the fate that she wishes to avert from her brother. If she
buries him, it will please him (89). She feels instinctively that
this is her duty. She knows that it is right. Her different arguments arise from the single dominating conviction that she must
bury Polynices. If that is right, she will face the consequences.

The audience would understand Antigone's feelings and would
agree that on principle the dead man should be buried and that
this duty lay primarily with his next of kin. If the family neglected
it, the burial was the duty of the deme.[6] The general recognition
of the duty is shown by the festival of Demeter at Athens, when a
curse was invoked on all who should leave a corpse unburied.[7]
For this there were good religious reasons. First, the presence of
an unburied corpse was thought to pollute the sun.[8] And secondly,
its right place was in the earth. That was why the Athenians
buried the Persian dead at Marathon, believing that it was 'in
every way holy to cover a man's corpse with earth'.[9] It was right
that a body should go back to the earth whence it came. Burial
was both a public and a domestic duty. If it was withheld, disas-

---

[1] *Il.* xxiii. 71–4.   [2] *Od.* xi. 72–3.   [3] Lys. xiii. 46, Eur. *Med.* 1032 ff.
[4] Eur. *Supp.* 540.
[5] 29–30   ἐᾶν δ' ἄκλαυτον, ἄταφον, οἰωνοῖς γλυκὺν
                θησαυρὸν εἰσορῶσι πρὸς χάριν βορᾶς.
[6] Dem. xliii. 57–8.   [7] Schol. Soph. *Ant.* 255.   [8] Aelian fr. 242.
[9] Paus. i. 32. 5.

ters might come. The ghost of the unburied might haunt the neighbourhood, and to deprive it of burial 'is worse for the with-holder than for him to whom it is refused'.[1] For Antigone it was mainly a private duty, but when the Guard finds a little dust scattered on the body, he thinks that the rite has been paid to avoid the pollution that the unburied corpse may bring (256). Antigone's action does something to avert this, but she is foiled because Creon orders the body to be uncovered. She differs from the average man only because she does not admit any difference between a traitor and another man so far as burial is concerned. To her it is clear that she must bury her brother because he is her brother. So, too, in Attic law a son had to bury his father even though that father had treated him disgracefully and lost any right to be kept by him.[2] The audience might not agree with Antigone and even feel that a traitor was rightly punished in this way, but they would surely see that she is impelled to act as she does because she loves her brother and honours holy domestic ties.

Antigone naturally finds it hard to express the strictly personal and intimate character of her resolution. She feels it so strongly that explanations do not come easily to her. But in her last speech, when disputes are finished and she knows that she must pay for what she has done, she has some remarkable words about her motives. The gist is that only for a brother would she have done what she has:

> For not for children's sake if I had borne them,
> Nor for a husband mouldering in death,
> Would I have braved the world and done this task.
> What law demands that I should speak like this?
> One husband dead, I might have had another,
> A child by another man, in his lost place.
> But father and mother being laid in death,
> No brother could be ever born to me.[3]

Antigone would not have taken this supreme risk for a husband or a child; for these can be replaced by others, but a brother whose

---

[1] Isocr. xiv. 55.   [2] Aeschin. i. 13.
[3] 905–12   οὐ γάρ ποτ' οὔτ' ἂν εἰ τέκνων μήτηρ ἔφυν
οὔτ' εἰ πόσις μοι κατθανὼν ἐτήκετο,
βίᾳ πολιτῶν τόνδ' ἂν ᾐρόμην πόνον.
τίνος νόμου δὴ ταῦτα πρὸς χάριν λέγω;
πόσις μὲν ἄν μοι κατθανόντος ἄλλος ἦν,
καὶ παῖς ἀπ' ἄλλου φωτός, εἰ τοῦδ' ἤμπλακον,
μητρὸς δ' ἐν Ἅιδου καὶ πατρὸς κεκευθότοιν,
οὐκ ἔστ' ἀδελφὸς ὅστις ἂν βλάστοι ποτέ.

parents are dead cannot be. These lines are certainly strange, and their relevance has been questioned. Their main sentiment at least belongs to the fifth century. Herodotus makes the wife of Intaphrenes use a similar kind of argument to Darius and by it secure her brother's life: 'O King, if the gods will, I may have another husband and other children when these are gone. But as my father and mother are no more, it is impossible that I should have another brother.'[1] If Sophocles, as is possible, took his idea from Herodotus, he used it differently. For Polynices is dead and the Persian brother is alive. What Antigone means is that she feels a closer relationship to her brother than she ever could to children or husband, and is willing to do for him after death what she would not do for them. He cannot be replaced; the fact that he is dead and needs her help only makes her feels this nearness all the more. She agrees with the wife of Intaphrenes in feeling that more is demanded of a sister than of a wife or mother. The point may seem strange to us, but it is what she means.

The devotion of brother and sister, the special affinity between them, would not seem unreal to a Greek audience. They might recall the story of Althaea who, because her son Meleager has killed her brothers, curses him and destroys him. She certainly felt that her brothers came before her son and that her first duty was to their angry spirits. If a brother is closer than a son, he is also closer than a husband; for he has more of the same blood, and in such calculations it is the degree of consanguinity that counts. No doubt the idea goes back to times when family ties were extremely close and holy. The theme is common enough in the folk-song and folk-lore of many lands, including modern Greece.[2] It could be applied in different ways. In the Border Ballad of *The Douglas Tragedy*, for instance, the parents are alive and a different problem arises, but again consanguinity wins and the love for a father comes before love for a husband:

> 'O hold your hand, Lord William!' she said,
>   'For your blows they are wondrous sair:
> True lovers I can get many an ane,
>   But a father I can never get mair.'

Sophocles, and with him Herodotus, may derive the notion from common talk and story, not from literature but from the street and the market-place. That is no doubt why Aristotle found an ele-

---

[1] iii. 119.

[2] Cf. L. D. Barnett, *C. R.* 1903, p. 209; W. H. D. Rouse, ib. 1904, p. 386; J. Mavrogordato, ib. 1925, p. 151.

ment of the incredible in the passage, but none the less accepted Antigone's reasons as valid.[1] It is the strangeness that counts. Antigone is no ordinary woman, and she breaks ordinary rules for a remarkable reason. But the reason is real to her and in the end quite simple. She is moved by an intense love for her brother, a feeling that her relation to him is unique and demands a special loyalty. So she explains herself in this unsophisticated, even primitive way. At heart what moves her is a deep sense of kinship and what is owed to it.

None the less it has been argued that Antigone's speech does not suit her circumstances as those of the wife of Intaphrenes suit hers.[2] The wife has husband, brother, and son alive; the choice between them is imperative and actual. But Antigone's brother is dead; Haemon is not yet her husband; she has no children. Nor is any choice put to her as it is to the wife. She says merely what she would have done if she had been forced to choose. So we may wonder why Sophocles used the Herodotean theme. The answer is surely that he wished to display the special character of Antigone's devotion to Polynices. She compares him with the husband who is not yet hers, with children who are not yet born. In her life her love for Polynices is the strongest tie she has known. It is a reality like nothing else, deeply rooted in the sense of kinship which means so much to her. She considers what she might have done, and decides that only for a brother would she have taken so great a risk and incurred so heavy a penalty. She could have neglected her brother and lived safely with Haemon. She has chosen otherwise, to satisfy her love for her brother at the cost of her life. If we take her words as they come, they are deeply touching and perfectly natural.

The intimate and special sense of kinship which Antigone feels for Polynices finds some commentary in what Aristotle has to say about the friendship that exists between brothers. He says that brothers love one another, 'as being born of the same parents; for their identity with them makes them identical with each other, which is the reason why people talk of "the same blood", "the same stock", and so on'.[3] Aristotle's 'identity' is the philosophical counterpart of the common notions which he then mentions. He feels that there is a special relation between members of the same blood simply for that reason. He then explains what this means. The

[1] *Rhet.* 1417 a 29.
[2] e.g. by D. L. Page, *Actors' Interpolations in Greek Tragedy*, pp. 86–90.
[3] *Nic. Eth.* 1161 b 32.

friendship of brothers, he says, is like that of comrades and of men
who are alike 'inasmuch as they belong more to each other and
start with a love for each other from their very birth, and inasmuch
as those born of the same parents and brought up together and
similarly educated are more akin in character'.[1] Brothers, in fact,
have more in common than other men less closely related. Here
too Aristotle accepts the fact of kinship as a special bond, and
though he speaks only of brothers, what he says, and the popular
conceptions behind it, are almost equally applicable to brothers
and sisters. Such naturally love one another, as Antigone loves
Polynices. Her feeling for him is based on a kinship which means
more to her than any other relation. It means so much that she
knows it to be sacred and cannot endure to be false to it.

In this last speech Antigone speaks from her inmost being. This
is her personal, final explanation. In it she uncovers her feelings,
her convictions, which are not the less powerful for being in some
sense irrational. Before this she has made her noble defence to
Creon, and in that she states her case in answer to his accusation,
rebuts his claims, justifies herself by appealing to the sacred laws
of family life. The two speeches complement each other and show
Antigone as she is alone with her feelings and as she is when she
has to explain her action to her enemy. In her there is no conflict
between love and duty, between what she wishes to do and what
she knows to be right. She is not even a case of that 'noble in-
continence' which Aristotle noted as an interesting possibility in
the moral life.[2] She does the last services to Polynices because she
loves him and because the gods demand it. In this there is no
contradiction, no dual purpose, no ambiguity. She does what she
must because she is that sort of woman. She obeys the gods because she does out of love what she knows to be right and has no
thought of denying it. She is of such a kind as to choose the good
without hesitation. She knows what she is doing, and when she is
pressed, she explains. But of course explanation is not necessary
to her. She is glad to do what she must.

The conflict between Antigone and Creon is partly in character
and outlook. What count for her are holy domestic ties, for him
position and power. Each goes as character demands, she to duty
through love, he to brutality through pride. Yet, as we have seen,
their conflict is also of principle. Each claims to stand for something important, and we can understand that each will have
partisans. Some might feel that burial is a paramount duty, others

---

[1] *Nic. Eth.* 1162 a 9 ff.   [2] Ib. 1146 a 19.

hat the laws must be obeyed. Sophocles sees this issue and makes
his characters represent opposing principles. Each claims that law
is on his or her side. If Creon claims that Antigone has broken the
aws, her answer is that his edict is no real law, that she is right to
lisobey it, and that he is wrong to make it. The controversy be-
ween them almost turns on the nature of law. It is not presented
lialectically, as Euripides might have presented it, but with the
full emotional background of a tragic situation. The two charac-
ers have entirely different views of law because they are themselves so different. Between these views a choice must, sooner or
ater, be made. The gods decide for us when in the end they
condemn Creon and show that he is wrong. But before this
happens Creon himself reveals the flaws in his belief. Sophocles
is far from suggesting that human laws are of no importance. But
he does suggest that they are not everything, that not all laws are
necessarily right, that Creon's edict is perhaps not a law at all.
Though Antigone appears to be lawless and is condemned for so
being, it is gradually made clear that she and not Creon stands
for a true notion of legality.

The average Athenian might have no very clear notion of what
a law is, but would at least think that it is a rule rigidly enforced and
rightly obeyed. He would know of the established laws of Solon,
which were held in great honour and regarded as the indispensable foundation of Athenian life. He would agree in principle
with Heraclitus that 'the people must fight for the law as for a
wall',[1] and accept the eloquent defence of legal order which Hero-
lotus gives to Demaratus.[2] But law could have a less august significance and be used for any decision of the governing power. In
answer to a question of Alcibiades Pericles is reported to have
said, 'Laws are all the rules approved and enacted by the majority
in assembly, whereby they declare what ought and what ought not
to be done',[3] and Aeschylus makes his young tyrant Zeus make laws
which are against right.[4] It is therefore not surprising that Creon
should call his edict a law. He speaks naturally when he asks
Antigone:

And did you dare to disobey these laws?[5]

or says that she acted

In disobedience to th' established laws.[6]

[1] Fr. 44. [2] vii. 104. 4–5. [3] Xen. *Mem*. i. 2. 42. [4] *P. V*. 150.
[5] 449 καὶ δῆτ' ἐτόλμας τούσδ' ὑπερβαίνειν νόμους;
[6] 481 νόμους ὑπερβαίνουσα τοὺς προκειμένους.

4790 H

In so far as he has the consent of the people as represented by the
Chorus, he may even claim popular support. Ismene has no legal
knowledge, but she is not far wrong when she says that Antigone
will act 'in defiance of the citizens',[1] and when Antigone repeats
the words,[2] she implicitly admits that Creon has support for his
decree. Creon's view of a law is natural and intelligible, but it is
precisely this that Antigone refuses to accept. She claims that a
law is something different, and that Creon's edict is no law because it conflicts with the laws of the gods and has no authority
against them.

   Against Creon's edict Antigone sets the claim of what she believes to be the only real laws, those of the gods. In answer to
his question about her disobedience she says:

> It was not Zeus, I think, made this decree,
> Nor Justice, dweller with the Gods below,
> Who made appointment of such laws to men.
> Nor did I think your edicts were so strong
> That any mortal man should override
> The Gods' unwritten and undying laws.
> Their life is not to-day and yesterday
> But always, and none knoweth whence they came.[3]

In the third line Antigone picks up Creon's word 'laws' and uses
it in his sense, but ironically. He called his edict a law, and so for
the moment does she, but this is the only place where she does.
Later she calls it an edict or decree, and contrasts it with what
are for her the real laws. And this view and this vocabulary she
maintains. In her first dialogue with Ismene she has harped on it
(27, 32, 34). To call Creon's order an edict is apt; for this method
of enforcing power was characteristic of tyrants such as Periander
and Cleisthenes.[4] For Antigone Creon's 'law' is a mere proclamation; it has none of a real law's binding force. She makes an
absolute distinction between it and the laws of the gods. She has
already anticipated this when she says to Ismene:

---

[1] 79 βίᾳ πολιτῶν.   [2] 907.

[3] 450–7   οὐ γάρ τί μοι Ζεῦς ἦν ὁ κηρύξας τάδε,
                 οὐδ' ἡ ξύνοικος τῶν κάτω θεῶν Δίκη
                 τοιούσδ' ἐν ἀνθρώποισιν ὥρισεν νόμους.
                 οὐδὲ σθένειν τοσοῦτον ῳόμην τὰ σὰ
                 κηρύγμαθ' ὥστ' ἄγραπτα κἀσφαλῆ θεῶν
                 νόμιμα δύνασθαι θνητὸν ὄνθ' ὑπερδραμεῖν·
                 οὐ γάρ τι νῦν ⟨γε⟩ κἀχθές, ἀλλ' ἀεί ποτε
                 ζῇ ταῦτα, κοὐδεὶς οἶδεν ἐξ ὅτου 'φάνη.

[4] Hdt. iii. 52. 1, v. 92. 3.

If that is your belief,
Hold in irreverence what the Gods revere.[1]

he now presents her case with logic and clarity. It is her answer
o those who, like the Chorus, think it wrong to disobey Creon's
o-called law.

Against these false laws Antigone sets up the real laws ordained
y Zeus and Justice. She does not invoke Zeus in his special
haracter of Guardian of the Dead but as the god who looks after
ight and wrong. The Unwritten Laws are born on Olympus[2]
nd come from Zeus. With him is Justice, the daughter of Themis
r Right,[3] who also watches over men's actions and has the special
uty of exacting punishment from the proud.[4] So when Antigone
ays that she obeys Justice, she denies any charge of impious arro-
ance. Her position may be compared with that of Aethra in the
uppliant Women of Euripides who also pleads the cause of the un-
uried dead and appeals to divine authority.[5] But Aethra has not
hought out her position so clearly. She is content with a vague
onviction that it is right. Antigone knows that the laws of the gods
re the basis of human order and morality. Her Zeus is the source
f all real laws as he was for Protagoras, her Justice the principle
vhich holds cities together, 'sure foundation of cities' as Pindar
alls her.[6] When she appeals to these powers, she answers the
ritics who claim that her action undermines the structure of civic
rder. On the contrary, she seems to say, her authorities are the
ery basis of that order.

Antigone's insistence that burial is commanded by an unwritten
aw of the gods, impressive and sincere though it is, might not at
nce appeal as being indisputably right. Like other traditional
otions, that of Unwritten Laws was more powerful than precise.
Vhen Gorgias in his Funeral Speech attempts to define their con-
nts, he gives mere rules of good behaviour.[7] In the fourth century
1e philosophers were interested in them and tried to reduce them
o order. While Aristotle's distinction between a 'particular law',
vhich is defined by the community for itself, and a 'common law',
hich is concerned with universal right and wrong,[8] looks like a
hilosophical simplification, Plato seems to appeal to older ideas
hen he says that 'what the many call Unwritten Laws' are

[1] 76–7   σοὶ Δ' εἰ Δοκεῖ,
τὰ τῶν θεῶν ἔντιμ' ἀτιμάσασ' ἔχε.

[2] *O. T.* 867.   [3] Hes. *Theog.* 902, Pind. *Ol.* xiii. 7.   [4] Solon fr. 3. 15 ff.
[5] *Supp.* 301.   [6] *Ol.* xiii. 6 βάθρον πολίων ἀσφαλές.   [7] Fr. 6.
[8] *Rhet.* 1373 b 10.

ancient, hereditary, and the bonds that hold every city together,
and even that they are embodied in all laws that have been made
or will be made.[1] He assumes that the only real basis for human
laws are divine rules. This had been stated before him by Heraclitus, when he said 'All human laws are fed by the one divine law',[2]
and it has much in common with Antigone's position. But in
practice most men of the fifth century would have drawn a simple
distinction between the ordinary laws of the State and the Unwritten Laws which concern conscience and religious duty. Such
a distinction was explicitly drawn by Pericles,[3] even though he
thought that the State should sometimes take action against those
who offended against the Unwritten Laws.[4] Naturally enough, the
Unwritten Laws were specially concerned with domestic sanctities. No doubt it was this which made Empedocles, in his belief
that all living beings belonged to a single family, proclaim a law
'which extends everywhere, through the wide-ruling air and the
infinite light of heaven'.[5] In ordinary life and among more
ordinary people the Unwritten Laws concerned especially the
relations between members of a family. That is why Xenophon's
Socrates says that they are broken by incest between parents and
children.[6] To the ordinary Athenian the Unwritten Laws would
be rules, of dateless antiquity and unknown origin, which protected
the sanctities of family life.

This is how Antigone sees them. For her they apply to her
brother. His burial is a domestic duty demanded by the gods.
Like Pericles, she feels that no one knows the origin of these laws[7]
and that any breach of them is shameful.[8] But unlike the philosophers and statesmen, she sees that there can be a conflict between
the Unwritten Laws and the laws of men. Pericles seems to have
thought that the two kinds of law supplemented each other, Socrates that 'legal' and 'just' are the same, Plato that the Unwritten
Laws are embodied in the written, Aristotle that all men feel the
authority of the Unwritten. Antigone sees no such harmony and
feels no such confidence. She knows that Creon's edict breaks the
Unwritten Laws and is therefore wrong and cannot be obeyed.
In making Antigone so state her case Sophocles advances two
important considerations. The first is that burial is universally
commanded by the gods and that no exceptions, even for traitors,
are permissible. In this he appeals to the conscience, to deep feelings of sanctity due to the dead. It is not a point that can be

---

[1] *Laws* vii. 793 a.   [2] Fr. 114.   [3] Thuc. ii. 37. 3.   [4] Lys. vi. 10.
[5] Fr. 135.   [6] *Mem.* iv. 4. 20.   [7] Lys. vi. 10.   [8] Thuc. ii. 37. 3.

argued, but it can be proclaimed with a sincerity that awakes powerful approval and shows itself to be right. This is what Antigone does. Her appeal to the Unwritten Laws is really an appeal to deep-seated feelings of holiness. Secondly, Sophocles displays and stresses the possible conflict between the two kinds of law. It was easy to praise the Unwritten Laws as the foundation of political and domestic life, but what if political power acted against them? Many might think it right to obey political power, but were its edicts, necessarily temporary and man-made, really more important than the everlasting rules of the gods? Once the question was put, there could be only one answer. The audience would be forced to admit that Antigone is right. Sophocles has in fact his own theory of law as much as Pericles or Socrates had his. It is that the laws of men must conform to the laws of the gods. Otherwise disaster will follow. Plato might assume a harmony between the two kinds; Sophocles saw that it was not inevitable and dramatized a case of discord between them.

Antigone's defence to Creon establishes her rightness for most who hear it. If the Chorus and Creon fail to accept it, that is their fault. Creon is blinded by pride and unable to see the truth; the Chorus is another example of the inability of the human herd to discern true merit.[1] Yet right though Antigone is, she is undeniably formidable. If a woman acts like this, she will not resemble most of her kind. Antigone is not the type praised by Ajax or Pericles or Aristotle. She intervenes in public affairs with no uncertain touch, and the awful thing is that the gods are behind her. A similar situation might have arisen with Euripides' Macaria, but she has none of Antigone's uncompromising temper, and is careful to explain that she knows her place.[2] Antigone shows no respect for Creon, though he is king of Thebes and the head of her family. She does not observe the economy of words which was thought proper for young women to use to their elders.[3] Her duty compels her to speak the truth. By her ruthless regard for it she brings home its urgency. It overrides such considerations as the position of women. In effect she gives support to the Socratic doctrine that the virtue of a woman is the same as that of a man,[4] or at least she shows that when duty to the gods is in question, there is no distinction between the sexes. Many in the audience might resist this conclusion, but Sophocles drives it home. He leaves no doubt what his own views are.

Antigone comes into irreconcilable conflict with Creon, who

[1] Pind. *Nem.* vii. 23 ff.   [2] *Heracl.* 476–7.   [3] Soph. fr. 64.   [4] Plato, *Meno* 72 c.

neither understands nor respects the divine laws. No compromise is possible between her and him. The issue can only be tragic. But the fault which brings the catastrophe is not Antigone's but Creon's. His refusal of burial to Polynices is an error of judgement which arises out of a grave defect of character. Creon's conceit and arrogance grow until they dominate his whole nature and transform him from a respectable citizen into a tyrannical brute. He suffers from a real blindness of spirit. Because of it he withstands the appeals to higher motives which Antigone makes to him. Other, different appeals are made, and in the end he is brought to his senses. The later part of the play is a demonstration of the doctrine that men learn by suffering[1] and consists first of the attempts made by Haemon and Teiresias to shake Creon, then of the repentance which comes too late when disaster has already begun its course and cannot be stayed.

The first assault on Creon's obstinate convictions comes from Haemon, who is important less because he is Creon's son than because he says what public opinion thinks of Antigone's condemnation. He is the voice of the ordinary conscience, of common morality, and through him Sophocles shows his trust in the average man when it comes to a real question of right and wrong. Public opinion approves Antigone's action and must be regarded seriously. Sophocles makes dramatic use of what Aeschylus had seen when he said that the angry talk of citizens performs the duty of a public curse.[2] The Athenians were true enough democrats to believe that on some important matters popular judgement was final and that, if it condemned, it must be respected. So when Haemon reports what the people think, Creon should listen to him. Popular approval of Antigone is as unqualified as is disapproval of her punishment:

> That of all women she the least deserving
> Foully perishes for deeds most honourable.[3]

It is thought that she should rather be rewarded:

> Is she not worthy of a golden prize?[4]

By this appeal Creon is quite unmoved. He pursues his own line of abuse for Haemon's impudence, accuses him of being the slave of a woman (746), and threatens him with punishment (754). He

---

[1] Aesch. *Ag.* 177 πάθει μάθος.   [2] Ib. 456–7; cf. Dem. xviii. 130, xix. 70.

[3] 694–5   πασῶν γυναικῶν ὡς ἀναξιωτάτη
κάκιστ' ἀπ' ἔργων εὐκλεεστάτων φθίνει.

[4] 699   οὐχ ἥδε χρυσῆς ἀξία τιμῆς λαχεῖν;

is on good ground in so far as Haemon loses his temper and treats his father with disrespect, but he is wrong in refusing to listen to public opinion. He falls into the tyrant's common fault of shutting himself off from other men, like Deioces who established the rule that a king should see no one,[1] or Pausanias who, when his head was turned by success, made himself inaccessible.[2] In this mood Creon fails to understand either Haemon's reasons for coming to him or the public opinion behind him. The result is that he loses his son, who is determined to stand by Antigone and to share her doom (762–5). This is the price which Creon pays for his obstinacy. The gods have no direct part in it; it is the human and social consequence of wrongdoing.

Yet though Creon does not admit it and hardly knows it himself, he has to some extent been touched by Haemon. He shows it in two ways. First, though he has previously decided to punish Ismene as well as Antigone, now, at the mere suggestion of the Chorus, he agrees that she is innocent and says that he will do nothing to her (771). In this his obstinacy begins to weaken. About Antigone he still believes himself on good ground, but about Ismene he has qualms and lets her go. This shows that he is not a bloodthirsty brute but the victim of illusions. Reality has pierced through to him at one point. Soon he will be fully enlightened. This concession, small though it is, is surely made because Haemon has stirred his conscience. Secondly, though Creon is still determined to punish Antigone, he now changes the character of her punishment and gives his reasons. He will shut her up in a rocky cavern away from man (773–4) and give her enough food to keep her alive. His motives for this are mixed and show his confused mind. In the first place he hopes that by this the city will escape the pollution of her death (776). He seems to think that after all he cannot kill one of his own kin, but he will not forgo his right to punish her. He hopes that by the change of penalty he will avert the anger of the gods and yet save his own dignity. His second reason is that perhaps confinement will force Antigone to repent:

> Or she will learn perhaps, although too late,
> That reverence for the dead is wasted toil.[3]

Like other deluded wrongdoers, he seems to have persuaded himself that the punishment will be for the victim's good. It is hard to

[1] Hdt. i. 99.   [2] Thuc. i. 130.

[3] 779–80   ἢ γνώσεται γοῦν ἀλλὰ τηνικαῦθ' ὅτι
πόνος περισσός ἐστι τὰν Ἅιδου σέβειν.

say how sincere he is in this. But the combination of the two
reasons show that he is shaken and uneasy. He is not yet ready to
admit that he is wrong, but he tries to change the punishment and
to make it look as if it were really for the best. He fails. Antigone
kills herself, and her death falls heavily upon Creon.

The change of punishment is no alleviation for Antigone. She
does not fear death, indeed she desires it, but the prospect of a
subterranean, sunless prison appals and shakes her. She who has
appeared so adamant and unflinching is now human and pathetic.
She feels that she is going to be deprived of two worlds, that she
will belong neither to the living nor to the dead (850–2), and more
subtly, she contrasts this life underground with her hopes of
marriage and sees in it a new kind of marriage, a travesty and
perversion of marriage, in which there is no wedding-song, no
bridal bed, no bridegroom but Acheron (813–16, 917). She will
be neither dead nor alive, but suffer a living death, a death in life
(920). She even seems to have turned her thoughts to killing herself (895 ff.), though not yet with clearness. Her immediate fate
robs her even of her hope of seeing her brother. No wonder that
she has lost some of her old confidence, that she now concentrates
her thoughts on her love for Polynices. For it is the satisfaction of
this that she is now to lose. And it is her obedience to the gods
which has brought her to this pass. She has hitherto been sustained
by love and piety, but the first seems to be frustrated of its hopes,
the second to be unrewarded. That is why she almost turns against
the gods who have recompensed her devotion with a name for
impiety (922–3), why she even doubts whether after all she acted
rightly (925–6). In this she is quite humble. She admits that
perhaps she is wrong and that the gods will tell her if she is.
She has no longer even an appearance of pride. In a sense Creon's
change of punishment really does humble Antigone, but not to
his satisfaction or according to his design. It wins to her side any
who have hitherto had doubts about her or been repelled by her
uncompromising character. She is human and touching after all.
But Creon gains nothing from it. She does not give in to him, but
chooses to kill herself rather than live without her brother. Creon
is wrong in this, as in other calculations.

The change in Antigone, the disappearance of her last vestiges
of pride, leaves the Chorus puzzled and uneasy. They can no
longer condemn her for arrogant obstinacy. Their song, 944–87,
is mysterious and comes to no definite conclusion. It seems to
indicate the doubts which they feel, their inability to come to a

decision. They compare Antigone with three other persons of high degree, Danaë, Lycurgus, and Cleopatra, in whose lives imprisonment played an important part. The mere parallel of imprisonment—and in Cleopatra's case it is uncertain and not mentioned —cannot explain all that the song means. It must have some more pertinent reference to the situation. The three stories seem to suggest different interpretations of what is happening and to hint that any one of them may be right. Danaë comes first. In her case the miseries of prison were due simply to the strange power of fate and turned to her good. So, perhaps, we may feel, Antigone's imprisonment is after all part of a divine plan to glorify her in the end. The second case is Lycurgus, who was mad, reviled Dionysus, and was imprisoned by him. The punishment was lenient for one who insulted a god, and was certainly deserved. The Chorus have said that Antigone is mad and more recently that she has a storm in the soul (929–30), and this is their way of saying that perhaps she deserves what she gets, that she has been proud to the verge of madness, and her punishment is lighter than it might have been. The third case is more difficult to unravel. It seems clear that Antigone is compared to Cleopatra; for the Chorus say:

> But upon her too
> The age-old Fates bore hard, my child.[1]

But the legends about Cleopatra vary, and the precise point of comparison is not stated. It is not even certain that Cleopatra was imprisoned, though some say that she was.[2] But in any case Cleopatra is an example of great and undeserved suffering, the innocent and helpless victim of gross cruelty. The Chorus use her to suggest that there may perhaps be no defence for Antigone's punishment, that it is just an act of wanton brutality. The three parallels are different ways of interpreting what happens to Antigone. The Chorus have begun to waver. For the moment they temporize and cannot make up their minds. They have weakened more than Creon, and their weakening makes them more ready to accept the message of the gods when it comes.

If Haemon represents ordinary men, Teiresias represents the gods. When Antigone leaves the stage for her rocky prison, she has already said what she thinks about her persecutors:

---

[1] 986–7   ἀλλὰ κἀπ' ἐκείνᾳ
Μοῖραι μακραίωνες ἔσχον, ὦ παῖ.
[2] Diod. iv. 42.

If theirs the fault is, may to them befall
No worse than they have wrongly done to me![1]

She means 'may they suffer as I suffer'. She feels that if Creon
has punished her for doing what is right, he should pay for it. Her
prayer is answered, and Teiresias is the first agent in its consummation. In presenting the old seer Sophocles uses traditional de-
vices of Greek narrative, but so works each into the play that it
is hardly recognizable and certainly not obvious. The first is the
appearance of Teiresias, who warns Creon not to insult the dead.
This is the device of the Warner. In the *Odyssey* when the gods
warn Aegisthus through Hermes not to kill Agmemnon or to marry
Clytaemnestra, Aegisthus rejects the warning and comes to a
hideous end. The moral is drawn by Zeus:

Monstrous it is that men should blame the gods for misdoing,
Saying that we are to blame for the evils they suffer; but rather
They in their impious folly find woes that were never predestined.[2]

The warning absolves the gods from all responsibility; thenceforward the warned man is to blame for his own fate. In the *Prometheus Bound* Hermes performs a similar duty when he warns the
daughters of Oceanus not to support Prometheus and tells them
that if they do they will not be able to say that their fate is unfor-
seen.[3] In political life Solon appears as a Warner to Athens[4] and
tells his countrymen that if they fall into disaster it will be with
their eyes open.[5] The advantage of this scheme is that it gives an
intelligible explanation of suffering and attributes a degree of cle-
mency to the gods. Men get their chance, but disregard warnings
about their evil ways and cannot justly complain if they persist in
them and are punished. On this structure Sophocles builds the
last section of his play. Creon is warned by Teiresias, but disregards the warning until it is too late.

Teiresias speaks with an authority which Creon claims to accept
(993), and begins with a solemn command:

Take thought! you stand upon a razor's edge.[6]

Creon has still time to save himself, and Teiresias warns him that
he stands on the edge of a great crisis. Then in a speech instinct

[1] 927–8   εἰ δ' οἵδ' ἁμαρτάνουσι, μὴ πλείω κακὰ
πάθοιεν ἢ καὶ δρῶσιν ἐκδίκως ἐμέ.
[2] *Od.* i. 32–4   ὢ πόποι, οἷον δή νυ θεοὺς βροτοὶ αἰτιόωνται·
ἐξ ἡμέων γάρ φασι κάκ' ἔμμεναι· οἱ δὲ καὶ αὐτοὶ
σφῇσιν ἀτασθαλίῃσιν ὑπὲρ μόρον ἄλγε' ἔχουσιν.
[3] *P. V.* 1071–9.   [4] Fr. 3. 30 ff.   [5] Fr. 1. 67.
[6] 996   φρόνει βεβὼς αὖ νῦν ἐπὶ ξυροῦ τύχης.

with uncanny horror he tells of the evil signs, the confused jargon of the birds, the sacrifices which will not burn (999–1011). For all these he blames Creon:

> Your will has brought this malady to the state.[1]

The gods refuse sacrifice because altars are tainted with carrion from the corpse of Polynices; the birds give no clear message because they have tasted of his blood. Teiresias knows that something is desperately wrong and that the gods have been angered by Creon's impious edict. Into these horrors Sophocles has infused so strange and so strong a poetry that we do not ask if the situation is real or not. It is enough that the gods' spokesman proclaims it. He speaks with knowledge, and his word must count; for it is through prophets that the gods reveal their mind to men. Nor indeed would it seem strange that a whole city should be so punished for an impious act. The fall of Sybaris was thought to have come because the inhabitants slew some envoys from Croton and let their bodies be devoured by dogs outside the walls, 'and this was the beginning of their misfortunes; for the god was angry'.[2] So Teiresias describes a natural state of affairs. To him the cure is easy; Creon must change his mind and bury the body of Polynices. He is not angry with Creon, though he thinks that he is criminally presumptuous (1028). He warns him for his own good and expects the warning to be accepted.

Creon fails to appreciate the warning or the goodwill which prompts it. In his folly he reverts to his old hallucination that his critics have been bribed, and just as he thought that love of money lay behind the first rites done to Polynices (293–303), so now he thinks that Teiresias has been paid to threaten him (1033–9). He has no inkling that he himself may be wrong, but believes that he is the victim almost of conspiracy, certainly of unjust attack (1033–4). In this state he is incapable of seeing how urgent Teiresias' warning is. He attempts to counter it:

> You shall not hide him in a tomb,
> Not though God's eagles wish to ravage him
> And take him off for food up to God's throne.
> I shall not fear defilement even so
> Or yield him burial. I know well enough
> No human being can pollute the gods.[3]

---

[1] 1015   καὶ ταῦτα τῆς σῆς ἐκ φρενὸς νοσεῖ πόλις.

[2] Phylarchus fr. 45 Jacoby.

[3] 1039–44   τάφῳ Δ' ἐκεῖνον οὐχὶ κρύψετε,
οὐδ' ἢν θέλωσ' οἱ Ζηνὸς αἰετοὶ βορὰν

He says not that he does not care if Zeus is defiled by the carrion-bearing birds but that Zeus cannot be so defiled. In other circumstances his argument might carry weight. When the Euripidean Heracles feels himself so defiled that he must hide his head from the light of day, Theseus says to him:

> Why? Mortal, you cannot defile the gods.[1]

This is unquestionably reverent. For Theseus the defilement which Heracles feels after killing his children is nothing in comparison to his essential innocence of a crime committed in madness. In his view the gods cannot be angry with Heracles, and since he is really innocent, he cannot pollute them. This is a sincere opinion, but it is not what Sophocles held. For him the pollution is a real fact, caused by the impiety of Creon and guaranteed by the inspired knowledge of Teiresias. Creon is not even innocent as Heracles is. His belief that the gods cannot be defiled is an infatuate delusion, an unconscious means to cover his own wrongdoing. He shows again his old fault of knowing better than the gods what they demand of men. His pride is at work and prevents him from correcting his fault just as originally it drove him to it.

Teiresias has delivered his warning; Creon has rejected it. The inevitable nemesis follows. The evil that might have been avoided must come to pass. Teiresias prophesies that before long Creon will lose the son of his loins in requital for the unburied Polynices and the buried Antigone. This punishment will come from the avenging gods:

> Therefore Destroyers who come late but sure,
> Furies of gods and death, lie hid for you,
> To catch you in the self-same sufferings.[2]

If Creon had heeded the warning, he would have escaped the penalty. Teiresias foretells it only when he knows that Creon is obdurate. There is no question of his being pursued by a malignant fatality; he must suffer because he has done wrong and refused to undo his wrong in time. The gods do not wish merely to exact retribution from him; they wish him to learn

> φέρειν νιν ἁρπάζοντες ἐς Διὸς θρόνους·
> οὐδ' ὡς μίασμα τοῦτο μὴ τρέσας ἐγὼ
> θάπτειν παρήσω κεῖνον· εὖ γὰρ οἶδ' ὅτι
> θεοὺς μιαίνειν οὔτις ἀνθρώπων σθένει.

[1] *Her.* 1232   τί Δ'; οὐ μιαίνεις θνητὸς ὢν τὰ τῶν θεῶν.

[2] 1074-6   τούτων σε λωβητῆρες ὑστεροφθόροι
λοχῶσιν Ἅιδου καὶ θεῶν Ἐρινύες,
ἐν τοῖσιν αὐτοῖς τοῖσδε ληφθῆναι κακοῖς.

To keep a quieter tongue
And better thought than now his spirit has.[1]

These last words of the seer sum up his warning, the need for sound sense. If man will not find it for himself, the gods will force it on him against his will. It is the Aeschylean doctrine that modesty comes even to those who would not.[2] The difference between the first stage and the last is that whereas the enlightenment might have come without suffering, now it must come through it.

Once Teiresias has gone, disasters follow thick and fast. Complaint has been raised that this kind of catastrophe is not really dramatic and that the last part of the play lacks the fullness of the first part. But this is to misunderstand it. The conclusion shows that when the gods set to work, they work swiftly and surely. They may be slow to start, but they are undeniably certain. It is the rapidity and accumulation of events that drive Creon's lesson home to him. He has had his chance and missed it. Now his punishments follow one after the other. Into this conclusion Sophocles weaves another traditional theme, 'Too late'. Creon is one of those who see the truth, but too late for it to help him. So in Euripides' *Bacchants*, when Agave complains of the doom pronounced on her and Cadmus by Dionysus and claims to repent, the god replies:

Too late you knew me. When you should, you knew not.[3]

The theme is ancient, its moral that if a good action is put off for too long, it will cease to be effective or even good. For Sophocles the scheme so presented had obvious advantages. It enabled him to show Creon in a mood of repentance and yet unable to avert the catastrophe which his actions have brought upon him. And more subtly he could portray as active but futile in well-doing the same man who has been opinionated and obstinate. Creon does not change his character all at once with his decision. It is only at the very end that he sheds all his stiff-necked self-satisfaction. Finally, the theme of 'Too late' drives home the moral that, though the gods may bear with faults for a time, there is a limit to their patience, and once this is reached, sorrows come. Creon has gone too far. It is now impossible for him to escape the lesson which the gods intend to teach him.

[1] 1089–90   τρέφειν τὴν γλῶσσαν ἡσυχαιτέραν
τὸν νοῦν τ' ἀμείνω τῶν φρενῶν ὧν νῦν φέρει.

[2] Aesch. *Ag.* 180–1.

[3] *Bacch.* 1345   ὄψ' ἐμάθεθ' ἡμᾶς, ὅτε δὲ χρῆν οὐκ ᾔδετε.

In the scheme of 'Too late' Creon has a change of heart. When Teiresias has gone, the Chorus, who are usually one move ahead of Creon, say that they have never known the prophet to be wrong. Creon agrees, but still hesitates:

> 'Tis hard to yield, and yet to stand and strike
> My pride with ruin, that is no less hard.[1]

He is torn between pride, which counsels obstinacy, and fear that he may suffer. His hesitation does not last. A strong word from the Chorus, followed by advice to release Antigone and bury Polynices, clinches his decision (1091 ff.). The Chorus see the dangers of delay and urge speed:

> And, master, lose no time. Swift-footed haste
> The hurts of heaven to cut short foolishness.[2]

Yet even now Creon shows traces of his old self. His conversion is only skin-deep. He has as yet no regret, no sense of guilt. What impresses him is the force of circumstance. He finds it difficult to yield, but admits

> I cannot fight against necessity.[3]

This is not repentance but common sense. For even the gods do not fight against necessity.[4] In this frame of mind Creon sets out to undo the evil which he has begun.

A change of purpose such as Creon's might seem to justify modest hopefulness but hardly the wild ecstatic joy which it evokes in the Chorus. In an excited hymn they summon Dionysus to help and protect Thebes. It is true that his help is needed if Thebes is to be saved from pollution and that he has a special place in its cults, but what surprises is the note of wild exaltation that fills the song, the glamour of midnight revelries (1129–35), of nocturnal rites and voices (1146–8), of mad Maenads who follow the master (1151–2). Of course this joyful spirit serves a dramatic purpose; it creates an atmosphere of exultant hope which is soon to be shattered, and makes the onslaught of disaster all the more painful when it comes. But this is not to explain the song in the action. It has its meaning there too. The Chorus have in the past con-

---

[1] 1096–7   τό τ' εἰκαθεῖν γὰρ δεινόν, ἀντιστάντα δὲ
                   ἄτῃ πατάξαι θυμὸν ἐν δεινῷ πάρα.

[2] 1103–4   ὅσον γ', ἄναξ, τάχιστα· συντέμνουσι γὰρ
                   θεῶν ποδώκεις τοὺς κακόφρονας βλάβαι.

[3] 1106   ἀνάγκῃ δ' οὐχὶ δυσμαχητέον.

[4] Simonides fr. 24. 21; Soph. fr. 256, fr. 757; Eur. *Hel.* 513; *Alc.* 965; Aesch. *P. V.* 105.

demned Antigone for holding high hopes. Their words come back
on them, and now it is they who will suffer bitter disillusionment,
the 'deception of light-minded desires' which they foretold for her.[1]
And in them this hope rises out of their partial blindness. Their
vision of the truth is still imperfect; they have not grasped the
stark grimness of the situation. Their song shows that they are too
confident, too satisfied that all will soon be well. For them, as for
Creon, there is a lesson in store. Their mood reflects his, though
perhaps their confidence is more exaggerated. It is the lyrical
expression of a wild, unreasonable spirit and a prelude to bitter
disillusionment.

Creon has two tasks, to release Antigone and to bury Polynices.
In this order Teiresias (1069–71) and the Chorus (1100–1) have
placed them. And with reason; for Antigone's life can be saved by
immediate intervention, while the burial of Polynices can wait
until the more urgent task is done. Creon thinks and acts otherwise. He first gives a full burial to Polynices, then goes to release
Antigone from her prison. He is too late. She has already hanged
herself, and with her is Haemon, who kills himself over her body
in his father's presence. This gives a truly tragic climax. To have
reversed the order of events would have lessened the horror and
spoiled the catastrophe. Since disaster must come, it should come
at the end. And this order is psychologically right. It follows from
Creon's character. At first sight we might think that the natural
course would be for him first to rescue Antigone and then to bury
Polynices. But Sophocles is right to make Creon act otherwise. Of
his two tasks he thinks the burial more important. In his warning
Teiresias has spoken emphatically about the wrong done to Polynices and not mentioned Antigone till later; the discordant birds
and the unburned sacrifices are due to the unburied body; it is
the denial of burial which causes the conflict with Antigone. So
it takes first place in Creon's mind. He pursues his own habits of
thought and fails to save Antigone or Haemon.

Creon is punished by the death of his son and by the death of
his wife, Eurydice, who kills herself on hearing the news. The
Chorus, awake at last to the true significance of events, point the
moral of 'Too late':

Alas, it seems you see the right too late.[2]

Before she dies Eurydice blames Creon for the deaths both of
Haemon and of Antigone:

[1] 617   ἀπάτα κουφονόων ἐρώτων.
[2] 1270   οἴμ' ὡς ἔοικας ὀψὲ τὴν Δίκην ἰδεῖν.

> Aye, for the guilt of his and of her death
> Were you accused by her who lies dead here;[1]

and Creon admits that this is right (1319). He has been punished,
as the seer foretold, by the loss of those whom he loves, his son
and his wife. Their deaths are directly due to him. If he had not
forbidden the burial of Polynices and sentenced Antigone for carrying it out, none of these disasters would have come. They would
not even have come if he had changed his mind in time. His responsibility is made clearer and his doom harder by the hatred
which his son and wife feel for him in their deaths. Haemon spits
on him and refuses to speak to him (1231-2); Eurydice denounces
him as the slayer of their son (1305). No wonder that he feels
annihilated and wishes to die.

He does not die. He goes into the house knowing that he is only
a foolish man (1339), and not knowing where to look or where to
rest (1344). A crushing fate has fallen on him. And this humiliation and conviction of guilt are the lesson which the gods have
taught him. The Chorus close the play with a reflection on the
dangers of pride and irreverence (1348-53). They speak of a
wisdom which lies in recognizing man's humble state before the
gods. Just as the spectacle of the mad Ajax taught Odysseus that
before the gods man is a mere phantom, so Creon has learned,
from his own sufferings, a similar lesson:

> Take me away with speed, take me away from men;
> Less than a thing of nought, I am nothing at all.[2]

The lesson of the play is that man must be humble and reverent,
that he must avoid pride and the illusions which it engenders.
This lesson, finally and emphatically proclaimed by the Chorus,
has already been made clear by events. The fearful reversal in
Creon's fortunes from pride to humiliation, from illusion of power
to knowledge of his impotence, from complacency to misery, is
more effective than any moral. Sophocles gives his lesson mainly
through the characters and their misfortunes. He provides a
demonstration in which events lead inevitably to a conclusion and
a lesson.

The conclusion accords with Greek religion. Creon's fall would
have appealed to Pindar as the rightful punishment of one who

---

[1] 1312-13   ὡς αἰτίαν γε τῶνδε κἀκείνων ἔχων
                πρὸς τῆς θανούσης τῆσδ᾽ ἐπεσκήπτου μόρων.

[2] 1324-5   ἀπάγετέ μ᾽ ὅτι τάχος, ἄγετέ μ᾽ ἐκποδὼν
                τὸν οὐκ ὄντα μᾶλλον ἢ μηδένα.

defied the gods. Sophocles makes it more actual by showing that
it follows directly from his character. He even makes it more
merciful by giving Creon a chance to redeem his errors. In all
that concerns Creon the play presents sound theology and would
be accepted by the reverently minded. Even the deaths of Haemon and Eurydice would be accepted as part of the divine plan
to punish Creon. For in their deaths he finds the sorrow which
humbles him. They are the innocent instruments of his enlightenment. Many would see in their fates a proof of Solon's view that
when divine justice is at work, the innocent may be punished with
the guilty:

> Innocent are punished,
> Children, and their children after them.[1]

The theological outlook which Sophocles shows is in some sense
traditional, but it is worked out with a careful logic and a full
sense of its implications. Above all he stresses man's responsibility
for his actions. Greek thinkers hesitated between taking this responsibility to themselves and ascribing it to the gods. We find the
contradiction in Theognis, who at one place attributes all evils to
the gods (113–42) and at another puts the blame on men's violence,
covetousness, and pride (833–6). In the *Antigone* Sophocles holds
the second view and almost anticipates the doctrine of Plato's
myth in which unborn souls choose their destinies on the principle
that 'the blame is his who chooses; God is not to blame'.[2] In the
case of Creon divine justice is reconciled with human responsibility.

Creon's fate is explained, but what of Antigone's? What are we
to make of a divine order which allows her to perish for carrying
out the divine will? The Chorus have tried to explain it by the
hereditary doom of her family, but events have proved them
wrong. Sophocles does not attempt to justify the death of Antigone, but he does explain it. It is the result of Creon's folly, and
of course this is right. It must be clear to anyone that human
beings will make mistakes like Creon's and that the innocent may
suffer from them. But, according to Sophocles, the gods are not
blind to such suffering. The part of the play which follows Antigone's last departure is devoted to the punishment of Creon for
his treatment of her. That is why the play has a unity more
essential than the formal unity provided by the part which Creon

---

[1] Fr. i. 31–2   ἀναίτιοι ἔργα τίνουσιν
         ἢ παῖδες τούτων ἢ γένος ἐξοπίσω.
[2] *Rep.* x. 617 e αἰτία ἑλομένου· θεὸς ἀναίτιος.

plays. If it had stopped with the departure of Antigone, our indignation at such injustice would be intolerable. Creon's fall atones for it. He pays for it, as Teiresias has foretold that he will. Antigone's death is indeed a tragic disaster, but it is due to the folly of man and does not remain for long unrequited.

In retrospect, then, the *Antigone* is a tragedy of human folly. The folly is of a special kind, a blindness of soul which makes a man in high position do what is wrong. With his illusions the play is much concerned, and indeed its conflict takes place at a level where the illusions of men resist and rebut the claims of reality and truth. On the one side is pride which believes that it is justice, on the other justice which many take to be pride. Sophocles certainly intended this contrast. It is shown by his use of what is commonly called tragic irony, when what a character says has one meaning for himself and another, more sinister, meaning for those who know the plot. This is particularly clear in Creon. The admirable thesis that government shows the man (175–7) is ironically fulfilled; government shows him for the weak tyrannical creature that he is. A little later he says that he will never be silent if he sees ruin coming on his country (185–6), but when his actions threaten Thebes with the wrath of the gods, he resists attempts to avert it. In his answer to Antigone he makes much play with the inevitable collapse of obstinate natures (473–8), but it is his own obstinacy which ruins him and his family. To Haemon he praises the man who is good in his family and useful to the State (661–2), but he himself breaks the sacred ties of the family and thereby endangers the State. Creon is an example of a man who does not attend to the Delphic command 'Know thyself'. Many of his words come with cruel ironical force to the audience, who know how unlike them his actions will be proved to be.

This irony reaches beyond Creon into the very structure of the play. With great skill Sophocles makes his characters attribute to Antigone faults which are later seen to be Creon's. She even seems to claim them for herself. She speaks of her folly (95), but in the end Creon knows that his folly has caused the general havoc (1269), and Teiresias and the Chorus warn him of his need of wisdom (1050, 1098). Creon is lavish in accusations of pride against Antigone (309, 480, 482), but it is his pride in speech and action which the Chorus condemn in their last words. He tells Antigone that she is not in a position to have big thoughts (479), but before long Teiresias tells him to cultivate a humbler spirit himself (1090). The Chorus believe that Antigone is the victim of infatuation (584,

614, 624–5), but it is clear that the infatuation is on the side of Creon. The main charges against Antigone are untrue of her and true of him. By this irony Sophocles shows the degree of error and illusion in which Creon and the Chorus judge their fellows. He seems to think that men are subject to errors of a peculiarly poignant kind. They wrongly accuse others of faults which are their own. Such illusions belong to the human state, but their results may be deadly. They prosper in that pride which makes a man think that he knows more than the gods and end by flouting them. In the *Antigone* Sophocles dramatizes this fault with great insight and understanding and shows to what disastrous conclusions it may lead.

IV

THE WOMEN OF TRACHIS

IN the *Antigone* the conflict between a man and a woman leads to disaster for both; in the *Women of Trachis* Sophocles again made his protagonists of opposite sexes and again brought both to a tragic finale. But while the fates of Creon and Antigone arise from their irreconcilable differences, those of Heracles and Deianira come from the woman's love for the man. By this the lives and deaths of the two characters are bound together, and in the dramatic action each is as important as the other. The central subject of the play is neither Heracles nor Deianira but the destiny which involves each in the other's ruin. So intimately are the characters and their fates connected that Sophocles can defy the critics by never representing both on the stage together. By delaying the appearance of Heracles until after the death of Deianira he uses the so-called 'diptych' construction, as in the *Ajax* and *Antigone*,[1] but differently. In the *Ajax* the hero, though dead, is still on the stage, still the chief character who holds the play together; in the *Antigone*, though the interest shifts from Antigone to Creon, he has always been an important character and his fate is required to make amends for his treatment of Antigone. But in the *Women of Trachis*, though Deianira is on the stage longer than Heracles, she is not more important than he is. He is always present in her mind and in ours. Throughout we think of her in relation to him and of him in relation to her. Even at the end, when his last hours almost absorb our attention, she is not entirely absent from our thoughts. The subject of the play is the single, shared destiny of a man and a woman. So with reason it is named not after Heracles or Deianira but after the Chorus who provide a link between the two and remain before us through most of the action.

The main theme of the *Women of Trachis* is a woman's tragic love for her husband. In her desire to keep him for herself she kills him without meaning to do so, and has to kill herself. Such a theme could be treated in different ways, but we know so little about the antecedents of the legend that it is difficult to compare Sophocles with any of his predecessors in it or to image what the audience would expect from a play on the subject. The story was treated succinctly in the Hesiodic *Catalogues*,[2] but though the fatal shirt of

---

[1] T. B. L. Webster, *Sophocles*, p. 105.　　[2] Pap. Berol. 9777 and Pap. Oxy. 2075

Nessus played its part there, we have no indication what the poet
thought of Deianira beyond calling her 'thoughtful'. If the name
Deianira, Δαϊάνειρα, conveys anything about the original character
of its possessor, it suggests that in the oldest legends Deianira was
a kind of Clytaemnestra who slew her husband, perhaps out of
jealousy for another woman. Or it may have a different origin
and be connected with the common epithet for an Amazon, ἀντι-
άνειρα.[1] In that case Deianira would be a woman with the strength
of a man, and a faint echo of this may survive in a statement that
she drove a chariot and practised war.[2] But these dim hints tell
very little. If they were known to Sophocles, he neglected them
and presented quite a different Deianira. His heroine and his plot
bear some resemblance to a poem which was probably written
early in the fifth century, Ode XVI of Bacchylides. It gives a short
and poignant account of Deianira and makes her neither an
Amazon nor a murderess. For him her story is of a tragic mistake;
Deianira tried to win back her husband, but lost him. And this is
the substance of Sophocles' play. He may or may not owe something to the sketch of Bacchylides. His play is characteristically
his own. His peculiar touch may be seen in his formation of the
chief characters, in his implicit attitude to their actions, and in the
metaphysical background of the play.

The two chief characters, Heracles and Deianira, are man and
woman, husband and wife. They might be typical of any married
pair, and their tragedy private and domestic. We can imagine
how Euripides would have treated the subject, enlivening the
drama with shrewd observations from contemporary woman's lot
and making the man no better than the average. Sophocles did
not do this. His play is of universal interest because he makes his
woman extremely womanly and his man extremely manly. Each
character seems to possess in an advanced form the qualities commonly attributed to his or to her sex. This makes the conflict acute
and extreme. Deianira's sufferings are all the greater because she
is the woman that she is; the fall of so fine a man as Heracles is a
piteous spectacle to all who value the traditional grand qualities of
manhood. And the conflict between man and wife, unnecessary
as in some ways it is, is none the less the kind of conflict that may
arise when a dependent, highly feminine woman is deeply in love
with an independent, highly masculine man. By stressing the
peculiarities of the two sexes Sophocles creates a tragedy of married life, of the relations between man and woman. In his *Medea*

---

[1] O. Gruppe, *Griechische Mythologie*, p. 468, n. 1.   [2] Apollodor. *Bibl.* i. 8. 1.

Euripides too dramatized the story of a man who forsakes his wife for another woman. But neither his Jason nor his Medea is typical or representative of their sex as such. The mean motives of the one, the wild barbarian temper of the other, prevent them from being a typical pair. Their tragedy is not of married life but a special case of mixed marriage between Greek and barbarian.

For nearly two-thirds of the *Women of Trachis* Deianira is its dominating character. This shows what importance Sophocles attached to her, but more revealing is the evident care which he gave to her delineation. From the beginning he conveys both her charm and her pathos. Her first words, spoken before dawn after a care-ridden night, reveal the continual anxiety and unhappiness in which she has lived. Before marriage she was pursued by a monstrous suitor, the river-god Acheloüs; since marriage she has had little but cares. Her husband has nearly always been away from her, and she has had to live alone with her children, who are all but strangers to their father:

> And we have children, whom he saw erewhile,
> As a husbandman who has a foreign field,
> At seedtime and at harvest and no more.[1]

The comparison comes from contemporary life. In a time of war and foreign settlement there must have been many Athenian husbands who possessed lands which they saw only for short periods and at rare intervals. The simile makes Deianira's deserted state more vivid and actual. Indeed her loneliness was a familiar enough feature of Athenian life in the fifth century. The sorrows of the deserted wife are nobly described by Aristophanes' Lysistrata in language which leaves no doubt of their reality.[2] So, too, for Deianira the lonely unaccompanied night is a time for brooding and fear. Each new night brings a new care to take the place of the old:

> Night brings a trouble,
> And the next night with a new one drives it out.[3]

She speaks with truth of her experience as a deserted wife, and she suggests a comparison, as in other places, with Clytaemnestra, who tells in eloquent words what a woman suffers when her husband

[1] 31–3   κἀφύσαμεν δὴ παῖδας οὓς κεῖνός ποτε,
γῄτης ὅπως ἄρουραν ἔκτοπον λαβών,
σπείρων μόνον προσεῖδε κἀξαμῶν ἅπαξ.

[2] *Lys.* 591–2.

[3] 29–30   νὺξ γὰρ εἰσάγει
καὶ νὺξ ἀπωθεῖ διαδεδεγμένη πόνον.

leaves her alone at home.[1] Each has passed through the same state, but while loneliness drives Clytaemnestra to console herself with a paramour,[2] it has no such effect on Deianira. She longs for her husband to return; his absence mutilates her life.

When the play opens, Deianira has a new anxiety. She realizes that the fifteen months are over at the end of which Heracles must, according to prophecy, either die or live happily for the rest of his days. The sudden thought of this has woken and brought her out of doors:

> It made me leap up from my pleasant sleep
> In fear and terror, friends, lest I must live
> Deprived of him who is the best of men.[3]

We must imagine that this anxiety obsesses her at the beginning of the play. That is why her opening words are cast in so melancholy a tone. Heavy with cares and fears she contrasts her present state with the happiness of childhood, envies the unmarried, unworried life of the maidens in the Chorus, and sees in their care-free existence a type of woman's state before it is spoiled by marriage:

> The delicate plant grows in the sheltered place
> That is its own. And it the sun-god's heat
> Shakes not, nor rain, nor any wind that blows.
> It lifts its life up in untroubled joys
> Till that day when a maiden takes the name
> Of wife and finds at night her share of cares,
> Afraid for husband's or for children's sake.[4]

She looks back with longing to this wonderful time now lost to her and sees it in retrospect like the blissful existence of the Homeric gods:

> The winds do not shake it, nor rainstorm
> Soak it, nor does the snow fall down on it; always a cloudless
> Glory is spread thereon, and white is the brightness that covers.[5]

[1] *Ag.* 858 ff.   [2] *Cho.* 920.

[3] 175-7   ὥσθ' ἡδέως εὕδουσαν ἐκπηδᾶν ἐμὲ
φόβῳ, φίλαι, ταρβοῦσαν, εἴ με χρὴ μένειν
πάντων ἀρίστου φωτὸς ἐστερημένην.

[4] 144-50   τὸ γὰρ νεάζον ἐν τοιοῖσδε βόσκεται
χώροισιν αὑτοῦ, καί νιν οὐ θάλπος θεοῦ
οὐδ' ὄμβρος, οὐδὲ πνευμάτων οὐδὲν κλονεῖ,
ἀλλ' ἡδοναῖς ἄμοχθον ἐξαίρει βίον
ἐς τοῦθ', ἕως τις ἀντὶ παρθένου γυνὴ
κληθῇ, λάβῃ τ' ἐν νυκτὶ φροντίδων μέρος
ἤτοι πρὸς ἀνδρὸς ἢ τέκνων φοβουμένη.

[5] *Od.* vi. 43-5   οὔτ' ἀνέμοισι τινάσσεται οὔτε ποτ' ὄμβρῳ
δεύεται οὔτε χιὼν ἐπιπίλναται, ἀλλὰ μάλ' αἴθρη
πέπταται ἀνέφελος, λευκὴ δ' ἐπιδέδρομεν αἴγλη.

She seems to contrast her present anxious life with her girlhood as men might contrast their life with that of the gods. By this means Sophocles shows how much she has suffered already, what her adventures have cost her. She has lost the self-contained days of girlhood and found a life full of cares for husband and children. At the outset Deianira appeals to sympathy by her loneliness and her heavy burden of responsibilities. If the audience had any other picture of her in their minds, the opening scene dismisses it and presents a woman who is almost overwhelmed by distress and anxiety.

Deianira is still deeply in love with Heracles. He saved her from the monstrous Acheloüs, and since then her whole life has been centred on him. In his absence she feels herself pierced with cruel pangs (41-2). She is almost certain that something has gone wrong with him (43). In her anxiety about him she sees that her own and her children's safety are inextricably intertwined with his:

> Either we are saved
> If he be safe, or else are lost with him.[1]

This despairing spirit is reproved by the Chorus (124), who praise the virtues of hope and may have appealed to those who thought that a woman should not display her feelings too candidly. Deianira answers that anguish is eating her heart (142). For her Heracles is the 'best of all men' (176), and she is terrified that she will lose him. But in her complete dependence on him there is something passive and helpless. Sophocles suggests that she has always been more prone to wait for events to take their course than herself to take the initiative. When Heracles fought Acheloüs, she was too frightened to see the fight:

> I sat distraught with terror, lest my beauty
> Should bring me naught but sorrow in the end.[2]

This passivity now accounts for her inaction in finding where Heracles is and what he is doing. She seems content to suffer in ignorance until a suggestion from the Nurse that Hyllus should be sent to inquire stirs her to action. So too, though Heracles has left instructions with her what to do if he does not return after fifteen months, she has dismissed these from her mind until they come back to her with a sudden shock, and even then she is slow to

---

[1] 84-5
ἢ σεσώσμεθα
κείνου βίον σώσαντος ἢ οἰχόμεσθ' ἅμα.

[2] 94-5
ἐγὼ γὰρ ἤμην ἐκπεπληγμένη φόβῳ
μή μοι τὸ κάλλος ἄλγος ἐξεύροι ποτέ.

face their insistence. The thought of them has come to her at night
and driven her from her bed, and she gives a hint to the Nurse of
their importance (45–7). But once Hyllus has been dispatched in
search of his father, though the double-edged prophecy still
menaces, she seems to forget it. Though she has strong emotions,
her will to act is weak. She is not used to making decisions or to
planning ahead. Her melancholy is partly due to her conviction
of helplessness. The poet carefully prepares the ground so that
when she does decide to do something, she makes the wrong decision, as we might expect from one of her character.

Lonely and passive, Deianira is a prey to melancholy and fear.
This is clear from her own opening words, where she has doubts
even about the good fortune of having married Heracles:

> But Zeus, who rules the fight, ordained it well,
> If it was well.[1]

It shows itself in her worries about his absence (36 ff.) and the message which he has left (46–8). Sadness has habituated her to expect
the worst. The Chorus know this side of her character and compare her to a bird which has lost its mate and cannot stay its laments
(105 ff.). This tendency shows itself in her account of the tablet
which Heracles has left and of the prophecy which she has remembered about him.[2] At first she accepts the even chances of
happiness and unhappiness in the oracle (79–81), but as she pon-
ders over it, it seems to her to contain a more likely presage of
death than of relief (155–77). So when, without warning, she
hears that Heracles is really on the point of coming home, her
natural pessimism makes her slow to believe it. She greets the first
announcement with incredulity and seems hardly to have heard it:

> What are these words, old man, you say to me?[3]

When she is reassured, she asks what the Messenger's authority is
(187), and even then she asks why Heracles has not come in person
(192). Only when a satisfactory answer is given to this is she convinced; so deeply are fear and suspicion of evil ingrained in her
character.

Deianira is revealed in the first scene with great clearness.

---

[1] 26–7   τέλος δ' ἔθηκε Ζεὺς ἀγώνιος καλῶς,
                    εἰ δὴ καλῶς.

[2] At 46–8 Deianira refers obliquely to the prophecy contained in the document
left by Heracles. At 164 she discloses its contents to the Chorus, who use her information at 821 ff. The fifteen months are made up by the last year of Heracles' servitude,
spent with Omphale, and by three months in the sack of Oechalia. When at 647 the
Chorus speak of his twelve months' absence, they, or the poet, make a pardonable slip.

[3] 184   τίν' εἶπας, ὦ γεραιέ, τόνδε μοι λόγον;

Externally she is gracious and courteous to the Nurse, whose advice she takes with a gentle compliment (61 ff.). She has the air and the manners of a great lady, of the princess that she is. But she is used to depending on a husband whose will is far stronger than her own, and her natural inactivity and melancholy have been increased by the events of her life. Into her existence startling events are soon to break, and the poet has to convince us that when they come she acts in character. At the same time he does everything to make her sympathetic, to show her deep devotion to Heracles and her natural warmth of heart. His preparation both explains why, when the crisis comes, she acts as she does, and makes us find every excuse for her in it. The drama leads her, gradually and doubtfully, to one joyous moment of hope. The hope is never realized, and instead of joy she finds despair. When Deianira at last believes that Heracles is on his way home, she thanks Zeus for it and tells the Chorus to celebrate the good news (200–4). This is almost her only moment of happiness in the play. It presents a contrast with what follows and shows the irony of her momentary exaltation. The disillusionment begins almost when Lichas arrives with Heracles' captives. The hero himself is not yet there. Deianira's first question is about him—will he come back alive (233)? It is reasonable and real. The oracle is still at the back of her mind; she will not believe that Heracles has returned until she sees him. About him she asks questions—where is he, why is he sacrificing, and then, who are the captives? Instead of joy she feels doubt and disappointment; then the sight of the captives moves her to pity and foreboding. The melancholy spectacle of her husband's victims touches her deeply and makes her anxious. The heroic triumph of Heracles means nothing to her if he himself is not present with it.

From the very first Deianira notices the pitiful state of the captive women:

> And these, I pray you, whose are they, and who?
> Pitiful, if their plight deceives me not.[1]

After she has heard Lichas' story of Heracles' triumphant revenge for his injured honour, the spectacle is still before her. To the Chorus this is an occasion for joy:

> Now, lady, is your joy made manifest.[2]

[1] 242–3   αὗται δέ, πρὸς θεῶν, τοῦ ποτ' εἰσὶ καὶ τίνες;
           οἰκτραὶ γάρ, εἰ μὴ ξυμφοραὶ κλέπτουσί με.

[2] 291   ἄνασσα, νῦν σοι τέρψις ἐμφανὴς κυρεῖ.

Deianira says that she rejoices in her husband's good fortune, and
of course she means it. But she soon recurs to the captives:

> A dread compassion is upon me, friends,
> Seeing these outcasts in an alien land,
> Ill-fated, without father, without home.[1]

Her words are full of pity, but they arise out of her own fears. We
may imagine that in her long hours of waiting she has sometimes
dreaded that such a fate will befall her, and now she prays that it
may not befall her children (303–4). It is of them, not of herself,
that she thinks. As before, her responsibilities of wife and mother
rise in her and darken her joy. She sees this fear as a kind of
modesty, of prudence (296–7), which knows that a man who now
prospers may one day suffer a reverse. The thought is pious and
humble and based on her own experience. The marriage from
which she might have had so much happiness has brought years of
anxiety. She has learned their lesson and will not indulge in im-
moderate joy. This modesty is direct and natural to her, the fruit of
her life and character.

In the company of captives Deianira turns her attention to one
in particular, to Iole, whose identity and name she does not know,
nor why she is there. No suspicion enters her mind that Heracles
intends to make Iole his concubine. Deianira speaks to the captive
girl in words of charming simplicity and tenderness:

> Unhappy lady, tell me who you are.
> A maiden or a mother? From your looks
> All this is strange to you. But you are noble.[2]

When Iole, broken with misfortune and misery, does not answer,
Deianira does not press her, but turns her questions to Lichas, who,
though he keeps up his deceptions about Iole's identity and the
reason for her presence, is sorry for her and tells how she has not
spoken since she left her 'windswept land' (323 ff.). In answer to
him Deianira shows how free from pride and resentment she is.
She will not add to the girl's sorrows:

> Leave her alone to go into the house
> As suits her best, nor may she at my hands
> Find other griefs to crown those that are hers.[3]

[1] 298–300   ἐμοὶ γὰρ οἶκτος δεινὸς εἰσέβη, φίλαι,
               ταύτας ὁρώσῃ δυσπότμους ἐπὶ ξένης
               χώρας ἀοίκους ἀπάτοράς τ' ἀλωμένας.

[2] 307–9   ὦ δυστάλαινα, τίς ποτ' εἶ νεανίδων;
               ἄνανδρος, ἢ τεκνοῦσσα; πρὸς μὲν γὰρ φύσιν
               πάντων ἄπειρος τῶνδε, γενναία δέ τις.

[3] 329–31   ἡ δ' οὖν ἐάσθω καὶ πορευέσθω στέγας

The gentle nobility and modesty of Deianira cannot fail to recall another scene where a wife receives a woman to her home after a husband's long absence. In the *Agamemnon* Cassandra is brought home by Agamemnon, but Clytaemnestra does not treat her as Deianira treats Iole. She seems to suspect at once that she comes as a concubine, though she does not say so until she has killed her.[1] She dwells relentlessly on the humiliations of slavery, that await her.[2] When Cassandra, like Iole, remains silent and answers no questions, Clytaemnestra is impatient and angry and leaves her with threats of death.[3] The contrast between the two wives is absolute. Clytaemnestra is suspicious, brutal, abrupt, Deianira trusting, gentle, considerate. Surely Sophocles intended to remind his audience of Clytaemnestra, and to show that in a like situation Deianira acts completely unlike her.

From modest anxiety Deianira is flung into deep fear and misery. The Messenger tells her that the story which Lichas has told is untrue, that Heracles sacked Oechalia for love of Iole, that the captive girl is Iole, that Heracles intends to make her his concubine. Deianira at once knows that a deadly blow has been aimed at the heart of her life:

> What hidden curse have I made welcome here
> Beneath my roof? O woe is me.[4]

For the moment she is at a loss (385–6). Then on the advice of the Chorus she questions Lichas. In this incomparable scene she keeps her emotions in check and introduces the subject with dignified restraint. While the Messenger extracts the truth from Lichas, she keeps silence; then she makes a moving appeal to him to tell her everything (436–69). Some have thought that this is a deliberate deception, that Deianira has no intention of taking Iole into her house as a rival and only pretends to be willing that Lichas may more readily tell her all that she wishes to know. But such deception is alien to Deianira's character. Modest and simple, overcome by the appalling news, she would not have the hardness or the self-control to lie, still less the strength of character to come so early to so final a decision as to refuse to have Iole in her house. She means what she says. Her natural obedience to all that Heracles wishes, her acceptance of everything that he does, her habitual indecision

οὕτως ὅπως ἥδιστα, μηδὲ πρὸς κακοῖς
τοῖς οὖσιν ἄλλην πρός γ᾽ ἐμοῦ λύπην λάβοι.

[1] *Ag.* 1441 ff.   [2] Ib. 1037 ff.   [3] Ib. 1066 ff.
[4] 376–7   τίν᾽ ἐσδέδεγμαι πημονὴν ὑπόστεγον
λαθραῖον; ὦ δύστηνος.

and inactivity, are too strong to allow her to dispute even such a
demand as this from him. Although she has already seen the
dangerous claims of a rival

> Splendid indeed in beauty and in birth[1]

she still professes and really feels pity for Iole (463 ff.), both because of her present state and for all the destruction that she has
caused. She accepts the power of love as an excuse against which
there is no appeal (441 ff.). And in this spirit she closes the scene
by saying that she herself will go into the house. Her modesty and
acceptance are in the ascendant when she declares her resolution:

> No new plague shall I add to mine, nor fight
> A vain fight with the gods.[2]

With a final effort to do what is right she tells Lichas that she will
give him a gift to take to Heracles. There is in her promise a gruesome tragic irony, but she herself has no thought of double dealing.
She means simply to efface her own feelings, to do what a good
wife should. She feels that she must not fight against Love since
she is sure to lose. Up to this point Deianira is the faithful devoted
wife, like the woman in Sophocles' *Tereus* who says of marriage

> And just because a single night has joined us,
> We must give praise and think that all is well.[3]

Her decision would be approved by most as worthy of a good wife.
But during the next choral song many may have wondered how
Sophocles was going to make her send the fatal gift to Heracles.

This curiosity was soon satisfied. When Deianira comes out of
the house, she has changed. She seems in the interval to have
thought about the situation and decided that she cannot possibly
accept it. Her change is surprising, but no more than Ajax' decision to kill himself. It is meant to surprise, to cause a shock, to
bring home the violent revolution which has taken place in her
mind. Her new intentions are soon revealed. It is now clear to her
that she cannot welcome Iole under her roof. She feels like a ship's
captain who is called to take on merchandise that will wreck him
(537-8). She disclaims any anger against Heracles, whom she regards as suffering from a disease (543-4), but she cannot share him

---

[1] 379 ἦ κάρτα λαμπρά καὶ κατ' ὄμμα καὶ φύσιν.

[2] 491-2 κοὔτοι νόσον γ' ἐπακτὸν ἐξαρούμεθα
θεοῖσι Δυσμαχοῦντες.

[3] Fr. 583, 11-12 καὶ ταῦτ', ἐπειΔὰν εὐφρόνη ζεύξῃ μία,
χρεὼν ἐπαινεῖν καὶ Δοκεῖν καλῶς ἔχειν.

with another woman. The crux of her argument is that she is past
her first youth while Iole is in the beginning of hers:

> I see her youth has not yet come to bloom,
> While mine is fading. Men's eyes love to pick
> The bud, but from the other turn away.[1]

She fears that while Heracles is called her 'spouse', he will be the
'man' of Iole (550–1). Therefore she has made a desperate decision, to resort to magic, to the blood of the dead Centaur which he
promised should act as a charm to bring back Heracles if he were
ever unfaithful (575 ff.). Her case, so simply and naturally put
forward, sounds reasonable enough. If the charm works, we feel,
all will be well; if not, no great harm will have been done. But
that is not how the Greeks would have seen it, and Deianira is not
quite easy in her own mind about it.

Her uneasiness first shows itself when she comes out to tell the
Chorus secretly of her plan (533). Her secretiveness shows some
lack of faith in its rightness. Then at the end of her speech she defends herself against possible objections and shows that she has
serious doubts:

> But wicked daring may I never know
> Nor learn. Women who risk it I abhor.
> But if I can prevail against this girl
> With charms and spells laid upon Heracles,
> This have I schemed,—unless I seem to act
> In wantonness. If so, I will forbear.[2]

While she disclaims any liking for bold women, she is still afraid
that her own action may be wrong. She is even willing to give up
her plan if it is really thought wrong. And perhaps she would have
given it up if the Chorus had not expressed their approval of it and
if Lichas had not appeared in haste to depart with the gift to Heracles (599). Deianira's hesitations are overruled by the assurances
of the Chorus and by the need to act at once. Though she knows
that she may be guilty of evil daring, she is overborne by circum-

---

[1] 547–9   ὁρῶ γὰρ ἥβην τὴν μὲν ἕρπουσαν πρόσω,
          τὴν δὲ φθίνουσαν· ὧν ἀφαρπάζειν φιλεῖ
          ὀφθαλμὸς ἄνθος, τῶν δ' ὑπεκτρέπει πόδα.

[2] 582–7   κακὰς δὲ τόλμας μήτ' ἐπισταίμην ἐγὼ
          μήτ' ἐκμάθοιμι, τάς τε τολμώσας στυγῶ·
          φίλτροις δ' ἐάν πως τήνδ' ὑπερβαλώμεθα
          τὴν παῖδα καὶ θέλκτροισι τοῖς ἐφ' Ἡρακλεῖ,
          μεμηχάνηται τοὔργον, εἴ τι μὴ δοκῶ
          πράσσειν μάταιον· εἰ δὲ μή, πεπαύσομαι.

stances, holds to her decision, and hopes to win back her husband by magic.

By Greek standards Deianira is now open to severe condemnation. The good, faithful, resigned wife has taken the initiative against her husband, and her whole situation is changed. She not only runs a very grave risk but is moved by reasons most unsuitable for a woman. A wife's duty was to obey:

> For a sane woman must support her husband
> In everything.[1]

To attempt to force a man's will was an intolerable act of arrogance; for, as Democritus said, 'to be ruled by a woman would be the last indignity for a man'.[2] It was her duty to allow him to have a concubine if he wished. Concubinage was protected by Attic law, and the concubine and her children had their recognized place in the home.[3] The true wife would not complain if her husband introduced a concubine. Euripides saw this when he made his Andromache say that, though she was Hector's real wife, she looked after his bastards and did this out of virtue,[4] as if a perfect wife would and should act in this way. Ordinary opinion would expect Deianira to accept Iole without complaint as Heracles' concubine. Deianira, who has hitherto been the embodiment of submission and modesty, suddenly shows a dangerous tendency to assert herself against her husband. Her reasons can be easily understood, but to the average Athenian they would not excuse her. Her decision shows an unexpected and deplorable pride.

Even more disquieting are the means which Deianira chooses to win back Heracles for herself. To force his will by magic was both presumptuous and dangerous. The ambiguous character of love-charms was well known. They might do irreparable harm. When the Nurse in Euripides' *Hippolytus* presses Phaedra to use them to gain her step-son, she carefully argues that they will be harmless, but Phaedra is still suspicious and says that this is a kind of skill which recoils on itself.[5] She feels what most felt, that the risk is too great and that recourse to drugs does more harm than good. Alciphron portrays a woman who wishes to win back her man but admits that 'charms are wont to be untrustworthy and to lead to sudden destruction',[6] and Plutarch says that lovers won by such baits are like fish ruined by being caught, 'frantic and senseless and

---

[1] Eur. *El.* 1052–3 γυναῖκα γὰρ χρὴ πάντα συγχωρεῖν πόσει,
    ἥτις φρενήρης.
[2] Fr. 111. [3] Isaeus iii. 39, Lys. i. 31; cf. Dem. lix. 122. [4] Eur. *Andr.* 222–7.
[5] Eur. *Hipp.* 518. [6] *Ep.* i. 37.

ruined'.[1] Indeed the use of such charms was mainly a discreditable
secret confined to the worst women. Neither Theocritus' Simaetha
nor Lucian's Bacchis[2] are models for good wives. Since the use of
drugs might well lead to death, the law took account of them, and
though legal decisions and practice varied, it is worth noting that
in the island of Teos death was the penalty for anyone who used
destructive drugs,[3] while Plato prescribes death to anyone who
uses witchcraft on another, even though the result is not fatal.[4] It
may even be true that the Areopagus once sentenced a woman to
death for using magic.[5] We shall see that legally punishment did
not always attend users of charms and witchcraft, but the fact that
it sometimes did shows what public opinion was. Deianira's decision to use magic is not only wrong in a wife; it is wrong in anyone. It involves great risks and invites stern disapproval. It is a
kind of impiety because it is an attempt to control natural forces
by magic, and those who do so are thought to believe that the gods
do not exist or have no strength.[6]

Something has happened in Deianira to turn her from a sub-
missive wife into a practitioner of magic, from modest acceptance
to reckless risk. The violence of the change has been indicated by
the dramatic device which shows her mind not during her decision
but before and after it. The actual process is not dramatized: we
have to infer it. Yet it must be explained and made intelligible.
Sophocles keeps his explanation until Deianira begins to see that
something is desperately wrong with the Centaur's blood, and
comes out to tell of the uncanny frightening experience she has had
with the handful of wool with which she anointed the garment. It
has perished under her eyes in the sun and left no trace (693 ff.).
This hideous event has brought Deianira back to her senses. She
knows that she has done a terrible thing (706 ff.), that her lesson
is too late (711). In this chastened mood she looks back on her
action and the spirit that prompted it. It was wild hope, ἐλπίς.
She herself says:

> My heart sinks lest I soon be found
> To have done great ill from hope that promised well.[7]

The Greek notion of hope was not quite ours. It might sometimes
do good, but it could also do harm. It was a mood of wild confidence, of unreasonable assurance. Therefore Solon says that men

---

[1] Con. Pr. 5.　　　[2] Dial. Mer. 4. 5.　　　[3] S. I. G. 37.　　　[4] Laws xi. 933 d.
[5] Ael. V. H. v. 18.　　　[6] Hippocr. Sac. Mor. 4.
[7] 666–7　　　ἀθυμῶ δ' εἰ φανήσομαι τάχα
　　　　　κακὸν μέγ' ἐκπράξασ' ἀπ' ἐλπίδος καλῆς.

cherish it until they are taught by suffering,[1] and the Thucydidean
Pericles makes it the strength of the desperate and the opposite of
reasonable foresight.[2] It was a mood which, without cause or
reason, might descend on men and drive them to their doom. So
Herodotus makes it an important element in the fall of the great
king Croesus and brings it fifteen times into his story. So Deianira
has a sudden confidence in a wild undertaking which defies modesty and sense. For such a miscalculation a penalty follows. As
Democritus says, 'the hope of evil gain is the beginning of punishment'.[3] So it is for Deianira. She ought never to have thought that
she could win back Heracles by magic, and now she must pay for it.

This state of illusion and exaltation and blind, thoughtless confidence lasts for a very short time, from Deianira's decision to send
the robe to the moment when she sees the woollen tuft perish. Her
recovery, when it comes, is immediate. Such a confidence is too
alien to her nature to have a lasting hold on her. It has only dominated her at all because she feels such an aversion to taking Iole
into her household. She cannot keep the discovery to herself and
comes to confess it to the Chorus. She knows that she has gone too
far:

> Women, I tremble lest beyond the Mean
> All that I lately did may have been done.[4]

She knows now that she has acted wrongly, that she may well have
done irreparable harm to Heracles. She decides at once that if he
dies, she will die too. Her reasons befit her character and station:

> Life with a base name is not to be borne
> For one who prides herself not to be base.[5]

She has no word of blame or recrimination for the Chorus who
have supported and even strengthened her in the fatal decision.
She feels that this is her crime and that she must pay for it. So
when she hears from her son of Heracles' fearful torments in the
robe which she has sent him, she makes no answer or defence but
leaves him and the outer air without a word. The Chorus, who
know that she never intended to kill Heracles, say:

> Why go away in silence! Know you not
> That silence helps the accuser to your harm?[6]

[1] Fr. 1, 35–6.   [2] ii. 62. 5.   [3] Fr. 221 ἐλπὶς κακοῦ κέρδεος ἀρχὴ ζημίης.

[4] 663–4
γυναῖκες, ὡς δέδοικα μὴ περαιτέρω
πεπραγμέν' ᾖ μοι πάνθ' ὅσ' ἀρτίως ἔδρων.

[5] 721–2
ζῆν γὰρ κακῶς κλύουσαν οὐκ ἀνασχετόν,
ἥτις προτιμᾷ μὴ κακὴ πεφυκέναι.

[6] 813–14
τί σῖγ' ἀφέρπεις; οὐ κάτοισθ' ὁθούνεκα
ξυνηγορεῖς σιγῶσα τῷ κατηγόρῳ;

They do not really understand her. In thinking that her silence will be taken as an admission of guilt, they follow conventional lines. As Sophocles says elsewhere

> In time of trouble modesty is no help;
> For silence is confederate of the accuser.[1]

But Deianira is not concerned with her reputation or even to prove her innocence. She has taken a risk and failed; she has lost the one thing in her life that really matters to her, her husband. He is almost dead. All that she can do is to die too.

This sense of desolation, of ruin, fills Deianira's last moments, as the Nurse sees and reports them. Her actions resemble those of Euripides' Alcestis. Both approach the household altars,[2] go into the bridal chamber, address the bridal bed,[3] and have thoughts for their children.[4] But these last farewells are made in utterly different spirits. Alcestis dies in full honour, conscious that she is a good wife who dies for her husband; Deianira feels that she is an evil woman, fit only to die alone (903). Alcestis is resigned that another woman may sleep in her bed, but not a better woman than herself;[5] Deianira looks not to the future, which means nothing to her, but to the past:

> O bed and bridal room of mine,
> Good-bye for always now; for never shall
> You welcome me to sleep in you again.[6]

Alcestis says good-bye to her children in pride and love; Deianira shrinks from the sight of Hyllus and dies with his curse on her (819–20). The self-sacrifice which Alcestis makes enables her to die in peace and resignation; Deianira is tormented by guilt and shame. The house which she sees for the last time has been the centre of her existence. She touches the familiar household chattels (905–6), cries out to the familiar servants (907–8). Then with tragic appropriateness she goes into the bridal chamber, the sacred place of her wedded life, and kills herself in it. She seems to feel that all that has hitherto occupied her, her duties as wife and mother and mistress of the household, have ceased to have any meaning. She remembers what they have been to her and bursts into uncontrollable tears. The death of Heracles is the end of her

---

[1] Fr. 928   αἰδὼς γὰρ ἐν κακοῖσιν οὐδὲν ὠφελεῖ·
ἡ γὰρ σιωπὴ τῷγκαλοῦντι συμμαχεῖ.

[2] 904, *Alc.* 170.   [3] 913 ff., *Alc.* 175 ff.   [4] 911, *Alc.* 189 ff.   [5] *Alc.* 181–2.

[6] 920–2   ὦ λέχη τε καὶ νυμφεῖ' ἐμά,
τὸ λοιπὸν ἤδη χαίρεθ', ὡς ἔμ' οὔποτε
δέξεσθ' ἔτ' ἐν κοίτῃσι ταῖσδ' εὐνατρίαν.

domestic and married life. In destroying him she has destroyed herself.

This charming gracious woman comes to a tragic end because of a single terrible miscalculation, a mistake of judgement. Unlike Creon's, this mistake is not characteristic of her; it is indeed alien to her normal self and induced by the fearful situation in which she finds herself. Yet she has undeniably committed a great error. The judgement on it must wait for the moment in the hush of her death, though her son, in his new knowledge of the circumstances, has already forgiven her (936 ff.). The audience are left without guidance or instruction about her until the plot has travelled farther. They may still feel that she acted as no woman should, or they may have begun to have qualms about condemning her. But their attention is turned from her and from her responsibility to the visible results of her action, to Heracles, to the choral song with the slow movement and monotonous repetitions of a dirge which accompanies his arrival, to the piteous spectacle of a great hero lying asleep on a stretcher, borne by servants and accompanied by an old man. The sudden change of interest from Deianira to Heracles shows that the plot is equally concerned with both, that if Deianira has killed herself, she has also destroyed her husband. To appreciate the full extent of the tragic subject we must see what kind of man he is who thus perishes, what a loss Deianira's desperate decision has brought to the world.

If Deianira was not a familiar figure and Sophocles could fashion her as he chose, the same cannot be said of Heracles. Of all Greek heroes he is perhaps the most familiar. The poets, epic and lyric and dramatic, had celebrated his achievements; his many labours were the delight of painters and sculptors. Views of him might differ. According to one tradition, dating back perhaps to Stesichorus, he was a congenial, jovial figure, fond of food and drink and swayed by simple, even childish, emotions, an embodiment of physical and athletic prowess but not tragic and hardly serious. As such he was dramatized by Euripides in the *Alcestis*, and no doubt by Sophocles in his *Heracles at Taenarum*. On the other hand, Euripides gave a different vision of him in his *Heracles* as a noble tortured soul, whose long life of bloodshed turns at last to madness and makes him kill his own children. Behind these different interpretations was the simple popular view that he was a hero of great strength, an almost divine figure who delivered mankind from pests and monsters, the protector of the injured and, in the end, the equal of the gods. So Pindar celebrated him in *Nemean* I and

sang of his 'surpassing nature and power'.[1] Such he seems to be
when he is first mentioned in the *Women of Trachis* and Deianira
tells how he saved her from Acheloüs:

> In time that followed, and to my delight,
> Zeus' and Alcmene's famous offspring came.[2]

For the moment we feel that he may turn out to be just such a hero
as Pindar imagined, that his boundless strength will be matched
with a boundless endurance, that he will be revealed as the worthy
son of Zeus and peer of the immortals. Sophocles, however, does
not present him like this. His Heracles is his own original creation,
powerful, strange, and even forbidding.

The first full news of Heracles comes from Lichas. He arrives
with a great procession of captives, victims of the sack of Oechalia
and visible tokens of a fearful triumph. In their silent arrival there
is something pitiful, even horrible. Deianira feels it at once, and,
before she speaks to the captives, says to Lichas:

> I bid the herald hail, whose coming has
> Been long delayed,—if you bring aught of joy.[3]

Then this horror which is the reverse side of Heracles' glory grows
as Deianira questions Iole and learns that she has not spoken since
she left her home. The paradox of great physical prowess is already
clear. It is acclaimed with rejoicing, but its manifest results stir
pity and horror, which deepen as Lichas tells his story. It is of
course based on a lie, but most of the facts, apart from the explanations, in it are true. It is true that Heracles punished Eurytus by
throwing his son over a cliff and later sacked his city. The punishment seems excessive even when we know that Heracles acted not
from injured pride but from love. Even to the gods he is not
entirely pleasing; for they have punished him for slaying Iphitus
with a year's bondage to Omphale.

Heracles cannot be judged by humanitarian standards. His
legend dates from a heroic past when achievements like his were
universally admired, even though their painful results were recognized. Heracles is the son of Zeus, a hero, and he stands outside
ordinary rules of behaviour. Sophocles has created what he imagined such a hero to be, and he follows familiar beliefs. The sack of

---

[1] *Nem.* i. 56–7   ἐκνόμιον
λῆμά τε καὶ Δύναμιν.

[2] 18–19   χρόνῳ Δ᾿ ἐν ὑστέρῳ μέν, ἀσμένη Δέ μοι
ὁ κλεινὸς ἦλθε Ζηνὸς ᾿Αλκμήνης τε παῖς.

[3] 227–8   χαίρειν Δὲ τὸν κήρυκα προυννέπω, χρόνῳ
πολλῷ φανέντα, χαρτὸν εἴ τι καὶ φέρεις.

Oechalia is in character. Heracles was well known as a sacker of cities. Not only Oechalia but Troy[1] and Pylos[2] had fallen to him, so that Bacchylides rightly calls him 'breaker of gates'.[3] For an ordinary man to sack cities was an act of gross pride and likely to be punished. So the Chorus in the *Agamemnon*, conscious of the risks run by a conqueror, pray

> May I be no sacker of cities.[4]

In an earlier age real heroes like Achilles and Odysseus could be called 'sacker of cities'[5] without danger or dishonour. And no doubt Heracles shared their privilege. Moreover, Heracles, as the son of Zeus and half divine, was entitled to exercise the destructive anger of revenge. All heroes were harsh on those who crossed or insulted them. In this they differed little from gods, and Heracles displays in life the heroic temper which other heroes sometimes exercised from the grave. His violence is part of his strength, a necessary accompaniment of his power to destroy beasts and pests. Deianira is a human being, and it is right for her to pity the victims of misfortune, but Heracles is different and governed by different rules. If he chooses to sack Oechalia, it is not for ordinary men to pass judgement on him. They can only look on him with awe.

Heracles sacks Oechalia not for revenge on Eurytus, as Lichas has said, but for love of Iole. The revelation puts his action in a new light. What are we to think of a hero who is driven by passion to such extremes? The Messenger is naturally anxious to tell Deianira the truth:

> Love alone of gods
> Laid spell on him to do these acts of war,[6]

but he is anxious for its effect on her, not for the information it gives about Heracles. Deianira, still eager to behave as a good wife, accepts this as an unanswerable reason:

> Whoso challenges Love to have a round
> Of fisticuffs, has lost his wits; for he
> Rules even gods according to his will.[7]

When she says that she herself will not fight an impossible battle

---

[1] *Il.* v. 639 ff.   [2] *Ib.* xiv. 198.   [3] v. 56.

[4] Aesch. *Ag.* 472   μήτ' εἴην πτολιπόρθης.

[5] *Il.* xv. 77, ii. 278.

[6] 354–5   Ἔρως δέ νιν
μόνος θεῶν θέλξειεν αἰχμάσαι τάδε.

[7] 441–3   Ἔρωτι μέν νυν ὅστις ἀντανίσταται
πύκτης ὅπως ἐς χεῖρας, οὐ καλῶς φρονεῖ·
οὗτος γὰρ ἄρχει καὶ θεῶν, ὅπως θέλει.

against the gods (492), she means that she will not combat the passion of love in Heracles. She sees how powerful it is in him. Nor does she think it strange that it should force him to exact so fearful a satisfaction. The sack of Oechalia, which a Euripidean Chorus regard as a classic case of the limits to which love can drive a man,[1] is for her only natural in Heracles. She is swayed by strong emotions, but amazement and disapproval are not among them.

Her feelings are not necessarily those of the audience or of the average man. Yet it seems probable that these too would accept Heracles' passion for Iole as something inevitable. They might well deplore that such things should be, but perhaps they would not really blame Heracles for it. It was a common view that, whether it was desirable or not to resist love, it was sometimes impossible. To this view Sophocles himself gives some support not only when the Chorus of the *Antigone* sing of 'Love unconquerable in battle'[2] but in a remarkable fragment:

> For love is death, imperishable force,
> And love is raving madness, is desire
> Unmixed, is lamentation. And in her
> Is all that leads to action, peace or force.
> Deep into every living breast she sinks;
> Who is not prey to this divinity? [3]

A power of this kind cannot be resisted even by the gods. Nor was this a private view. Sophocles advanced it more than once. A character in his *Phaedra* insists that love troubles the souls of the gods,[4] and the lines just quoted go on to say

> What god but wrestles with her and is thrown? [5]

So when Deianira excuses Heracles on the same lines (443), she holds a tenable point of view. If the gods could not resist love, it was unlikely that Heracles, who is half a god, could. On this point she would find others to agree with her. It was useless, it might even be wrong, to resist. In his *Daughters of Danaus* Aeschylus made Aphrodite praise love in such a way as to make all resistance look

---

[1] *Hipp.* 546–54.   [2] Soph. *Ant.* 781 ff.

[3] Fr. 941. 3–8   ἔστιν μὲν Ἅιδης, ἔστι δ' ἄφθιτος βία,
ἔστιν δὲ λύσσα μανιάς, ἔστι δ' ἵμερος
ἄκρατος, ἔστ' οἰμωγμός· ἐν κείνῃ τὸ πᾶν
σπουδαῖον, ἡσυχαῖον, ἐς βίαν ἄγον.
ἐντήκεται γὰρ πλευμόνων ὅσοις ἔνι
ψυχή· τίς οὐχὶ τῆσδε δεύτερος θεοῦ;

[4] Fr. 684.

[5] Fr. 941. 13   τίν' οὐ παλαίουσ' ἐς τρὶς ἐκβάλλει θεῶν;

wrong,[1] and Euripides says that anyone who does not regard Love as the greatest of the gods,

> Is but a fool or, ignorant of all good,
> Knows not the greatest of all gods for men.[2]

Since Love was a god, it was almost impiety to oppose him. Such at least is what Gorgias argues in his *Praise of Helen* when he defends Paris. Conversely, he says, if love is not a god, it must be regarded not as an error but as a misfortune.[3] It follows that in either case we cannot blame anyone for being its victim. It may be deplorable that passion should drive Heracles to such extreme action as the sack of Oechalia, but nothing can be done about it, and he should not be blamed. When such a power as love falls on such a man as Heracles, the results are bound to be fearful.

Both in his treatment of Iphitus and his sack of Oechalia Heracles shows a superhuman power true to the heroic world but difficult to relate to the fifth century. We may legitimately ask what an Athenian audience would think when such a being was held up to them as 'the best of men'. He is certainly far removed from such ideal types as Odysseus in the *Ajax* or Theseus in Euripides' *Suppliant Women*. He has no modesty, mercy, or civic virtues. If something stands in his way, he removes it, at no matter what cost. He has not even the gentleness which the epic heroes show to their friends and their families. He stands for something else than the ordinary ideals of manhood whether Homeric or Athenian. In him Sophocles seems to have created a kind of superman, a hero of a new sort who is outside ordinary rules and standards. In doing so he may have been influenced by certain undercurrents of thought in his time. At a later date Aristotle recognized a 'heroic and divine excellence'[4] which is as far above ordinary excellence as the baseness of the beasts is below it. As an example he gives Priam's words on Hector:

> Nor bore he resemblance
> To any son of a mortal but seemed to be born of a god's seed.[5]

This is a natural conclusion from the popular notion that heroes were men who possessed superior qualities and resembled the gods

---

[1] Aesch. fr. 44.

[2] Eur. fr. 269   ἢ σκαιός ἐστιν ἢ καλῶν ἄπειρος ὢν
                    οὐκ οἶδε τὸν μέγιστον ἀνθρώποις θεόν.

[3] Fr. 11. 19.

[4] *Nic. Eth.* 1145 a 20 ἀρετὴν ἡρωικήν τινα καὶ θείαν.

[5] *Il.* xxiv. 258-9   οὐδὲ ἐῴκει
                    ἀνδρός γε θνητοῦ πάϊς ἔμμεναι ἀλλὰ θεοῖο.

by the degree of their power, Δύναμις. Men differed from the gods by being inferior in power, as Pindar says, when, after recognizing that men and gods have a single mother, the earth, he continues:

> But every power is distinct
> And keeps them apart.[1]

He adds that sometimes and in some ways men approach the gods in mind or in body. If they have a superior power, they may find a superior excellence, which we may regard as 'heroic or divine'. In his own way Sophocles applies these ideas to Heracles, who possesses power to such a degree that he is not really a man but something above man. The result is strange and forbidding, and Aristotle saw some of its implications when he said that some men do not need society to live in, 'He who is unable to live in society, or who has no need because he is sufficient for himself, must be either a beast or a god'.[2] He sees that a god is outside society and sufficient to himself. So is Sophocles' Heracles. He is self-sufficing not merely in his lack of a fixed abode and his disregard for ordinary human ties but in the more profound sense that he thinks chiefly of himself and of his own achievements. He is like the gods in his strong passions, his quickness to avenge an insult, his unfailing conviction that what he wants is right, his insensitiveness to the feelings and failings of ordinary men and women. He is an embodiment of power as the gods have it. Therefore he excites awe, even admiration. It is not for men to wish to be like him, but, when such a being exists, he is rightly admired.

The admiration for such a type is so plainly at discord with Greek views of modesty and the Mean that it may well excite surprise. Yet in the fifth century there were those who proclaimed that deeds of violence were justified if they led to glory, and envisaged an ideal of life in which power was more important than quiet. When Aeschylus dramatized the young Zeus of his *Prometheus Bound*, he attributed to the ruler of the universe qualities of unscupulousness and ingratitude which may not be attractive but are undeniably helpful to success. This doctrine is quite different from such crude beliefs as those of Thrasymachus that 'justice is the interest of the stronger'. It is a justification of violence for higher ends. Zeus works for the empire of the world. To consolidate this power he must use means which may well be deplored,

---

[1] *Nem.* vi. 2–3   Διείργει δὲ πᾶσα κεκριμένα
    Δύναμις.

[2] *Pol.* 1253 b 27 ὁ δὲ μὴ Δυνάμενος κοινωνεῖν ἢ μηδὲν Δεόμενος Δι' αὐτάρκειαν οὐδὲν μέρος πόλεως, ὥστε ἢ θηρίον ἢ θεός.

but as Pericles says in his Funeral Speech, such a policy secures
friends and does good.[1] So Heracles employs his extraordinary gifts
for the benefit of mankind. The long list of his achievements
which he himself gives (1089 ff.) may show his self-satisfaction but
is also a record of dangerous undertakings successfully completed
for the common good. No one but he could have done so much,
and he only because of the superior power that is his.

The cult of power and of glory, even for the good of others, may
well lead to hatred and envy. The Athenian imperialists of the
fifth century were fully conscious of this, and Pericles knew that
such will be incurred by all who wish to rule others. He adds that
since they must be incurred, it should be for the highest objects,
and he adds a consolation for those who suffer from it, that 'hatred
does not last for long, but what makes the glamour of the moment
and the glory of the future remains unforgotten'.[2] In this there is
a consistent thought. The glory of great achievements outweighs
their unpopularity. This may be applied to Heracles. In life he
may stir hatred among men like Eurystheus and Eurytus; he may
even fill us with horror. But the extraordinary success of his work
outbalances and outlives these feelings; his great qualities will be
remembered and his acts of violence forgotten. So the portentous
character of Heracles has its place in the pattern of Periclean
thought. He stands outside the ordinary ranks and cannot be
accused of arrogance; for he has special powers and a special mission. Pindar, who admired the Mean as the right rule of life, saw
that Heracles was not to be condemned for his neglect of it. He
quotes his seizure of the cattle of Geryon 'unasked and unbought'
as an example of a law:

> Law, king of everything,
> Of mortals and of immortals,
> Carries all with uplifted hand
> And makes right the most violent act.[3]

The 'law' here is the way of life proper to superior beings. What
is right for Heracles is wrong for ordinary men. So Sophocles presents Heracles not really as beyond good and evil but certainly as
governed by rules more appropriate to gods than to men. He does

[1] Thuc. ii. 40. 4–5.
[2] Thuc. ii. 64. 5 μῖσος μὲν γὰρ οὐκ ἐπὶ πολὺ ἀντέχει, ἡ δὲ παραυτίκα τε
λαμπρότης καὶ ἐς τὸ ἔπειτα δόξα ἀείμνηστος καταλείπεται.
[3] Fr. 152   νόμος ὁ πάντων βασιλεύς
            θνατῶν τε καὶ ἀθανάτων
            ἄγει δικαιῶν τὸ βιαιότατον
            ὑπερτάτᾳ χειρί.

in his sphere what Pericles imagines Athens to do in hers. His labours are in their own way like those which Athens endures for her glory. They impart nobility to him who surmounts them and bring glory, admiration, and awe. Heracles is a new kind of heroic figure, in whom old qualities of endurance and power are united to the Periclean notion that such qualities, however unpleasant they may be at the time, are justified by the good that they do and rewarded in the end by undying fame.

This physically splendid creature is destroyed in a peculiarly painful and horrible way. When he appears racked with agony and humiliation, his words must be judged in reference to his condition. So too, before he appears, we cannot condemn him for throwing Lichas over a cliff (777 ff.). For though Lichas is entirely innocent, Heracles, distraught with agony, sees in him an instrument of his sufferings and avenges them on him. It is what we should expect Heracles to do in the frenzy of pain. The horror of his condition is made clearer by the details which Hyllus gives of his paroxysms in the accursed garment. It clings to his limbs as if a skilful workman has fastened it; it racks his bones; it eats him as if it were a poisonous snake (767–71). For a people who admired physical perfection and strength so much as the Greeks did there would be something peculiarly painful in the destruction of such a man in this irresistible and hideous grip. The memory of the struggle is still vivid when Heracles is brought on to the stage. He is carried in a litter and is the wreck of what was the strongest and most enduring man in the world. When he wakes, his broken brief sentences show his weakness and pain. In this moment his only desire is for death as a relief from his agony. Mingled with this, and no less painful, is his feeling of dishonour. He cries out

What a ruin have you made of me, what a ruin![1]

Humiliation is not the least of his sufferings. Such is his pain that he denounces those around for not killing him at once (1011). Out of his torment emerges his hatred for Deianira whom he believes to be the deliberate cause of it. He wishes that she may die such a death as his (1037–8). The audience, seeing a spectacle so painful and the ruin of so grand a being, would feel pity for him and horror for what has happened. No doubt the effect was enhanced by music, but without it the scene is disquieting enough.

From this half-delirious state Heracles makes a slight recovery. He changes from agonized cries to more reasoned and coherent

[1] 996   οἵαν μ' ἄρ' ἔθου λώβαν, οἵαν.

speech. His mind is dominated by the contrast between his former
state and his present humiliation and helplessness. That is why
he enumerates his great labours (1091–1102) and speaks of his
lineage:

> I, whom, 'tis told, the noblest mother bore,
> I who am called the son of starry Zeus.[1]

The memory of the past makes the present all the more appalling.
Above all he looks at his wasting body which was once the source
of his strength, and he finds the sight intolerable, whether he uncovers his limbs to the onlookers:

> Look at my poor maimed body, all of you,
> Look at my misery, how pitiful![2]

or addresses his own limbs:

> O hands, my hands,
> O breast and shoulders, arms that were my own![3]

The contrast between present and past is bitter enough for one
whose whole life has been shaped by his physical strength, who has
found in it his means of service and his hope of glory, but it is made
the more bitter by the thought that this fearful change is the work
of a woman (1062–3). When Heracles says

> I who was such am now found womanish[4]

the extent of his fall is clear to him. A woman has brought him
down to her own level. That is a special and degrading shame.
Heracles who has all male qualities in excess is brought to ruin by a
gentle, unassuming, weak woman who is also his wife.

In his belief that Deianira has plotted his death Heracles naturally turns to thoughts of revenge. If she is guilty, as he believes,
this is his right, especially since his heroic character entitles him
to every freedom to punish wrongs. He calls her godless (1037)
and crafty-faced (1050), demands that she be brought forth for
him to kill (1067–70), and closes his speech with a wish that she
will come and proclaim the message that in death, as in life, he
punished the wicked (1109–11). He sees in her a kind of Clytaemnestra. Sophocles, who earlier in the play pointed to the vast gulf

[1] 1105–6   ὁ τῆς ἀρίστης μητρὸς ὠνομασμένος,
           ὁ τοῦ κατ' ἄστρα Ζηνὸς αὐδηθεὶς γόνος.

[2] 1079–80   ἰδού, θεᾶσθε πάντες ἄθλιον δέμας,
           ὁρᾶτε τὸν δύστηνον, ὡς οἰκτρῶς ἔχω.

[3] 1089–90   ὦ χέρες, χέρες,
           ὦ νῶτα καὶ στέρν', ὦ φίλοι βραχίονες

[4] 1075   νῦν δ' ἐκ τοιούτου θῆλυς ηὕρημαι τάλας.

between the two women, here makes Heracles show the extent of his mistake by using language which recalls Clytaemnestra. When he says of Deianira

> Upon my shoulders she set fast this net
> By Furies woven, and it brings me death,[1]

and later that he is

> By unimagined chains subdued[2]

he recalls the words of Electra and Orestes to their dead father about his murder:

> *El.* Remember the new net they made for you.
> *Or.* In chains but not of bronze they caught you, father.

If we wish to know what Heracles thinks of Deianira, we must think of Clytaemnestra. For him his wife is an abominable murderess like her.

The heroic power which calls for vengeance on Deianira is not satisfied with that. Heracles is so absorbed in his own fall that he is almost past listening to reason. He resists Hyllus' efforts to tell him the truth. Hyllus begins modestly and in general terms (1114–19), and Heracles does not resent what he says (1120–1). But the moment that he mentions Deianira and says that she erred unwillingly, Heracles burst into fury against him:

> Base scoundrel, you have breathed your mother's name,
> Your father's murderess, for me to hear.[4]

The mere mention of his wife is enough to put Heracles into an ungovernable frenzy of rage. Wrapped in his torments he either does not hear all Hyllus' words or pays no attention to them. Hyllus patiently presses the truth and says that Deianira is dead (1130). Heracles is pleased but not too pleased. He would rather that she had died by his hand (1133). So Hyllus repeats that she is innocent:

> This is the sum: she wished good but she failed.[5]

Even then Heracles has no word of forgiveness. He merely asks for more information. His obstinate refusal to hear his wife's case is

---

[1] 1051–2   καθῆψεν ὤμοις τοῖς ἐμοῖς Ἐρινύων
             ὑφαντὸν ἀμφίβληστρον, ᾧ διόλλυμαι.

[2] 1057   ἀφράστῳ τῇδε χειρωθεὶς πέδῃ.

[3] Aesch. *Cho.* 492–3 Ἠλ. μέμνησο δ᾽ ἀμφίβληστρον ὡς ἐκαίνισαν.
            Ορ. πέδαις δ᾽ ἀχαλκεύτοις ἐθηρεύθης, πάτερ.

[4] 1124–5   ὦ παγκάκιστε, καὶ παρεμνήσω γὰρ αὖ
           τῆς πατροφόντου μητρός, ὡς κλύειν ἐμέ.

[5] 1136   ἅπαν τὸ χρῆμ᾽, ἥμαρτε χρηστὰ μωμένη.

part of his heroic wrath. Since she has destroyed him, he hardly cares whether she did it on purpose or not. He is like those gods and heroes who punish insults even though they have been committed in mistake. What matters to him is his fall; he hardly pauses to consider the reasons which led to it. His hardness of heart is all part of his superior power, of the quality which makes him perform great tasks so well. His strength has made his life for him; when it is destroyed, there is no question of his forgiving the woman who has undone him.

Sophocles does not dwell on this. He simply shows how Heracles takes the truth from Hyllus; then he passes on to something else. For Hyllus' mention of Nessus recalls prophecies of Heracles' death. He knows now that he must die, that the old prophecy will be fulfilled. His thoughts turn from Deianira to his own death. Here, too, he is absorbed in himself, in his own downfall and his own destiny. Remote from human beings in life, he is no less remote on the verge of death. It is part of his heroic power that he has no thoughts for Deianira once she has ceased to affect him. Yet though he follows his own strange laws, there is modesty in his attitude towards death now that it is inevitable and near. His first realization of it is a great shock (1143 ff.), but he soon recovers himself and tells the truth in grave and reverent tones. He does not complain that the gods destroy him in this way. There is a noble simplicity in his ready acceptance of his doom from the dead Centaur:

> 'Twas the wild Centaur, as the holy word
> Foretold, who slew me living, being dead.[1]

Heracles may lack the kinder virtues, but he has his own splendour. The appalling horror of his end does not lead him to blaspheme against the gods who have brought it to him, the son of Zeus. Once he understands that it is fated by the gods, he is reasonable about it. The effort for one in his state to find such a mood must indeed be great, and Heracles shows that he is no ordinary man. Used to suffering, he is able at the last to face the worst when he knows the reason of it.

In this state Heracles gives his last orders and busies himself with arrangements for his end. Since his son Hyllus is the only one of his own kin with him, it falls to Hyllus to receive these orders. The first is that he should burn his father alive on Oeta. Heracles exacts a promise as if he had doubts about Hyllus obeying (1181),

---

[1] 1162-3   ὅδ' οὖν ὁ θὴρ Κένταυρος, ὡς τὸ θεῖον ἦν πρόφαντον, οὕτω ζῶντά μ' ἔκτεινεν θανών.

and closes a command with a threat that if Hyllus refuses, he will
be pursued by his father's wrath from the dead (1201–2). Hyllus
feels the greatest repugnance to obeying. At first he can hardly
believe what he hears (1203). Then he explains:

> Alas again, what do you ask of me,
> Father, to be defiled with murdering you![1]

He feels that the pollution of his father's blood will be on his hands.
Then Heracles yields, and insists only that Hyllus shall build his
pyre (1211). The short colloquy is illuminating. Heracles, concerned with his own end, does not stop to consider what Hyllus
will feel about it. When he knows, he yields. He is remote and
imperious, not absolutely brutal. Death presses hard on him; he
wishes to die, to be rid of his agony; he has no time to explain or
argue. Though he has been hard about Deianira, he has some
human feelings for his son. He trusts him enough to ask his help,
just as he called on him when he first put on the fatal robe (795–
802). He yields on the point of kindling the pyre.

The first order is followed by a second. Heracles speaks as if he
now knew how much he is demanding of Hyllus:

> Add for me
> One little grace to your large benefits.[2]

The purport is soon clear; he wishes Hyllus to marry Iole. To this
too Hyllus feels the greatest repugnance. For he regards Iole as
the cause of his mother's death and thinks that he would rather die
than marry such an enemy to his race (1233–7). Why does Heracles wish Hyllus to marry her, and why on this point is he obdurate, making no concessions and insisting that this is not a request
but a command? It is no explanation that in the saga Iole became
the wife of Hyllus.[3] Sophocles could have omitted such a detail
which is not of fundamental importance to the plot. Since he introduces it, he must have meant it to be significant. Surely he
shows an unsuspected trait of tenderness and justice in Heracles.
The great hero still loves Iole, for whom he has done so much and
for whom, in a sense, he dies. With the reticence of his kind he
does not deign to explain; his will must be enough for Hyllus.
But his words seem to show his love for the girl:

[1] 1206–7   οἴμοι μάλ' αὖθις, οἷά μ' ἐκκαλῇ, πατέρ,
φονέα γενέσθαι καὶ παλαμναῖον σέθεν.

[2] 1216–17   πρόσνειμαι Δέ μοι
χάριν βραχεῖαν πρὸς μακροῖς ἄλλοις Διδούς.

[3] Apollodor. Bib. ii. 15.

You know the maiden, child of Eurytus?[1]

Hyllus must marry her because he can be trusted to care for her.
Moreover, this is also an act of justice. Hyllus regards Iole with
horror, but she is as innocent as Deianira. She has lost her home
and her family, and she has not gained Heracles. She is utterly
abandoned and friendless. In no way is she to blame. Her misfortunes are not a punishment for anything that she has done. It is
right that she should receive some recompense. Heracles sees this
and does his best for her. By his own rules he is just, though his
justice overrides the natural and human scruples of Hyllus. Hyllus, torn between his duty to his dead mother and his duty to his
dying father, follows the latter. He will never be disloyal to him
(1184).

Through this scene Heracles, racked with pain and conscious of
coming death, has shown a tremendous fortitude and endurance.
If he is hard on others, he is harder on himself. The man whose
life has been given to labours does not flinch when his own strength
is stricken. With stern purpose he orders the men around him to
lift him, and his last words are characteristically addressed to himself, as he makes his final effort to control his cries of pain:

> Come now, before you awake this plague,
> Come, O my stubborn heart, and give
> Me a curb as of steel on lip's like stone.
> Let no cry come. Though you do it perforce,
> Think it something fit for rejoicing.[2]

The audience, seeing the departure of this heroic figure, would
carry as a last memory of him his unflinching courage in unequalled pain, his acceptance of the hideous end which the gods
have sent to him. They would also remember that in all his self-
sufficiency he gave in to his son in the matter of burning and had
at the last a thought for Iole. He is not a monster, but a superman,
a hero, a demi-god. His great gifts for good and for evil, his freedom from the limits set to human endeavour, show him as a fearful
and awe-inspiring figure. But behind the sternness and the brutality are great courage and even some tenderness. He has lived in
himself. But when death breaks him, he shows traces of a nature

---

[1] 1219   τὴν Εὐρυτείαν οἶσθα δῆτα παρθένον;

[2] 1259–63   ἄγε νυν, πρὶν τήνδ' ἀνακινῆσαι
νόσον, ὦ ψυχὴ σκληρά, χάλυβος
λιθοκόλλητον στόμιον παρέχουσ',
ἀνάπαυε βοήν, ὡς ἐπίχαρτον
τελέουσ' ἀεκούσιον ἔργον.

gentler than we have suspected. Like the gods, he is beyond criticism but not beyond respect. We can understand why his death is regarded as so great a disaster by the Chorus:

> Unhappy Hellas, what grief do I
> Foresee for her if she must lose this man![1]

Heracles may not be lovable, but there is something in him which inspires respect and wonder.

The human interest of the *Women of Trachis* lies in the contrasted characters of Heracles and Deianira. From their conflict the tragedy comes. Deianira depends entirely on Heracles. She cannot endure to lose his affection; therefore she resorts to the desperate expedient of magic. Heracles once cared for her, but since he is a creature of strong passions and follows them, he passes from her to Iole. Though he fought to win Deianira, he has ceased to care for her and does not think of her. Her utter dependence is at the mercy of his independence. The woman loses all that she values and dies; the man through her loses all that he values and also dies. This tragedy is not private, not something that rises from a particular collocation of personalities. It is the tragedy of the difference between man and woman. The man wants to go one way; the woman wants to go with him, but not with another woman to share his affections. She wants him to herself. The play might be regarded as the tragic dramatization of Aristotle's view that the courage of a man is shown in commanding, that of a woman in obeying.[2] Heracles commands; Deianira normally and gladly obeys. So far their union suits Aristotle's requirements. But it breaks down because Deianira is too anxious to remain as a wife to endure a rival or a partner in her husband's affections. The acuteness of the conflict and its hideous end come from the essential differences between manhood and womanhood. Heracles' strong will and independent spirit sever him from his wife just as they draw her to him and make her admire him beyond all other men. To the Greeks the tragedy would surely seem to rise naturally out of circumstances in which any characteristic man and woman might find themselves.

When man and wife differ so much as Heracles and Deianira, their children may well be the victims of divided loyalties, rival claims, and conflicting duties. So at least is Hyllus. He is caught in the conflict and flung from one kind of sorrow to another. When

---

[1] 1112–13   ὦ τλῆμον Ἑλλάς, πένθος οἷον εἰσορῶ
ἕξουσαν, ἀνδρὸς τοῦδέ γ' εἰ σφαλήσεται.

[2] *Pol.* 1260 a 23.

the tragedy first unfolds its hideous events, he is whole-heartedly
on his father's side. He tells Deianira that she has killed Heracles
(739–40). His first words to her show perhaps some hesitation or
inability to say what he feels:

> Mother, for you one of three things I'd choose,—
> That you were dead, or if not dead, not called
> Mother of mine, or else would change the heart
> That now is yours for something better far.[1]

He speaks with an awkward formality, as if he did not quite dare
to express his feelings to the full or hardly knew what they were.
The worst alternative comes first, that Deianira would be better
dead; it is followed by others less fearful but impossible to realize.
This is not yet a curse. It is still spoken with some kind of respect;
for Deianira is after all his mother. But as Hyllus unfolds his tale
and sees how hideous is the fate that she has brought to Heracles,
he overcomes his doubts and scruples, calls on Justice and the
Fury to punish her, and knows that it is right for him to do so (808–
10). His respect for his mother is overcome by his horror and indignation at what she has done. His feeling against her naturally
grows when she does not answer him but leaves him with the conviction that she is guilty of her husband's murder. Then he feels
that she has forfeited the name of mother and all title to respect
that it carries with it. He owes her no filial duty:

> Why should a mother's name bring her respect
> When all unlike a mother's are her deeds?[2]

In a gentler, less revengeful way he says of her what Electra says
of Clytaemnestra.[3] For the moment he is his father's champion
against his mother.

Later Hyllus learns the truth about Deianira. He would then,
if he could, have stayed her from killing herself (932 ff.). He is too
late (934), and suffers the misery of one who has unjustly accused
his mother. In a rush of affection for her he falls over her dead
body and kisses it, bitterly crying

> That he had struck her with a wrong, vain charge,[4]

---

[1] 734–7   ὦ μῆτερ, ὡς ἂν ἐκ τριῶν σ' ἓν εἰλόμην,
              ἢ μηκέτ' εἶναι ζῶσαν, ἢ σεσωμένην
              ἄλλου κεκλῆσθαι μητέρ', ἢ λῴους φρένας
              τῶν νῦν παρουσῶν τῶνδ' ἀμείψασθαί ποθεν.

[2] 817–18   ὄγκον γὰρ ἄλλως ὀνόματος τί δεῖ τρέφειν
              μητρῷον, ἥτις μηδὲν ὡς τεκοῦσα δρᾷ;

[3] El. 1194.

[4] 940   ὡς νιν ματαίως αἰτίᾳ 'μβάλοι κακῇ.

and that he has now lost both father and mother (941-2). Naturally he tries to make amends by telling Heracles that Deianira is
really innocent (1123, 1136). But in this, too, he fails. Just as he
unjustly accused his mother of murder and may have hastened her
death, so he is unable to convince his father of her innocence. He
is involved in both tragedies because he belongs to both his parents.
His quandary is even clearer when Heracles tells him to marry
Iole. He would like to refuse because Iole has brought death both
to his father and his mother, but his father's command is law, and
he has to obey. In the last resort his father is more important than
his mother, but that does not mean that obedience to him is easy or
willingly given. Hyllus is torn between two duties, and finds satisfaction in neither. At the end of the play it is he, and not the
Chorus, who complains of all the sorrow that has come to pass. He
is of course only a boy, and we must not expect too much character
in him, though his frank impulsive nature is true enough to his
years. His interest lies in his situation. He is subordinated to the
two tragedies which take place round him and sweep him into
them. His position is typical of any son whose parents are in conflict. He tries to be just, to carry out his loyalties, but he fails to do
any good and finds nothing but misery.

In the conflict between Heracles and Deianira the poet deliberately and consciously raises moral or ethical questions. Indeed the
drama almost turns on them, as the ambiguous position of Hyllus
shows. Nor can we doubt that a Greek audience would have
judged the characters by their actions or at least have asked
where right and wrong lie, particularly with Deianira. Sophocles
suggests by subtle hints that we should compare her with Clytaemnestra, the unconscienced murderess of her husband. The contrasts indicate that Deianira is not of this kind, but we still ask of
what kind she is and what would be thought of her. She is in some
sense responsible for the death of Heracles. In so far as she decides
to use magic on him, she acts wrongly. Of that there can be no
doubt. But it is not all. Even if she acts wrongly, how wrong is
she? and in what does this wrongness consist? In this matter it is
instructive to see what Bacchylides had said of her. He attributed
her fatal error to 'jealousy', φθόνος. She was its ill-starred victim:

> Ah, ill-fated, ah unhappy one, what did she plan!
> Powerful jealousy ruined her.

Bacchylides is sorry for her, but he also thinks that she was wrong.

---

[1] xvi. 30-1   ἆ δύσμορος, ἆ τάλαιν', οἷον ἐμήσατ[ο·
φθόνος εὐρυβίας νιν ἀπώλεσεν.

She is the victim of jealousy which works on a large scale. She ought to have been modest and submitted to circumstances, but jealousy drove her to a deadly expedient. But in Sophocles real jealousy has hardly any place. Deianira shows no hardness or hatred, hardly even suspicion, the usual attributes of jealousy. Even when she knows why Iole has come, she still says nothing against her. She rightly takes pride in the welcome that she has given her:

> You saw and know the welcome that I gave
> , The stranger, how I kindly greeted her.[1]

What she feels is an overwhelming desire to keep Heracles to herself, but this is not accompanied by the dark destructive hate which belongs to real jealousy. She even believes that her magic will do no harm. Sophocles makes Deianira's action as sympathetic as he can. He has already presented her in the most favourable light, and when she makes her fatal decision it seems to be prompted by no base or evil motive. He could have presented her otherwise, made her an admirable woman marred by a grave fault. But he does not. Her fault is a single slip, an error of judgement. It is undeniably wrong, but it is presented with every alleviating circumstance. The process that leads to it is made so natural that we feel that at least Deianira acted under strong provocation and is not lightly to be condemned.

A more general problem is whether Deianira would still be thought guilty of her husband's death. Hyllus does not think so. His words that she acted 'unwillingly' (1123) would suggest to an Athenian audience that she was legally innocent; for even Dracon allowed that no one was guilty of murder who acted unwillingly. But is Hyllus right? What would be thought of a case like this in which a very dubious action leads to the death of a woman's husband? Should not Deianira be condemned for attempting something which might well lead to Heracles' death? Was not the use of magic in itself a crime of no small gravity? On these important questions Athenian law seems to have come to different decisions, and this variety no doubt represents an uncertainty in public opinion. On the one hand are cases in which users of magic were condemned and heavily sentenced. For such practices Theoris was condemned to death.[2] Surely Deianira might be condemned on similar grounds. Yet other evidence shows that a different view

---

[1] 627-8   ἀλλ' οἶσθα μὲν δὴ καὶ τὰ τῆς ξένης ὁρῶν
προσδέγματ', αὐτή θ' ὡς ἐδεξάμην φίλως.

[2] Dem. xxv. 79.

might be taken, and that if magic led to death it might be regarded as a ground for acquittal. In the First Speech of Antiphon a woman is accused by her stepson of murdering her husband and his father. Her defence is that the death was due not to murderous intent but to an attempt to win the man back by love-charms.[1] Whatever the facts of the case may have been,[2] it is clear that this defence would not have been offered if the lawyers had not believed that it might secure the woman's acquittal. Legally, then, it might be maintained that Deianira was innocent. The more theoretical aspects of a case like hers are developed by Aristotle. In discussing actions which may be called involuntary because they are not accompanied by thought, he gives an account of what seems to have been a famous case tried before the court of the Areopagus:

'They say that once on a time a woman gave a love-potion to somebody; that the man died from the effects of the love-potion and the woman was tried before the Areopagus; on her appearance before which she was acquitted, just for the reason that she did not do it with design. For she gave it in love, but missed her mark; wherefore it was not held to be voluntary, because in giving the love-potion she did not give it with the thought of killing.'

The case is singularly like that of Deianira. The main facts are the same. The decision of the Areopagus, which follows correctly from the Athenian law concerning murder, is like the defence of Hyllus that Deianira acted 'unwillingly' (1123) and 'missed her mark' (1136). This surely is the conclusion that Sophocles intends us to form. He follows the Areopagus against other legal opinion and judicial decisions. In a matter where two views were possible he shows where his own sympathies are. Whatever the audience might feel about Deianira's attempt to dominate her husband they should at least admit that she was not a criminal, that she was guilty perhaps of a grave fault but not of a horrible crime.

Deianira's death follows from her fault. In killing herself she makes amends. Her tragedy takes place on a human plane. She is not punished by the gods and is hardly their victim. With Heracles it is different. His whole end is presented as the work of the gods. Oracles foretelling its time and manner are fulfilled. In his last hours he recognizes and accepts them. The process is differ-

---

[1] Ant. i. 9 οὐκ ἐπὶ θανάτῳ . . . ἀλλ᾽ ἐπὶ φίλτροις.

[2] K. J. Maidment, *Minor Attic Orators*, i, p. 11, argues persuasively that she was innocent.

[3] *Mag. Mor.* 1188 b 31 ff. Trs. St.G. Stock.

ent from the punishment of Ajax or Creon. Heracles is no ordinary
being who is struck down for pride. His fall is darker and less easy
to explain. Sophocles has no very clear explanation of it. Yet he
throws out hints and suggestions. It is not absolutely undecipherable. The fate which seems to work with such malignity is the will
of Zeus. It must be treated with respect; in the last resort it must
be right. It may not be fully intelligible, and it certainly is not to
be explained by any easy scheme. Here, too, Sophocles may have
learned something from tradition. For it is possible that the end of
Heracles was regarded as an example of inevitable fate. When
Bacchylides tells the story he assumes something of the kind. For
when Iole is coming:

> Then unconquerable doom
> Wove for Deianira
> A cunning device, full of tears.[1]

He puts some responsibility for Deianira's action on an irresistible
power which he does not specify. It must be fate, the superhuman,
anonymous power that shapes human ends. Sophocles takes the
hint from here or elsewhere and fashions it in his own way. He
depicts the working of fate, but this fate is the will of the gods. It is
they who foretell the end of Heracles and in due course fulfil it.

Bacchylides says nothing of oracles. Yet there is a hint of fatality
when he says that Deianira was undone partly by

> The dark veil of coming events[2]

The fated future was hidden from her and came in spite of her
efforts to secure a happy issue. Perhaps the legend illustrated the
dark ways of destiny which runs counter to human calculations
and desires. But whether the saga said this or not, Sophocles certainly gave it prominence. The central unifying character of the
Women of Trachis is not Heracles nor Deianira but the destiny which
unites them in a common doom. It is fated that Heracles shall die
as he does; Deianira is the instrument of his death. His fate takes
precedence; hers is incidental to his. The man is more important
than the woman, the superman than the human being. This destiny does not act so consistently and so relentlessly as that of Oedipus. It is not always present as an unavoidable menace which
bursts in at every stage of the play. We may even forget it for a

---

[1] xvi. 23–5
　　τότ᾽ ἄμαχος Δαίμων
　　Δαϊανείρᾳ πολύδακρυν ὕφα[νε
　　μῆτιν ἐπίφρον᾽.

[2] Ib. 32–3
　　Ἀνόφεόν τε κάλυμμα τῶν
　　ὕστερον ἐρχομένων.

time. But it is at work, and it is important to notice the place that Sophocles gives to it.

The first scene of the *Women of Trachis* has been called otiose and undramatic and accused of improbabilities. Why, it is asked, has Deianira not thought before of sending Hyllus in search of Heracles? Why should the Nurse think of him just at the moment when he is about to return? Why should Hyllus at the same time have heard news that his father is in Euboea? Yet to these questions there is a simple answer. The atmosphere in the opening scene is of a long inactivity and ignorance broken suddenly by inquiry and action. On Deianira's isolation and idleness the gods have begun to work, and when they begin, they work from different sides and in different ways. A similar situation exists at the beginning of the *Odyssey*. There, too, are the inactive wife sunk in hopeless lethargy, the young son eager to act but ignorant what to do, the faithful friends eager to help. The situation is suddenly changed because the gods have decided that Odysseus shall return. Telemachus is told by Athene that his father is alive and sets out in search of news of him just when Odysseus is about to come home. The converging rumours and purposes come from the gods. So Sophocles makes the gods stir the household of Deianira into action. She herself wakes with an anxious foreboding that a fated hour is near; the Nurse suggests inquiry; Hyllus, from some un-named source, has heard news from his father. In the darkness before dawn broods a spirit of doubt and indecision. But it is suddenly broken by news and hope. The gods have begun to act.

Homer explains his coincident events by the decision of the gods in council on Olympus; Sophocles uses more mysterious means. Years before an oracle has been given to Heracles at Dodona that after twelve years he shall either die or have peace and rest. Lost in her memories and miseries, Deianira has not thought of the oracle before the present moment, but now she broods over it and begins to see its menacing significance (79–85). She does this because the divine plan for Heracles is at work. Oracles are often forgotten until the moment when the gods decide to put them into effect. And so it happens here. The remembrance of the oracle fills Deianira with forebodings. She remembers how Heracles himself told her that, when fifteen months are past, the time for its fulfil-ment will come (44–5, 164–5); he has left instructions with her what to do when the time comes (46–8, 161–3). At first she is shy of speaking about the oracle, even perhaps of thinking about it; she mentions only its main contents and its instructions; later she

speaks about it first to Hyllus, then to the Chorus. As the time for
its fulfilment draws near, she sees more clearly what it is. It is ambiguous, but Deianira, who is used to suffering, takes the worse view
of it. She states its alternatives fairly, but she dwells on the darker
side when she tells Hyllus that they are at a dangerous turning-
point in their lives (82–5) and the Chorus that she is afraid of losing
her husband (176–7). Her anxiety suggests that there is something
in her fears, that a fatal hour is at hand when the divine intentions
for Heracles will, for better or for worse, be disclosed. This menace
hangs over the prologue and the first episode. The mention of
the oracle intensifies the sense of coming crisis, of powers at work
in darkness, of destiny intruding into quiet lives.

The oracle is not mentioned in the excited scenes between the
arrival of Iole and the sending of the robe. In her new excitement
Deianira forgets it. Her wild hope has driven it from her mind; to
her great harm, for the thought of it might have made her pause
before anointing the robe with the blood of Nessus. But once the
damage is done past remedy, the Chorus revert to the oracle. They
now see that the rest which it promised to Heracles is the rest of
death:

> For how could he who sees not the light,
> Have any longer the toil
> Of servitude, being dead? [1]

This too is the conclusion which Heracles himself reaches when he
knows that he is dying and that the oracle given long ago at Dodona is going to be fulfilled by his death (1163–73). In this there
is a difficulty. Deianira knows that the oracle offers alternatives of
death or rest; she does not say that it is double-edged or ambiguous. But Heracles has assumed that it is clear and offers only rest.
His understanding of it is different from Deianira's. He feels no
hint of a darker meaning, nothing but assurance of quiet years
after his labours. The solution is perhaps that Sophocles intended
the oracle to be obscure and susceptible of more than one interpretation. It promised rest. Deianira sees that such rest might be
either good or bad; Heracles believes that it will be good. The
different interpretations suit the different characters of the man
and the woman. Deianira, prone always to suspect the worst, suspects it here; Heracles, confident of his destiny, assumes that after
his labours all will be well. It happens that Heracles is wrong and

[1] 828–30   πῶς γὰρ ἂν ὁ μὴ λεύσσων
ἔτι ποτ' ἔτ' ἐπίπονον
ἔχοι θανὼν λατρείαν;

Deianira right. But that too is part of the fated scheme. For her insight is useless to her when she sends the fated robe; his knowledge comes to him only when he is already dying.

This oracle is supplemented by another, given earlier to Heracles by Zeus, that he shall not die at the hand of any living being. This too sounded reassuring, but in the result turns out to mean that he will be killed by the blood of the dead Centaur (1159–63). He is the victim of two deceptive oracles. The one foretold the time, the other the manner, of his death. Both seemed to encourage confidence, and both are fulfilled in a singularly merciless way. To us these oracles may seem remote and unreal, mere mechanism to develop the plot and surmount its improbabilities. We may find it hard to believe that an intelligent man of the fifth century could attach any more importance to oracles than Thucydides did.[1] But the fact remains that to most men of the time oracles were a real source of divine truth. Pindar always treated Delphi with devout respect, and even when it was wrong, as about the colonization of north Africa, he took some trouble to explain away its mistake. His views were held by men as different as Herodotus and Socrates. They even won official sanction. When in 447 B.C. the Athenian army of Tolmides was defeated at Coronea, the epigram on the fallen recorded that they had been misled by an oracle and added the surprising conclusion that the divine being who so deceived them established the truth of all oracles for ever:

> All men for the future
> Made he mark that oracles are sure.[2]

If a public monument could state so uncompromising a doctrine as this, we cannot doubt that oracles were accepted at Athens as vehicles of divine information and that it was thought unwise to distrust or neglect them.

In the *Women of Trachis* the oracles are of a special kind. Some oracles might be warnings which a man disregarded to his cost. Aeschylus, for instance, used an oracle of this kind in his account of Laius. The oracle warned Laius against having a son; he took no notice and was punished. The moral is emphasized:

> The oracles lose not their edge.[3]

But the oracles given to Heracles are not warnings. He cannot

[1] ii. 17. 2.

[2]
> βροτοῖσι Δὲ πᾶσι τὸ λοιπὸν
> φράζεσθαι λογίων πιστὸν ἔθηκε τέλος.

Cf. *C. Q.* xxxii, pp. 80–8.

[3] *Sept.* 844   θέσφατ' οὐκ ἀμβλύνεται.

avoid their fulfilment by taking this or that step. They show a
more fatalistic tendency than that given to Laius. They forecast
the inevitable, and they forecast it in dark ambiguous terms. So
when they are fulfilled, their victims almost feel that they have
been tricked. Heracles expects rest and finds death; he believes
that no dead being can hurt him, and he dies through the dead
Centaur. The oracles which Sophocles uses are of a familiar kind.
It was well known that oracles were hard to understand.[1] In this
case they are more than difficult; they are ambiguous. Of this
kind there are good examples in Herodotus. More than once he
tells of oracles which seem to promise one thing but are shown in
the result to have promised almost the opposite, something different and certainly less pleasant. Croesus received an oracle that if
he crossed the Halys he would destroy a great army.[2] He took this
as an encouragement, but the army destroyed was his own. Cambyses was told that he would die in Ecbatana, and thought that he
was safe for a long life since he was far from the Median Ecbatana,
but he died soon in a Syrian village of the same name.[3] So Heracles
believes that he will have peace and rest after his toils, but he finds
to his cost that he is wrong:

> I thought I should fare well.
> But this, it seemed, was nothing but my death;
> For the dead have no labours any more.[4]

He does not complain that the gods have deceived him, but we
cannot help thinking that he has been cruelly treated, that his
hopes have been unnecessarily encouraged only to be frustrated.

Such oracles served a special purpose in the divine governance
of men. They did not prevent a man from wrongdoing, as that
given to Laius might have. Such was not their use. But they
served to stress the helplessness of man before the gods and to
teach him a salutary lesson in humility. Croesus, who was the
victim of such an oracle, was told by the Pythian Priestess 'It is
impossible even for a god to escape his fated destiny',[5] and when he
realized what the oracle meant, he admitted modestly that the
fault was his and not the god's.[6] So, too, the presumptuous Cambyses, when he learned on his death-bed that the god had prophesied truly, accepted his fate in a modest frame of mind.[7] The

---

[1] Aesch. *Ag.* 1255 Δυσμαθῆ, Eur. *Suppl.* 138 Δυστόπαστ' αἰνίγματα.
[2] Hdt. i. 75.   [3] Hdt. iii. 64.
[4] 1171–3   κἀδόκουν πράξειν καλῶς·
                τὸ Δ' ἦν ἄρ' οὐδὲν ἄλλο πλὴν θανεῖν ἐμέ·
                τοῖς γὰρ θανοῦσι μόχθος οὐ προσγίγνεται.
[5] Hdt. i. 91. 1.   [6] Id. i. 91. 6.   [7] Id. iii. 64. 5.

fulfilment of the gods' plan taught humility. It does not matter
whether the learner is pious like Croesus or impious like Cambyses. If the gods decide to humble him, they may do so, and this
means is open to them. Heracles is humbled not merely by the
collapse of his strength and the bitter consciousness that he is
undone by a woman, but by the realization that the gods have
planned and foretold his death. As a hero and the son of Zeus,
he might have expected to avoid such humiliation. But when it
comes, he accepts it. If oracles were liable to have such ambiguities, it was all the more necessary to pay full attention to them.
Sophocles himself says:

> And such full well I know the god to be:
> The wise find riddles in his oracles,
> Fools think his lesson trivial and short.[1]

Fools are in due course taught that they are wrong. Heracles has
been like them in paying too little attention to the oracle and
assuming that it must have a favourable issue for him. Now he
knows that it did not portend what he thought.

The oracles induce in Heracles a mood of acceptance, almost of
humility. Nothing becomes him better than his resignation in the
face of death. Yet he is not proud like Cambyses or successful like
Croesus. It is not easy to see why the gods wish to humble him in
this way. He has their blood in his veins; he resembles them in
many ways. Yet we may suspect that they have their reason for
treating him as they do. In so dark a matter the poet does not
speak with assurance. He does not use Heracles like Creon to convey a direct lesson; he describes his fate and throws out hints of its
causes and character. The means he uses for this is the Chorus. It
speaks with some authority and advances propositions of great
import. It stands at some distance even from Deianira, and often
it does not know the full purport of its own words, as if the poet intended to use it as his own mouthpiece. In its first song it advances
as a counsel of hope the old Orphic or Pythagorean doctrine of the
wheel of things; joy succeeds sorrow and sorrow succeeds joy:

> To all they come, sorrow and joy,
> In circling round, like the turning
> Paths of the Bear.[2]

[1] Fr. 771

καὶ τὸν θεὸν τοιοῦτον ἐξεπίσταμαι,
σοφοῖς μὲν αἰνικτῆρα θεσφάτων ἀεί,
σκαιοῖς δὲ φαῦλον κἄν βραχεῖ διδάσκαλον.

[2] 129–30

ἀλλ' ἐπὶ πῆμα καὶ χαρὰ
πᾶσι κυκλοῦσιν, οἷον ἄρ-
κτου στροφάδες κέλευθοι.

Into the texture of the play this doctrine is woven in a close and special pattern. Heracles is cast down by the revolution of fortune, but his fall takes a form specially suited to his character and his actions.

This revolution may be seen most clearly in the part which love plays in Heracles' life and death. When the Chorus first grasp the significance of Iole's arrival, they sing a song which announces love's power and begins:

> Very great is the strength which the Cyprian plies
> Always to win.[1]

But this song continues in an unexpected way. It is a simple narrative of Heracles' wooing of Deianira. No judgement, no comment, is made on the actual situation and its fearful possibilities. Yet we may surely read into it an intention of the poet to point a moral on what is happening. In the past Heracles used violence to win Deianira; it is in his character to use it to win Iole. History repeats itself, and there is nothing strange in his last adventure. Love is irresistible and overcomes even Zeus and Death (500–1). To this hint we may add a second. When the coming doom of Heracles is known, the Chorus attribute the responsibility for the fall of Oechalia and for all that follows to Aphrodite·

> The Cyprian, working in silence,
> Is the manifest doer of all these things.[2]

It is quite true. Heracles' love for Iole has led him to sack her town. It is also true that Deianira's love for him has led to his death in the poisoned robe. Heracles is doubly the victim of love. His passionate character has turned on him and worked his destruction; the wheel has come full circle. The Chorus, not knowing all their meaning, give a right explanation. But on one point they are wrong. They claim that Love is stronger than Death. In this case Death defeats both Heracles' love for Iole and Deianira's love for him. For, as Sophocles himself says, Death is one

> Who knows not favour, no, nor equity,
> But only cares for Justice absolute;[3]

---

[1] 497–8   μέγα τι σθένος ἁ Κύπρις ἐκφέρεται
                    νίκας ἀεί.

[2] 861–2   ἁ Δ' ἀμφίπολος Κύπρις ἄ-
                    ναυλος φανερὰ τῶνΔ' ἐφάνη πράκτωρ.

[3] Fr. 770   ὃς οὔτε τοὐπιεικὲς οὔτε τὴν χάριν
                    οἶΔεν, μόνην Δ' ἔστερξε τὴν ἁπλῶς Δίκην.

Trs. W. E. Headlam.

and we know that he referred to the conflict of Death with Love. Death has his own rules and pays no attention to considerations of the heart or the conscience. So in the *Women of Trachis* he over-rides the claims of Love.

There is a real truth in this. The passionate intensity which burns in Heracles when he is in love and drives him to such excess-ive acts of self-assertion and violence as the sack of Oechalia may well turn against him, and, when it does, he suffers more than any-one. There is also a kind of justice in it, that Heracles should perish through the power that has made him destroy others. It is a special case of the rule which Sophocles expressed elsewhere in such maxims as:

> For he who does must pay with suffering[1]

and

> If hard your doings, hard your penalty.[2]

Now it is applied to Heracles. He has done violence to others, and he comes to a violent end. And this end comes not only through the appropriate agency of Love but by cruelly appropriate means. The blood of the dead Centaur which kills Heracles is tainted with the poison of the Hydra which Heracles slew. The memory of this poison flits through the play and suggests that there is a sequence of events which catches Heracles and kills him. When the dying Nessus gives his instructions to Deianira, he speaks with exactitude about the wound inflicted on him by Heracles:

> Where Lerna's growth,
> The snake, has tinged the arrow with black gall.[3]

From Nessus' blood this poison passes into the fatal garment. When it devours Heracles, Hyllus, not knowing how well his figure is chosen, describes the power that eats his father's flesh:

> As of some deadly cruel snake,
> The poison then began to feast on him.[4]

Later, the Chorus, knowing that Heracles is doomed and by what means, refer to the poison:

> Which death begat, and the shining serpent nursed.[5]

---

[1] Fr. 229   τὸν δρῶντα γάρ τι καὶ παθεῖν ὀφείλεται.
[2] Fr. 962   εἰ δείν' ἔδρασας, δεινὰ καὶ παθεῖν σε δεῖ.
Cf. Pind. *Nem.* iv. 32, Aesch. *Ag.* 1564.
[3] 573-4   ᾗ μελαγχόλους
ἔβαψεν ἰοὺς θρέμμα Λερναίας ὕδρας.
[4] 770-1   εἶτα φοινίας
ἐχθρᾶς ἐχίδνης ἰὸς ὣς ἐδαίνυτο.
[5] 834   ὃν τέκετο θάνατος, ἔτρεφε δ' αἰόλος δράκων.

Poison and death are closely connected. Death produced it, and the Hydra nursed it. Now both do their work on Heracles.

There is a poetical justice in this end. Heracles comes to it by the means with which he has brought death to others. The oracle that he shall die by no living person is more wise than it seemed. For it means that his own past has turned on him and destroyed him. But poetical justice is not the same as divine justice. The appropriateness of the means does not justify the end. We may still ask why the gods destroy Heracles. To this in the last resort Sophocles gives no clear answer. He may well have had no answer to give. He has shown the means and the method by which the gods work, and that there is in these a certain appropriateness. But he does not explain their reason. He does not end the play, like the *Antigone*, with a clear judgement on what has happened. His close raises more questions than it answers. When Hyllus is taking his dying father away, he says or chants:

> Lift him up, servants, and grant to me
> Full pardon for all that I must do;
> For you know the full heartlessness of the gods
> In everything that has come to pass:
> They bring men to birth, and a father's name
> Is theirs who look on such ills as these.[1]

He asks pardon for himself, since he has to assist in burning his father and to marry Iole, but he puts the blame for these duties and for far worse things on the cruelty of the gods. This is Hyllus' personal view. He himself has lost both parents, and he does not speak with absolute authority. Yet his view has something to be said for it. He complains of the way in which the gods treat their children. He knows now that the Chorus were wrong when they proclaimed that Heracles must be safe since the gods do not desert their own:

> For who yet saw
> Zeus so careless of his children?[2]

That confidence is shattered. The gods may treat their children with utter cruelty. Hyllus' words, coming so emphatically almost

[1] 1264-9   αἴρετ', ὀπαδοί, μεγάλην μὲν ἐμοὶ
τούτων θέμενοι συγγνωμοσύνην,
μεγάλην δὲ θεῶν ἀγνωμοσύνην
εἰδότες ἔργων τῶν πρασσομένων,
οἳ φύσαντες καὶ κληζόμενοι
πατέρες τοιαῦτ' ἐφορῶσι πάθη.

[2] 139-40   ἐπεὶ τίς ὧδε
τέκνοισι Ζῆν' ἄβουλον εἶδεν;

at the very end, certainly cause surprise and give food for thought. They are far removed from ordinary pious sentiment like that of Pindar, who spoke of the gods as

> Caring for good men exceedingly.[1]

But they are not the last words of the play, nor are they the poet's own opinion. They are what many might think, what might well seem reasonable, but they are wrong.

They are corrected and contradicted, quietly and gently, by the Chorus:[2]

> And stay you not, maiden, within the house,
> Where you have seen deaths great and strange,
> And many a sorrow of unknown shape,
> And nothing of these that is not Zeus.[3]

First Iole is urged to go with Hyllus, despite his feeling that it is wrong; then judgement is passed on what has happened. There have indeed been strange deaths and strange sufferings, but only one conclusion is right—all this is the work of Zeus. The Chorus demand an unquestioning complete acceptance of the divine will, and many would accord it to them. Such a conclusion urges humility before the unreckonable power of the gods. In a world where suffering is not confined to the wicked, this position would embody an indisputable truth. It was familiar that the gods could, if they chose, send suffering to men. So Homer's Priam says to Helen:

> I do not hold you to blame: all blame belongs to the gods here;[4]

and Herodotus' Croesus tells Adrastus, who has unwittingly killed Atys, 'It is not you who are to blame for this evil, except so far as you dealt the blow unwillingly; one of the gods is to blame.'[5] This attribution of responsibility to the gods is not a cry of revolt or complaint but obedient acceptance of the divine will. The Chorus agree with Hyllus that Zeus is behind all that has happened, but

---

[1] *Nem.* x. 54   μάλα μὲν ἀνδρῶν δικαίων περικαδόμενοι.

[2] These four lines are given variously by the MSS. to the Chorus and to Hyllus. The " maiden " must be Iole, and they seem more likely than he to address her. Moreover, except in the *O. T.*, Sophocles seems to like to give the last words to the Chorus. But the real reason for not giving them to Hyllus is that their temper is different from his indignant protest.

[3] 1275–8   λείπου μηδὲ σύ, παρθέν', ἐπ' οἴκων
μεγάλους μὲν ἰδοῦσα νέους θανάτους,
πολλὰ δὲ πήματα καὶ καινοπαγῆ,
κοὐδὲν τούτων ὅ τι μὴ Ζεύς.

[4] *Il.* iii. 164 οὔ τί μοι αἰτίη ἐσσί, θεοί νύ μοι αἴτιοί εἰσιν.

[5] i. 45. 2.

they do not approve his accusations of cruelty and callousness. Earlier they saw that Aphrodite caused the fall of Heracles, but now behind her they see the all-pervading power of Zeus. The play ends with the announcement of his responsibility for all that has happened. It is enough that he has so acted. Human beings must not complain. The utterance of the Chorus, more detached and more informed than that of Hyllus, corrects his natural human impulse and shows what the audience should think.

In the saga Heracles, after ascending his pyre on Oeta, was taken in glory to Olympus, made a god, and married to Hebe.[1] His arrival on Olympus was familiar to the poets and favoured by archaic artists like the sculptors of the Amyclean Throne[2] and the old poros pediment on the Acropolis at Athens. Its popularity is shown by its frequent representation on vases dating back to the early part of the sixth century. Pindar regarded this glorification as an amends and saw Heracles as

> Winning a choice reward
> Of peace for his mighty toils.[3]

Whatever Heracles might have endured or suffered, he was rewarded in the end. He was the very type of man whom the gods burden with labours that they may at last show justice and gratitude to him. Sophocles knew this. In the *Philoctetes* his Heracles tells how his toils have won him undying glory (1419 ff.). It is therefore strange that in the *Women of Trachis* no word is said of apotheosis or life on Olympus or marriage to Hebe, no word of amends for suffering or reward for labours. The tragic events take place in a human world; nothing is said of the hereafter. The plot is rigidly restricted to the mortal existence of Heracles which ends in a tragic calamity. The future glory is treated as if it had nothing to do with the play. Indeed, so painful and effective is the play, so strong the will of the gods revealed in it, that we hardly look outside it. In the annihilation of its close there seems to be no place for hope or reward or amends. It is enough that the gods have worked their will and that it must be accepted.

In the main this is undeniably true. Yet in one small point Sophocles seems to have noticed the legend and referred to it allusively but unmistakably. The saga told of the building of a pyre. In his *Philoctetes* Sophocles refers to this (801 ff., cf. 727–9),

---

[1] *Od.* xi. 602–3, Hes. *Theog.* 950–5.   [2] Paus. iii. 18. 11.

[3] *Nem.* i. 70   ἡσυχίαν καμάτων
                       μεγάλων ποινὰν λαχόντ' ἐξαίρετον.

and in the *Women of Trachis* Heracles gives precise orders for such a pyre:

> Abundant wood of the deep-rooted oak
> Cut down, and hew therewith the masculine
> Wild-olive tree, and on it set my body,
> And taking a bright torch of flaming pine
> Set fire to it.[1]

It might be thought that this fine piece of writing is no more than Sophocles' own version of a traditional theme, that he chose to mention the pyre because it belonged to the story and to show what he could do with it. This is a tenable view. Heracles wishes his body to be burned and will have no mistakes made. But the audience knew that from this pyre Heracles was saved and taken to Olympus. On hearing these words they might think of this and see a hint that in the end all would be well with him. Even though they hear no more of it, the hint would make its effect and bring a small ray of consolation. There is too another hint of some end that awaits Heracles. In the middle of his last lamenting words Hyllus says

> What is yet to come no man can behold.[2]

Just as Heracles knows nothing of his own future, so Hyllus knows nothing of it. His words are no more than a pious hope, if indeed they are so much. But the audience might see in them another hint from the poet that the darkness and misery will not last for ever, that in the unseen future things may be better than now.

These are the faintest and most shadowy of hints. They might easily be neglected or missed, and they carry very little weight against the overwhelming disasters which have occurred and leave their ineffaceable trace even on those who survive them. The *Women of Trachis* remains a peculiarly painful play in which suffering is not less poignant because it is foreordained and foretold. The agony of Heracles and of Deianira is more tragic, in the modern sense, than that of Antigone; for Antigone chooses her own destiny and for that reason stirs admiration rather than pity. In this play the effect of unescapable disaster is enhanced because it falls on two characters so dissimilar as Heracles and Deianira.

[1] 1195-9 πολλὴν μὲν ὕλην τῆς βαθυρρίζου δρυὸς
κείραντα, πολλὸν δ' ἄρσεν' ἐκτεμόνθ' ὁμοῦ
ἄγριον ἔλαιον, σῶμα τοὐμὸν ἐμβαλεῖν,
καὶ πευκίνης λαβόντα λαμπάδος σέλας
πρῆσαι.

[2] 1270 τὰ μὲν οὖν μέλλοντ' οὐδεὶς ἀφορᾷ.

We see what a price has to be paid by the proud, independent man and the quiet, dependent woman. In both cases it is equally painful. Each character may show faults, but each is struck in that part of his life which most excites our admiration, Deianira in her love for her husband, Heracles in his superhuman strength and power. The one loses her home, the other his body. Sophocles displays almost the extremes of human suffering in these widely divergent characters. The fact that they are so different and that both are struck at the root of their lives adds to the great painfulness of the play. Yet against this violence Sophocles sets something which abates its horror and makes the play noble. The tenderness and love for her husband which is Deianira's to the last, the endurance of Heracles in his helpless and hopeless agony, stress the positive gains that emerge from the tragic situation and the waste.

V

KING OEDIPUS

NO Greek story has such pain and horror as that of Oedipus, who, after answering the riddle of the Sphinx and being made king of Thebes, discovered that he had killed his father and married his mother, then blinded himself and became an outcast beggar. The bare outlines must have been known to everyone. Homeric poetry had touched on the story;[1] it had been told in the lost epics of the *Thebaid* and *Oedipodea*; Aeschylus had devoted to it the second play of a trilogy on the House of Laius; it appealed strongly to Euripides, who wrote an *Oedipus* and dramatized related themes in his *Antigone* and *Phoenician Women*. Apart from its great dramatic and tragic possibilities the story appealed to poets because it raised dark questions about the treatment of men by the gods. Oedipus, who seemed the very type of fortune's favourite, was suddenly cast down and ruined. He was an eminent example of the prosperity which falls. In the prologue to his *Antigone* Euripides made this point in its simplest form:

> A happy man was Oedipus at first,
> Then he became the wretchedest of men,[2]

and it was inherent in any version of the story. Moreover, this appalling reversal of fortune was commonly attributed to the direct action of the gods. It had been foretold in oracles and duly came to pass. For Homer Oedipus' rule in Thebes was due to 'the dire counsels of the gods.'[3] For Pindar the most significant element in the tale was the fulfilment of the oracle:

> His fated son encountered Laius
> And slew him, fulfilling the oracle
> Spoken in Pytho long before.[4]

For Aeschylus the whole tragedy followed a divine plan,[5] and for Euripides fate determined Oedipus' life from the beginning.[6] It was almost inevitable that any poet who told the story should stress

---

[1] *Od.* xi. 271–80.
[2] Frs. 157–8 ἦν Οἰδίπους τὸ πρῶτον εὐτυχὴς ἀνήρ·
     εἶτ' ἐγένετ' αὖθις ἀθλιώτατος βροτῶν. Trs. B. B. Rogers.
[3] *Od.* xi. 276   θεῶν ὀλοὰς διὰ βουλάς.
[4] *Ol.* ii. 38–40   ἔκτεινε Λᾷον μόριμος υἱὸς
     συναντόμενος, ἐν δὲ Πυθῶνι χρησθὲν
     παλαίφατον τέλεσσεν.
[5] *Sept.* 766 ff.   [6] *Phoen.* 1595–6, 1614.

both the magnitude of Oedipus' fall and the part played in it by the gods.

Sophocles' play is so grand and so tragic that it is easy to misinterpret his fundamental ideas and to find explanations for the fall of Oedipus which are not really his. A story like this can hardly fail to invite some kind of explanation, and it is legitimate to look for Sophocles'. The tragic collapse of Oedipus cries for comment or justification. It could be justified in different ways, and in fact has been—as due to a hereditary doom or curse on the House of Laius; as a punishment for Oedipus' own pride; as caused by some mistake or faulty judgement of his. For each arguments may be found, but none is entirely satisfying. Sophocles might have used any of them. Of most he seems to have been in some degree conscious, so that he makes his characters assume one or other of them at different moments in the play. But if we follow him carefully, it is clear that not one of these theories meets every need, that Sophocles' central idea was something else. He had his own explanation for the fall of Oedipus, and it too had its roots in Greek thought.

Aeschylus explained the fall of Oedipus by hereditary guilt, by the sin of the father visited upon the son. Laius begat a child in defiance of the Delphic oracle, and the son paid for the father's fault. This explanation is embodied in the *Seven against Thebes*, and may be assumed to have provided the scheme of Aeschylus' *Oedipus*. It reappeared in Euripides' *Phoenician Women*, where Jocasta makes it the source of all the woes that befall the House of Laius.[1] The idea of such a hereditary curse was perfectly familiar to Sophocles, who made his Chorus apply it to Antigone, though it was not his own explanation of her sufferings. If he did not hold it in the *Antigone*, we should be wary of believing that he held it in *King Oedipus*. Nor does he seem to have held it. If he had meant to trace the sufferings of Oedipus to a hereditary doom, he would surely have stressed its source, Laius' defiance of the oracle which told him not to beget a child. But he does not. As he describes it, the oracle left no choice to Laius but simply foretold that he would be killed by his son (711–13). This change must be intentional. Sophocles must have felt that for Oedipus, as for Antigone, the theory of inherited doom was unsatisfactory. On the other hand, in two passages he makes Oedipus speak in language which has been taken to show that he believes himself the victim of such a doom. When Oedipus

[1] *Phoen.* 13 ff.

discovers that he has married his mother, he cries out that he is one who

> Stands naked now. Shamefully was I born:
> In shame I wedded: to my shame I slew.[1]

It has been thought that the shame of his birth proves that Laius was forbidden to have a child. But in the context this is surely wrong. For all three shames, of birth, wedlock, and killing, are on the same level; they are all things that should not have been. Oedipus sees himself as accursed in all three, but he puts no blame on Laius and certainly does not make him the cause of his sufferings. He means simply that it would have been better if he himself had never been born. Again, when Oedipus says:

> But now—but now—godless am I, the son
> Born of impurity, mate of my father's bed[2]

it is claimed that the 'impurity' refers to Laius' disobedience to Apollo. No doubt it does, but all that it proves is that Oedipus feels himself to be born of polluted stock. To these two passages we might add a third, when Oedipus speaks of himself as

>   the man,
> Proved of the gods polluted—Laius' son.[3]

The emphatic last words certainly gain in point if Oedipus feels that he comes of an accursed race. Nor need we question that he means this. But for him to think that the gods hate his family or that his father was impious is not the same as to see his whole destiny as determined by a single act of Laius which brings down the anger of heaven on father and son alike. The words are entirely natural in one who finds that he is the son of one known to be godless, but they mean no more than that, and tell nothing about the poet's main intention.

It might equally be thought that Oedipus is punished for his own presumptuous insolence, his ὕβρις. This could be maintained if Sophocles had made him kill Laius in wanton aggression. He would then be a murderer, and his punishment would be deserved. But Sophocles says something different. When Oedipus describes the killing, he shows that Laius was the aggressor and got what he deserved (800–13). The attack is made with violence

---

[1] 1184–5   ὅστις πέφασμαι φύς τ' ἀφ' ὧν οὐ χρῆν, ξὺν οἷς τ'
            οὐ χρῆν ὁμιλῶν, οὕς τέ μ' οὐκ ἔδει κτανών.

[2] 1360–1   νῦν δ' ἄθεος μέν εἰμ', ἀνοσίων δὲ παῖς,
            ὁμογενὴς δ' ἀφ' ὧν αὐτὸς ἔφυν τάλας.

[3] 1382–3   τὸν ἐκ θεῶν
            φανέντ' ἄναγνον καὶ γένους τοῦ Λαΐου.

(805). Legally Oedipus would be innocent of deliberate homicide, and by the law of Dracon would be acquitted.[1] He would be polluted and would have to be exiled, but that is another matter. Oedipus kills Laius in self-defence and is legally innocent of murder as he is morally innocent of anything that can be called insolence in the encounter. It has even been thought that a special exception was made for a man who killed another 'on a journey',[2] and if so, Oedipus would be acquitted. But the exception is doubtful, and we cannot put much trust in it. It is enough that Oedipus acts in self-defence, and even though he kills his own father and thereby incurs an appalling pollution, he is none the less innocent of any criminal intent or of acting consciously against what he knows to be right. It seems unlikely that Sophocles intended to portray Oedipus as punished for wanton pride; for the proud are punished by the gods for acts of quite a different character.

The view that Oedipus is punished for insolent pride can, however, be stated and defended in a different way. It can be claimed that he is punished not for the single act of killing Laius but for being in general proud and aggressive, as he certainly shows himself in the scenes with Teiresias and Creon. This is more persuasive and brings positive advantages. For in these scenes Oedipus transgresses the Mean and is almost swept away in a blind frenzy of pride when he accuses Teiresias of fomenting conspiracy (380 ff.) or wishes to kill Creon on a baseless suspicion (623). Moreover, the Chorus are distressed by Oedipus and afraid that he may prove to be a tyrant. They express their fears in guarded and general terms, but when they sing

> Insolence it is that breeds
> A tyrant[3]

it is easy to conclude that they have Oedipus in mind. He may not yet be a full-fledged tyrant, but he shows the signs. Yet despite this, we may doubt whether Sophocles intended his Oedipus to be punished for aggressive insolence. Even Teiresias does not speak of his coming woes as if they were a punishment; the Chorus do not return to their suspicion but form a different view of Oedipus' fall when it comes; Oedipus himself, in the horror of his humiliation, does not think that it is a punishment for pride. The only possible

---

[1] *S. I. G.* 111 καὶ ἐὰν μὴ ἐκ προνοίας κτείνῃ τίς τινα, φεύγειν.

[2] Lex ap. Dem. xxiii. 53 ἐν ὁδῷ καθελών. Cf. J. H. Lipsius, *Das attische Recht*, p. 616. ἐν ὁδῷ has been altered to ἐν συνόδῳ by Drerup and to ἐν ὅπλῳ by Keil. Aristot. *Rep. Ath.* 57. 3 and Plat. *Laws* ix. 865 A on similar cases of involuntary homicide suggest that the text is corrupt. [3] 873 ὕβρις φυτεύει τύραννον.

hint that he holds such a view is when he says to his children:

> Be your prayer to live
> Where fortune's modest measure is, a life
> That shall be better than your father's was.[1]

All that he does here is to contrast the modest, middle state
which he desires for his children with his own life thrown between
extremes of prosperity and downfall. He appeals to the familiar
doctrine:

> Seek not too much; the Mean is best in all things.[2]

He himself has known the extremes; his prayer is that his children
may avoid them and have an even, quiet life, far better than his
own. He is not concerned with his or with their pride. Proud he
may be, but pride is not the direct cause of his fall.

More subtle and more persuasive than any of these theories is
Aristotle's, that Oedipus falls through a mistake.[3] He does not say
that he means Sophocles' Oedipus, but his admiration for the play
is so great that it is hard not to think that he does. The question
is what he means by mistake. If he means simply an intellectual
mistake, an error of judgement, his own views would lead to
Oedipus' acquittal. For he says that such mistakes originate not
in vice or depravity but in ignorance of fact or circumstance, are
not voluntary, and should be forgiven.[4] Now it is perfectly true
that when Oedipus kills Laius he makes a mistake of this kind. He
acts in ignorance that Laius is his father, and this is the beginning
of his downfall. For it leads to the plague, the curse, the discovery
of the truth, and Oedipus' blinding of himself. Because of his
mistake Oedipus changes from good to bad fortune. It is, however,
possible that Aristotle means a different kind of mistake, something more like a fault of character which leads a man to see things
wrongly. He does not say this, but it is possible that he meant
it. If so, he came very near to the truth. For Oedipus' character
is undeniably connected with the form that his downfall takes.
But even this is not quite adequate. Neither interpretation of
Aristotle's view of a tragic mistake meets all the facts of the
play. Whichever we prefer, Aristotle still missed one vitally
important element in *King Oedipus*. He says nothing about the
part taken by the gods in the rise and fall of Oedipus. His omission

---

[1] 1512–14   νῦν Δὲ τοῦτ' εὔχεσθέ μοι,
                οὗ καιρὸς αἰεὶ ʒῆν, βίου Δὲ λᾠονος
                ὑμᾶς κυρῆσαι τοῦ φυτεύσαντος πατρός.

[2] Theogn. 401 μηΔὲν ἄγαν σπεύΔειν· καιρὸς Δ' ἐπὶ πᾶσιν ἄριστος.
Cf. Hes. *Op.* 694, Pind. *Pyth.* xi. 52–3, Theogn. 219–20, 331–2.

[3] *Poet.* 1453 a 16.   [4] *Nic. Eth.* 1135 b 12, 1110 b 31.

is understandable since he was, apparently, not interested in this aspect of tragedy and did not discuss it in his *Poetics*. But it seriously impairs his view. For though Oedipus' mistake in killing his father leads to other disasters, it is itself foreordained by the gods. The tragic career of Oedipus does not begin with it. His doom is fixed before his birth.

The activity of the gods is an essential part of *King Oedipus*. Oedipus is their victim. They have ordained a life of horror for him, and they see that he gets it. He is even the instrument by which their plans are fulfilled. The prophecy that he will kill his father and marry his mother leaves him no escape. He fulfils it in ignorance of what he is doing, but he must fulfil it. In this respect he is like Heracles in the *Women of Trachis*. Both do what has been foretold and cannot do otherwise. The difference between them is in the oracles that concern them. For Heracles the oracle concerns only his death. The thought of it does not haunt or shape his life. He has long known it, but has interpreted it favourably, almost dismissed it from his mind. But Oedipus' oracle is not even ambiguous, though for a moment he plays with the idea that it may be (969–70). It can have only one meaning. That is why he tries to avoid its fulfilment by leaving Corinth. Nor is it concerned merely with his end. It shapes his whole life. Because of it Jocasta tries to have him exposed in infancy, and later he himself leaves Corinth to come, so disastrously, to Thebes. At both stages an effort is made to avoid what has been foretold, and both efforts are frustrated. So in the play itself, when the crisis of revelation is near, false hopes and beliefs delay it until at last it comes and is all the more horrible because it has been delayed. The fated doom of Oedipus is more insistent than that of Heracles. It dogs him at every step. Nor does it come through an external power. He fulfils it himself. It is he who curses the murderer of Laius and takes the lead in finding who he is, he who blinds himself when he discovers the truth. The foreordained sufferings of Oedipus are far more closely interwoven with his life than the foreordained end of Heracles is with his. More even than the *Women of Trachis*, the play shows how human life is at the mercy of the gods.

The part which the gods take in the fall of Oedipus is emphasized by Sophocles. Jocasta goes back to the oracle given to Laius

that he should die
Some day, slain by a son of him and me.[1]

---

[1] 713–14   ὡς αὐτὸν ἕξοι μοῖρα πρὸς παιδὸς θανεῖν,
ὅστις γένοιτ' ἐμοῦ τε κἀκείνου πάρα.

At the very start of Oedipus' existence, even before it, the gods have decreed that he shall kill his father. Later at Corinth he hears rumours about his parentage. He inquires of Apollo, who tells him:

> Thou shalt defile thy mother, show mankind
> A brood begot by thee intolerable,
> And shalt be thy own father's murderer.[1]

His doom is unqualified and unambiguous. In due course the oracle is fulfilled; Oedipus kills Laius and marries Jocasta. In both cases he acts in ignorance and innocence. He kills Laius in self-defence. He seems to marry Jocasta, as he inherits the kingdom of Thebes, as a reward for solving the riddle of the Sphinx. Sophocles does not directly say so, but this was the story as Euripides knew it,[2] and it is not incompatible with Oedipus' own words:

> To-day, since I am King where he was King,
> The husband of his bride.[3]

At each stage the gods' will is fulfilled. It cannot be otherwise. When the gods make a decision, it cannot be cancelled or withdrawn.[4]

Sophocles' play deals directly with Oedipus' discovery of the truth and with the effect of this on him. This crisis in his fortunes is sufficient to provide a complete tragedy in which he is changed from a powerful and beloved king into a blind and abhorred outcast. In it Oedipus finds out what he has done and who he is. The process of discovery, intensely exciting and painful as it is, would not make its full impression if what is discovered did not arouse horror and even dismay. The lurking, awful truth that Oedipus has killed his father and married his mother comes to light and overwhelms him. It is therefore important to see what a Greek audience would feel about Oedipus' parricide and incest. For the tragic power of the play depends on the horror which these evoke. Oedipus is not legally or morally guilty of murder or of incest since he acted in ignorance. But he is something no less horrible; he is a polluted being, a man to be shunned as if he literally had some revolting and infectious plague. So far

---

[1] 791–3   ὡς μητρὶ μὲν χρείη με μειχθῆναι, γένος δ'
ἄτλητον ἀνθρώποισι δηλώσοιμ' ὁρᾶν,
φονεὺς δ' ἐσοίμην τοῦ φυτεύσαντος πατρός.

[2] *Phoen.* 45–54.

[3] 259–60   ἔχων μὲν ἀρχάς, ἃς ἐκεῖνος εἶχε πρίν,
ἔχων δὲ λέκτρα.

[4] Soph. fr. 414.

as the gods are concerned, it makes no difference whether he has
acted in ignorance or not. Incest and parricide pollute him. Even
Euripides, who treats Heracles with much sympathy when he has
killed his children, has to admit that he is defiled and must be
purified.[1] Offences against the gods had always to be atoned, and
until they were, the offender was an abominable being who
carried plague and destruction with him. So Antiphon says that
the presence of a homicide causes barrenness in the land and brings
disaster to men's undertakings.[2] Blood-guiltiness was felt to be
a physical reality; it made no difference whether it had been incurred voluntarily or not. For it was believed that in any violent
death the dead man called for vengeance. Plato explicitly says that
even when such a death is inflicted involuntarily, the dead man
'is angry with the doer'.[3] What applied to violent death applied
still more to parricide, which violates the sacred bonds of the family
and makes the wrath of the slain all the greater. Oedipus, who
has killed his father, is a thing of abomination. He himself feels
intensely the horror of his position, and others feel it hardly less.
Above all the gods feel it, as they show when they send the plague
to Thebes. The parricide is impious and unholy. For a great king
to find himself such is enough to make a tragedy.

Oedipus has also committed incest with his mother. This too
is a breach of the divine laws, and his ignorance in committing it
does not help him to avoid pollution or the wrath of the gods.
Xenophon's Socrates expressly says that such unions are against
the Unwritten Laws and are punished even in this world.[4] It is
true that the punishment which he names, the production of un-
healthy children, hardly meets the case, but there is no doubt
of the general horror with which incest was regarded. It was
indeed thought to be so grossly against nature that it could hardly
exist; for, as Xenophon says elsewhere, 'fear and law are enough to
stop such love'.[5] The normal feeling about it is that of the orator
who regards the alleged relations of the younger Alcibiades with
his sister as one of the worst things in an utterly depraved and
impious life.[6] Plato thought that such unions were 'hateful to the
gods and the most shameful of shameful things', and that it was
right for those who, like Oedipus, Thyestes, and Macareus, have
found themselves to have committed incest in ignorance to wish
to kill themselves.[7] Even to dream of such things was an evil sign,
and Plato says that in his sleep the tyrannical man does not shrink

[1] *Her.* 1322 ff.   [2] *Tetr.* 1. i. 10.   [3] *Laws* ix. 865 d.   [4] *Mem.* iv. 4. 20 ff.
[5] *Cyr.* v. 1. 10.   [6] Lys. xiv. 28 and 41.   [7] *Laws* viii. 838 c.

from trying to sleep with his mother,[1] thinking perhaps of the dream which the Athenian tyrant, Hippias, had before Marathon,[2] but certainly regarding even a dream of this kind as appalling and polluting. Incest, even though involuntary, excited the same kind of horror as parricide. The mother, with whom her son slept, seems to have felt towards him much as the slain father felt towards his killer. Her curse was on him. So Homer makes Oedipus' mother bequeath woes to him,

> Many indeed, nay all that a mother's Furies accomplish.[3]

Her vengeance is at work, and that is why Teiresias tells Oedipus that he will be pursued by a double curse:

> Twin-scourged, a mother's Fury and thy Father's,
> Swift, fatal, dogging thee, shall drive thee forth.[4]

When the most holy ties of the family are broken, the injured parents become avenging spirits and wreak their anger on the ignorant sinner.

It is wrong to think that the pollution exists only in the human mind, that Sophocles did not believe in it but built his tragedy about Oedipus' natural horror at what he has done. Oedipus certainly has these feelings, but we are expected to share them and to accept the pollution as an undeniable fact. This is proved by the plague which the gods send because the land is polluted by the death of Laius and the presence of his slayer in it (97–8). His death must be avenged either by the death or by the exile of the slayer (100–1). A plague as punishment for bloodshed is quite usual. Herodotus says that when the Lemnians killed their children by Athenian wives, their land ceased to bear fruit and their women and flocks to bear young.[5] Antiphon lays down that the presence of an unpunished murderer brings famine and disaster to a city.[6] The symptoms of blighted crops and miscarriages are to be found in Sophocles' Thebes. The Priest speaks of the land:

> A blight is on her budding fruits, a blight
> On pastured cattle, and the barren pangs
> Of women,[7]

---

[1] *Rep.* ix. 571 c. [2] Hdt. vi. 107. 1.

[3] *Od.* xi. 280 πολλὰ μάλ', ὅσσα τε μητρὸς Ἐρινύες ἐκτελέουσι.

[4] 417–18 καί σ' ἀμφιπλὴξ μητρός τε καὶ τοῦ σοῦ πατρὸς
ἐλᾷ ποτ' ἐκ γῆς τῆσδε δεινόπους ἀρά.

[5] vi. 139. 1. [6] *Tetr.* I. i. 10.

[7] 25–7 φθίνουσα μὲν κάλυξιν ἐγκάρποις χθονός,
φθίνουσα δ' ἀγέλαις βουνόμοις, τόκοισί τε
ἀγόνοις γυναικῶν.

and the Chorus sing:

> The fruits of the mighty mother Earth increase not.
> Women from their tempest of cries and travail-pangs
> Struggle in vain. . . no birth-joy followeth.[1]

These curses are sent from the gods. This plague is not like that of 430–429 B.C. whose details Thucydides noted with meticulous science. This comes from an older, more god-ridden world. Its characteristics are such as Hesiod noted as coming to men when their rulers are proud and sinful.[2] Yet the plague of Thebes and the historical plague of Athens have one point in common which shows how differently their recorders judged them. Thucydides tells how the sick crowded to supplication in the temples and to divination, just as the Priest tells of the crowd sitting

> at the shrines of Pallas,
> And by Ismenus' oracle of fire[3]

and the first great song of the Chorus is a kind of Paean to the gods asking for help. But while Thucydides emphasizes the futility of the supplications—'all was useless, and in the end they gave them up'[4]—Sophocles indicates that only the gods can cure what the gods have sent. Creon is sent to Delphi with this thought, and the message of polluting bloodshed with which he returns shows that the plague is an act of the gods, an assertion of their rights and of their inviolable laws. If the play was written, as has been thought, soon after the plague at Athens, it is possible that Sophocles noted the irreligion which it engendered and was careful to draw a different lesson from his own plague.

Oedipus is polluted. Custom recognized the existence of cases like his and prescribed what should be done. As one who had the blood of a kinsman on his hands, he would by Attic law have to be exiled for a period.[5] In answer to Creon the oracle seems to have ordered such exile for the murderer of Laius:

> Phoebus the King enjoins with clear command:—
> A fell pollution, fed on Theban soil,
> Ye shall drive out, not feed it past all cure.[6]

---

[1] 171–3   οὔτε γὰρ ἔκγονα
            κλυτᾶς χθονὸς αὔξεται οὔτε τόκοισιν
                          ἰηίων
            καμάτων ἀνέχουσι γυναῖκες.

[3] 20–1   πρός τε Παλλάδος Διπλοῖς   [2] Op. 238–47.
            ναοῖς, ἐπ᾽ Ἰσμηνοῦ τε μαντείᾳ σποδῷ.

[4] Thuc. ii. 47. 4.   [5] Schol. Eur. Hipp. 35.

[6] 96–8   ἄνωγεν ἡμᾶς Φοῖβος ἐμφανῶς ἄναξ
            μίασμα χώρας, ὡς τεθραμμένον χθονὶ
            ἐν τῇδ᾽, ἐλαύνειν μηδ᾽ ἀνήκεστον τρέφειν.

By these rules Oedipus should be exiled and purified. So too his impiety in marrying his mother would also demand not punishment but atonement. For his action is involuntary and resembles the class described by Aristotle as including Aeschylus' involuntary profanation of the Mysteries. These may be forgiven, but none the less 'an action of this kind must be painful and involve repentance'.[1] The doer is naturally pained by what he has done and sorry for it. We might expect Oedipus to make amends and so to find peace with his country, with himself, with the gods who guard his family. In any case the doom of a blind beggar which falls to him seems far harsher than anything we should expect in atonement for what he has done in ignorance. Sophocles has to explain how his doom comes so heavily to Oedipus. Though it has sometimes escaped notice, his explanation is clear.

The truth is that Oedipus lays a curse on the murderer of Laius, and the curse falls on himself. It has to be fulfilled. Since it calls down appalling penalties, his own fate is much worse than it might otherwise have been. Instead of exile and purification, he must be deprived of all rights and ties, and suffer misery and poverty. The oracle does not order such a doom, but once Oedipus has pronounced his curse, there is no escape from it. He is the instrument to make his own fate worse than it might have been. In his desire to do what the gods require he brings on himself a heavier punishment. He sees this when he first begins to realize that he may be the murderer of Laius. That is why he calls himself the most miserable of men and says:

> And this—'twas I,
> No other, on myself invoked the curse.[2]

He says much the same when he has blinded himself; he has shut himself off from everything in Thebes:

> whereof, alas!
> I robbed myself—myself, I spoke that word.[3]

He knows that his own curse will add to the burden of his suffering.

This curse would be entirely real to the audience. The solemnity and elaboration with which Oedipus pronounces it show that Sophocles meant it to be taken with great seriousness and close

---

[1] *Nic. Eth.* 1111 a 20.
[2] 819–20   καὶ τάδ' οὔτις ἄλλος ἦν
ἢ 'γὼ 'π' ἐμαυτῷ τάσδ' ἀρὰς ὁ προστιθείς.
[3] 1381   ἀπεστέρησ' ἐμαυτόν, αὐτὸς ἐννέπων.

attention. Oedipus curses with a double authority, sacred and
profane. He gives his qualifications:

> Thus I take up my fight for the dead man's cause
> And for the god.[1]

The god is the Delphian Apollo who has commanded the punishment of the murderers. Because Oedipus acts as his agent, his curse
is formidable and irresistible like that which the Amphictyons,
at Apollo's suggestion, laid upon themselves if they failed to protect Delphi. It called down barrenness, defeat, and the utter
destruction of themselves, their households, and their descendants.[2]
On the other hand, Oedipus curses on behalf of Laius, as head of
the State and of the family. Great powers are again with him and
behind him. In the family a father could curse with terrible effect,
as when Amyntor cursed Phoenix for sleeping with his concubine:

> The gods accomplished his curses,
> Zeus, dweller under the earth, and awful Persephoneia.[3]

But Oedipus is also head of the State, and this too gives him powers
to curse. States enforced their ordinances with curses, and Plato
follows usage when he sanctifies his laws with a curse.[4] Oedipus
does the right thing, and even follows correct precedent when he
enumerates the ancestors of the dead man whom he helps and
whose family he represents:

> The child of Labdacus and Polydorus,
> Agenor's offspring and great Cadmus' son.[5]

So Herodotus' Xerxes swears that he will avenge himself on the
Athenians and shows his authority by quoting the names of his
ancestors for nine generations.[6] No less kingly and correct is the
way in which Oedipus closes with a threat to those who disobey
him that their wives and fields shall be barren (269–72). For Cambyses, in exacting a promise from his nobles, asks that if they carry
it out their land may bear fruit and their flocks and wives offspring,
but if they fail, 'I call down the opposite of these things to happen
to you'.[7] The whole proceedings of Oedipus' curse are in order,
right, and real.

---

[1] 244–5   ἐγὼ μὲν οὖν τοιόσδε τῷ τε δαίμονι
             τῷ τ᾿ ἀνδρὶ τῷ θανόντι σύμμαχος πέλω.

[2] Aeschin. iii. 111.

[3] Il. ix. 456–7   θεοὶ δ᾿ ἐτέλειον ἐπαράς,
             Ζεύς τε καταχθόνιος καὶ ἐπαινὴ Περσεφόνεια.

[4] Laws ix. 871 b.

[5] 267–8   τῷ Λαβδακείῳ παιδὶ Πολυδώρου τε καὶ
             τοῦ πρόσθε Κάδμου τοῦ πάλαι τ᾿ Ἀγήνορος.

[6] vii. 11. 2.   [7] Id. iii. 65. 7.

The curse is both defensive and offensive. It protects the city from pollution and it imposes penalties on the murderer. The order that he shall not be addressed nor received by anyone nor be allowed to take part in prayers or sacrifice or lustral rites (238 ff.) follows Attic practice as Dracon had settled it.[1] The murderer's presence at such ceremonies might well do harm, and as Antiphon says, it is dangerous for a defiled person to profane divine precincts or to pollute the innocent by sitting at their tables.[2] This injunction by Oedipus defends his people. From it he advances to the offensive against the murderer and demands

> As was the deed, so be his life accurst![3]

He must be shut out from human life and perish miserably. Since Oedipus is himself the murderer, we should conclude that he will end in such a way. But does he? Is the curse really fulfilled on him? When he first begins to suspect that he has killed Laius, he certainly believes that it will be (817–20). But all depends on the end of the play. It is easy to lay stress on Creon's kind feelings for Oedipus, to show that the Chorus pity him. All that is true. But human behaviour does not alter what has to be, and the gods demand that Oedipus shall carry out the curse which he has so solemnly pronounced in their name. We may be sure that at the end of the play his woes are not finished. His departure from the stage is the prelude to his departure to a life of wandering. In *Oedipus at Colonus* Sophocles was to tell more about Oedipus, and differently. But we cannot look to it for enlightenment on *King Oedipus*. Here the future of Oedipus is forecast by Teiresias. Just as the seer is right in his knowledge of the hidden past, so he must be right about the future:

> A beggar, once so rich, in a foreign land
> A wanderer, with a staff groping his way.[4]

Teiresias has already said that Oedipus will be driven out by the united curse of his father and mother (416–17), and this curse is now strengthened by Oedipus' own curse. He becomes the instrument for its fulfilment. It means that he will be turned out of Thebes and sent, blind and helpless, into the wild places of the mountains. Such is the fate in store for him, and though the play closes without emphatically proclaiming it, we must assume

---

[1] *Dem.* xx. 158.   [2] *Tetr.* I. i. 10.

[3] 248   κακὸν κακῶς νιν ἄμορον ἐκτρῖψαι βίον.

[4] 455–6   καὶ πτωχὸς ἀντὶ πλουσίου ξένην ἔπι
σκήπτρῳ προδεικνὺς γαῖαν ἐμπορεύσεται.

that it awaits Oedipus. If Oedipus had not cursed himself, he would surely have suffered less heavily.

Throughout the gods' will is done, and in the usual way. Pollution follows a violent death and must be removed; a curse pronounced with full authority is amply fulfilled; oracles which seemed unlikely to be true are proved all too true; human pity is stirred but can do nothing against the irrefragable decrees of the gods. That Sophocles intended to show the gods at work is seen not only by the part which they take in events but by the dramatic effects which the poet secures by displaying the futility of Jocasta's and Oedipus' scepticism. It is Jocasta's disbelief which leads to Oedipus' discovery that he may be the slayer of Laius (707 ff.), his own dismissal of the oracles (971–2) which precedes the revelation of his true origin, his wild hope that he is the son of Luck (1080 ff.) which comes just before the final shattering truth. The play shows the power of the gods at every important turn in its development and leaves no doubt about the poet's theological intention.

King Oedipus shows the humbling of a great and prosperous man by the gods. This humbling is not deserved; it is not a punishment for insolence, nor in the last resort is it due to any fault of judgement or character in the man. The gods display their power because they will. But since they display it, man may draw a salutary lesson. This is kept till the end of the play when the Chorus, or perhaps Oedipus himself, point to the extent of his fall, and comment:

> And, being mortal, think on that last day of death,
> Which all must see, and speak of no man's happiness
> Till, without sorrow, he hath passed the goal of life.[1].

That this moral was thought suitable is clear from its close imitation at the end of Euripides' *Phoenician Women*, though it may not be from his hand. After the hideous and harrowing events this finale of *King Oedipus* may seem a little tame. Yet it provides a quiet end, such as the Greeks liked, and it is Sophocles' conclusion on what has taken place. The old lesson of Solon which it repeats accounts, simply enough, for undeserved suffering[2] and may be used of Oedipus as Herodotus used it of Croesus. That it meant something to Sophocles may also be seen from a fragment of his *Tyndareos*:

[1] 1528–30   ὥστε θνητὸν ὄντ' ἐκείνην τὴν τελευταίαν ἰδεῖν
                 ἡμέραν ἐπισκοποῦντα μηδέν' ὀλβίζειν, πρὶν ἂν
                 τέρμα τοῦ βίου περάσῃ μηδὲν ἀλγεινὸν παθών.

[2] Hdt. i. 32; cf. Eur. *Andr.* 100 ff., *Tro.* 510, *Heracl.* 865.

We should not, when a man is fortunate,
Call his luck good, until his whole life's course
Is finished and has reached its final end.
For in the shortest, smallest space of time
Fate's evil gift destroys his wealth and bliss,
Just when it changes and the gods decide.[1]

The context of this and its application are not known, but its
fullness shows that Sophocles understood the idea and made use
of it. Its lesson is that men must be modest in prosperity and remember that at any moment the gods may destroy it. It is a warning not so much against pride as against any confidence or sense
of security. To drive this warning home the gods have made an
example of Oedipus. From the very beginning he has been chosen
to show by his misfortunes the need for modesty in times of
success.

Such, reduced to its most abstract and impersonal form, is the
theological scheme in *King Oedipus*. In it there is nothing new. It
would be accepted by men so different as Herodotus, Pindar, and
Euripides. What counts in it is the opportunity which it gives of
presenting human greatness in disaster and evoking tragic emotions
from such a spectacle. It is much more tragic than the scheme
which informs the *Antigone*. But its chief interest is the particular
form which it takes. It shows the fortunes of an individual man in
an intensely dramatic form. And in doing this it naturally raises
questions about the justice of the gods, who treat Oedipus simply
as a means to enforce a lesson on others. It is not like this that we
expect the gods to act. Sophocles, perhaps, might not have felt
our qualms, but he sees the difficulties of his theological scheme
and does something to answer possible critics. When the gods
humiliate Oedipus they create a situation of great complexity in
which much is concerned beside the general main lesson. There is
above all the individual problem of Oedipus himself. If they force
him to break their own laws, as he does when he kills his father
and marries his mother, they should provide means of reconciliation by which he, polluted as he is, can make his peace with them
and restore the breach in the divine order which he has made.
Sophocles was conscious of this need and took steps to meet it.

[1] Fr. 646   οὐ χρή ποτ' εὖ πράσσοντος ὀλβίσαι τύχας
ἀνδρός, πρὶν αὐτῷ παντελῶς ἤδη βίος
Διεκπεραθῇ καὶ τελευτήσῃ δρόμον.
ἐν γὰρ βραχεῖ καθεῖλε κὠλίγῳ χρόνῳ
πάμπλουτον ὄλβον δαίμονος κακοῦ δόσις,
ὅταν μεταστῇ καὶ θεοῖς δοκῇ τάδε.

The play shows not only the crisis which humbles Oedipus and reveals to him that he is polluted but also the first steps by which he begins to overcome the gulf between himself and the gods, to find again a place in the ordered system of things. In this the gods help him.

This reconciliation is the meaning of Oedipus' action in blinding himself. Hard enough to hear of from the Messenger, it is almost unendurable when the king comes out of the palace with his bleeding sightless eyes. The moment is of such tragic import that it is easy to assess its meaning wrongly and to miss what Sophocles intends to show by it. Both ancient and modern critics have thought that Oedipus' action is wrong and should be condemned. There is something to be said for their view, and it must be considered seriously. It goes back to Aelian, who condemns Oedipus because he tries 'to heal by an incurable evil evils that have already occurred'.[1] Aelian appeals to a common rule of Greek morality that it was wrong to try to cure one evil by another,[2] to try to make a right out of two wrongs. Sophocles himself was familiar with the notion and makes the Chorus of his *Ajax* use it when his hero calls on them to kill him. In a fragment of his *Aleadae* the doctrine is stated in plain gnomic words:

> All men's affairs are sick in such a case,
> When they would do a wrong to heal a wrong.[3]

The maxim rings authoritatively, even if it does not express the poet's own opinion. Aelian appeals to a firm body of support. Yet in *King Oedipus* no character condemns Oedipus on this ground, and we have no reason to think that Sophocles did. Like all maxims, it had its exceptions, and when Oedipus blinded himself, it may have been one of them. Modern critics have followed another line, and contend that in blinding himself Oedipus sins against the doctrine that men should accept what the gods decide. The doctrine is well established even for Sophocles, in whose *Tereus* someone said:

> Manifest, Procne, is its pain, and yet
> Since the gods send it, men must not complain.[4]

---

[1] *N. A.* iii. 47 κακῷ ἀνηκέστῳ Ἰᾶσθαι κακὰ τὰ ἤδη παρελθόντα.

[2] Aesch. fr. 349, Eur. *Hec.* 306, Thuc. v. 65. 2, Hdt. iii. 53. 4.

[3] Fr. 77   ἐνταῦθα μέντοι πάντα τἀνθρώπων νοσεῖ,
            κακῶς ὅταν θέλωσιν Ἰᾶσθαι κακά.

[4] Fr. 585   ἀλγεινά, Πρόκνη, δῆλον· ἀλλ' ὁμῶς χρεὼν
            τὰ θεῖα θνητοὺς ὄντας εὐπετῶς φέρειν.

Cf. frs. 680 and 964.

Resignation before the gods' will is familiar. It follows that if Oedipus resists the doom which they have sent, he is wrong. The argument looks irreproachable, but it is not. There is no real evidence that in blinding himself Oedipus resists the will of the gods or refuses to accept his lot. If he had so chosen, Sophocles could have pointed this lesson. But he gives a different explanation and invites a different judgement.

The chief witness against the innocence of Oedipus is the Messenger who reports the death of Jocasta and the blinding of Oedipus. Before he tells his story, he says with noble emphasis

> Can Ister or can Phasis wash this house—
> I trow not—with their waters, from the guilt
> It hides. . . Yet soon shall publish to the light
> Fresh, not unpurposed evil. 'Tis the woe
> That we ourselves have compassed, hurts the most.[1]

The Messenger makes a distinction between the old and the new pollution in the House of Laius. The new, which will soon be revealed, is 'not unpurposed'; there seems to be a distinction between the old incest and parricide, which were committed unwittingly, and the new violence of Jocasta's suicide and Oedipus' blinding. The distinction follows that of Attic law and suggests that the new evils are blameworthy. In fact the Messenger is thought to condemn Oedipus for blinding himself as he does not condemn him for his other acts. Yet this view, convincing as it may seem, is open to objection. First, it is extremely dangerous to assume that the Messenger is the voice of Sophocles. Sophocles has a way of suggesting that his characters have acted wrongly and then proceeding to show that they are right, as he does with the Chorus and Antigone. Secondly, the Messenger refers in general to what has taken place in the palace. It has incurred a new pollution, and so far as pollution is concerned, only Jocasta can be in question. Oedipus' violence against himself creates no new pollution. Thirdly, and most important, the Messenger speaks not about the rights and wrongs of what has happened but about the miseries Oedipus and Jocasta have brought on themselves. What moves him is not the wickedness of what has been done but its horror, and a special element in this is that the sufferers have inflicted the

---

[1] 1227–31　οἶμαι γὰρ οὔτ' ἂν Ἴστρον οὔτε Φᾶσιν ἂν
νίψαι καθαρμῷ τήνδε τὴν στέγην, ὅσα
κεύθει, τὰ δ' αὐτίκ' ἐς τὸ φῶς φανεῖ κακὰ
ἑκόντα κοὐκ ἄκοντα· τῶν δὲ πημονῶν
μάλιστα λυποῦσ' αἱ φανῶσ' αὐθαίρετοι.

injuries on themselves. The Messenger does not condemn Oedipus
for blinding himself, nor does the poet through him.

Sophocles gives his own opinion and explanation in a more indi-
rect but more impressive way. He tells us what happens and then
makes his characters comment upon it. It is that when Oedipus
blinds himself, he is prompted and guided by a *daimón*, a divine
spirit which rules his actions for him. The word has no exact
equivalent in English and is variously translated 'fate', 'destiny',
'god', and 'spirit'. It has something of all these in it. It is a supernatural power which is inferior to a true god and is closely concerned with an individual man's fortunes. The first hint of it
appears when Oedipus finds that he himself may have killed
Laius:

> If any judge my life and find therein
> Malignant stars at work, he hath the truth.[1]

This is no more than a hint. It is soon followed by another. When
the Chorus, not yet knowing that Oedipus has blinded himself,
but deeply horrified by the revelations about him, lament his life,
they comment:

> Thine, O unhappy Oedipus,
> Thine is the fatal destiny,
> That bids me call no mortal creature blest.[2]

In the Messenger's story this spirit is at work and forces himself on
the attention. Supernatural powers drive Oedipus to find the place
where Jocasta has hanged herself:

> As thus he raged, some god—
> 'Twas none of us—guided him where she lay[3]

and when he bursts in upon her, he is, as it were, led by some unseen power:

> And he, as guided, with a terrible shout
> Leapt at her double door.[4]

[1] 828-9   ἀλλ' οὐκ ἀπ' ὤμου ταῦτα Δαίμονός τις ἂν
κρίνων ἐπ' ἀνδρὶ τῷδ' ἂν ὀρθοίη λόγον;

[2] 1193-6   τὸν σόν τοι παράδειγμ' ἔχων,
τὸν σὸν Δαίμονα, τὸν σόν, ὦ
τλᾶμον Οἰδιπόδα, βροτῶν
οὐδὲν μακαρίζω.

[3] 1258   λυσσῶντι Δ' αὐτῷ Δαιμόνων Δείκνυσί τις.

[4] 1260-1   Δεινὸν Δ' ἀΰσας ὡς ὑφηγητοῦ τινος
πύλαις Διπλαῖς ἐνήλατ'.

When Oedipus comes out blinded to the Chorus, they ask him:

> What evil Spirit from afar,
> O Oedipus, O wretched!
> Leapt on thee, to destroy.[1]

There is indeed no reason why they should refer to this spirit, but the poet seems to think it is necessary to keep the idea before our minds. A few minutes later Oedipus speaks to it himself:

> Alas! Curse of my Life, how far
> Thy leap hath carried thee.[2]

The Chorus now connect the blinding with the work of a spirit, and ask Oedipus how he came to act like this:

> Oh, dreadful deed! How wert thou steeled to quench
> Thy vision thus? What Spirit came on thee?[3]

Towards the end when Oedipus thanks Creon for bringing the children to him and wishes better fortune for him than he has had himself, he still dwells on the *daimôn*:

> Be happy, and for treading this good way
> A kinder fate than mine defend thy steps.[4]

The *daimôn*, the spirit, is undeniably given prominence. It is an active power which determines Oedipus' life and makes him act as he does, especially when he blinds himself.

In a theological conception of this kind too much precision is hardly to be expected. But the *daimôn* works on and through Oedipus and has a definite enough character. It is almost his individual destiny, his accompanying spirit, the power which arranges his life for him. Such an idea may have been familiar in the fifth century, as it certainly was in the fourth when Plato refers to 'each man's spirit which has taken possession of him in life'[5] and anticipates some famous lines of Menander:

> A spirit stands at each man's side at birth
> To guide him through the mysteries of life.[6]

---

[1] 1300–2   τίς ὁ πηδήσας
μείζονα Δαίμων τῶν μακίστων
πρὸς σῇ Δυσδαίμονι μοίρᾳ;

[2] 1311   ἰὼ Δαῖμον, ἵν' ἐξήλου.

[3] 1327–8   ὦ Δεινὰ Δράσας, πῶς ἔτλης τοιαῦτα σὰς
ὄψεις μαρᾶναι; τίς σ' ἐπῆρε Δαιμόνων;

[4] 1478–9   ἀλλ' εὐτυχοίης, καί σε τῆσδε τῆς ὁδοῦ
Δαίμων ἀμεῖνον ἤ 'μὲ φρουρήσας τύχοι.

[5] *Phaedo* 107 d.

[6] Fr. 550   ἅπαντι Δαίμων ἀνδρὶ συμπαρίσταται·
εὐθὺς γενομένῳ μυσταγωγὸς τοῦ βίου.

The orator Lysias had something of the same kind in mind when he spoke of 'the spirit who is master of our destiny',[1] and that this was a fairly common view may be deduced from Socrates' denial of it in the *Republic*, where his statement 'A spirit shall not choose you but you shall choose a spirit',[2] is surely unexpected and unusual. We need not be too precise about the spirit which works on Oedipus, but it is at least compatible with such spirits as these. It is a kind of supernatural power, and it is assumed by the Messenger, the Chorus, and Oedipus himself to be at work at least when he blinds himself, and probably also throughout his life.

The fact that Oedipus is driven or instigated by a *daimôn* to blind himself does not necessarily make him right. A *daimôn* might be a power for evil. But Sophocles follows a different plan. He makes the *daimôn* an instrument of the gods to carry out their demands. That it could stand in this subordinate position to the gods is shown by Pindar, who says to Arcesilas, king of Cyrene:

> The great mind of Zeus
> Is pilot of the doom of the men whom he loves.[3]

There the doom, the *daimôn*, is favourable and brings happiness; it is the agent of Zeus and obeys his will. It could also work ill, as it does in the lines already quoted from the *Tyndareos* where the *daimôn* starts to destroy a prosperous house when the gods decide that it shall. Oedipus' *daimôn* certainly seems to work ill, and it too is the instrument of the gods. Sophocles hints this at first vaguely, when Oedipus realizes that he has killed Laius and breaks out in the terrible words:

> O Zeus, what is it thou wilt do to me?[4]

Here he ascribes to Zeus the fate which later he ascribes to a cruel *daimôn*. This by itself carries little weight, but later Oedipus makes the position clearer. In the first moment after his appearance from the palace he claims that Apollo is really responsible for what has happened:

> Apollo! 'Twas Apollo, friends,
> Willed the evil, willed, and brought the agony to pass!
> And yet the hand that struck was mine, mine only, wretched.[5]

[1] *Epitaph.* 78.   [2] *Rep.* 617 e.
[3] *Pyth.* v. 122–3   Διός τοι νόος μέγας κυβερνᾷ
                        δαίμον' ἀνδρῶν φίλων·
[4] 738   ὦ Ζεῦ, τί μου δρᾶσαι βεβούλευσαι πέρι;
[5] 1329–32   Ἀπόλλων τάδ' ἦν, Ἀπόλλων, φίλοι,
                        ὁ κακὰ κακὰ τελῶν ἐμὰ τάδ' ἐμὰ πάθεα·
                        ἔπαισε δ' αὐτόχειρ νιν οὔ-
                        τις, ἀλλ' ἐγὼ τλάμων.

The hand that works the destruction is that of Oedipus, but the power behind the action is Apollo. This does not contradict the part assigned elsewhere to the *daimôn*. The *daimôn* bridges the gulf between Apollo who decides and dictates and the human agent Oedipus who carries out the decision. Apollo ordains; Oedipus fulfils. The *daimôn* connects the first cause and the final agent.

Oedipus, then, acts under the influence and pressure of a supernatural power which is in its turn determined by the gods, Zeus or Apollo. If the gods decide to treat a man like this, they have their reasons for it, though these vary with circumstances and persons. It would, for instance, be possible to keep the main lines of the scheme and to assume that the gods make Oedipus mad before destroying him. In that case his blindness is inflicted in a madness sent by the gods. This would be quite familiar to Greek minds. Men who destroyed themselves were thought to be all but mad. Herodotus gives two examples, Cambyses who died from a self-inflicted wound and Cleomenes who killed himself in a peculiarly horrible way. Both were more or less mad, and in both this madness was in some quarters believed to be a punishment for impious acts, to Cambyses for killing the Bull of Apis and to Cleomenes for blasphemous behaviour at Argos. So some might think that Oedipus too is punished for impious acts by a mad fury which impels him to blind himself. This would be consonant with the belief that the gods make mad those whom they wish to destroy. An anonymous tragic fragment states the position:

> When anger of the gods assails a man,
> It does this first,—it empties from his heart
> All noble sense, and turns it to worse thoughts
> That he may choose the wrong in ignorance.[1]

Such seems to have been Aeschylus' explanation of Oedipus' action. His Oedipus acts in 'madness of heart'.[2] Sophocles might have adopted this view, and he was conscious that it was tenable. For when the Chorus first see Oedipus after he has blinded himself, they suggest that he has acted in madness:

> Alas, unhappy one,
> What madness came on thee?[3]

---

[1] Tr. Ad. 296   ὅταν γὰρ ὀργὴ Δαιμόνων βλάπτῃ τινά,
τοῦτ' αὐτὸ πρῶτον, ἐξαφαιρεῖται φρενῶν
τὸν νοῦν τὸν ἐσθλόν· εἰς Δὲ τὴν χείρω τρέπει
γνώμην, ἵν' εἰΔῇ μηΔὲν ὧν ἁμαρτάνει.

[2] *Sept.* 781   μαινομένᾳ κραΔίᾳ.

[3] 1299–1300   τίς σ', ὦ τλᾶμον,
προσέβη μανία;

But Sophocles soon shows that Oedipus was not mad, that he knew what he was doing and had his reasons for it. These must be taken seriously. Oedipus is not the victim who does not know what he is doing. His good sense is not destroyed.

The Chorus, naturally enough, do not at first applaud Oedipus' action. But their words do not really condemn it:

> In this I know not how to call thee wise,
> For better wert thou dead than living—blind.[1]

They mean no more than that his life of blindness will be even more miserable than death. They do not understand that he cannot and will not die because in death he would have to face his parents, and that he cannot do (1371-4). The real explanation of his decision to blind himself is in his own words. When he does it, he cries out that his eyes shall no longer see such horrors as he has been doing and suffering and henceforth must look on the dark (1271-4). This is not a momentary fancy. Oedipus returns to it and almost argues his case:

> Nay, give me no more counsel. Bid me not
> Believe my deed, thus done, is not well done[2],

and says that he could not look on his parents, his children, his city and its temples from which he has excluded himself by his own curse (1377-83). He develops this thought and advances to a new stage. He wishes to be shut off altogether from the converse of the living. If he could have choked the fount of hearing, he would have done this too,

> Sweet for the mind
> To dwell withdrawn, where troubles never come[3].

He ask to be thrown out of the city (1436-7) that he may live alone on the mountains; for there Cithaeron will be a living tomb to him (1451 ff.). He has blinded himself because he wishes to be cut off from the living and from the dead.

Oedipus' explanation suggests that he sees himself as a kind of scapegoat, a φαρμακός or κάθαρμα, a polluted being whose expulsion from the city will purify it. When grave impiety had been committed, it was right to send out such a scapegoat who might well be the defiling or guilty person himself. In his fierce attack on

---

[1] 1367-8   οὐκ οἶΔ' ὅπως σε φῶ βεβουλεῦσθαι καλῶς·
κρείσσων γὰρ ἦσθα μηκέτ' ὢν ἢ ζῶν τυφλός.

[2] 1369-70   ὡς μὲν τάΔ'.οὐχ ὧΔ' ἔστ' ἄριστ' εἰργασμένα
μή μ' ἐκΔίΔασκε, μηΔὲ συμβούλευ' ἔτι.

[3] 1389-90   τὸ γὰρ
τὴν φροντίΔ' ἔξω τῶν κακῶν οἰκεῖν γλυκύ.

Andocides for impiety, 'Lysias' demands that Athens should expel
the criminal and so purify the city. The expulsion is called 'sending out a scapegoat'.[1] So Oedipus wishes to be treated. He feels
that such a punishment is right for him because of the curse which
he has laid upon himself. Nor is expulsion enough for him. His
blindness too is necessary to complete his severance from the light
of day and the company of men. Only by this can he really cut
himself off and carry out the penalty which he has called down on
the murderers of Laius. He must not live like other men. He
must have a special, separate life such as he can have if he is blind
and an outcast. He will rid the city of pollution; he will carry out
to the full the curse which he has laid on himself.

Neither the Chorus nor Creon says that Oedipus has acted
wrongly. The Chorus feel pity and horror, but that is different.
They even accept his view that Apollo is the real power behind
what he has done:

> 'Twas even as thou sayest.[2]

When Creon tells Oedipus that he must not pollute the sun by
staying out of doors, he does not refer to his blindness. What
pollutes the sun is the presence of the parricide. It is this that is
so foul

> that neither Earth
> Nor Light nor Heaven's rain may welcome it.[3]

Euripides' Heracles, bowed with guilt on killing his children, hides
his head from the sun. And this was right. The sun was a 'pure
god' and must not be defiled by the sight of any polluted thing.
Such a thought seems to have been present to Oedipus' own mind
when he found out the truth and cried:

> Light, let me look on thee for the last time.[4]

The sun may not look on those who are defiled, and they may not
look on it. Therefore Oedipus must hide himself. When Creon
demands that he should go inside, the demand is right and proper.
But it contains no condemnation of Oedipus for blinding himself.

Oedipus blinds himself because of his curse. He does it both
deliberately and by divine prompting. The Greeks would make
no real distinction between the two and would certainly praise

---

[1] Lys. vi. 53 φαρμακὸν ἀποπέμπειν.
[2] 1336   ἦν ταῦθ᾽ ὅπωσπερ καὶ σὺ φής.
[3] 1427–8   τὸ μήτε γῆ
              μήτ᾽ ὄμβρος ἱερὸς μήτε φῶς προσλέξεται.
[4] 1183   ὦ φῶς, τελευταῖόν σε προσβλέψαιμι νῦν.

Oedipus for acting as the gods desire and see that the *daimôn's* pressure on him was part of their scheme. As a parricide and incestuous he will exile himself from Thebes which he pollutes and from human society with which he can have no normal relations. To carry out his curse he inflicts a fearful injury on himself. The curse has still to finish its course. Oedipus knows this, makes no attempt to resist it, rather does his best to help it. There is no question of guilt and its punishment, but once pollution has been incurred, once the powers of heaven have been invoked with such solemnity, they cannot be countermanded. There is much to pity when Oedipus blinds himself, but much also to admire. His willingness to shoulder the burden of his pollution, his desire to do at all costs what is right, show that even in the worst crisis of his fortunes he keeps his essential nobility. In his angry scenes with Teiresias and Creon he has lost some of our sympathy and revealed dangerous tendencies in his character, but once he knows who he really is, he throws aside his faults and acts with inspired resolution in his fearful sacrifice. He is not to be condemned for resisting his destiny, but to be admired for accepting it in all its horror and for being ready to work with the god to see that he makes his full amends. He who has been the victim and the sufferer regains the initiative and takes his destiny into his own hands.

The gods have chosen Oedipus for this fate. In so far as he is to be an example to others it is enough that he is a great king. But the lesson that he himself has to learn must be suited to his own nature. The man who is to be taught his own utter insignificance must be endowed with special gifts of character and intellect; for only in such conditions is the lesson worth learning. Such Oedipus undeniably is. But in presenting him Sophocles has boldly faced certain difficulties inherent in the legend and turned them to good account. His Oedipus must be a man who has killed his father, solved the riddle of the Sphinx, married his mother, and become king of Thebes, and at the same time he must be convincing enough to win sympathy in his fate and fall. Sophocles shirks none of these difficulties. The past events of Oedipus' life are worked into the play in the most natural way possible. Through the greater part of it Oedipus shows himself as the sort of man to defend himself when attacked, to answer riddles and assume great responsibilities. But the same characteristics which brought him to success make his downfall more tragic and are almost instruments to it. It is because he is such a superior being, angry when attacked, capable of brief and brilliant action, self-confident and rapid in decision, that his discovery of the truth takes so tragic a turn. His fated life is his own life. It is his character, his typical actions, that make his mistakes so intelligible and fit so naturally into the gods' plan to humble him.

Even in retrospect the solving of the Sphinx's riddle plays little part in the play, but it lies behind certain situations. It accounts for Oedipus being king of Thebes, and it is typical of his intellectual activity and curiosity. Both are important. First, the kingship. Oedipus is no tyrant. He did not seize or demand power. The city gave it to him in gratitude for delivering it from the Sphinx (1198–1203). He is king by right of natural superiority, the deliverer and protector of his people. Sophocles displays the theme in all its grandeur. When the play opens, Oedipus is presented as the great king. In some ways he recalls the Homeric monarch who is 'gentle as a father'[1] to his people, but he is drawn from nearer home than that. Despite their detestation of tyrants, the Greeks of the fifth century, even the democratic Athenians, respected a good king. Just as Pindar stresses the opposite characters and opposite fates of Tantalus and Pelops, of Phalaris and Croesus, so Herodotus distinguishes between brutal tyrants like Periander and good kings like Amasis. With the first words of the play it is clear to which class Oedipus belongs. When he speaks to his people,

> My children, sons of Cadmus, and his care,[2]

he is *pater patriae* like Croesus whom Cyrus called 'more than a father to the Lydians',[3] or Cyrus himself who was called 'father' because he 'was gentle and contrived everything'[4] for his people. He fulfils Socrates' demand that a king should be chosen not to take care of himself but for the good of those who have chosen him[5] and should differ from his subjects by his forethought and love for them.[6] Unlike tyrants who shut themselves up, Oedipus comes forward himself to find what is the matter with his people:

> Whereof I would not hear the tale, my children,
> From other lips than yours. Look! I am here.[7]

It is abundantly clear that he is no tyrant.

In his care for his people Oedipus shares their sufferings and is

---

[1] *Od.* ii. 47.
[2] 1   ὦ τέκνα, Κάδμου τοῦ πάλαι νέα τροφή.
[3] Hdt. i. 155. 2.   [4] Id. iii. 89, 3.   [5] Xen. *Mem.* iii. 2. 2.
[6] Id. *Cyr.* i. 6. 8.
[7] 6–7   ἀγὼ δικαιῶν μὴ παρ' ἀγγέλων, τέκνα,
                 ἄλλων ἀκούειν αὐτὸς ὧδ' ἐλήλυθα.

active on their behalf. When he says⌉

> Well I know the hurt whereby
> You are all stricken—and not one of you
> So far from health as I,[1]

he shows his almost personal affection for them. Their woes are
his. He has given, as a king should, unsleeping thought to them:

> You rouse not one that sleeps. Through many tears
> And many searchings on the paths of thought,
> By anxious care . . .[2]

Oedipus has done all that he can think of to help, sent Creon to
inquire of the Delphic Oracle (70 ff.), and summoned Teiresias
for consultation (287 ff.). He receives with courtesy the Chorus's
suggestions for relief, though he has already anticipated what they
ask and taken steps for it (282 ff.). His denunciation of the
murderers of Laius is delivered with a mounting severity. He
begins with an appeal for information, but when none comes, he
moves to stern threats and to his awful curse. The change of
temper when he says:

> What! You are silent still? If any fear
> For a friend or for himself, and will not speak,
> Then I must play my part. Attend what follows,[3]

shows that with all his gentle considerateness he will allow nothing
to prevent him from doing his duty to the city.

Oedipus is not a tyrant. Nor is he more than man. He is not
even 'god-born' or 'peer of the gods' like the Homeric kings. The
Priest knows this when he says:

> We count you not a god, I and these children,
> That thus we seek your hearth. Of human kind
> We judge you first in the common accident
> Of fate; in the traffic of the gods with man
> Greatest of men.[4]

[1] 59–61   εὖ γὰρ οἶδ' ὅτι
                  νοσεῖτε πάντες, καὶ νοσοῦντες ὡς ἐγὼ
                  οὐκ ἔστιν ὑμῶν ὅστις ἐξ ἴσου νοσεῖ.

[2] 65–7   ὥστ' οὐχ ὕπνῳ γ' εὕδοντά μ' ἐξεγείρετε·
                  ἀλλ' ἴστε πολλὰ μέν με δακρύσαντα δή,
                  πολλὰς δ' ὁδοὺς ἐλθόντα φροντίδος πλάνοις.

Cf. Aesch. *Sept.* 1–3.

[3] 233–5   εἰ δ' αὖ σιωπήσεσθε, καί τις ἢ φίλου
                  δείσας ἀπώσει τοὔπος ἢ χαὐτοῦ τόδε,
                  ἐκ τῶνδε δράσω, ταῦτα χρὴ κλύειν ἐμοῦ.

[4] 31–4   θεοῖσι μέν νυν οὐκ ἰσούμενόν σ' ἐγὼ
                  οὐδ' οἵδε παῖδες ἐζόμεσθ' ἐφέστιοι,
                  ἀνδρῶν δὲ πρῶτον ἔν τε συμφοραῖς βίου
                  κρίνοντες ἔν τε δαιμόνων συναλλαγαῖς.

Oedipus receives the respect due to the man who is pre-eminent
both in the ordinary affairs of men and in those more difficult
matters in which the gods have a hand. The Priest treats him
rather as Pindar treats Hieron:

> Your portion of Felicity attends you.
> On the Prince who rules his people, if on any,
> Is the eye of mighty Fate.[1]

So far as mortal man may find happiness, it seems to belong to
Oedipus as to Hieron. Their kingship is a sign of their good
fortune no less than of their superior abilities. This kind of respect
for a king bears no resemblance to the subservience paid to Oriental
autocrats or exacted by Greek tyrants. Oedipus is honoured
because in the past he has saved his people and is now called to
save them again. He bears a resemblance to Aristotle's heroic
king who rules willing subjects and is himself 'a benefactor in arts
or arms.'[2] Oedipus' first thoughts are for his people. He is one of
those who, to continue with Aristotle, are made kings 'because
they were benefactors, and benefits can only be bestowed by
good men'.[3]

Yet, just because Oedipus is a great king, he is exposed to great
perils both from the gods and from himself. Because he is after all
a monarch who acknowledges no mortal superior and no law above
himself, he is liable to presumption and pride. He illustrates the
question which Herodotus makes Otanes ask: 'How can monarchy
be a well-adjusted thing when it allows a man to do what he likes
without being answerable?'[4] All is well with his character so long
as he prospers, but when his will is thwarted, his kingly temper
verges on the tyrannical. Both with Teiresias and with Creon he
steps far beyond the bounds of decency and humanity, blusters,
abuses, and threatens. His threats fail. Teiresias departs un-
harmed, having said the last, most deadly word; Creon is saved by
the intervention of Jocasta and shows later that he bears no malice.
But the great and good king shows how small is the barrier between
royalty and tyranny, between authority and pride. He has lost
some of his nobility, forfeited some of our admiration. He has even
come nearer to Aristotle's tragic hero who is not pre-eminently
virtuous or just.[5] Consequently his sufferings stir compassion
but do not awake an intolerable indignation against the gods as

---

[1] *Pyth.* iii. 84–6   τὶν δὲ μοῖρ' εὐδαιμονίας ἕπεται·
λαγέταν γάρ τοι τύραννον Δέρκεται,
εἴ τιν' ἀνθρώπων, ὁ μέγας πότμος.

[2] *Pol.* 1285 b 5.   [3] *Ib.* 1286 b 11.   [4] iii. 80. 3.   [5] *Poet.* 1453 a 8.

they might if he had shown no human faults. And for him these outbursts of unbridled temper add to the horror of his collapse. Because he is furious with Teiresias, he is unable to grasp the seer's message and fails to see that he himself has killed Laius, so that the revelation of the truth is postponed and comes with all the greater effect when it finally breaks on him.

Because Oedipus is a great king, he might be liable to the 'envy' of the gods. So at least Herodotus would have thought. Sophocles does not suggest this, but he seems to hold a view not far removed from it, that all high positions are insecure and dangerous, and that at any moment the mighty may be overturned. His Oedipus stands on a precipice. He is too full of confidence for his happiness to last. Because he felt that the great ones of the earth were liable to this mood, Pindar often, if indirectly, warned princes and victors of their insecurity. He tells Hieron that for every good thing the gods send a pair of sorrows,[1] and the warning is not so much against pride as against confidence and self-satisfaction. Sophocles, too, was fully conscious of the insecurity which attends human happiness. When he wrote in his *Tereus*:

> The life of man is changed
> In every season by sorrow's
> Cunning-hearted calamities,[2]

he referred to the dangers that threaten the great in their own thoughts or in powers beyond their control. Oedipus' high position has been given to him by the gods, and what the gods have given, they can take away. He is insufficiently aware of this. The Priest modestly says to him:

> Your own wit, touched by some god,
> Men say and think, raised us and gave us life.[3]

Oedipus himself admits no such divine help; in his view he answered the Sphinx by his own unprompted intelligence:

> I, the fool,
> Ignorant Oedipus—no birds to teach me—
> Must come, and hit the truth, and stop the song.[4]

---

[1] *Pyth.* iii. 81.

[2] Fr. 592. 4–6
τὰν γὰρ ἀνθρώπου ζόαν
ποικιλομήτιδες ἆται
πημάτων πάσαις μεταλλάσσουσιν ὥραις.

[3] 38–9
προσθήκη θεοῦ
λέγῃ νομίζῃ θ' ἡμὶν ὀρθῶσαι βίον.

[4] 396–8
ἐγὼ μολών,
ὁ μηδὲν εἰδὼς Οἰδίπους, ἔπαυσά νιν,
γνώμῃ κυρήσας οὐδ' ἀπ' οἰωνῶν μαθών.

To the audience this confidence and this power would certainly seem fraught with danger. They would know that anyone so highly placed was liable to fall, and that it was a bad sign in Oedipus to be unconscious of his risks.

Oedipus' royal gifts are a source of danger to him. The same may be said of his intelligence. He solved the riddle of the Sphinx. On his own claim, he did it through his wits (398), but whether the gods helped him or not, he succeeded where others failed. So Sophocles makes him a man of powerful intelligence and shows that it is of the kind to solve problems. Just as he must have answered the Sphinx by a sudden stroke of insight, so now the gift of reaching rapidly the answer to a problem, of asking pertinent questions, of finding his own answers to them, is still with him. His energy in looking for the murderer of Laius, his courageous and unflinching desire to know the truth about himself, belong to his vigorous mental equipment. But by a hideous irony, this time the answers are all wrong. They are based on some kind of evidence; they sound plausible. But they do not touch the truth. The man who could answer riddles is still keen-witted and live-minded, but he is no longer right. He is in fact really the 'ignorant Oedipus' such as in mock modesty he thinks that he once was (397). This failure is apparent in his dealings with Teiresias. The prophet, like the Sphinx, begins by speaking in riddles which seem to bode no good and to show a malevolent heart. Oedipus complains:

Riddles again! All subtle and all vague![1]

He thinks he knows what it means. He suspects corruption, that Teiresias had a hand in the death of Laius (346–8) and has been bribed by Creon, who wishes to become king (385–6). The idea has been, in a vague form, present with him for some time. But what was a mere possibility in his first inquiries (124–5) has now taken definite shape and become an obsession. It is quite false. Yet it has a certain speciousness Oedipus is so sure that he himself is not the murderer and so incensed by what looks like Teiresias' malignant refusal to speak out that he forms a theory of corrupt motives, and with characteristic decisiveness is at once convinced that he is right. This conviction dominates him and even grows in his interview with Creon until it explodes in violent anger. It leaves Oedipus only when his mind is turned to the grave possibility that he himself may be the murderer. Just as his fall is all the

[1] 439   ὡς πάντ᾿ ἄγαν αἰνικτὰ κἀσαφῆ λέγεις.

greater because he is a great king, so it is all the more poignant because despite his acute intelligence he is unable to see the truth until it is forced upon him.

Oedipus, said the legend, married his mother. Sophocles faced the extremely difficult task of making this a real relation and worked it into his tragic scheme. His triumph is extraordinary. Jocasta is both wife and mother, and yet we do not feel that her affection for Oedipus is in any way unnatural or strange. Oedipus is deeply attached to her, almost always speaks to her with courtesy, even with strong affection:

> Tell me, Jocasta, wife of my dear love.[1]

He curbs his anger against Creon because she wishes him to do so (671–2), listens with respect to her doubts about oracles and later almost shares them (964–72), and for a moment accepts her view that chance rules everything (984 ff.). He treats her with deference, yields to her influence, accepts her ideas, is considerate of her feelings. She is older than he is, and in his affection there is an element of respect. We understand how she who is his mother can also be his wife. The only time that he is harsh to her is when he begins to know the real truth from the Messenger. Then his passion to hear it prevents him from seeing how she suffers. To all appearance this union is full of that 'union of hearts', ὁμοφροσύνη, which Odysseus praised to Nausicaa as the best thing in marriage.[2] As Democritus says, 'union of hearts makes friendship,[3] and there is a real friendship between Oedipus and Jocasta. But this union is accursed. Its impious character must reveal itself. There must be a flaw in it, and the flaw lies precisely in the closeness of the bonds which bind the two together. Because of this Oedipus begins to lose his trust in oracles, to be uncertain about the divine government of the world. In the circumstances neither he nor she can be blamed for a scepticism which seems to be well warranted by the facts. But the scepticism is wrong, and contributes to their undoing and to the destruction of their harmony. Once she knows her error Jocasta goes to kill herself. Oedipus, still buoyed up by hope, places his trust in irrational Luck. Neither is really impious, but both have lost their proper respect for the gods. And after this the gods are sure to strike them. Moreover, this union, simply because it is accursed, ends in tragedy. Jocasta goes to her doom with the terrible words:

---

[1] 950   ὦ φίλτατον γυναικὸς Ἰοκάστης κάρα.
[2] *Od.* vi. 180–5.   [3] Fr. 186.

> O Wretched, Wretched utterly! that name
> I give you, and henceforth no other name.[1]

The man whom she has loved, her husband and her son, is now nothing to her but 'wretched'. That is the end for them in this world, and in the after-world her injured spirit will pursue him (418). For his part he hardly cares whether she leaves him or not. He thinks, again wrongly, that she despises his humble birth, and that is his last thought of her until he sees her hanging dead.

By such subtle strokes Sophocles makes the curious features of the archaic story fit his Oedipus. Whatever improbable or grotesque elements the legend had are transmuted with consummate skill into this convincing and coherent plot. No less subtle is the delineation of Oedipus' personal qualities, of the force in him which brings him to power and then to disaster. The predominant quality of Sophocles' Oedipus is his high temper, his θυμός. This was an ambiguous quality. On the one side it worked for good and made men active and enduring. So Plato gave it a prominent place in his psychology and made it the ally of the reason against the appetites.[2] As the self-assertive principle whose object is honour it is part of the mental equipment of any active man and especially of a king and leader like Oedipus. In his earlier career he has shown it in full measure, and it is no less strong when he sets to work to stop the plague by finding the murderer of Laius. But it had another side. It was not necessarily nor always allied to reason. As Plato saw, it could have a destructive side when it was allied to unreasoning violence.[3] So in Oedipus, his high spirit and temper, admirable when the end is good, are liable to get out of control and to do damage. That he is a man of this kind is seen by Jocasta, who says of him when he is convulsed after her first fatal revelation:

> For Oedipus excites too much his spirit
> With every distress.[4]

His anxieties arouse Oedipus' temper, and Jocasta is afraid of what will happen. Again, when he accepts her intervention between himself and Creon but still cherishes his anger, Creon says:

---

[1] 1071–2   Ἰοὺ ἰού, Δύστηνε· τοῦτο γάρ σ' ἔχω
                μόνον προσειπεῖν, ἄλλο Δ' οὔποθ' ὕστερον.

[2] *Rep.* iv. 441 a.   [3] *Laws* ix. 863 b.

[4] 914–15   ὑψοῦ γὰρ αἴρει θυμὸν Οἰδίπους ἄγαν
                λύπαισι παντοίαισιν.

You yield, but still you hate; and as you pass
From passion, you are hard. 'Tis very plain.
Such men—'tis just—reap for themselves most pain![1]

There is in Oedipus a tendency to uncontrolled anger, to unreasonable passion. This is part of his high spirit and essential to his
character.

This appears in his pride of kingship, even in his relentless pursuit of what he believes to be the truth. But it is more important
in another part of his life and goes back to his killing of Laius. He
is a man who retaliates with force and does not shrink from killing
an aggressor. In such a man his spirit soon passes into anger, as
Aristotle saw when he compared men acting in such a spirit to
beasts which rush at those who have enraged them.[2] So Oedipus
himself describes the fatal encounter with Laius:

> But I
> When one that led the horses jostled me,
> Struck him in anger,[3]

and no doubt he slew Laius in the same spirit. Even in his account
of the episode to Jocasta we can see the excitement which a man
of action feels in recounting his exploits, and the thrill of battle
which the memory of them revives. In this case law and morality
unite in excusing Oedipus. His wrath is justifiable, for he has
been attacked. But it is not always so. He is an example of what
Theognis says about anger:

> Nothing is worse than anger. Base the pleasure
> That it gives your temper, to your bane.[4]

Oedipus is like the Homeric Achilles whose anger is an inevitable
part of his disposition but none the less does him grievous harm.

The mood in which Oedipus slew Laius reappears in the crisis
of his fortunes, and this time there is less excuse for it. With
Teiresias and Creon he loses all control of himself. His outburst
of temper might seem to be consonant with his kingly bearing;
for as Homer says,

Mighty a king who is wroth with a man who is baser than he is—[5]

---

[1] 673–5   στυγνὸς μὲν εἴκων δῆλος εἶ, βαρὺς δ' ὅταν
                θυμοῦ περάσῃς· αἱ δὲ τοιαῦται φύσεις
                αὑταῖς δικαίως εἰσὶν ἄλγισται φέρειν.

[2] *Nic. Eth.* 1116 b 24.

[3] 806–7   κἀγὼ τὸν ἐκτρέποντα, τὸν τροχηλάτην,
                παίω δι' ὀργῆς.

[4] 1223–4   οὐδέν, Κύρν', ὀργῆς ἀδικώτερον, ἢ τὸν ἔχοντα
                πημαίνει θυμῷ δειλὰ χαριζομένη.

[5] *Il.* i. 80   κρείσσων γὰρ βασιλεὺς ὅτε χώσεται ἀνδρὶ χέρηῑ.

but Oedipus' anger is not turned against men really inferior but against the representative of the gods and the embodiment of modest reasonableness. Such anger is not kingly but tyrannical, and can do Oedipus no good. Nor is there any justification for it. Neither Teiresias nor Creon is really plotting against Oedipus. He accuses them unjustly because he is angry and finds it hard to abandon his suspicions. His whole behaviour is dominated by his high temper both for better and for worse. It is the clue to his actions, and to his mistakes. In the past it has not harmed him; it has even served him well. But now it turns on him, spoils his character, and adds to his troubles. It has blunted his insight and encouraged what there is of the bully in him. We might apply to him Heraclitus' saying, 'It is hard to fight against anger; for what-soever it wishes, it buys at the cost of the soul'.[1] When Oedipus indulges his angry temper, he pays for it with the loss of judge-ment and decency. But the intellectual aspects of the struggle are more important than the moral. For the play what counts is that Oedipus' tendency to anger prevents him from seeing the truth, even when it is told him and induces a state of illusion in which he lives until reality is forced upon him. When Euripides says,

> Great strength of spirit ruins many men,
> And lack of thought, two banes to them that have them,[2]

his words may be applied to Oedipus. His high temper breeds almost a state of thoughtlessness.

This state of obstinate belief is of great importance to the play. It explains Oedipus' slowness to see the truth and the appalling horror which he feels when at last he learns it. He is a man of action, not given to meditation. He accepts facts as he hears them, and in this case his illusion turns on a small point, the common belief that Laius was killed by a band of men. Even Creon, in reporting the reply of the Delphic Oracle, speaks of 'the mur-derers' (107). This was the current belief in Thebes, and Creon may be affected by it, or the Oracle may have spoken unclearly or ambiguously. For a moment, in tragic irony, Oedipus speaks of 'the slayer' (124), but when he pursues his inquiries the plural again appears in the Chorus' answer:

> He died, they said, at the hand of travellers.[3]

---

[1] Fr. 85 θυμῷ μάχεσθαι χαλεπόν· ὃ τι γὰρ ἂν θέλῃ, ψυχῆς ὠνεῖται.

[2] Fr. 257 πολλοὺς δ' ὁ θυμὸς ὁ μέγας ὤλεσεν βροτῶν
ἥ τ' ἀξυνεσία, δύο κακὼ τοῖς χρωμένοις.

[3] 292 θανεῖν ἐλέχθη πρός τινων ὁδοιπόρων.

This stays in Oedipus' mind and prevents him for suspecting that
he himself is the murderer. Before Teiresias comes and tells him
that he is, this is natural enough. We are not surprised when
Oedipus speaks to him about 'the killers' (308). But before long
Teiresias has broken the hideous secret:

> Thou seekest, and thou art, the murderer.[1]

Oedipus fails to understand him or to think that there can be anything in what he says, simply because his anger is aroused and
undermines his judgement. His only answer is that Teiresias shall
not say this kind of thing twice (363). When the exact truth is told
to him, the wise Oedipus is too angry to grasp it.

In his anger with Teiresias Oedipus has formed the false notion
that Creon is plotting to dispossess him (385–7). This hallucination dominates him even more powerfully when Creon comes to
defend himself against the charge. So strong is it that Oedipus
ends by wishing to kill Creon and would have committed some
violent act but for the intervention of Jocasta. Yet for a moment
we may detect signs of a struggle in him between truth and
illusion. He recovers his balance enough to question Creon about
the death of Laius, and in the solemn, hesitating tone of his
words we may surely see the workings of a truer insight or at least
the beginnings of an honest doubt:

> Oe. How long ago, tell me, did Laius . . .
> Cr. What, that he did? I have not understood.
> Oe. Pass, by that stroke that slew him, from men's sight?[2]

But the doubt fades away. Oedipus asks what Teiresias was doing
at the time, and his temper rises again. He pursues his violent
course and follows his fantasies. The Chorus warn him against any
precipitate decision (656–7), but in the self-righteousness of delusion he answers that he is dealing with a traitor. He is incapable
of a truly balanced or rational judgement. He shows that fault
which Diodotus censured in the Athenians, 'I think that two things
are most inimical to good counsel, haste and anger'.[3] Oedipus'
hasty temper robs him of the capacity to think coolly. So angry is
he, so full of his fancies, that when Jocasta asks him how the quarrel
with Creon began, he says:

> He says I am the murderer of Laius.[4]

---

[1] 362   φονέα σέ φημι τἀνΔρὸς οὗ ϡητεῖς κυρεῖν.

[2] 558–60   Οι. πόσον τιν' ἤΔη ϡῆθ' ὁ Λάιος χρόνον . . .
           Κρ. ΔέΔρακε ποῖον ἔργον; οὐ γὰρ ἐννοῶ.
           Οι. ἄφαντος ἔρρει θανασίμῳ χειρώματι;

[3] Thuc. iii. 42. 1.

[4] 703   φονέα μέ φησι Λαΐου καθεστάναι.

Not Creon but Teiresias has said this (362). In his furious belief
that the two are conspiring against him, Oedipus does not trouble
to distinguish between them but justifies himself by saying that
Creon has sent Teiresias to say this (705–6).

When Jocasta intervenes Oedipus' fury abates, but his illusion
remains, even in the terrible scene in which she tries to discredit
all oracles. When, in all ignorance of its meaning for him, she tells
of the place where Laius was killed,

> Now, the King . . . strangers, robbers murdered him,
> So runs report, at a place where three roads meet,[1]

it arouses his darkest doubts and anxieties:

> Wife, as I heard you speak, within my soul
> What trouble stirred! What fearful doubt was born![2]

In effect he has not heard or marked anything that Jocasta says
after the mention of the cross-roads. Yet her later words are no
less relevant to him. The child whose ankles were pierced (718)
might well remind him of his own pierced ankles which, as he says
later, were an old source of shame to him (1033). Yet he fails to
take notice of this or to suspect that he may be not only the
murderer of Laius but his son. He might perhaps have drawn a full
conclusion from Jocasta's words. But he seizes only on one point,
and that is appalling enough. The blow to his pride is fearful. He
cannot be expected to grasp all the truth at once. At least he
abandons his suspicions about the corruption of Teiresias and
says:

> I have dread misgivings that the seer may see,[3]

and he says nothing more about Creon. The first shock has
destroyed some of his illusions, but he still fights against the
irresistible truth which is being forced upon him.

It is characteristic of Oedipus' spirit, in the best sense of his high
confidence and courageous temper, that he still clings to hope and
refuses as yet to accept the facts as he has heard them. He bases
his last hope on the existence of a witness to the death of Laius; the
attendant who was present on the fatal day and escaped can still
say whether Oedipus is the murderer or not. To this Oedipus
clings. And we can see why. He still holds his earlier belief that

---

[1] 715–16   καὶ τὸν μέν, ὥσπερ γ᾽ ἡ φάτις, ξένοι ποτὲ
λησταὶ φονεύουσ᾽ ἐν τριπλαῖς ἁμαξιτοῖς.

[2] 726–7   οἷόν μ᾽ ἀκούσαντ᾽ ἀρτίως ἔχει, γύναι,
ψυχῆς πλάνημα κἀνακίνησις φρενῶν.

[3] 747   Δεινῶς ἀθυμῶ μὴ βλέπων ὁ μάντις ᾖ.

there was more than one murderer, and in that case he himself
cannot be guilty:

You said

> This was the tale, that robbers slew the King,
> Robbers. If he confirm it, if he speak
> Of robbers still, it was not I, not I,
> That slew. One man is not a company.[1]

In this he has recently received some support from Jocasta's use of
the plural 'robbers' (716), and she again asserts that this is so and
that the whole city knew it at the time (850). Against the rest of
the evidence perhaps this carries little real weight, but Oedipus
puts great trust in it. For the moment he seems to think that the
surviving witness will prove him innocent. He demands to see him.
His temper makes him trust in the one chance which seems to
favour him. His confidence is a kind of courage, part of his
great character. Aristotle perhaps would think him more sanguine
than truly brave because he thinks that he will not suffer,[2] but the
distinction between the two is slight and not always easy to mark.
At least Oedipus is not afraid of what he will find.

Oedipus' confidence rises when, still waiting for the absent witness, he hears of Polybus' death. He feels that after all the oracles
are wrong, and he half accepts Jocasta's view that Luck rules all.
There is a note of triumph in his words:

> Anyhow, he is dead, and to his grave
> Has carried all these oracles—worth nothing,[3]

and though he is still cautious about the second part of the oracle
that he will marry his mother (976, 985–6), his mind is for the
moment light with hope and confidence. In this mood he questions
the Messenger from Corinth, refuses to listen to Jocasta's warnings and entreaties, disregards her efforts to keep him from knowing the whole truth which is clear to her so soon as she hears that
Oedipus is the child who was once exposed on Cithaeron. The
quest of the truth enthrals him, and nothing can hold him back.
He probes the past with unflinching curiosity and courage. In
this excited mood he pays little attention to Jocasta's tremendous,
tragic departure. He may be the murderer of Laius, but for the

---

[1] 842–5   λῃστὰς ἔφασκες αὐτὸν ἄνδρας ἐννέπειν
             ὡς νιν κατακτείνειαν· εἰ μὲν οὖν ἔτι
             λέξει τὸν αὐτὸν ἀριθμόν, οὐκ ἐγὼ 'κτανον·
             οὐ γὰρ γένοιτ' ἂν εἷς γε τοῖς πολλοῖς ἴσος.

[2] *Nic. Eth.* 1117 a 13.

[3] 971–2   τὰ δ' οὖν παρόντα συλλαβὼν θεσπίσματα
             κεῖται παρ' Ἅιδῃ Πόλυβος ἄξι' οὐδενός.

moment he forgets it; he may not be the son of Polybus but he is the son of Luck. He will spare no effort to find out his origin, and in a mood of wild exaltation he proclaims his new trust:

> I am Luck's child. Deeming myself her son,
> I shall not be disowned. She lavishes
> Good gifts upon me, she's my nature's mother!
> Her moons, my cousins, watched my littleness
> Wax and grow great.[1]

It is his last bid for freedom from his destiny, his last illusion.

It is not quite easy to see what Oedipus means. Indeed he is so excited that it may be wrong to demand any clear thought from him. But his words have an emotional value. He does not care who his parents are; what matters is he himself. He is a self-made man who will be remembered not as the son of someone but as the man who answered the Sphinx's riddle and became king of Thebes. He trusts in Luck. It looks after him and has shaped his life from small to great. He does not shrink from the possibility that his birth may be humble (1079). What matters for him is the sense of freedom, of irresponsibility, which is for the moment his. He feels that Luck looks after him and that therefore all is well. This confidence is unfounded and irrational, a mere feeling, a manifestation of Oedipus' confident spirit in its least reasonable form. It is his version of the belief that 'Fortune favours the brave'.[2] But Oedipus is wrong. There is no reason to think that Luck looks after him. Democritus' words, 'The hopes of the thoughtless are without reason',[3] may well be applied to him. There is no need to accuse him of irreverence, of denying the rule of the gods. Implicitly perhaps or logically he does, but he cannot be judged by such standards. He is wildly excited, carried away by a last desperate hope. He wishes to know who he is, but with an exaltation that is on the edge of delirium he assumes that the discovery will bring him joy. A few minutes later, after the Servant has told him the truth, his hopes are all broken. Even in the dread colloquy Oedipus still keeps his high temper, his princely self-control, but it does not help him. The truth comes out. He knows who he is. His last illusion is shattered, the whole of his confidence gone.

[1] 1080–3   ἐγὼ δ' ἐμαυτὸν παῖδα τῆς Τύχης νέμων
             τῆς εὖ διδούσης οὐκ ἀτιμασθήσομαι·
             τῆς γὰρ πέφυκα μητρός· οἱ δὲ συγγενεῖς
             μῆνές με μικρὸν καὶ μέγαν διώρισαν.

[2] Soph. fr. 927, Men. fr. 572, Hdt. vii. 50. 2.

[3] Fr. 292 ἄλογοι τῶν ἀξυνετῶν αἱ ἐλπίδες.

Sophocles stresses this wild confidence in a very remarkable way. The little song, 1086–1109, which the Chorus sing after his declaration that he is the son of Luck, is in so airy and care-free a spirit that it has caused much trouble to the commentators. The Chorus, who have hitherto shown themselves serious and even critical about Oedipus, now share all his unreasonable expectations. They go even farther than he does. He says that he does not care who his father is, but they form the pretty fancy that he is of divine birth, the son of a Nymph by Pan or Apollo or Hermes. They look forward to feasting in honour of the discovery and are convinced that they have prophetic insight into the situation. Their mood is certainly surprising. A little earlier they were shocked at the unbelief of Jocasta and Oedipus; they have good reason to think that Oedipus killed Laius and that his presence pollutes Thebes. Yet all this is forgotten in the song. Of course there is a dramatic gain in this. The wild hopes of the Chorus present a vivid contrast to the bitter disillusion that follows. But such an explanation is not enough. The song must have its place in the psychological development of the play. Surely what Sophocles intends to convey is that the Chorus have caught Oedipus' mood and even enhanced it with their own hopes. His irrational confidence is infectious. For a few minutes even the grave Theban elders are bewitched by it. The song shows the climax of tragic illusion in the play, the moment before disaster. Hope, as the Athenians tell the Melians, can only be indulged by those who have abundant resources, but those who put all their trust in it see the truth only when they are ruined.[1] Such is the notion which Sophocles follows when he makes Oedipus and the Chorus indulge in wild and tragic optimism.

The character of Oedipus, then, is based on the legend of his exploits and is so developed as to explain why he falls as he does. The gods have decided to humble him, but they do so through his own gifts. The whole process comes naturally through himself. The play depicts a conflict between two worlds, the world of gods and the world of a man. The first drives home its truth to the second. Oedipus learns it at last. But before he learns it he resists, not indeed consciously but with all the force of his unconscious nature. The tragic conclusion lies in the fearful character of the truth. The gods insist that their victim shall know who and what he is. And this conflict is all the more stubborn and painful because Oedipus is the high creature that he is, born to command and to think, a

[1] Thuc. v. 103. 1.

man of action and a friend to other men. The horror of his fall
is great because he is a superior being, gifted with great possibilities of nobleness. Even his fine qualities prolong and make
more painful the process by which he comes to see himself as
he really is. His love of action, his desire to know everything,
his occasional ruthlessness in forcing the truth from an unwilling
witness, lead to nothing but his own humiliation. The core of
the drama is Oedipus' discovery of the truth about himself.
Sophocles has dramatized the illusions and the ignorance of
Oedipus and their collapse. In their ruin is his climax, in their
discord with reality his conflict, in their failure to resist the truth
his tragic fall.

A conflict of this kind, between divine truth and human illusion,
would not be strange to men of the fifth century. The actual situation recalls some lines of Theognis:

> Many men with base natures have good fortune;
> For them what seems evil turns to good.
> But others with good counsel and bad fortune
> Labour, and their actions find no end.[1]

Oedipus has good intentions and a bad fortune; his purposes are
frustrated. The parallel from Theognis goes farther than this.
His distinction between real and apparent evil is important for
the play. When transposed to dramatic action, it is the difference
between human appearance and opinion on one side and divine
being and knowledge on the other. The Chorus see this when they
know the truth about Oedipus:

> Ah! Generations of mankind!
> Living I count your life as nothingness.
> None hath more of happiness,
> None that mortal is, than this:
> But to seem to be, and then,
> Having seemed to fail.[2]

[1] 161–4 πολλοί τοι χρῶνται δειλαῖς φρεσί, δαίμονι δ' ἐσθλῷ,
οἷς τὸ κακὸν δοκέον γίνεται εἰς ἀγαθόν.
εἰσὶν δ' οἱ βουλῇ τ' ἀγαθῇ καὶ δαίμονι δειλῷ
μοχθίζουσι, τέλος δ' ἔργμασιν οὐχ ἕπεται.

[2] 1186–92 ἰὼ γενεαὶ βροτῶν,
ὡς ὑμᾶς ἴσα καὶ τὸ μη-
δὲν ζώσας ἐναριθμῶ.
τίς γάρ, τίς ἀνὴρ πλέον
τῆς εὐδαιμονίας φέρει
ἢ τοσοῦτον ὅσον δοκεῖν
καὶ δόξαντ' ἀποκλῖναι;

Their words contain a doctrine of human life. In Oedipus the Chorus find a lesson on the vanity and nothingness of mortal man, but the lesson is of a special kind. The nothingness of man lies in his knowing nothing, in his living in a world of illusory appearances. Such a view is not Homeric. It seems rather to be a product of religious and philosophical thought.

A clear distinction between the worlds of reality and appearance, of knowledge and opinion, is made by Parmenides. He knows that the senses are no sure guide,[1] that there is no certainty in opinions,[2] that men

> Both deaf and blind are they, in a stupor, crowds undiscerning.[3]

Heraclitus would agree with him when he contrasts the ignorance of man with the knowledge that belongs to God—'the way of man has no wisdom but the way of God has'[4] and 'man is called a baby by God, even as a child is by a man'.[5] A similar view was held by the scientific Alcmaeon of Croton, who said: 'About what is invisible, about what is mortal, the gods have clear knowledge, but to us as men only inference on what is coming is possible.'[6] Such men were primarily concerned with philosophy and natural science, but the distinction which they make has its counterpart in religion. In his comparison of gods and men Pindar makes the ignorance of men an important part of the contrast. Both are born of a single mother, but the gods have an abiding place, while men do not know what lies before them:

> We know not by day or in the nights
>   To what goal
> Fate has written that we shall run.[7]

He dwells on the ignorance of man,[8] especially about his own destiny.[9] Behind his theory of life lies a strong belief in the uncertainty of human existence and in the darkness in which men

---

[1] Fr. 1. 35.   [2] Fr. 1. 30.

[3] Fr. 6. 7   κωφοὶ ὁμῶς, τυφλοί τε, τεθηπότες, ἄκριτα φῦλα.

[4] Fr. 78 ἦθος γὰρ ἀνθρώπειον μὲν οὐκ ἔχει γνώμας, θεῖον δὲ ἔχει.

[5] Fr. 79 ἀνὴρ νήπιος ἤκουσε πρὸς δαίμονος ὅκωσπερ παῖς πρὸς ἀνδρός.

[6] Fr. 1 περὶ τῶν ἀφανέων, περὶ τῶν θνητῶν σαφήνειαν μὲν θεοὶ ἔχοντι, ὡς δὲ ἀνθρώποις τεκμαίρεσθαι καὶ τὰ ἐξῆς.

[7] Nem. vi. 6–7   καίπερ ἐφαμερίαν οὐκ εἰδότες οὐδὲ μετὰ νύκτας
                        ἄμμε πότμος
                        ἄντιν' ἔγραψε δραμεῖν ποτὶ στάθμαν.

[8] Nem. vii. 23–4.

[9] Ol. ii. 30–3.

live. The gods have 'a sure dwelling for ever'[1] and know the
truth.[2]

Poets and philosophers might agree that there are two worlds,
the one real in which dwell the all-knowing gods, the other illusory in which dwell ignorant men. Such a conclusion was natural
enough for a people who believed that human life was directed by
immortal, powerful gods. But the two worlds, though far asunder,
must somehow come into contact with one another. Men sometimes get a little nearer to the knowledge, security, and power
of the gods; the gods sometimes interfere, for weal or woe, in the
lives of men. Of this interpenetration the fragments of Parmenides
say nothing. We do not know what relation, if any, he established
between the Way of Knowledge and the Way of Opinion, between
the One and the Many. But Pindar certainly knew that such a
relation must exist, and preferred to dwell on its brighter side.
He believed that sometimes for short periods men might approxi-
mate to something remotely resembling the state of the gods, 'in
greatness of heart or of body',[3] that in moments of joy or triumph
a man is helped by the gods to a partial resemblance of their own
gifts,[4] that the highest glory in human life is a god-given bright-
ness.[5] In a way, too, he is concerned with knowledge. For these
bright moments come to those who know their human limitations,
conduct themselves as the gods wish, and show their inherited
qualities in fine achievements. Sophocles, too, postulates two such
divided and different worlds and marks a point at which they
meet. But for him this meeting is a tragic conflict. Oedipus has
broken the laws which the gods have made and to which they
demand obedience. He has to know what he has done, and they
force the knowledge on him. It brings pain and humiliation.
Therefore its human recipients, Jocasta and Oedipus, resist it as
strongly as they can without understanding what they are doing.
Their resistance is overcome, the might and knowledge of the gods
are vindicated, and a lesson is given to all men not to be too confident of any prosperity or happiness in this world.

As we have seen, Oedipus resists the truth through his high
temper which makes him follow false clues and cling to illusions
rather than recognize the facts. His resistance is typically human.
For it arises out of his self-confidence. And in a deeper sense he
resists simply because he is a man, because the ways of the gods

[1] Nem. vi. 3   ἀσφαλὲς αἰὲν ἕδος.
[2] Pyth. iii. 29–30.
[3] Nem. vi. 4–5.   [4] Ol. xi. 10.   [5] Pyth. viii. 96.

are always hard for men to understand, not least because they are presented in symbols and riddles. This is partly the significance of the scene between Oedipus and Teiresias. Teiresias is no god, but he is possessed of a knowledge far greater than that of other men. It ranges over heaven and earth, over

> all the signs
> That move in heaven and earth—the secret things
> And all that men may learn.[1]

He alone of men knows the truth about Oedipus. But like all who possess the gods' secrets, like burnt offerings and birds of augury, he is hard to understand. It is natural for him to speak in riddles, to clothe the truth in magnificent or menacing ambiguities. Like Heraclitus' god of Delphi, 'he neither utters nor conceals but hints.'[2] Yet he is also human, a man with feelings like other men, not weaker because he is old. He knows the hideous truth, but he is unwilling to reveal it to Oedipus. We can see why. Oedipus' destiny must be fulfilled and nothing that Teiresias says can alter it. Naturally he shrinks from such a task. He comes because he has been summoned, but the moment he arrives he knows that he should not have come:

> Ah me! it is but sorrow to be wise,
> When wisdom profits not. All this I knew,
> But had forgot it. Else I had not come.[3]

His knowledge cannot help. Now he wishes to return without speaking (320–1). Since the gods are at work and their will must be fulfilled, no revelation can be of use. Teiresias feels that he can do nothing, and in that case he had better keep silence.

In this intention Teiresias fails. He stays, is enraged by Oedipus, and in his rage lets out the truth, Oedipus fails to understand. This quarrel with its futile conclusion shows how men fail to deal rightly with the gods or to understand them. Oedipus' human temper prevents him from seeing the truth. His anger both forces Teiresias to speak and prevents any understanding of what he says. The lack of agreement is inevitable. Teiresias knows that Oedipus is doomed, that he is polluted and accursed. He cannot feel well dis-

---

[1] 300–1   διδακτά τε
             ἄρρητά τ', οὐράνιά τε καὶ χθονοστιβῆ.

[2] Fr. 93.

[3] 316–18   φεῦ φεῦ, φρονεῖν ὡς δεινὸν ἔνθα μὴ τέλη
            λύει φρονοῦντι· ταῦτα γὰρ καλῶς ἐγὼ
            εἰδὼς διώλεσ'· οὐ γὰρ ἂν δεῦρ' ἱκόμην.

posed to him; for he is an object of hatred to the gods. Oedipus, on the other hand, lives in his illusory world and fails to make anything of the prophet's words. This is the special irony of human illusion. Man thinks that he knows the truth, but so far is he from it that he cannot see it when it comes. This is his condition before the gods. In ignorance or passion he breaks their laws, but so ignorant is he that often he does not even know that he has done so. The greatest obstacle between him and the truth is the sense of his own importance. In Oedipus this takes the form of self-confidence. His whole attitude to Teiresias is that of men who after hearing oracles or warnings from the gods refuse to accept them because they cannot believe what they say. In this scene Sophocles shows the two sides of the conflict. The old seer can do nothing to remedy a hopeless situation. He tells the truth, but makes no effect. The man, anxious to do his best, quite fails to understand what is said, and no solution is reached. The gods pursue their plans undeterred, and Oedipus finds his destiny.

In this world of illusions Jocasta is no less deceived than Oedipus. If his temper makes him impervious to the truth, she is hardly less so, but for a different reason. Her sacrifice to Apollo shows (919–23) that she is no sceptic or unbeliever as are certain characters in Euripides. But experience has discouraged her from believing in oracles. She believes that the oracle which foretold the death of Laius by their son has been nullified by facts. Therefore she claims not to believe in it or any other oracle:

> On soothsaying
> Nothing depends.[1]

She argues that if the child who was to kill his father is already dead, there is no cause for belief in oracles now or henceforth:

> Since that, for all the soothsayers can tell,
> I go straight on, I look not left nor right.[2]

But we may suspect that her distrust is not so strong as it seems, and is partly dictated by a natural desire to comfort Oedipus. For she tries to discredit the authority of the oracle by a reason which is not really consistent with her view that no oracles are to be trusted. When she says

[1] 708–9   ἐστί σοι
βροτεῖον οὐδὲν μαντικῆς ἔχον τέχνης.

[2] 857–8   ὥστ' οὐχὶ μαντείας γ' ἂν οὔτε τῇδ' ἐγὼ
βλέψαιμ' ἂν οὕνεκ' οὔτε τῇδ' ἂν ὕστερον.

An oracle once came
To Laius—I'll not say it came from Phoebus,
But from his ministers . . .[1]

she implicitly admits that what is wrong is not oracles as such but
the source from which this particular oracle came; the servants
of Phoebus are not so reliable as their master. Her unbelief is
feminine and subjective, not based on any clear or argued doubt.
In the present crisis it brings her comfort. If the oracle is wrong,
there is nothing for Oedipus to be troubled about. She wishes to
let things alone, to prevent Oedipus from asking too much (1060
ff.). But this passive scepticism can in the end resist the truth no
more than Oedipus' active illusions.

Jocasta's doubts are proved wrong. But before the full revelation comes the Chorus sing a powerful song which is directly inspired by them. In 863–910 they tell of duties owed by men to the
gods. This song should make the audience suspicious of Jocasta's
scepticism and alive to the risks that it runs of creating impiety.
The Chorus are anxious. They feel that Jocasta and Oedipus have
gone too far and are near to grave wrongdoing. The song tells of
this danger, and proclaims that if Jocasta is right the whole structure of religion and morality is undermined. It presents a strong
case for the maintenance of religion in the State. The argument
is closely woven and advances from general considerations to the
definite conclusion that oracles must be trusted. The Strophe proclaims the everlasting nature of the divine laws, rather as Antigone
proclaims it, and prepares the way for the special law which
decrees the punishment of presumptuous insolence. Of this the
Antistrophe tells, and we cannot but detect an oblique reference
to the dangers which Oedipus runs by behaving as he just has to
Creon. It seems to hint that if he continues like this, the gods will
strike him. The second Strophe adds new possibilities. New
dangers, such as love of splendour (888) and unjust gains (889),
which are not visible in Oedipus, are descried on the horizon. Once
a tyrant begins to act in character and to override the gods' rules,
such results follows. And if these things are honoured, religion is
meaningless:

If doing such things as these be countenanced,
What mean religion's holy dance and hymn?[2]

[1] 711–12   χρησμὸς γὰρ ἦλθε Λαΐῳ ποτ', οὐκ ἐρῶ
                Φοίβου γ' ἀπ' αὐτοῦ, τῶν δ' ὑπηρετῶν ἄπο.

[2] 895–6   εἰ γὰρ αἱ τοιαίδε πράξεις τίμιαι,
                τί δεῖ με χορεύειν;

Then the second Antistrophe takes the special case of oracles.
They are, as it were, a test case of religious belief. If men really
despise them, the whole structure of faith totters:

> They fade, nor is Apollo glorified
> In worship any more. Religion dies.[1]

The Chorus are gravely disturbed. They fear the threats which
hang over religious belief and the potentialities of tyrannical behaviour in Oedipus. They do not mention him or Jocasta, but it
is clear that their thoughts are inspired by both of them. They are
in a dilemma. If Oedipus and Jocasta are right, religion is ruined;
if they are wrong, to what evils will they not, in their unbelief,
proceed?

The comment is justified. The Chorus are more likely to accept
the second horn of the dilemma than the first, and if their rulers are
proved wrong, they will unhesitatingly condemn them. The audience would surely find the song puzzling. They know that the
oracles are true and have been fulfilled; they might feel that therefore they should condemn Oedipus and Jocasta. And so to some
degree they should. The scepticism which both have displayed
may have its reasons, but it is wrong. It grows out of a situation
which is itself wrong because in it the laws of the gods have been
broken. Oedipus is doubtful about oracles because his life has
been so shaped that he does not know of his parricide and incest,
Jocasta because the child who should have perished on Cithaeron
has lived to kill his father. This unnatural situation has lasted
because of the ignorance which surrounds those who are most
concerned in it. This drives Oedipus and Jocasta to a scepticism
which is alien to their real natures and would not be entertained
by them if they did not live in a false world. Just as they do not
know who and what they are, so they do not understand the truth of
oracles. Their doubts are another sign of their severance from the
gods and from the right way of life. The situation is really fraught
with peril, and the Chorus understand something of what it means.

But the song has a second meaning, unknown to the Chorus yet
clear enough to the audience. Each section of it can be applied to
Oedipus or Jocasta, as we know from the sequel. The Unwritten
laws, whose power is proclaimed,

> A god in them is great. He grows not old,[2]

---

[1] 909-10   κοὐδαμοῦ τιμαῖς Ἀπόλλων ἐμφανής,
             ἔρρει δὲ τὰ θεῖα.

[2] 872   μέγας ἐν τούτοις θεὸς οὐδὲ γηράσκει.

concern Oedipus, who has broken them by parricide and incest.
Since they are everlasting and protected by the gods, he will
infallibly pay for violating them. The insolent pride which the
Chorus suspect in him may not yet dominate his whole nature,
but because he is a king and above ordinary restrictions he is
liable to be struck down, and we know that he will be. The horror
which the Chorus have begun to feel at Oedipus and Jocasta is
partly justified by their scepticism, but both have committed acts
which the gods regard with abhorrence and for which they exact
amends. The searching question:

Then from the arrows of the gods what mortal man shall save his soul
  alive?[1]

is all too applicable to them. Finally, the oracles have been called
in doubt and Apollo's word distrusted. Before long the oracles
will be proved right and Apollo's truthfulness abundantly justified.
This subsidiary, secondary meaning of the song, conveyed with a
typically Sophoclean irony, prepares for the general conclusion.
The gods' will is fulfilled; religion is not discredited; it is useless
to fight against the gods. We see more than the error which deludes
Oedipus and Jocasta; we see that if the divine dominion of the
world is real, they will come to disaster.

The process of decay and disorder continues in Jocasta. When
she hears of Polybus' death she feels even more justified in her
doubts:

Why, what should a man fear? Luck governs all!
There's no foreknowledge, and no providence!
Take life at random. Live as best you can.[2]

The words may easily be underestimated. Though they are not
the language of complete unbelief, they show a grave irresponsibility and culpable ignorance of what the gods are. Luck was not
unreal or always unworthy of respect. So long as it was associated
with some higher power, it was even pious to take note of it. There
is nothing wrong when Pindar calls Luck the daughter of Zeus.[3]
But it was a different matter to substitute the rule of Luck for
that of the gods, and this is what Jocasta does. She is perilously

---

[1] 893-5   τίς ἔτι ποτ' ἐν τοῖσΔ' ἀνὴρ βέλη θεῶν
              ἔρξεται ψυχᾶς ἀμύνων;

[2] 977-9   τί Δ' ἂν φοβοῖτ' ἄνθρωπος ᾧ τὰ τῆς τύχης
              κρατεῖ, πρόνοια Δ' ἐστὶν οὐΔενὸς σαφής;
              εἰκῇ κράτιστον ʒῆν, ὅπως Δύναιτό τις.

[3] *Ol.* xii. 1.

near to denying the power of the gods altogether and displays a scepticism like that of Euripides' Talthybius:

> O Zeus, what shall I say? that you regard
> Mankind? Or are the gods an idle fancy
> And Luck the only governor of the world?[1]

or his Odysseus:

> Or should we think Luck a divinity,
> And everything divine less strong than she?[2]

Since Jocasta denies the rule of the gods, she also denies human responsibility towards them and thinks that it is best to live at random, without purpose or plan. She can be contrasted with the pious Nicias who thought it unwise to trust in Luck,[3] and her real motives are well illustrated by Democritus' searching words that 'Men have made an image of Luck as an excuse for their own lack of wisdom'.[4] By exalting Luck Jocasta defies the gods and denies her responsibilities. This is not only impious; it is imprudent. It means that she has no foresight for the future. Thucydides distrusts those who believe in Luck and says that we attribute to it anything that turns out contrary to our reckoning.[5] When Jocasta says that providence or foresight is impossible and that it is best to live at random, she deprives life of order and security. She offends against religion, morality, and common prudence. The audience would expect her to be corrected, and before the scene is over she has been.

The truth is forced on Jocasta against her will and against her convictions. While Oedipus questions the Messenger and finds that he himself is the child who was years ago exposed on Cithaeron, Jocasta listens in silence. The truth must be clear to her as soon as she knows that Oedipus is this child and therefore her son (1025). For some agonizing moments she says nothing. Then, true to her belief that life should be lived at random, she tries desperately to persuade Oedipus to stop his questions (1056–7, 1060–1). She wishes to keep him at least in ignorance, and almost her last words to him are:

---

[1] *Hec.* 488–91 ὦ Ζεῦ, τί λέξω; πότερά σ' ἀνθρώπους ὁρᾶν;
ἢ δόξαν ἄλλως τήνδε κεκτῆσθαι μάτην,
τύχην δὲ πάντα τἀν βροτοῖς ἐπισκοπεῖν;

[2] *Cyc.* 606–7 ἢ τὴν τύχην μὲν δαίμον' ἡγεῖσθαι χρεών,
τὰ δαιμόνων δὲ τῆς τύχης ἐλάσσονα;

[3] Thuc. v. 16.

[4] Fr. 119 τύχης εἴδωλον ἐπλάσαντο πρόφασιν ἰδίης ἀβουλίης.

[5] Thuc. i. 140. 1.

Alas! I pray you may not know yourself.[1]

But her attempts fail. Oedipus pursues his inquiries without flinching. Jocasta leaves him with her last terrible words and goes to her death. When she prepares for it, her thoughts turn away from this false marriage with her son to her real husband. She calls on Laius and laments her life with Oedipus (1245–50). It is her confession before death, her attempt to make peace with her real husband and with the gods. The shock of the truth has brought her to herself. Her death is a sign that she cannot endure to live any longer as she has been living with Oedipus. With her, as with Oedipus, truth triumphs at the last. It wins against the man's active illusions and the woman's passive scepticism. At the end of the play the truth is revealed, and those who learn it pay a heavy price. Yet by this suffering Oedipus and Jocasta are restored to the proper order of things. Jocasta goes to her dead husband in Hades; Oedipus goes to face his life of amends. The gods cannot leave them in ignorance. Like Heraclitus' sleeper, Oedipus has lived in a 'private universe'[2] which is broken when the 'common universe' of the gods and of reality comes into conflict with it. In his struggle Oedipus may well arouse pity and admiration, but he is bound to lose. And his failure is a lesson on the omnipotence of the gods and the insecurity of man.

By modern standards the gods who decide on Oedipus' fate before he is born and then inflict it on him without mercy treat him cruelly. But this is not a view that Sophocles would have held or admitted. He would more probably hold that men cannot judge the gods and might even agree with Heraclitus that 'For God all things are beautiful and good and just, but men think some things unjust and others just.'[3] For he states emphatically that the gods must be honoured, and shows that their word must be believed. Nor is it legitimate to argue that their word is sometimes hard to understand. That, too, arises from the ignorance and blindness in which man lives. He can only do his best to understand the gods by what means he possesses, to recognize that his own judgement may be wrong. The gods, who know everything, are right. Nor may man complain of them. He must humble himself before them and admit that he is nothing and that he knows nothing. This is the lesson of *King Oedipus*. The last words draw attention to it. Oedipus is

---

[1] 1068 ὦ δύσποτμ', εἴθε μήποτε γνοίης ὃς εἶ.   [2] Fr. 89.

[3] Fr. 102 τῷ μὲν θεῷ καλὰ πάντα καὶ ἀγαθὰ καὶ δίκαια, ἄνθρωποι δὲ ἃ μὲν ἄδικα ὑπειλήφασιν ἃ δὲ δίκαια.

That Mighty King, who knew the riddle's mystery.[1]

But his knowledge is of no avail in dealing with the mysteries of
the gods. On this note of ignorance and humiliation the play ends.
It is hardly a quiet end. Oedipus is still an abhorred and defiled
creature who may not remain in the daylight and is fated to suffer
more. Creon, who does correctly what the gods require, insists on
his going indoors. His manner may seem rigorous, but he does his
religious duty. He cannot do otherwise, and Oedipus, now fully
conscious of his nothingness before the gods, knows that Creon is
right. He asks to be sent out of the land (1518); he knows that the
gods abhor him (1518). What will happen next must, as Creon
sees (1438-9), wait on the gods' decision. We know that Teiresias
has prophesied more miseries for Oedipus and that they will infallibly come. The play ends in the anguish of humiliation and the
anticipation of more to come. But at last the truth is out, and the
gods have had their way.

The gods humble Oedipus as a lesson to men not to trust in
their happiness or their knowledge. The horror of his fate and his
fall is fore-ordained that others may learn from it. But though
this plan determines all that happens, the actual events follow a
pattern which is tragic and Sophoclean. When Oedipus kills his
father and marries his mother the inviolable laws of the gods are
broken and the divine order of things sustains a grievous wound.
The wound must be healed, the order restored. Before this can be
done, the evil that has been, albeit unconsciously, committed, must
show its full force. This it does in the growth of Oedipus' illusions
when the plague forces a crisis on him. From illusions he moves to
dangerous acts. His fits of fury, his moments of scepticism, his
certainty that he is right, are the natural products of his state.
Such a condition cannot last, and it is broken by the events which
follow the death of Polybus. As Oedipus comes to see the truth
and to punish himself for his past actions, he makes his peace with
the gods. He does what is right, accepts his position, knows the
truth. Through resignation and suffering the rightful harmony of
things is restored. By divine standards Oedipus at the end of the
play is a better man than at the beginning. His humiliation is a
lesson both to others and to him. Democritus' words, 'the foolish
learn modesty in misfortune',[2] may be applied to Oedipus, who
has indeed been foolish in his mistakes and illusions and has been

[1] 1525   ὃς τὰ κλείν' αἰνίγματ' ᾔδει καὶ κράτιστος ἦν ἀνήρ.
[2] Fr. 54   οἱ ἀξύνετοι δυστυχέοντες σωφρονέουσι.

taught modesty through suffering. The lesson which the gods convey through his fall is all the more impressive because he is the great king and the great man that he is. In the eyes of the gods what matters is that he should know who and what he really is. To secure this end his power and his glory must be sacrificed. In his acceptance of his fall, his readiness to take part in it, Oedipus shows a greatness nobler than when he read the riddle of the Sphinx and became king of Thebes.

VI

ELECTRA

BY a whim of choice or chance there survives from each of the three Attic tragedians a play on the revenge which Orestes exacted from his mother and her paramour for the murder of his father. Whatever may be responsible for the preservation of the *Libation-bearers* of Aeschylus, the *Electra* of Sophocles, and the *Electra* of Euripides, the gruesome old story which they tell has enough dramatic claims to justify its popularity. But it also contains a complex ethical situation such as appealed to Greek poets and called for that dramatic casuistry in which they delighted. A son is told by Apollo to kill his mother because she has murdered his father. The audience might ask if Orestes was right to kill his mother and would expect the poet to provide them with something like an answer, though he might not give one. Homer, for instance, knew about Orestes and refers more than once to the vengeance exacted by him for the murder of Agamemnon. But though the Homeric gods regard the killing of Aegisthus as an exemplary act of filial devotion, they say nothing, or next to nothing, about the death of Clytaemnestra. Homer certainly thought that she was a murderess,[1] but he does not say that Orestes killed her. Once he mentions her death, when, after telling of the death of Aegisthus, he says of Orestes:

> When he had killed him, he gave a funeral-feast to the Argives
> Over his mother accurs'd and the cowardly dastard Aegisthus.[2]

Aristarchus was uncertain what the lines meant, and while he admitted that 'Clytaemnestra was destroyed with Aegisthus', he added the reservation, 'but it is uncertain if by Orestes'.[3] We are in his position. Homer's reticence has been variously explained. Some have thought that in the story as he knew it Clytaemnestra killed herself. For this there is no evidence in ancient art or literature, and it is strange that Homer who recounts the suicide of Epicaste[4] should be silent on that of Clytaemnestra. On the other hand, it is surely typical of his temper to avoid so painful a subject

---

[1] *Od.* xi. 421–34.

[2] Ib. iii. 309–10 ἦ τοι ὁ τὸν κτείνας Δαίνυ τάφον 'Αργείοισι
μητρός τε στυγερῆς καὶ ἀνάλκιδος Αἰγίσθοιο.

[3] Schol. ad loc. συναπώλετο Αἰγίσθῳ ἡ Κλυταιμήστρα· τὸ δὲ εἰ καὶ ὑπὸ 'Ορέστου ἄδηλον.

[4] *Od.* xi. 277–9.

as the killing of a mother by her son. Just as he refers to the
parallel story of Eriphyle without saying that her son Alcmeon
slew her,[1] so he may have kept a similar decent silence about the
manner of Clytaemnestra's death. Whatever his reasons were,
Homer said nothing about it. What he emphasized was the
righteous punishment of the murderous paramour Aegisthus.

Other poets did not observe a similar reticence. Both Aeschylus
and Euripides saw that the story raised a difficult problem, and
each answered it in his own way. Aeschylus makes Orestes the
victim of two duties, one to his father and to Apollo who commands
him to exact vengeance, the other to his mother who is protected by the Furies. Perhaps his solution of the problem may
seem a little hollow to us. Yet it is based on a real consideration
of the facts. Apollo argues, and Athene agrees, that when there
is a conflict between the claims of a man and the claims of a
woman, those of a man must win. Apollo supports his contention
with the biology of his age,[2] and Athene says boldly:

> I praise the male in all things.[3]

This preference was natural enough in a society which, at least in
theory, kept women in some kind of subjection. But Aeschylus'
solution goes deeper. The Furies, who champion Clytaemnestra's
spirit, are the old guardians of family rights; Apollo stands for
the new order of state and law as it is embodied in the Council
of the Areopagus. Against this new authority the old rights cannot
prevail. Orestes is acquitted because his action is necessary for
the preservation of society and cannot really be wrong. His task
has been extremely painful to him. He has been harassed by the
Furies, who are the embodiment of all the guilt and misery that
a man must feel if he kills his mother. But he has done the right
thing. Blood must be paid for in blood, but the last decision rests
with the State. The vengeance of Orestes is right.

Euripides found an answer which is almost diametrically
opposite to this. In his *Electra* Apollo orders Orestes to kill his
mother, but once the fell deed is done, neither Orestes nor Electra
finds any satisfaction in it. The god's command is shown to be
repugnant to the human conscience, and the Dioscuri, who speak
with authority at the end, make Apollo the villain of the piece:

> Wise is he, but his order was not wise.[4]

[1] *Od.* xi. 326–7.
[2] G. Thomson, *Oresteia*, ii, p. 293, quotes Diod. i. 80 and Stob. i. 64.
[3] *Eum.* 737   τὸ δ' ἄρσεν αἰνῶ πάντα.
[4] *El.* 1246   σοφὸς δ' ὢν οὐκ ἔχρησέ σοι σοφά.

A similar view appears in the *Iphigeneia in Tauris*[1] and *Orestes*.[2] The meaning of Clytaemnestra's death for those who have worked it is shown in the *Electra* by the duet which brother and sister sing after it. It is a song of guilt and grief. They feel defiled and deceived. Euripides would admit that since Clytaemnestra is a murderess she must be punished, but he thinks it wrong that this punishment should be executed by her son. The Dioscuri say to Orestes:

> Her doom is right, but not right what you do.[3]

Euripides sets a son's feelings before the reasons of state and public morality which carried weight with Aeschylus. He puts the blame on established religion and on Apollo for commanding an action so abhorrent to human feelings. He may be to some extent maintaining a paradox and showing that what is ascribed to the gods is not always right. Therefore he stresses his conclusion in a sense opposite to Aeschylus. But he was not alone in his disapproval. Dio Chrysostom certainly felt that Orestes was wrong and argued that, since Apollo cannot have ordered him to kill his mother, he must have misunderstood the oracle which seemed to command it.[4] It was no mere desire to be different that made Euripides take up the position that he did.

Finally, there were those who, while they saw the dramatic, even tragic, elements in the story, thought that Orestes was right and did not recognize any real problem. If we may judge by the few remains of Stesichorus' *Oresteia*, he dealt with the story in a spirit which celebrated the triumph of the oppressed over their oppressors. A spirit similar in some ways but certainly serious and profound pervades the myth of Pindar's *Pythian* xi. It illustrates the divine wisdom of Apollo:

> Of holy Themis and Pytho
> And the straight justice of the navel of the world[5]

and closes with the deaths of Clytaemnestra and Aegisthus. Though Pindar speculates on the motives of the royal murderess in a way that recalls Aeschylus, he has no excuse for her and thinks that her death is right. There is no regret or hesitation in his emphatic close with the return of Orestes:

---

[1] *I. T.* 570-1, 711.   [2] *Or.* 28-30, 160-5, 581-601, 955-6.
[3] *El.* 1244   Δίκαια μέν νυν ἥδ' ἔχει, σὺ δ' οὐχὶ δρᾷς.
[4] *Or.* x. 27
[5] *Pyth.* xi. 9-10   Θέμιν ἱερὰν Πυθῶνά τε καὶ ὀρθοδίκαν
γᾶς ὀμφαλόν.

Yet Ares at the last
Brought him to slay his mother, and lay Aegisthus in blood.[1]

The double death fufils the god's design. Pindar sees no problem.
What Apollo orders is right and must be obeyed.

When Sophocles chose to write an *Electra*, several ways of
handling the subject were open to him. He could hardly follow
Homer and avoid the issue of Clytaemnestra's death. By his time
this had become an essential part of the story and could hardly be
omitted from a tragedy on the subject.[2] But he might agree with
Aeschylus in justifying Apollo's command as due to the superior
claims of a father to a mother's, of public to domestic duties, or
with Euripides in placing human feelings before religious or social
obligations,[3] or with Pindar in seeing the simple triumph of right
over wrong. Or he might go his own way and find a new solution.
Our task is to find how Sophocles approached the story of Orestes
and what conclusion he expected his audience to draw from his
play. The drama itself is so tense and the poetry often so brilliant
that we are liable to conclude that nothing else matters. If so, we
fail to see the play's meaning. To understand it rightly we must
see how a Greek audience would receive his characters and their
fortunes. Nor is this easy. Sophocles gives hardly any clue to his
general meaning. The Chorus are too partial to be his mouthpiece;
there is no independent witness like Odysseus in the *Ajax*; even
the play itself can be acted in different ways and produce quite
different effects. Modern critics have held various views of it,
and if we can see where these fail, we may be nearer the truth.

To the modern world Euripides' view that Apollo violates deep
and holy feelings by ordering Orestes to kill his mother is undeniably sympathetic. It is therefore not surprising that some
who know and love Sophocles should claim that he too felt this
and that his play is based on it. J. T. Sheppard[4] follows Dio
in thinking that the whole fault lay with Orestes, who was not
told by Apollo to kill his mother but, assuming this to be
his duty, asked the god how to do it, and that the god, as
was his wont when asked a question simply about means to
an assumed end, told him what to do but did not express his
approval. Now there are undoubtedly cases in which oracular

---

[1] Ib. 36–7   ἀλλὰ χρονίῳ σὺν Ἄρει
πέφνεν τε ματέρα θῆκέ τ' Αἴγισθον ἐν φοναῖς.

[2] Aristot. *Poet.* 1453 b 22.

[3] This must not be taken to mean that Sophocles' play is later than Euripides'.
On this vexed question cf. J. D. Denniston, *Electra*, pp. xxxiii ff.

[4] *C. R.* xli (1927), pp. 2–9. Cf. G. Perrotta, *Sofocle*, pp. 301 ff.

deities were willing to answer questions which assumed an end of which they did not approve. A classic example is that of the Cymaeans, who asked the oracle of Branchidae what they should do with a suppliant, Pactyes, who had taken refuge with them. The god replied, 'Give him up to the Persians.' When pressed, he repeated his decision and added, 'I do command it, that so for your impiety you may the sooner perish and not come here again to consult my oracle about the surrender of a suppliant.'[1] In other words, if men asked an oracle about something evil, the god might well drive them on to gather the full fruits of their wickedness. It is claimed that this happens to Orestes, that he merely asks how to kill his mother, that this killing is a bad thing and disapproved by the god, and that the god tells him how to do it in the knowledge that it will bring him nothing but harm and misery. If this view is right, Sophocles' *Electra* resembles Euripides' play in making the vengeance completely unsatisfying to Orestes and Electra but at the same time manages to save the character of Apollo.

Yet this interpretation, subtle and sensitive as it is, is open to objections. First, it assumes that Apollo would not order the matricide and would indeed condemn it. Sophocles does not say this, and we must believe that the audience would feel so strongly about Orestes killing his mother that they would assume it without being helped by the poet. But surely many in the audience would, even if not approving the matricide, know that it was part of the story and that Apollo commanded it. Since Sophocles does not deny this, they would legitimately assume that the god played his usual part. And in that case they would fail to see that Orestes is wrong or why he goes wrong. In fact if Sophocles intended to build his play on behaviour so untraditional on the part of Apollo, he would surely have given some hint of it. Otherwise we naturally assume that he follows the usual tradition. When Dio blames Orestes on these lines he says nothing about Sophocles. On the contrary he considers the case of Orestes 'in the tragedies', and surely he is thinking of the familiar story and giving his own interpretation of it, as if it were a chapter of history. In his view the only explanation is that Orestes misunderstood the oracle. He is entitled to hold such a view, but he tells us nothing about Sophocles or even about his own opinion of what Sophocles meant.

A second objection is that such indications as Sophocles does give about Apollo suggest that he told Orestes to kill his mother. This was so familiar that it needed no description but could be

referred to lightly in passing. The only long account of it is given
by Orestes to the Paedagogus.

> I went to Delphi, to the oracle
> Of Phoebus, with my question, by what means
> I could do justice on the murderers.
> Now listen. Thus, or nearly thus, the god
> Spoke: 'With no force of armed men, alone,
> By cunning do the righteous deed of blood.'[1]

From this it might look as if Orestes simply asked the god how to
kill the murderers, not whether he ought to kill them. Yet even if
it does this, the god's answer is quite emphatic that the vengeance
is 'righteous'. It certainly does not suggest that the god disapproved of the end for which he advised the means. And in
other places Sophocles indicates that the god both approves and
expects the vengeance of Orestes on Clytaemnestra and Aegisthus.
When Orestes says that he comes

> Justly with cleansing as God's minister[2]

he himself is convinced that the gods have sent him. When the
Paedagogus tells Orestes not to listen to his sister's cry but to get
on with their business:

> No! We must try to do the god's command
> First, before everything[3]

he refers to the work of vengeance as ordered by the god. Lastly,
when after Clytaemnestra's death Orestes says to Electra:

> In the house
> All's well, if Apollo's oracle was well,[4]

he may doubt if what he has done is good, but he is certain that
Apollo commanded it. The poet leads us to think that Orestes
acts on the god's orders. Nor can we assume that he is deluded.
For if Apollo had not given the order, the poet should and would

---

[1] 32–7   ἐγὼ γὰρ ἡνίχ' ἱκόμην τὸ Πυθικὸν
                μαντεῖον, ὡς μάθοιμ' ὅτῳ τρόπῳ πατρὸς
                Δίκας ἀροίμην τῶν φονευσάντων πάρα,
                χρῇ μοι τοιαῦθ' ὁ Φοῖβος ὧν πεύσῃ τάχα.
                ἄσκευον αὐτὸν ἀσπίδων τε καὶ στρατοῦ
                Δόλοισι κλέψαι χειρὸς ἐνδίκους σφαγάς.

[2] 70   Δίκη καθαρτὴς πρὸς θεῶν ὡρμημένος.
This seems to be an echo of Aesch. *Cho.* 941 θεόθεν εὖ φραδαῖσιν ὡρμημένος.

[3] 82–3   μηδὲν πρόσθεν ἢ τὰ Λοξίου
                πειρώμεθ' ἔρδειν κἀπὸ τῶνδ' ἀρχηγετεῖν.

[4] 1424–5   τἀν Δόμοισι μὲν
                καλῶς, Ἀπόλλων εἰ καλῶς ἐθέσπισεν.

have made it plain. We must find his meaning in what he says, and his text indicates that Apollo approves of Orestes' vengeance on his father's murderers.

Critics of this view have gone to the opposite extreme and claimed that Sophocles does his best to minimize the importance and horror of Clytaemnestra's death, that so far from feeling his task odious Orestes feels very little about it, and that we are expected to feel the same.[1] Sophocles, it is claimed, goes back to Homer and tries to lay as little stress as possible on the death of Clytaemnestra. In the first place we can hardly speak of Sophocles going back to Homer, for Homer avoids the whole incident and Sophocles chooses it as something critical in his play. It is equally unsound to argue that Sophocles minimizes the horror of Clytaemnestra's death. On the stage it provides a moment of breathless horror and is the climax of the whole play. The mere fact that it comes before the death of Aegisthus in no way reduces its effect. The Greek preference for a slackening of tension towards the close suggests that it is more important than the vengeance on Aegisthus. Finally, it is not true, as is claimed, that we are kept in the dark about the forthcoming death of Clytaemnestra as if the poet did not like to draw too much attention to it. Dark hints suggest and foretell it. Electra names her mother as a murderess in her first monody (97). Her use of the plural shows that she associates her with Aegisthus in her demand for vengeance:

> God in the Height, hear me!
> Let them suffer, let them pay for all.[2]

She surely has her in mind when she bids Chrysothemis pray for vengeance on their father's enemies (455-6). There can be little doubt about her secret desire when she says to her mother:

> If life for life
> Were always to be taken, you yourself
> Must be the first to die, if you have Justice.[3]

Hint upon hint suggests that Clytaemnestra deserves death and will find it. Her death is not a surprise when it comes. Her dream has shown that all is not well with her. We know that Electra clamours for vengeance, that Orestes has been told to exact the

---

[1] A. S. Owen, C. R. xli (1927), pp. 50-3.

[2] 209-10   οἷς θεὸς ὁ μέγας ᾿Ολύμπιος
πoίνιμα πάθεα παθεῖν πόροι.

[3] 582-3   εἰ γὰρ κτενοῦμεν ἄλλον ἀντ᾿ ἄλλου, σύ τοι
πρώτη θάνοις ἄν, εἰ Δίκης γε τυγχάνοις.

last penalty from the murderers (34). We are prepared for
Clytaemnestra's death, and when it comes it is the consummation
of what has gone before.

The truth seems to lie in neither of these views. Nor should we
expect Sophocles either to condemn the matricide outright or to
belittle its importance. To make it part of his plot and then to
attach small importance to it would spoil his drama at its chief
point. He would hardly expend his strength in preparing for an
action which has in itself little significance. Nor was he likely to
condemn matricide as unequivocally wrong. It was, as he indicates, ordered by Apollo, and he was not one to agree with
Euripides in condemning a god. In fact Sophocles may well have
seen the problem in a different way and with more respect for
the accepted ideas of his time. He must have known that the
story of Orestes presented a problem and that the choice of
evils in it would be clear to any intelligent Athenian. If we
can get a rough idea what an ordinary person would feel about
the issues involved, we should be able to see more clearly what
Sophocles meant. This is not to say that his view was that of the
ordinary man, but it gains in significance from being shown in
relation to it.

Orestes is faced with a dilemma. If a father is murdered, the
duty of vengeance falls on his next of kin, and primarily on his
son if one exists. That is why Homer's Orestes avenges Agamemnon and is approved by the gods for it.[1] In Attic law, if murder
was done, proclamation against the murderer was made in the
market-place by his family, whose duty it was to join in the prose-
cution,[2] and this duty extended to quite remote kinsmen.[3] They
had to see that the murderer was brought to justice. This was an
obligation not to be shirked. The sentiments which informed this
belief may be seen in the First Speech of Antiphon in which a
son prosecutes his step-mother for murdering his father. He has
no doubt that he must do it, and the arguments with which Antiphon provides him were calculated to appeal to the judges. He
is the dead man's 'helper' and 'avenger'.[4] He claims that the duty
of vengeance is laid on him by laws which come from the gods and
from his ancestors,[5] that his half-brother acts abominably in
taking the part of the step-mother,[6] that the punishment of the
murderess is an act of kindness and justice to the murdered.[7] It
is clear that the son's first duty is to avenge his father. Plato

[1] *Od.* iii. 307.   [2] *S. I. G.* 111.   [3] Dem. xlvii. 72.
[4] Ant. i. 2, 4, 21, 22.   [5] Ib. 3.   [6] Ib. 21.   [7] Ib. 25.

accepted this duty so emphatically that he even prescribes punishments for those kinsmen who do not take steps to avenge a murdered man.[1] It was undoubtedly Orestes' duty to avenge his father's death. That is why Apollo, the god of justice, tells him to do so.

On the other hand, a son owed a very special respect to his mother, and to kill her was in any circumstances a hideous thing. Plato lays down that if a man slays his mother he must in another life take on a woman's nature and be killed by his own children.[2] He seems to feel that no punishment is adequate for such an act, even though the killer has acted under violent emotion;[3] for his mother is the author of his being. Herodotus, who sometimes liked to criticize the Greeks by comparing them unfavourably with virtuous barbarians, may have such stories as that of Orestes in his mind when he says that the Persians refused to believe that any man ever killed his mother.[4] It is on this feeling that Euripides bases his condemnation of Orestes' vengeance. His Neoptolemus reproaches Orestes with it,[5] and in the *Iphigeneia in Tauris* Thoas, the barbarian king, exclaims:

> Apollo! no barbarian would do it.[6]

In the *Orestes* Strophius expels Pylades from his home for having helped Orestes in the matricide.[7] Euripides appealed to a natural feeling that it is a horrible thing to kill one's mother and that the man who does it is an object of hideous pollution. Sophocles was certainly aware of this feeling, for in his *Epigoni*, which told how Alcmeon killed his mother for killing his father, Adrastus says to Alcmeon:

> You killed the mother who gave birth to you,[8]

and we can imagine with what force the words sounded on the stage. The peculiar sanctity of motherhood needs no explanation. It is enough to note that it existed and carried great weight.

Orestes, then, would be faced with conflicting duties, and everyone would know it. If he fails to avenge his father he will be haunted by his angry spirit; if he kills his mother he will take on an appalling pollution and violate deep feelings of sanctity. Much of the plot's interest turns on this conflict of duties. Sophocles was fully aware of it. He has no solution like Aeschylus' argument

---

[1] *Laws* ix. 871 a.   [2] *Laws* ix. 872 e.   [3] Ib. 869 c.   [4] Hdt. i. 137.2.
[5] *Andr.* 977–8.
[6] *I. T.* 1174   Ἄπολλον, οὐδ' ἐν βαρβάροις ἔτλη τις ἄν.
[7] *Or.* 765–7.
[8] Fr. 187. 2   σύ δ' αὐτόχειρ γε μητρὸς ἥ σ' ἐγείνατο.

that the male is superior to the female, and he does not make his
characters discuss the rights and wrongs of the vengeance. But
this does not mean that he is not interested. On the contrary he
shows by many touches and hints that he had given much thought
to the implications of his theme. He presents it as a drama, and
what counts most is what the characters do and say. His conclusions must be drawn from the actual events that he portrays
and from the effect which his characters make on us. The result
may not be so clear as it is in Aeschylus, but it may well be more
satisfying. For Aeschylus' solution seems a little abstract and remote. Moreover, Sophocles was interested not merely in the rights
and wrongs of his theme but in its human aspects. He constructed
a play which showed how this kind of thing might have happened
and what in life and practice it meant.

Sophocles assumes that vengeance is demanded by the murdered man. In this he follows the belief of his time. Antiphon
shows what common sentiment on such a matter was. In his
Tetralogies, which are model speeches to .be studied by young
orators, he makes use of several notions which clustered round
murder. His view is that if no expiation is made, the dead man
will haunt the consciences of those who ought to avenge him.[1]
These powers of vengeance are a kind of demons[2] to whose help
the dead man appeals.[3] They will not only haunt the criminal but
bring disaster and famine to the State. So too Aeschylus speaks of
the wrath of 'those below' and must refer to the dead Agamemnon
and his protecting spirits.[4] His Orestes knows that if he shirks his
duty of vengeance he will suffer a terrible punishment.[5] Plato
holds that the murdered man has power to send all kinds of horrors
to his murderers.[6] So in Sophocles' *Electra* Agamemnon's spirit
demands vengeance and is powerfully at work. The Chorus compare him to Amphiaraus, who though below the earth

> Ruleth in plenitude of princely power[7]

and pray that he will hear of the wrongs which befall his house.
When Clytaemnestra is killed they claim to see his hand at work
and the manifestation of his power:

> The curses are at work. The dead are living.
> They are draining back the blood from those who slew.[8]

[1] *Tetr.* I. iii. 10.   [2] Id. III. i. 4, ii. 8, iv. 10.   [3] Id. III. i. 4.
[4] *Cho.* 39–40.   [5] Ib. 273 ff.   [6] *Laws* ix. 865 d.   [7] 841 πάμψυχος ἀνάσσει.
[8] 1417–21   τελοῦσ' ἀραί· ζῶσιν οἱ
                  γᾶς ὑπαὶ κείμενοι.
          παλίρρυτον γὰρ αἶμ' ὑπεξαιροῦσι τῶν
          κτανόντων οἱ πάλαι θανόντες.

When Orestes kills his mother he does not act entirely unaided
and on his own. His father's spirit works with him.

The gods are equally concerned. Antiphon says that a murderer 'both sins against the gods and confounds the ordinances of
men'.[1] The belief that murder was primarily a religious offence was
shown at Athens by the conduct of murder trials. At the beginning both sides took an oath in the name of the Erinyes;[2] each of
the three days of trial was sacred to one of the Dread Goddesses,[3]
and the acquitted made sacrifice to them.[4] This association of
civil proceedings with religious shows that in the Athenian mind
murder concerned the gods. So they demand the punishment of
Agamemnon's murderers. Aeschylus' Orestes knows that he is
driven to vengeance by 'the god's commands',[5] and in the *Electra*
Apollo's command shows what the gods desire. In turn different
characters show that they expect the gods to aid the vengeance.
Orestes' first thought is to do what they have commanded
(32 ff.). The Paedagogus insists that before anything else offerings
must be made at Agamemnon's tomb; he knows that this is indispensable to success:

> This, I say,
> Is victory. This shall prosper all we do.[6]

He means that if he carries out the right religious duties the gods
will aid his cause. On her first appearance Electra bursts into an
appeal for vengeance to the gods of the nether world:

> O House of Hades and Persephone,
> O Hermes, Lord of the Dead, O spirit of the Curse,
> And you, ye dreadful daughters of the Gods, ye Furies, . . .
> Come to me! come to my aid! Avenge our father's murder.[7]

She knows that they will help her. Soon afterwards the Chorus
announce that the gods are keeping watch for her:

> Zeus is in his heaven,
> Child, beholding, overruling all,[8]

[1] *Tetr.* III. i. 1.   [2] Din. *In Dem.* 47.   [3] Schol. Aeschin. i. 188.
[4] Paus. i. 28. 6.   [5] *Cho.* 300.
[6] 84–5   ταῦτα γὰρ φέρειν
νίκην τέ φημι καὶ κράτος τῶν δρωμένων.
[7] 110–16   ὦ Δῶμ' Ἅιδου καὶ Περσεφόνης,
ὦ χθόνι' Ἑρμῆ καὶ πότνι' Ἀρά,
σεμναί τε θεῶν παῖδες Ἐρινύες. . . .
ἔλθετ', ἀρήξατε, τείσασθε πατρὸς
φόνον ἡμετέρου.
[8] 174–5   ἔτι μέγας οὐρανῷ
Ζεύς, ὃς ἐφορᾷ πάντα καὶ κρατύνει.

and that the god who rules by Acheron remembers (184). Each character trusts in the gods for help because they watch over the murdered man and demand requital.

To this trust and these appeals the gods respond. The vengeance succeeds. But the god's part is not confined to this vague assistance. It may be seen directly in Clytaemnestra's dream. This theme was as old as Stesichorus[1] and may have been thought necessary to the story, since in different ways Aeschylus[2] and Euripides[3] refer to it. For Aeschylus and Stesichorus it was simply a presage of punishment—Clytaemnestra suckles a snake which turns into her son or is known to be he. But Sophocles changes the dream and its meaning. The snake has disappeared. Clytaemnestra dreams that Agamemnon comes back, takes his sceptre, and plants it on the hearth:

> There, they say, it grew
> Into a lusty sapling, which at length
> O'ershadow'd the whole Mycenean land.[4]

She is frightened and sends Chrysothemis to make offerings to Agamemnon's spirit (426–7). Neither the Chorus nor Electra have any doubt about the dream's meaning. Electra forbids her sister to make the offerings, and believes that the dream comes from her father:

> I think, I think, some stirring of his spirit
> Mov'd him to send these evil-seeming dreams.[5]

A little later the Chorus sing an exultant song of hope which proclaims that vengeance will soon come. The dream shows that it is near, but there is more in it than that.

Sophocles changes the imagery of the dream from a snake to a tree. For this he must have had a reason, and perhaps we may guess it. The snake of course is thoroughly sinister and threatening. It is the type of treachery[6] and, even more appropriately, of violence to a mother;[7] for young snakes were believed to gnaw a passage through the womb. Not without reason does Aelian comment: 'What are all your Orestes and Alcmeons to that, my

---

[1] Fr. 15. [2] *Cho.* 523 ff. [3] *Or.* 618.

[4] 421–3 ἔκ τε τοῦδ' ἄνω
βλαστεῖν βρύοντα θαλλόν, ᾧ κατάσκιον
πᾶσαν γενέσθαι τὴν Μυκηναίων χθόνα.

[5] 459–60 οἶμαι μὲν οὖν, οἶμαί τι κἀκείνῳ μέλειν
πέμψαι τάδ' αὐτῇ δυσπρόσοπτ' ὀνείρατα.

[6] Aristot. *H. A.* 488 b 16. [7] Hdt. iii. 109. 2.

dear tragedians?"[1] But the parallel with Orestes is too good. It makes him exact vengeance in too odious a spirit. It obliterates the part of the gods in his action. Sophocles does well to be rid of it. But he does more than this. In Aeschylus the dream has only one meaning. It is a plain threat which Clytaemnestra can hardly misinterpret. It merely informs her of an inevitable doom. But not all dreams were so clear, and Sophocles presents something more complex and more ambiguous. He may have been influenced by Herodotus, who tells of Xerxes' third vision in which he is crowned by the branch of an olive-tree; from this boughs spread and cover the earth, then suddenly the garland vanishes from his brow.[2] Clytaemnestra's dream has something in common with this. It is not a direct menace of vengeance; it combines what looks like a presage of good with a presage of ill. The Chorus and Electra understand it, but Clytaemnestra does not. She is frightened, but she does not quite know what she fears. She prays to Apollo for a favourable fulfilment:

> This night I saw
> Strange shapes and doubtful dreams. Lycean King,
> If they be good, I pray thee grant fulfilment:
> If they be evil, let my enemies
> Be haunted by them.[3]

Perhaps, after all, she seems to think, the dream may prove to be good. It serves not to make her conscious of her doom but to show that she lives in a false world and does not foresee her peril. The dream tests her infatuation. The gods who intend to punish her do not warn her clearly, but at least they give her a chance, a hint, which if she were not wholly blind and corrupted, she ought to take. And in fact she does see that the dreams are 'doubtful'. Such ambiguity should arouse her suspicion and caution. For a moment she seems to see this; then she forgets it and relapses into her old self-satisfaction.

The double character of the dream lies in its two main events. the reappearance of Agamemnon in the world of the living and the flowering of his sceptre on the hearth. Neither in itself is very strange, and it is possible that both were familiar to interpreters of dreams, and that their collocation helps to increase the ambiguity.

---

[1] N. A. i. 24.   [2] vii. 19. 1.

[3] 644–7   ἃ γὰρ προσεῖδον νυκτὶ τῇδε φάσματα
Δισσῶν ὀνείρων, ταῦτά μοι, Λύκει' ἄναξ,
εἰ μὲν πέφηνεν ἐσθλά, δὸς τελεσφόρα,
εἰ δ' ἐχθρά, τοῖς ἐχθροῖσιν ἔμπαλιν μέθες.

To see the dead was a bad sign. For Artemidorus the reappear-
ances of the dead portend troubles and harm,[1] and Achmes actually says that they foretell the punishment of the guilty.[2] The
Hippocratic author who discusses dreams from a more medical
point of view is less dogmatic, but he too says that it is a bad sign
if the dead carry something[3]—as Agamemnon carries his sceptre.
We may at least assume that Clytaemnestra is made uneasy by
the appearance of her murdered husband and sees in it a prospect
of evil, as Atossa is made uneasy by the appearance of the dead
Darius.[4] On the other hand, the great shade-giving bough which
grows out of the sceptre seems to portend good. To the medical
man it would be a sign of health.[5] To Artemidorus tall trees are a
sign of security,[6] and to Achmes of success.[7] Just as Xerxes is
emboldened to attack Greece by his dream of a tree whose
branches cover the earth, so Clytaemnestra may be encouraged
by this side of her dream. It is the combination of this hopeful
presage with the dark portent of the dead man that makes her
dream 'doubtful'. But, like Xerxes, she neglects the unfavourable
signs for the favourable. He forgets about the withering garland,
she about the appearance of Agamemnon. The gods are ready to
destroy both, but they seem to leave a small loophole of escape. If
either has the sense to read the dream aright, he may still avoid his
doom. Clytaemnestra recognizes the ambiguity but decides to
take notice only of the favourable signs. She is deluded into thinking that if a dream is told to the day its threatening character is
averted. She has already told her dream to the sun (425–6).
This, so far as it goes, is correct. A character in Sophocles'
Acrisius says:

> Have courage, lady. Many fearful things
> That breathed dark dreams at night are soothed by day.[8]

But this is not enough when the gods send the dream. Its warning
cannot be so dismissed. Clytaemnestra deceives herself. She would
rather continue in the enjoyment of evil than face the dread
possibilities which the gods suggest to her. When the gods send
such a dream it is dangerous to reject or neglect it. So Hippias
was warned ambiguously that his end was near, but rejected the
warning and was killed.[9] In the *Electra* Clytaemnestra's dream

---

[1] ii. 67.   [2] p. 3, 26 Drexl.   [3] *Diaet.* iv. 92.   [4] Aesch. *Pers.* 210.
[5] *Diaet.* iv. 90.   [6] iv. 13.   [7] p. 107, 6.
[8] Fr. 65   θάρσει, γύναι· τὰ πολλὰ τῶν Ζεινῶν ὄναρ
                πνεύσαντα νυκτός, ἡμέρας μαλάσσεται.
[9] Hdt. v. 56. 2.

gives her a last faint chance to make amends. She dismisses it, and after that she is a victim ready for punishment.

The dream which perplexes Clytaemnestra brings joy and confidence to her enemies. To the Chorus it is a clear sign that Agamemnon has not forgotten (482–3), and that justice will soon be done. They are full of courage after hearing of it (479 ff.). Then in ringing words they proclaim its message, its meaning:

> Yea, with the clash of many swords, the noise
> Of many trampling feet, forth from the lair
> Vengeance, brazen-footed Fury, ambush'd
> Now in darkness, cometh soon.[1]

They feel that they have prophetic powers (473) and know what the dream portends. They are more confident than Electra that it comes from Agamemnon. This confidence is a little surprising, until we realize that it is itself inspired by the gods. It is they who make men seers, and the Chorus now feel that they have mantic powers. They have a conviction which the result will justify. For the moment they state and defend it:

> Or else there is no truth in mortal dreaming,
> And vain is prophecy,
> Unless this dream prove true.[2]

Just as in *King Oedipus* the Chorus assert that if one oracle is proved false, all belief in all oracles is undermined, so here the Chorus associate dreams with oracles and prophecies and give them the same importance. If this dream is proved false, the whole structure of dream-interpretation will collapse. The thought is remarkable. For few Greeks would regard dreams as quite on the level of oracles. Yet the Chorus have their reason. The dream is so impressive with its reappearance of Agamemnon to his murderess that it must be true. It is a test case. The only conclusion is that this dream will not be proved false. And we know that it will not, that Orestes has arrived on his mission of vengeance and will soon advance to its fulfilment.

The gods and his dead father work with Orestes. They approve,

---

[1] 489–91   ἥξει καὶ πολύπους καὶ πολύχειρ ἁ
Δεινοῖς κρυπτομένα λόχοις
χαλκόπους Ἐρινύς.

[2] 497–502   ἦ-
τοι μαντεῖαι βροτῶν
οὐκ εἰσὶν ἐν δεινοῖς ὀνεί-
ροις οὐδ' ἐν θεσφάτοις,
εἰ μὴ τόδε φάσμα νυ-
κτὸς εὖ κατασχήσει.

demand, and further his vengeance. We need no other proof that
Sophocles thinks the vengeance right. At the level of ordinary
morality he would find some support, as we know from the First
Speech of Antiphon. There the prosecutor is not in Orestes'
position since the alleged murderess is only his stepmother and he
owes no filial duty to her. But his half-brother and her son is
precisely in Orestes' place. His father is thought to have been
murdered by his mother, and his duty should be to take action
against her. In fact he supports her, and for this the prosecutor
attacks him and asks if he thinks that his duty as a son lies simply
in being loyal to his mother, 'I think it is a far greater sin to forego
the vengeance of the dead man'.[1] His argument is that in such a
conflict of duties vengeance comes before loyalty to the guilty
party. If the stepmother is guilty, as we know Clytaemnestra to
be, she has no right to reverence from her son. The prosecutor
considers that his half-brother's appeal for the murderess will be
'unlawful, sinful, impossible, and not to be heard by gods or
you'.[2] It is clear that in this ordinary world the claims of the dead
father carried great weight. With this Sophocles agrees. The
main direction of his thought is quite in accord with common
belief.

Sophocles, however, does not leave the matter at that. He
understands that a matter of this kind has other than theological
or legal interest, that it involves consideration of other, less tangible
factors. The gods command the death of Clytaemnestra because
if murder passes unpunished a great rule is violated and many
high things are set at naught. At three prominent places Sophocles
makes this point with emphasis. They are his answer to those who
think that the duty may be shirked. At the end of the long colloquy
with the Chorus, in which the whole question of vengeance has
been posed and almost been discussed, Electra says:

> For if the dead must lie
> A heap of negligible dust, and they,
> The slayers, pay not death for death,
> There will be left no Modesty
> Nor Righteousness on earth.[3]

---

[1] i. 5.   [2] Ib. 22.

[3] 245–50   εἰ γὰρ ὁ μὲν θανών, γᾶ τε καὶ οὐδὲν ὤν,
                    κείσεται τάλας,
                    οἱ δὲ μὴ πάλιν
                δώσουσ' ἀντιφόνους δίκας,
                ἔρροι τ' ἂν αἰδὼς
          ἁπάντων τ' εὐσέβεια θνατῶν.

The words are more than her answer to difficulties and doubts raised by the Chorus. They come with such resonance that special attention is bound to be paid to them. Electra says that if murder is left unpunished there is an end of modesty and righteousness. The two things are related but separate. The first is the feeling of respect and honour due to the sacred ties of family which Clytaemnestra has violated and which Electra wishes to see maintained. She sees that if this crime remains unrequited, morality will receive a deadly blow. This feeling is associated with reverence, since the gods are the protectors of the family and forbid bloodshed. If sin is allowed to flourish, respect for them is undermined. The gods demand vengeance, and not to exact it is to treat them with contempt.

Electra's opinion is tested by stern facts. If what she says is right, decency and piety demand the punishment of Clytaemnestra. Nor does she shrink from such a conclusion. When Orestes and Pylades go into the house to exact vengeance Electra prays to Apollo to prosper them, and ends with the words:

> And show the world what wages by the gods
> Are granted to reward impiety.[1]

The gods punish the wicked. If men know this, they will be more careful to avoid sin. To save other men from thinking that sin prospers Clytaemnestra must be punished. Aeschylus saw that impiety begets greater impieties; Sophocles follows him and builds the idea into his play. It is his answer to those who thought that the gods do not care whether men act well or badly, or to such as agreed with the Euripidean sentiment that the gods do not punish wrongdoing because

> Either they are more foolish than men are
> Or else they value clemency more than right.[2]

In this case the wrongdoing is also impiety, and the gods punish it. The deaths of the murderers are a vindication of divine laws and power. The language is legal. The 'wages' of which Electra speaks are the damages owed to the gods, and they are no less than the lives of the murderers which must be paid in requital. This alone will vindicate the authority of the divine laws against bloodshed.

[1] 1382–3
καὶ δεῖξον ἀνθρώποισι τἀπιτίμια
τῆς δυσσεβείας οἷα δωροῦνται θεοί.

[2] Fr. 645. 5–6
ἢ τἄρα θνητῶν εἰσιν ἀσυνετώτεροι
ἢ τἀπιεικῆ πρόσθεν ἡγοῦνται Δίκης.

At a third emphatic place, almost at the end of the play, when Orestes is driving Aegisthus to his death, his last words are:

> When men are of a mind to break the law,
> One forfeit should be fix'd for all. Were Death
> Required, this world would grow less villainous.

This time not divine laws but human laws and justice are in question. They are based on divine commands, but have their separate importance for human society. In the *Antigone* the laws of men are not valid if they conflict with the laws of the gods. Here is the other side of the picture. The laws of men are eminently valid if they embody what the gods command. The old law, that blood must be paid for blood, must be applied to Aegisthus. Otherwise law and justice will be imperilled and discredited. We can almost hear Plato's judgement that laws are 'an example to other men against wrongdoing'.[2] Sophocles sees farther. He sees in law a defence against wickedness. Without it, human life is reduced to chaos. As Menander says,

> We must in no way give in to the wicked,
> But stand against them. Otherwise our life
> Turns upside down without our knowing it.[3]

The triumph of Clytaemnestra and Aegisthus in their misdeeds has been an outrage on legality and justice. They cannot go longer unpunished. Sophocles marks this for all that it is worth, and must have intended it to be noticed. The punishment of the murderers is necessary if right and goodness are to thrive in the world.

By these means Sophocles builds up the religious, moral, and legal case for the matricide. The gods approve, and human justice demands it. On this all the characters, except the murderers themselves, are agreed. Against this well-built argument we may set the doubts raised by Euripides: is it right in any circumstances for a man to kill his mother, and why, if Clytaemnestra must be killed, is she not killed by someone else than her son? The two questions are closely related, and though the second is subsidiary to the first, it may be taken first. The answer is simply that no

---

[1] 1505-7   χρῆν δ᾽ εὐθὺς εἶναι τήνδε τοῖς πᾶσιν δίκην,
ὅστις πέρα πράσσειν γε τῶν νόμων θέλοι,
κτείνειν· τὸ γὰρ πανοῦργον οὐκ ἂν ἦν πολύ.

[2] *Laws*, ix. 862 e.

[3] Fr. 5   οὐ παντελῶς δεῖ τοῖς πονηροῖς ἐπιτρέπειν,
ἀλλ᾽ ἀντιτάττεσθ᾽· εἰ δὲ μή, τἄνω κάτω
ἡμῖν ὁ βίος λήσει μεταστραφεὶς ὅλος.

one but Orestes can kill Clytaemnestra. It is true that when she believes that he is dead Electra makes her great resolve to carry out the vengeance herself, but we may doubt if a woman would succeed. Otherwise there is no one. Agamemnon's other children are both women, and, to judge by Chrysothemis, have made their peace with the established powers. The Chorus of Argive women are equally powerless. Even the Paedagogus, who has brought up Orestes for this sole end (14), is an old man and presumably no match for Aegisthus. In the play the vengeance falls to Orestes and to a lesser degree to Electra because they alone have the will and the power to exact it. By seizing authority the murderers have set themselves above the law. It cannot operate against them. Therefore the duty of killing them must come from outside, from individuals beyond their control. Nor is this an artificial situation. When the sources of power are in the hands of those who have no respect for law, justice can only be re-established by individuals who are willing to perform what may look like criminal acts. Moreover, it is even right that Orestes should kill his mother. His dead father demands it of him; the duty falls on him as next of kin. The duty is undeniably painful, even revolting, and Sophocles does not shrink from showing this. But it is none the less urgent, and it falls primarily to Orestes.

Orestes' own feelings are another matter, a question not of right and wrong but of the human heart. We may well ask how Sophocles presents a man who has to kill his mother. The conflict that must arise in him cannot be avoided. Aeschylus dramatized it in the Furies who haunt Orestes and showed it in the terrible colloquy between him and his mother before her death. His Orestes knows that what he has to do is fearful, but that is because worse wrongs have been committed. He says to Clytaemnestra:

You slew whom you should not; what you should not, take.[1]

Euripides so developed the conflict that his Orestes is shown to be wrong in killing his mother. When Iphigeneia says of him

An evil justice has he finely done,[2]

she may feel that the vengeance, though repulsive, is justified, but in the *Orestes* this justice is shown to be at variance with something more sacred:

Chorus. In justice. *Electra.* But wrongly.[3]

[1] *Cho.* 930   κάνες γ' ὃν οὐ χρῆν, καὶ τὸ μὴ χρεὼν πάθε.
[2] *I. T.* 559   ὡς εὖ κακὸν Δίκαιον εἰσεπράξατο.
[3] *Or.* 194   Χο. Δίκᾳ μέν.   Ηλ. καλῶς Δ' οὔ.

The Chorus even advance the paradox that such an action is impious:

> To sin for the good is subtle impiety,
> Madness of evil-hearted men.[1]

There was plainly something to be said for those who felt that in no circumstances should Orestes kill his mother. It was not enough for Sophocles to emphasize the justice of the act; he must also show that Orestes could do it without being an unnatural monster.

For this difficulty Sophocles has his solution. We might put it briefly and say that in his presentation Clytaemnestra has ceased to be a mother. But such a summary does little justice to his bold conception of her. He makes us know her for what she is and see that Orestes need feel no ultimate qualms about killing her. He takes a hint from Aeschylus and elaborates it until his portrait of her is something new. In the *Libation-bearers* Electra says of Clytaemnestra

> My mother, though the name she has fits not
> The godless spirit that her children know.[2]

Sophocles shows the stages, if not the process, by which Electra comes to see that Clytaemnestra does not deserve the name of mother. Her first doubt appears when she tells the Chorus how Clytaemnestra sleeps with her paramour in Agamemnon's bed:

> if the name
> Of mother suits the assassin's concubine.[3]

It is clearer when Electra comes into personal conflict with her mother and defends herself from the charge of disrespect:

> Mother? No,
> Tyrant you are, and mistress, but not mother!
> What is my life? What have I found from you—
> You, and your mate—but only persecution?[4]

Later, when she believes that Orestes is dead and knows that Clytaemnestra is glad at the news, such reservations as she may

---

[1] *Or.* 823–4   τὸ δ' εὖ κακουργεῖν ἀσέβεια ποικίλα,
              κακοφρόνων τ' ἀνδρῶν παράνοια.

[2] *Cho.* 190–1   ἐμὴ δὲ μήτηρ, οὐδαμῶς ἐπώνυμον
              φρόνημα παισὶ δύσθεον πεπαμένη.

[3] 273–4   μητέρ' εἰ χρεὼν
              ταύτην προσαυδᾶν τῷδε συγκοιμωμένην.

[4] 597–600   καί σ' ἔγωγε δεσπότιν
              ἢ μητέρ' οὐκ ἔλασσον εἰς ἡμᾶς νέμω,
              ἣ ζῶ βίον μοχθηρόν, ἔκ τε σοῦ κακοῖς
              πολλοῖς ἀεὶ ξυνοῦσα τοῦ τε συννόμου.

have had are gone, and she calls her 'mother most unmotherly'.[1]
This is the view that she communicates to Orestes when she tell^
of the hardships which she suffers from Clytaemnestra:

> One much unlike her name. She is call'd my mother.[2]

In Electra's opinion Clytaemnestra has ceased to count as a mother
because her actions are unmotherly. She summarizes the case
against Clytaemnestra and shows that she has lost all claim to
affection or respect from her children.

Clytaemnestra forfeits her rights for two reasons. She has murdered her husband and she maltreats her children. The first is
summed up in all its horror by Electra:

> This is the truth. You say you kill'd my father.
> Justly or not, could there be anything
> More shameful to confess?[3]

Electra knows that her mother is a murderess. Moreover, Clytaemnestra glories in her crime and its evil fruits. She has exalted her
paramour to the honours that once were Agamemnon's. He sits
on the dead man's throne (267), wears his clothes (268), pours
libations on the hearth where the murder was committed (269–70),
and sleeps in his bed (273 ff.). Clytaemnestra even holds monthly
festival in celebration of the murder (277 ff.). She has not only
murdered her husband but glories in the crime. So hardened is she
that she even hopes to placate Agamemnon's angry spirit without
surrendering her ill-gotten advantages. So she sends Chrysothemis
to make offerings at his grave. The action is characteristic of her.
Electra knows that it is not right or holy for Chrysothemis to do
this for her mother (432–3). A good wife should of course make
offerings to her dead husband's spirit, but Clytaemnestra has, so
to speak, ceased to be his wife. She has no right to do anything
of the kind.

Clytaemnestra is also a bad mother. She has failed in love and
care for her children. Aristotle nobly says that a mother's love
for her children is desirable for its own sake and for the reason
that it lies in loving rather than in being loved.[4] But Clytaemnestra
does not love Electra and Orestes. Not only does she threaten
and abuse Electra; she has reduced her almost to the condition of
a slave. Electra describes it:

[1] 1154   μήτηρ ἀμήτωρ.
[2] 1194   μήτηρ καλεῖται, μητρὶ δ' οὐδὲν ἐξισοῖ.
[3] 558–9   καὶ δὴ λέγω σοι. πατέρα φὴς κτεῖναι. τίς ἂν
            τούτου λόγου γένοιτ' ἂν αἰσχίων ἔτι;
[4] *Nic. Eth.* 1159 a 28.

Like a stranger and a beggar,
Dwelling in my father's house, thus,
In rags and shame,
I steal the scraps from empty tables when the feast is done.[1]

When she believes that Orestes is dead, she foresees the misery
that awaits her:

> and I once more
> A drudge among these deadly enemies,[2]

and later she tells Orestes that she endures enforced slavery (1192).
Here too Sophocles picks up a theme from Aeschylus, whose
Electra says that she is no better than a slave,[3] but means little more
than that she is cut off from her legitimate position and inheritance. Sophocles' Electra is almost literally a slave, compelled to
do humble tasks and scantily supplied with food and clothing. Her
treatment has worked havoc on her appearance, so that Orestes
pities her:

> Ruined and shamed by wanton cruelty![4]

and later learns how Clytaemnestra has maltreated her

> Brute force, shame, hardship—every kind of wrong.[5]

Nor is this maltreatment enough. In her fear and hatred of Electra
Clytaemnestra has decided to get rid of her, to lock her up in a
sunless prison (380 ff.). All human feelings that she may ever have
had for her daughter are dead.

Clytaemnestra's brutality may be seen especially in one point.
Electra is unwedded. She laments that she has no children (164)
and no husband (165), that life holds out no hopes for her

> Who withers away in childlessness.[6]

She has no one to love or cherish, and for a Greek this is a
fearful deprivation. The horror of such a state is among the
miseries of Antigone.[7] It was evidently part of the tradition about
Electra; for both Aeschylus[8] and Euripides[9] refer to it. Without a
husband or children she lives a mutilated life. For, as Aristotle

---

[1] 189–92   ἀλλ' ἀπερεί τις ἔποικος ἀναξία
οἰκονομῶ θαλάμους πατρός, ὧδε μὲν
ἀεικεῖ σὺν στολᾷ,
κεναῖς δ' ἀμφίσταμαι τραπέζαις.

[2] 814–15   ἤδη δεῖ με δουλεύειν πάλιν
ἐν τοῖσιν ἐχθίστοισιν ἀνθρώπων ἐμοί.

[3] Cho. 135.

[4] 1181   ὦ σῶμ' ἀτίμως κἀθέως ἐφθαρμένον.

[5] 1196   καὶ χερσὶ καὶ λύμαισι καὶ πᾶσιν κακοῖς.

[6] 187   ἅτις ἄνευ τεκέων κατατάκομαι.

[7] Ant. 813 ff., 917 ff.   [8] Cho. 487.   [9] Or. 306, 1050.

says, by marrying men and women, who have different functions by nature, complement each other and 'throw their gifts into the common stock'.[1] Electra cannot fulfil her proper functions and is therefore miserable. The absence of children means that she cannot be tended in old age or remembered after death. She lacks the support of which Sophocles himself says:

> Children are anchors to a mother's life.[2]

Without children Electra is unprotected, isolated, and friendless. To spoil her life in this way is outrageous. Yet Clytaemnestra acquiesces in it because Aegisthus wishes it. His reasons are clear. He will not allow Electra to breed a possible avenger upon himself:

> You can never hope
> To marry now—Aegisthus is no fool.
> He'll have no children got on you or me
> As ministers of revenge,—no hope of that.[3]

In this last humiliation of her daughter Clytaemnestra shows that she is utterly heartless and has for all real purposes ceased to be a mother.

Clytaemnestra's feelings for Orestes are different but hardly less discreditable. She does not know him, and cannot persecute him like Electra, but she is afraid of his return. When she hears rumours of it, she becomes like a mad woman (294) and bursts into tirades against Electra. She shows her real feelings when she hears the false news of his death. At the first mention of it she is extremely excited (675), and at once asks for details (678-9). When she has heard the story, she says:

> O Zeus, what shall I say? Is this thing good,
> Or terrible, though it save me? Must my life
> Be saved by such a grief? Alas, it hurts.[4]

Surely she speaks the truth. She knows that her son's death is to her advantage, but she still has some small qualm about saving her own life at the cost of his. That is why she goes on to say:

---

[1] *Nic. Eth.* 1162 a 23.

[2] Fr. 685   ἀλλ' εἰσὶ μητρὶ παῖδες ἄγκυραι βίου.

[3] 963–6   καὶ τῶνδε μέντοι μηκέτ' ἐλπίσῃς ὅπως
τεύξῃ ποτ'· οὐ γὰρ ὧδ' ἄβουλός ἐστ' ἀνὴρ
Αἴγισθος ὥστε σόν ποτ' ἢ κἀμὸν γένος
βλαστεῖν ἐᾶσαι, πημονὴν αὑτῷ σαφῆ.

[4] 766–8   ὦ Ζεῦ, τί ταῦτα; πότερον εὐτυχῆ λέγω,
ἢ δεινὰ μέν, κέρδη δέ; λυπηρῶς δ' ἔχει,
εἰ τοῖς ἐμαυτῆς τὸν βίον σῴζω κακοῖς.

It is strange to be a mother. Though they hurt,
These children that we bear, we cannot hate them.[1]

For a moment her mother's love fights with her fear and hatred.
She feels the inexplicable bond between herself and the child of her
womb. In similar words Euripides noted the curious power of
motherhood:

It is strange to be a mother; great the charm
That makes all labour for their children's good.[2]

But in this struggle inside Clytaemnestra wrong wins. Her desire
for security triumphs, and when she next speaks she feels that the
news is good and that she can pass her days in peace, rid at last
of the endless menaces which have hung over her (773–87). The
mood of relief turns almost to insensate triumph. In her perverse
heart she feels that Nemesis is on her side and has done well (793).
She goes off in high spirits with laughter on her lips (807). For
her children she has ceased to care. She wishes good only for
those who will help her. She even has the effrontery to pray that
she may stay in the enjoyment of power:

Happy among the friends with whom to-day
I live, and with my children—such of them
As neither hate nor hurt me cruelly.[3]

What she really cares for is her position, the fruits of her crime.
She has killed any real maternal love that was in her and deserves
all that Electra says of her.

Clytaemnestra is no true mother. Because she has murdered her
husband and ceased to love her children she has forfeited all claim
to respect or love from them. Yet she might still have some personal
force or dignity, some power which though evil excites a kind of
admiration and makes us feel that she deserves a word of excuse.
For us, as no doubt for the Greeks, it is impossible to approach
Sophocles' Clytaemnestra without memories of her great predecessor in Aeschylus. We expect her to have the same characteristics
and the same criminal grandeur. When we find that she has not,
we are liable to lose interest in her or at least to make little attempt

---

[1] 770–1   Δεινὸν τὸ τίκτειν ἐστίν· οὐδὲ γὰρ κακῶς
             πάσχοντι μῖσος ὧν τέκη προσγίγνεται.

[2] I. A. 917–18   Δεινὸν τὸ τίκτειν καὶ φέρει φίλτρον μέγα
             πᾶσίν τε κοινὸν ὥσθ' ὑπερκάμνειν τέκνων.

[3] 652–4   φίλοισί τε ξυνοῦσαν οἷς ξύνειμι νῦν
             εὐημεροῦσαν καὶ τέκνων ὅσων ἐμοὶ
             Δύσνοια μὴ πρόσεστιν ἢ λύπη πικρά.

to see her as she really is. In fact she owes more by contrast than by resemblance to Aeschylus' Clytaemnestra. Sophocles may have been conscious that comparisons would be made between the two murderesses, and he seems to have decided to create an entirely new character. His Clytaemnestra lacks the implacable courage of the Aeschylean and is more like a real murderess as she would be some years after her crime. She is hardly even the 'pitiless woman' that she was to Pindar.[1] She is more odious, more contemptible, more petty.

Aeschylus' Clytaemnestra is bold to the point of recklessness. She is 'all-daring',[2] as her actions show. She makes no attempt to dissemble her crime and threatens dire punishment to those who oppose her. There is something magnificent about the way that she passes the limits of her sex and proudly proclaims that she, a woman, has murdered a man.[3] Though she is in love with Aegisthus she is by no means subservient to him and curbs his desire for a fight with affectionate but firm words.[4] In the *Libation-bearers* she is willing to consult him as head of the house,[5] but she can take decisions and act on them without him. When she knows that he is dead and cannot help her, she faces her own death bravely alone.[6] In the *Electra* Clytaemnestra has none of this courage and independence. She is in Aegisthus' power and lacks confidence to act without him. She admits that when he is away Electra does not to listen to her:

> Aegisthus is not here! What do you care
> For me?[7]

Her decision to imprison Electra cannot be put into force until Aegisthus comes home (386). In her death she is helpless without him and calls in vain for his help (1409). Though she abuses Electra with such titles as 'godless wretch'[8] and 'shameless child'[9] and threatens her with vague punishments (291, 298), she fails to cow her or to curb her tongue. She depends on her lover for her authority and in herself lacks power to command. In no sense has she a 'heart of man's counsel'.[10] The result is that we do not feel the admiration that we feel, despite ourselves, for Aeschylus' Clytaemnestra. Still less do we feel that she has something to be

---

[1] *Pyth.* xi. 22.   [2] *Ag.* 1237.   [3] Ib. 1231.   [4] Ib. 1654 ff.
[5] *Cho.* 673, 715–17.   [6] Ib. 893 ff.
[7] 519–20   νῦν δ' ὡς ἄπεστ' ἐκεῖνος, οὐδὲν ἐντρέπῃ
            ἐμοῦ γε.
[8] 289 δύσθεον μίσημα.   [9] 622 θρέμμ' ἀναιδές.
[10] Aesch. *Ag.* 11 ἀνδρόβουλον κέαρ.

said for her because of outstanding qualities. We are the more
ready to see vengeance exacted from her by her son.

Clytaemnestra is a murderess, and we naturally wish to know
the motives for her crimes and judge her by them. In the *Agamemnon* she has two reasons for killing her husband: he has killed her
child, Iphigeneia, and he has been unfaithful to her. They do not
justify murder, but they are human and sincere. The first is the
only one to which Sophocles pays attention. He says nothing
about Cassandra, and to this degree makes Agamemnon less to
blame than Aeschylus did. But he pays considerable attention to
Clytaemnestra's claim that she killed her husband in punishment
for the death of Iphigeneia. Such a motive has its worth, and both
Aeschylus and Pindar felt its imaginative appeal. The first makes
Clytaemnestra defend the murder because

> He slaughtered his own child, my dearest travail,
> To be a charm against the winds from Thrace,[1]

and the second inquires into her motives:

> Was it Iphigeneia,
> Slain at Euripus far from her land,
> Who stung her to uplift
> The wrath of her heavy hand?[2]

For them she was at least a woman with a great injury which
dictated, if it did not excuse, the murder of her husband. Sophocles takes up this theme and treats it in a novel way.

To Electra Clytaemnestra defends her murder of Agamemnon.
She claims that Justice acted through her:

> And yet not I alone, but Justice slew him,[3]

and we anticipate that her defence will repeat what Aeschylus
had made her say, that she is an avenging spirit[4] or that not she
but Fate is responsible.[5] But as she unfolds her arguments they
carry little conviction. She says nothing of any curse on the House
of Atreus; she concentrates on the wrong done to Iphigeneia. She
has none of the Aeschylean passion of resentment, of a mother's
love turned to crime by revenge. Her only point is that Agamem-

---

[1] *Ag.* 1417–18   ἔθυσεν αὑτοῦ παῖδα, φιλτάτην ἐμοὶ
            ὠδῖν', ἐπῳδὸν Θρῃκίων ἀημάτων.

[2] *Pyth.* xi. 22–3   πότερόν νιν ἄρ' Ἰφιγένει' ἐπ' Εὐρίπῳ
            σφαχθεῖσα τῆλε πάτρας
            ἔκνιξεν βαρυπάλαμον ὄρσαι χόλον;

[3] 528   ἡ γὰρ Δίκη νιν εἷλεν, οὐκ ἐγὼ μόνη.

[4] *Ag.* 1501.   [5] *Cho.* 910.

non should have sacrificed one of Menelaus' children instead of his own (537 ff.). She tries to brazen it out:

> I think of what I did with no regrets,
> No heaviness of heart.[1]

That is of course true, not because she really believes in her defence but because she enjoys what the murder has brought to her. Electra's answer to this is twofold, almost at two levels. She dismisses the argument based on the sacrifice of Iphigeneia by saying that Agamemnon had to sacrifice his daughter to appease the wrath of Artemis:

> No other way
> To bring his men safe home, or cross to Troy.[2]

There was nothing else for him to do. This answer may seem artificial or inhuman. In a sense it is. For it is not the real answer to Clytaemnestra but the refutation of her defence. It meets her on her own ground and shows her wrong even on that. The real answer is more fundamental.

Electra knows that Clytaemnestra's true motive for killing Agamemnon was her love for Aegisthus. In this Sophocles hardly agrees with Aeschylus, whose Aegisthus is indeed an adulterer and a murderer but is not said to be the main cause of the crime. Pindar went farther when he speculated about Clytaemnestra's motives:

> Or was she broken in to a paramour's bed
> And the nightly loves
> Turned her mind?[3]

Sophocles makes Clytaemnestra's guilty love the real and only motive for her crime. The Chorus hint at it:

> Craft the plotter, Lust the slayer,[4]

and Electra makes it the main element in her attack on her mother. She brushes aside as false the excuses about Iphigeneia:

> No, Justice was the pretext, not the cause,[5]

and knows what the real motive was:

[1] 549–50   ἐγὼ μὲν οὖν οὐκ εἰμὶ τοῖς πεπραγμένοις
            δύσθυμος.

[2] 573–4   οὐ γὰρ ἦν λύσις
            ἄλλη στρατῷ πρὸς οἶκον οὐδ' εἰς Ἴλιον.

[3] Pyth. xi. 24–5   ἦ ἑτέρῳ λέχει δαμαζομέναν
                 ἔννυχοι πάραγον κοῖται;

[4] 197   δόλος ἦν ὁ φράσας, ἔρος ὁ κτείνας.

[5] 584   ἀλλ' εἰσόρα μὴ σκῆψιν οὐκ οὖσαν τίθης.

But I shall say
You did not kill for justice, but persuasion
Of a base man. You are living with him now.[1]

In her view Clytaemnestra has been carried away by the temp-
tation of love, the false persuasion which it exerts, and of which
Sophocles himself says:

Swift walks Persuasion on the road of Sin.[2]

Clytaemnestra has gone on this road and added one evil to another.
Electra appeals to facts. She knows that Clytaemnestra lives with
her husband's murderer, bears children to him, and has cast out the
children of her first marriage (585–90). Such a life is no vengeance
for a lost daughter (592). Of course Electra is right. She has only
to say this to be quite convincing. Against her Clytaemnestra has
no real defence. She can only accuse her of insolence (613) and
shamelessness (615). It is clear that her motive for killing Agamemnon was nothing but adulterous passion for Aegisthus. There can
be no pardon for it. It is, as Pindar says,

That sin in young wives
None forgives,[3]

and enough to rob Clytaemnestra of any claim to compassion.

Clytaemnestra, then, has not the grandeur which sometimes
belongs to criminals. She is haunted by fear, anxious to enjoy
her evil gains, subjected to the worthless Aegisthus, odious to her
children, unable even to assert authority. She is singularly lacking in attractive qualities. She has forfeited all right to respect.
Her death should excite no qualms and no pity. She deserves it
because she is a murderess and because she refuses to give up the
advantages which murder has brought to her. In her we see the
devastating effects of crime on the criminal. Because she has
murdered her husband, she has sunk into a life of brutality and
luxury which has killed any decent feelings that she may once have
had. Her soul is full of unquiet and disorder. Despite her air of
effrontery she is tormented by fear that Orestes will return and
punish her. Her attempts to cow Electra would be pathetic if
they were not prompted by base motives. She loses her last title
to sympathy when she finds in Orestes' death an occasion for joy.

[1] 560–2   λέξω δέ σοι,
ὡς οὐ Δίκη γ' ἔκτεινας ἀλλά σ' ἔσπασεν
πειθὼ κακοῦ πρὸς ἀνδρός, ᾧ τανῦν ξύνει.

[2] Fr. 870.   ταχεῖα Πειθὼ τῶν κακῶν ὁδοιπορεῖ.

[3] Pyth. xi. 26   τὸ δὲ νέαις ἀλόχοις
ἔχθιστον ἀμπλάκιον.

It is then clear that all goodness has died in her, that she is irreme-
diably corrupted, a lost soul. It is characteristic of Sophocles' unfaltering instinct for the truth that this corrupt state has no kind
of attraction. It is ugly and base. A woman like this makes no
appeal even to pity. The world is better without her. And this
conclusion is forced on Orestes and Electra. It explains why they
are able to encompass her death.

Sophocles shows clearly the situation which Clytaemnestra's
crime has created. In it wrong is uppermost, and other evils follow.
Above all, Electra is forced into a position which she knows to
be in some sense wrong but none the less inevitable. It is impossible
for her to behave well by common standards when she has such
a mother and lives such a life. The atmosphere of hate and brutality explains why Electra and Orestes behave as they do. If we
ask if it is right for them to kill their mother, the answer is that
though the vengeance is evil there are occasions in life so evil that
another evil is required to correct them. The situation denies the
adage that evil cannot be cured by evil, and suggests the opposite.
For this too there was support in proverbial wisdom. The Greeks
had their version of

> Diseases desperate grown
> By desperate appliance are relieved.

The Hippocratic *Aphorisms* give the specifically medical form in
the words, 'For extreme diseases extreme strictness of treatment
is most efficacious',[1] but Sophocles himself provides something
more general when he says

> With bitter drugs men wash out bitter bile.[2]

The avengers of Agamemnon's death are forced to a hideous
action by the hideous situation which crime has created.

Electra knows this and explains that circumstances leave her no
alternative. When the Chorus tell her that she is merely adding
to her troubles by resisting those in power she says:

> I know. I am not ignorant of my own spirit.
> I am not free. Necessity,
> Fearful Necessity of evil holds me   While I live
> I shall not make an end, though evil grow.[3]

---

[1] *Aph.* i. 6 ἐς δὲ τὰ ἔσχατα νοσήματα αἱ ἔσχαται θεραπεῖαι ἐς ἀκριβείην κράτισται.
[2] Fr. 854   πικρῷ πικρὰν κλύζουσι φαρμάκῳ χόλην.
[3] 221–5   Δεινοῖς ἠναγκάσθην, Δεινοῖς·
    ἔξοιδ', οὐ λάθει μ' ὀργά.
    ἀλλ' ἐν γὰρ Δεινοῖς οὐ σχήσω
    ταύτας ἄτας
    ὄφρα με βίος ἔχῃ.

She knows that she is moved by ugly passions, that the vengeance which she desires is horrible, but she cannot and will not act otherwise. She feels that despite its horror it is right. So when she has told the Chorus of the hopes that she places in Orestes she concludes:

> Friends, is there any room for modesty
> Or good religion here? Set in the midst
> Of evil, we must practise evil still.[1]

She knows that she cannot accept the situation as a modest woman should or pay to a mother the respect that should be due to her. Her excessive conduct looks like an outrage on common decency, her contempt and hatred for her mother like a violation of divine rules. In her evil circumstances she is driven to an evil course. There is no alternative to dishonouring her mother. When Clytaemnestra chides her for insolence, Electra defends herself:

> No shame? You may be sure I am ashamed
> Although you think not so. I understand.
> I know that what I do passes all bounds
> And is unworthy of me, but your hate
> Forces me, and your evil deeds compel me
> To forget shame because my life is shameful.[2]

This is her situation. When things are as wrong as they are in this household, they make other wrongs to grow. Electra has to be insolent to her mother, and we look beyond the superficial meaning of her words to something else. The base deeds of Clytaemnestra and Aegisthus teach her to be base and to wish for her mother's death.

Sophocles accepts the evil and makes no attempt to minimize it. He does, however, suggest that the task which lies before Electra and Orestes and which excites a natural horror is necessary and right. Only through such means can a fearful state of affairs be corrected. And that such exists in the house of Clytaemnestra he takes pains to show. In fact that is perhaps why his play is called *Electra* and its chief character is not Agamemnon's son but his

[1] 307-9

ἐν οὖν τοιούτοις οὔτε σωφρονεῖν, φίλαι,
οὔτ' εὐσεβεῖν πάρεστιν· ἀλλ' ἐν τοῖς κακοῖς
πολλή 'στ' ἀνάγκη κἀπιτηδεύειν κακά.

[2] 616-21

εὖ νυν ἐπίστω τῶνδέ μ' αἰσχύνην ἔχειν,
κεἰ μὴ δοκῶ σοι· μανθάνω δ' ὁθούνεκα
ἔξωρα πράσσω κοὐκ ἐμοὶ προσεικότα.
ἀλλ' ἡ γὰρ ἐκ σοῦ δυσμένεια καὶ τὰ σὰ
ἔργ' ἐξαναγκάζει με ταῦτα δρᾶν βίᾳ·
αἰσχροῖς γὰρ αἰσχρὰ πράγματ' ἐκδιδάσκεται.

daughter. For she, not Orestes, has lived in the presence of evil
for many years and has been deeply affected by it. She knows it
from acute personal experience. Crime and cruelty have left a
deep brand on her. She is a living example of the extremes to
which a noble and loving character may be driven by the wickedness of others, of the excesses of temper produced by unnatural
circumstances. Electra is not to be blamed or even excused. Her
temper is the natural result of her circumstances, and it is right.
For only through such implacable resolve can the evil figures of
Clytaemnestra and Aegisthus be eradicated from the world. Her
immodesty, her hatred for her mother, her outbursts of insolence
and disobedience, all make her an instrument of vengeance.
Judged by ordinary standards she offends. Sophocles was conscious of this. He knew that many would disapprove of Electra as
of Antigone. He knows that she is right, but he takes steps to
answer her critics and to show that what looks like weakness in
her is really strength, what looks like hatred grows out of love.

A casual observer might accuse Electra of over-indulgence in
grief for her dead father. In general, it was thought that grief
should be kept in proper bounds,[1] and the Chorus reproach Electra
for her insatiable sorrow and point out that such lamentations
exceed the Mean and bring no profit; for they will not bring the
dead man back to life (137–42). They advance the old empty
comfort that Electra is not alone in her loss (153–4). These sentiments are admirable for an ordinary situation. But they do not
suit Electra, and she has her answer to them. It amounts to saying that her grief is nothing else but love for her father. She feels
that he has nobody but her to remember him and that she cannot
but lament him. Then she addresses his spirit:

> There is no sign of pity anywhere,
> Except from me, O father,
> For thy pitiful, dishonourable death.[2]

She shows the depth of her love and pity for him, her conviction
that she alone remembers him. She thinks of him as her 'unhappy
father' (133) and recalls with horror that most hateful of days
when he was killed (201 ff.). Her excess of grief is prompted by
love.

Electra conveys her sorrow by two haunting and significant

---

[1] Archilochus fr. 67 a 5, Theognis 657, *Il.* xxiv, 524.

[2] 100–2   κοὐδεὶς τούτων οἶκτος ἀπ' ἄλλης
                  ἢ 'μοῦ φέρεται, σοῦ, πάτερ, οὕτως
                  αἰκῶς οἰκτρῶς τε θανόντος.

images, the nightingale and Niobe. When she first appears she
says that like the nightingale she will never cease from mourning
(106–9). She feels it close to her:

> I love the wakeful, sorrowful nightingale.
> Is not her ceaseless cry for 'Itys, Itys'
> Importunate? And yet she is the bird of Zeus the Father,[1]

and her laments are wings to her (242–3). The Chorus accept the
comparison and see her as 'the sorrowful nightingale'.[2] Behind
this imagery lies Homer's simile in which Penelope compares
herself to the nightingale weeping for her lost child.[3] The nightingale is the type of grief which is inconsolable because it is faithful.
She cannot forget her lost child and sings everlastingly in lament
for him.[4] So Electra laments for one violently done to death and
justifies her unceasing grief:

> Only the fool forgetteth
> His father, pitifully taken from him.[5]

This is her answer to the criticisms of the Chorus. She knows that
her grief is right because it rises out of love and loyalty. That is
perhaps why she calls the nightingale the bird of Zeus (148). Its
unceasing plaint is the voice of Zeus the avenger. Electra's laments
are a sign to her dead father that he is not forgotten but still has
someone who loves him.

Electra also compares herself to Niobe, and this too comes from
Homer, whose Achilles tells her story to Priam. There she is the
type of inconsolable sorrow. Even when she has been turned to
stone she continues to lament for her children.[6] Her state is
certainly not of joy. Though Niobe prayed for it, it is not a consolation for what she has suffered but a perpetuation of her sorrow.
There is even something horrifying in this unending stony grief:

> In summer's heat and in the winter's cold
> She changes night's grief for the grief of day.[7]

Her fate was a display of divine power. It should instil awe and
humility. Niobe on Sipylus is not what an ordinary man or woman
would wish to be. When Antigone compares herself to Niobe, it

---

[1] 148–9   ἀλλ' ἐμέ γ' ἀ στονόεσσ' ἄραρεν φρένας,
ἀ Ἴτυν, αἰὲν Ἴτυν ὀλοφύρεται,
ὄρνις ἀτυζομένα, Διὸς ἄγγελος.

[2] 1077 ἀ πάνλυρτος ἀηδών.   [3] Od. xix. 521–3.   [4] Eur. Hel. 1107 ff.

[5] 145–6   νήπιος ὃς τῶν οἰκτρῶς
οἰχομένων γονέων ἐπιλάθεται.

[6] Il. xxiv. 617.

[7] Tr. Ad. 7   θάλπουσα καὶ ψύχουσα καὶ πόνῳ πόνον
ἐκ νυκτὸς ἀλλάσσουσα τὸν μεθ' ἡμέραν.

is because of the fearful doom that awaits her. Turned into stone and beaten by storm and snow, Niobe is indeed 'most piteous'.[1] No one should envy her lot. But Electra does:

Ah, Niobe, who art all tears, I count thee more than mortals happy,
Because, although thou weepest,
Thou art changed; thou art a stone.[2]

In such an existence she sees the absolute loyalty in grief which she herself feels for her father. So by an extreme paradox she calls Niobe divine. The gods are happy, and for Electra Niobe's everlasting grief is itself a kind of happiness, a perfect satisfaction; Niobe is a goddess because she never ceases from mourning.

By these comparisons Electra shows the nature of her grief, its intensity and its justification. It is based on love for her father, and she feels that it is right because he needs it as a sign of that love. But it is not passive or negative; she is not content merely to lament like the nightingale or Niobe, enviable though their state may be. Her grief shows itself positively in a desire to exact justice from the evil-doers. Electra moves from the first comparison of herself to the nightingale to a great appeal to the nether powers for vengeance on the murderers of her father (110–16). A little later she prays that Zeus may requite them for what they have done (209–12). This desire for vengeance rises from her loyalty. Punishment is right, as she knows through her love for her dead father, through her horror at this death, through her unceasing sorrow at his loss. Her great conclusion follows that if such crimes are unrequited there is an end to all modesty and reverence. Her conviction that murder must be punished is based mainly on her own feelings, and chief among these is her devotion to her father. So when Chrysothemis pleads for submission and acceptance of circumstances, Electra is impatient with her to the point of scorn. Here too what counts is love for Agamemnon. She blames her sister for forgetting him (342), for not helping the work of vengeance (350), for consorting with his murderers (358), for betraying him (368). She scorns her prudence and faces her with a stark choice:

Choose. Either be impolitic with me,
Or use your policy and forget your dearest.[3]

[1] *Ant.* 823 ff.
[2] 149-52 ἰὼ παντλά-
μων Νιόβα, σὲ δ' ἔγωγε νέμω θεόν,
ἅτ' ἐν τάφῳ πετραίῳ
αἰεὶ δακρύεις.
[3] 345-6 ἔπειθ' ἑλοῦ γε θάτερ', ἢ φρονεῖν κακῶς,
ἢ τῶν φίλων φρονοῦσα μὴ μνήμην ἔχειν.

For herself she must be 'impolitic' because she is loyal to the dead.
In the same uncompromising spirit she forbids Chrysothemis to
take Clytaemnestra's offerings to Agamemnon's tomb, and makes
her offer instead a prayer for vengeance (431 ff.). And here too
her final appeal is based on love for her father:

> Dear sister, do this office for my sake
> And yours, and his, belov'd in spite of death
> More than the world, my father and your own.[1]

By a natural process Electra's love for her father leads her to
desire vengeance on his murderers.

Electra feels this all the more because she stands almost alone.
Her sister is not willing to help her; her brother is, as she believes,
far away, and she almost despairs that he will ever come (164 ff.).
None the less she fastens her hopes on him. She prays to the nether
gods for his coming (117–18). In her long waiting for him she
feels her own life failing:

> What of me? I wait, and wait,
> Lost, utterly lost. Orestes will not come.[2]

She tells Chrysothemis to pray for his return (453 ff.). She tells
her mother that she would gladly have reared Orestes to take
vengeance if she had been able to do so (603–5). He is her one
hope of success, and he is the only living person whom she feels
that she can love. When she hears that he is dead she suffers a
double, deadly blow. At the first news she feels completely lost
and can only break into cries of utter despair:

> Ah woe is me! Oh, I am lost, quite lost.[3]

> Forlorn and utterly wretched! Lost, quite lost.[4]

After she has heard the full story from the Paedagogus she is silent
for a while and breaks her silence only to chide her mother's unnatural joy. When Clytaemnestra departs triumphant, Electra
unburdens her misery. The death of Orestes has robbed her not
only of her hope of vengeance (809–11) but of her one friend
(819). No wonder that she wishes to die.

From this despair Electra gradually recovers. If Orestes is

---

[1] 461–3 ὅμως δ', ἀδελφή, σοί θ' ὑπούργησον τάδε
              ἐμοί τ' ἀρωγά, τῷ τε φιλτάτῳ βροτῶν
              πάντων, ἐν Ἅιδου κειμένῳ κοινῷ πατρί.

[2] 303–4 ἐγὼ δ' Ὀρέστην τῶνδε προσμένουσ' ἀεὶ
              παυστῆρ' ἐφήξειν ἡ τάλαιν' ἀπόλλυμαι.

[3] 674   οἲ 'γὼ τάλαιν', ὄλωλα τῇδ' ἐν ἡμέρᾳ.

[4] 677   ἀπωλόμην δύστηνος, οὐδέν εἰμ' ἔτι.

dead, she will carry out the vengeance without him. Her resolve
is in no way weakened because Chrysothemis refuses to help:

> I must do my task
> Alone. We cannot leave this work undone.[1]

With this decision in her mind she receives the alleged ashes of
her brother, and again we see how closely the desire for vengeance
is linked to deep and real love. This time her love turns not to her
dead father but to her dead brother. She remembers him as she
knew him in childhood (1130 ff.), when she nursed him (1145),
and loved him more than his mother loved him (1146). The
force of her affection comes out when she clings to the urn which
she believes to hold his ashes:

> O sad memorial of the life I priz'd
> Beyond all other lives, my lov'd Orestes;[2]

in the feeling of annihilation which his death brings to her:

> You gather'd up my life
> And, like a whirlwind, left me;[3]

in her longing to join him in the grave (1168–70). Behind Electra's
desire for vengeance and her hatred for her mother lie a great
capacity and need for love. She expends it on her dead father
and on the brother whom now she believes also to be dead. It is
because she can love like this that she can also hate. By the time
that Orestes reveals himself to her Electra has shown all the springs
of her nature. We see that she is what she is because she has
suffered abominably and lived in a household which has little to
give her but crime, abuse, and humiliation. When such things
flourish, human nature may well show its harder and harsher side.

Orestes stands in sharp contrast to Electra. The evil life which
has so affected her has not touched him. He has not lived at
home since childhood nor experienced the corrupting results of
Agamemnon's murder. At the beginning of the play Sophocles
marks the difference between him and his sister. Supported by
his faithful Paedagogus he faces his task without qualms and with
a serene confidence in his own powers. The whole setting suggests
hope, action, and readiness. It is early morning, and the wonder-

---

[1] 1019–20   ἀλλ' αὐτόχειρί μοι μόνῃ τε δραστέον
τοὔργον τόδ'· οὐ γὰρ δὴ κενόν γ' ἀφήσομεν.

[2] 1126–7   ὦ φιλτάτου μνημεῖον ἀνθρώπων ἐμοὶ
ψυχῆς Ὀρέστου λοιπόν.

[3] 1150–1   πάντα γὰρ συναρπάσας,
θύελλ' ὅπως, βέβηκας.

ful lines which describe the dawn hint that the dark shadows have
passed and that light brings hope:

> The bright beams of the sun already wake
> The morning voices of sweet birds to song.
> The black night wanes, and there are no more stars.[1]

This sets the note for Orestes' mood. He feels safe in the company
of his old attendant, whose warlike qualities he praises in the language of a young prince who knows the points of a horse (25-8).
The god has told him what to do, and his plans are laid (32 ff.).
The plan is little more than a trick. About the whole question of
revenge he has no qualms, still less about any deceit that his
stratagem may involve. He rather glories in it:

> I fear no harm from any tale that pays.[2]

He is sure of his mission (70) and hopes soon to recover the wealth
and state which rightly belong to him (71-2). Few enterprises of
so forbidding a nature could begin with so simple a confidence
and so easy a conscience. Orestes is a young man, sure that what
he does is right and that he can do it. So revealed, he is a convincing character. He has been brought up away from home, and
for years he has been taught that his duty is to avenge his father's
death. He hardly knows his mother and has no feeling for her.
What counts is his training. This has bred him to believe that he
has been unjustly treated. The Paedagogus has brought him up
for the single purpose of vengeance (13-14), but Orestes hardly
knows what in reality this means. He does not distinguish between
his mother and her paramour, but classes them together as the
murderers (34), and even for his dead father his feelings amount
to little more than a pious sense of duty. He will pour libations and
place a lock of hair on his tomb because the god has told him to do so
(51-2). Him too he hardly knew, and he cannot be expected to feel
any love for him. He does what he has been taught and told to do.
His strongest emotion at the beginning seems to be his desire to recover his inheritance (71-2). His nature has not found its full range;
he does not yet understand the nature of the task that awaits him.

In immediate contrast to him is Electra. Even with her first
cry behind the scene

> Ah me! O wretchedness! O sorrow![3]

[1] 17-19   ὡς ἡμὶν ἤδη λαμπρὸν ἡλίου σέλας
            ἐῷα κινεῖ φθέγματ' ὀρνίθων σαφῆ
            μέλαινά τ' ἄστρων ἐκλέλοιπεν εὐφρόνη.

[2] 61   Δοκῶ μέν, οὐδὲν ῥῆμα σὺν κέρδει κακόν.

[3] 77   ἰὼ μοί μοι Δύστηνος

we know that the sister's state is not like the brother's. And when after his exit she comes out, we cannot fail to mark the full difference between them. For Orestes the task is of abstract right, for Electra of intimate knowledge and intensely personal feelings. The dawn which blithely summons him to action is for her no more than a release from night with its tears (86–92). The murder which is for him a matter of history is for her a vivid loathsome memory. She recalls how her father fell:

> My mother, my own mother, with her bedfellow Aegisthus,
> Like woodcutters cutting an oak
> With an axe cleft his head.[1]

Orestes is full of confidence; Electra feels that her strength is coming to its end (186). He has the support of the Paedagogus; she is almost alone. At each point we feel the contrast between them. The evil world in which she lives has left deep scars on her, while he has lived outside it unscathed. He faces with a light heart the stratagem by which he will be thought to have died:

> And I have seen this often, men of wit
> Falsely reported dead: mark how they grow
> In reputation when they live again.[2]

But when the false story is told, it comes near to breaking Electra's heart. In the same superficial spirit the Paedagogus tells his story. In its wealth of circumstantial detail, its air of sporting knowledge, its inhumanity and its heartlessness, the speech has only one object, to convince and delude Clytaemnestra. We must expect no more from it than that. It is not the record of a tragic event but a lie intended to secure a certain result. As such it succeeds. But its effect on Electra is appalling. Neither the Paedagogus nor Orestes has foreseen this or given any thought to it. Their world is so different from hers that they fail to consider what her feelings will be. They are intent on their purpose. But Electra, whose life is tied to a single slender hope, collapses on hearing the false story. At this point the contrast between brother and sister reaches its

---

[1] 97–8 μήτηρ δ' ἡμὴ χὠ κοινολεχὴς
Αἴγισθος ὅπως δρῦν ὑλοτόμοι
σχίζουσι κάρα φονίῳ πελέκει.

[2] 62–4 ἤδη γὰρ εἶδον πολλάκις καὶ τοὺς σοφοὺς
λόγῳ μάτην θνῄσκοντας· εἶθ', ὅταν δόμους
ἔλθωσιν αὖθις, ἐκτετίμηνται πλέον.

climax. It seems that their different lives have set them immeasurably apart.

The different feelings of Orestes and Electra help the audience to see the vengeance from two points of view. So far as Orestes is concerned we feel that it is indeed awful that a son should have to kill his mother, but from Electra we see the necessity of the hideous duty, the ravages which the murder of Agamemnon has caused, and the ultimate rightness of punishment. If we are to get rid of our uneasy feelings for Orestes, it is essential that he too should come to see the situation as it really is and to know the true nature of his task. Sophocles makes him do this and so saves us from feeling that the god has commanded him to do something unbearable. When Orestes brings in the urn which is supposed to contain his ashes and gives it to Electra, he is still a man of action whose chief thought is success in his undertaking. He takes pleasure in acting his part and telling his story, in saying that he is a Phocian (1107), or drawing attention to the smallness of the urn (1113). Though he does not yet know that it is his sister who bursts into tears on hearing him (1115), and still keeps up his assumed part when he gives her the urn, he is clearly touched when she begs him to let her keep it (1123–5). Natural feelings have begun to work in him even before he hears Electra's long lament. At the end of it his jauntiness has all gone. He knows that this unhappy woman is his sister; he has been deeply touched by her, and he finds difficulty in controlling his speech (1174–5). He is appalled by what he hears from her and by what he sees, her sad state, her wasting neglected body (1181), her unmarried miserable condition (1183). He realizes that for all these years he has lived in ignorance of the truth:

I find I did not know my own misfortunes.[1]

His whole outlook has been changed. A new overwhelming factor has come into his life. His pity for his sister grows as he learns more about her sufferings:

Alas! Unhappy one, I pity you.[2]

She too, not knowing who he is, feels gratitude to him since he is the only person who has shown sorrow for her (1200). Then, when the recognition comes, each forgets himself in the other with a sense of fathomless relief, love, and satisfaction:

[1] 1185   ὡς οὐκ ἄρ' ἤδη τῶν ἐμῶν οὐδὲν κακῶν.
[2] 1199   ὦ δύσποτμ', ὡς ὁρῶν σ' ἐποικτίρω πάλαι.

El. O happy light!

Or.   A light of joy indeed!

El. Voice, you have come!

Or.   My voice shall be your answer.

El. Here in my arms?

Or.   Here, where I still would be.[1]

Electra's despair has turned to unbounded joy; Orestes' calculated dissembling disappears in the reality of his sister's presence.

This recognition is an important part of the reconciliation which Sophocles finds for the tragic situation of the *Electra*. The disorder, waste, and evil that have grown from the murder of Agamemnon can only be countered by the growth of opposite forces of order, trust, and love. If these can be re-established, the powers of wickedness must yield. The recognition gives a foretaste of how this works and what it means. Electra turns from hate to love, from despair to hope, from solitude to intimate companionship. Orestes is shaken from his superficial and partial view of his task into a finer and deeper discernment. He now knows what his father's murder means in its results, the misery and wickedness to which it has led, the life that it has spoiled. Hitherto brother and sister have lived in different worlds, but now they are not only brought together iñ union and harmony but enabled to face their stern task together and in the same spirit. Both know what they must do and why. Orestes now knows what kind of a woman his mother is and that it is right for him to kill her. What was before an abstract duty takes a definite shape and gains a new strength. In this mood he becomes more resolute. When Electra addresses him in excited lyrical words, he answers in plain iambic speech. While she gives vent to her unbounded joy, he is already thinking of the next step (1251–2), and is even apprehensive about his sister's excessive gladness (1271–2). He pulls her up and directs her thoughts to vengeance. He knows what the truth is, what Clytaemnestra and Aegisthus really are:

> No word save to the purpose, now. No need
> To prove my mother's wickedness, no need
> To tell me that the prodigal Aegisthus
> Battens on my inheritance, scattering
> And wasting.[2]

[1] 1224–6   Ηλ. ὦ φίλτατον φῶς. Ορ. φίλτατον, ξυμμαρτυρῶ.
                 Ηλ. ὦ φθέγμ', ἀφικοῦ; Ορ. μηκέτ' ἄλλοθεν πύθη.
                 Ηλ. ἔχω σε χερσίν; Ορ. ὡς τὰ λοίπ' ἔχοις ἀεί.

[2] 1288–91   τὰ μὲν περισσεύοντα τῶν λόγων ἄφες,
                 καὶ μήτε μήτηρ ὡς κακὴ Διδασκέ με
                 μήθ' ὡς πατρῷαν κτῆσιν Αἴγισθος Δόμων
                 ἀντλεῖ, τὰ Δ' ἐκχεῖ, τὰ Δὲ Διασπείρει μάτην.

He has learned the facts from seeing his sister in her misery and degradation. His pity and love for her have opened his eyes and become a potent impulse to exact vengeance from their mother. He need not now be told that Clytaemnestra is wicked. He has heard and seen enough to know that she is.

Inspired and strengthened Orestes goes to his task. The Paedagogus hurries him, but his intervention is necessary only to show the need for haste. Orestes' temper needs no whetting, and his sister has already urged him on (1323–5). Orestes feels that he enters on a solemn task and addresses a reverent prayer to his father's gods (1374–5). He knows that they demand and approve his undertaking. He takes the lead while Electra gives him her spiritual support. She waits outside and offers a prayer to Apollo for the punishment of the wicked (1376–83). The moment is tense and solemn. In action so dread as this the gods must help. The anxiety and desire that beset Electra are revealed in the unrestrained words of her prayer:

> I beg and pray and ask, be good to us;
> Help and promote and bless this enterprise.[1]

Then in the death and its consequences the tasks of brother and sister differ. While Orestes acts, Electra listens at the door and marks every stage with a fierce, ecstatic joy. She tells the Chorus that the men are at work (1399), that they are at Clytaemnestra's side (1400–1). When Clytaemnestra cries out that slayers are in the house, Electra notes with excitement:

> Someone cried out within. Did you not hear it?[2]

In the same mood she hears her mother's next cry (1410), and when Clytaemnestra begs for mercy, Electra, knowing that the time of judgement has come, is adamant in her pitilessness; since Clytaemnestra did not spare Agamemnon, she herself has no right to be spared (1411–12). The same spirit makes her cry out for a second blow when her mother has been struck (1415) and then wish that Aegisthus too may be struck (1426). When Orestes comes out, Electra excitedly asks him if their mother is dead, and only at this moment does she show any sign of tenderness for her, and that is small enough, the adjective 'unhappy' (1436). Except for this transient qualm she shows no shred of pity. She is athirst for justice, for blood, and satisfied only when she gets it.

---

[1] 1380–1   αἰτῶ, προπίτνω, λίσσομαι, γενοῦ πρόφρων
                ἡμῖν ἀρωγὸς τῶνδε τῶν βουλευμάτων.
[2] 1406   βοᾷ τις ἔνδον· οὐκ ἀκούετ', ὦ φίλαι;

Electra hates her mother and knows that it is right for her to
die. Her joy in the death satisfies her. But with Orestes it is
different. Though his sister's miseries have awakened him to the
necessity of his task and to its meaning, he has no personal hatred
for Clytaemnestra. When he kills her, the death cannot fail to
convey horror. Clytaemnestra is alone and unarmed. She feels
that she is trapped, and there is a terrible anguish in her words:

> Alas!
> Home, destitute of friends, full of destroyers![1]

In her despair she cries in vain for Aegisthus (1409). Then we
hear her last awful appeal to Orestes:

> My child, my child,
> Pity your mother.[2]

Electra has her answer to this, but the horror of Orestes' act is
none the smaller for it. The words need no elaboration. Then
come the last two cries when she is struck and struck again:

> Ah! I am struck.[3]
> Ah! struck again.[4]

They recall the last words of Agamemnon in Aeschylus' play:

> Ah! I am struck a deadly blow within.[5]
> Ah! struck again a second deadly blow.[6]

Surely the echo is intentional. It suggests that hateful though this
killing is, it is none the less an act of justice, of blood paid for
blood. The revenge has to be taken, but Sophocles does not
shrink from the truth. He shows that what is right may still be
horrible. Only by evil can this evil be cured.

Orestes has not flinched in his odious task, but when he comes
out he does not share his sister's triumphant spirit. When she
asks how it fares with him he answers:

> In the house
> All's well, if Apollo's oracle was well.

[1] 1404–5   αἰαῖ· ἰὼ στέγαι,
                    φίλων ἔρημοι, τῶν δ' ἀπολλύντων πλέαι.
[2] 1410–11   ὦ τέκνον, τέκνον,
                    οἴκτιρε τὴν τεκοῦσαν.
[3] 1415   ὤμοι πέπληγμαι.
[4] 1416   ὤμοι μάλ' αὖθις.
[5] Ag. 1343   ὤμοι πέπληγμαι καιρίαν πληγὴν ἔσω.
[6] Ib. 1345   ὤμοι μάλ', αὖθις, δευτέραν πεπληγμένος.

In these words there is no calm confidence such as has been found
in them. For the moment Orestes still feels the horror of his deed,
but tries to comfort himself with the thought that Apollo ordered
it. A great demand has been made of him and he is shaken. But
he finds a consolation. His next words to Electra:

> You need not fear
> Your mother will insult you any more,[1]

show that he knows what a relief the death of Clytaemnestra
brings to his sister. In his new-found love his thoughts turn to her
and he finds comfort from his horror. Once again things positive
and negative, love and hate, devotion and destruction, are united
in a complex whole. The mutual affection of Orestes and Electra
rises out of the criminal actions of Clytaemnestra and is sealed
by her death. It is the gain that comes out of the waste.

Aegisthus has still to be killed, and in his death not Orestes but
Electra is the moving spirit. She has special reasons for hating
him. For he has been the active instigator of her sufferings. We
know what she thinks of him:

> Puny, devilish, pestilent coward,
> Fighting his battles with a woman still
> His weapon.[2]

No shame or guilt need be felt about killing him. As a murderer
and adulterer he is twice guilty. To kill a man taken in adultery
was not an offence in Attic law.[3] So Aeschylus' Orestes says of
Aegisthus' death:

> He has the adulterer's doom, as law demands.[4]

We may assume that Sophocles held the same view. He makes no
attempt to make Aegisthus attractive or to defend him. Even
Euripides makes him entirely contemptible and disagreeable. Yet
in dealing with him Orestes shows a hesitation which he did not
feel in undertaking the death of Clytaemnestra. He needs, and
gets, the encouragement of Electra, and is kept by her to his task.
There is psychological truth in this. Orestes has discovered that
the death of his mother is an appalling thing. It has shaken him far
more than he foresaw. He has no rational qualms about killing
Aegisthus, but he shrinks from it and has to be kept to it.

[1] 1426–7   μηκέτ᾽ ἐκφοβοῦ
μητρῷον ὡς σε λῆμ᾽ ἀτιμάσει ποτέ.
[2] 301–2   ὁ πάντ᾽ ἄναλκις οὗτος, ἡ πᾶσα βλάβη,
ὁ σὺν γυναιξὶ τὰς μάχας ποιούμενος.
[3] Lex ap. Dem. xxiii. 53.
[4] *Cho.* 990   ἔχει γὰρ αἰσχυντῆρος, ὡς νόμος, Δίκην.

The second death begins with a warning from the Chorus. Orestes says that he is ready (1435-6), Electra assumes a double task, first to cheat Aegisthus into a sense of false security, second to urge Orestes on. The first she achieves with great skill and self-command. In her words with Aegisthus there is a fierce irony. When she says that the strangers have found a way to the hostess

> Within. They found a hostess to their mind;[1]

that Aegisthus can see what he wishes to see:

> Yes, he is here, and no glad sight to see;[2]

that Aegisthus may find the news good:

> If you find joy in this, I give you joy;[3]

her words are venomously double-edged. This is not the usual Sophoclean irony but the ironical speech of hate and legitimate exultation over an enemy. So when the doors are opened for Aegisthus and we know that he will see Clytaemnestra's body, Electra clinches the situation:

> For me the lesson's finished. Time has brought
> Discretion, and my master's will is mine.[4]

Aegisthus thinks that she is still subservient to him, but she means the opposite. She feels that now the stronger are on her side, that her long waiting has been rewarded, that she will not fail in her task.

She does not fail. For a moment she fears that Orestes will waste time and words on Aegisthus. She cuts the talk short:

> Do not let him talk!
> In God's name, brother, do not let him talk![5]

She bids her brother kill Aegisthus at once and have him buried out of their sight:

> Kill him at once. When you have done it, fling
> The carrion to the buriers it deserves,
> Out of our sight.[6]

---

[1] 1451 ἔνδον· φίλης γὰρ προξένου κατήνυσαν.

[2] 1455 πάρεστι δῆτα καὶ μάλ' ἄζηλος θέα.

[3] 1457 χαίροις ἄν, εἴ σοι χαρτὰ τυγχάνει τάδε.

[4] 1464-5 καὶ δὴ τελεῖται τἀπ' ἐμοῦ· τῷ γὰρ χρόνῳ
     νοῦν ἔσχον, ὥστε συμφέρειν τοῖς κρείσσοσιν.

[5] 1483-4   μὴ πέρα λέγειν ἔα,
     πρὸς θεῶν, ἀδελφέ, μηδὲ μηκύνειν λόγους.

[6] 1487-9 ἀλλ' ὡς τάχιστα κτεῖνε καὶ κτανὼν πρόθες
     ταφεῦσιν ὧν τόνδ' εἰκός ἐστι τυγχάνειν,
     ἄποπτον ἡμῶν.

This does not mean, as has commonly been thought, that Aegisthus shall have no burial or that his 'buriers' will be birds of prey. Homer certainly says that Aegisthus was left unburied and that the dogs and birds devoured him,[1] and Euripides' Orestes gives orders for the disposal of the corpse in like fashion until they are countermanded by the Dioscuri, who insist on burial.[2] Since Sophocles' Electra says nothing about leaving the corpse unburied, we may assume that she does not wish the body to be treated in this impious way. All she wishes is to have Aegisthus out of sight at once. For her the death of Aegisthus is both a punishment and a deliverance. Her house will at last be rid of this man who has for so long defiled it. After her words Orestes hesitates no longer and drives Aegisthus to his death.

Aegisthus deserves his end, and no tears need be shed over him. Yet in this brief presentation Sophocles makes him live and have his place in the play. Aeschylus and Euripides had both made Clytaemnestra dominate him. Sophocles reverses the roles. Clytaemnestra is subordinate to him. He must therefore have some personality. He is of course thoroughly brutal, but he has a certain authority. He has heard that Orestes is dead and he must know what this means to Electra. With brutal directness he asks her about it:

My question is for you—you, who were once
So bold. Yes, you must tell me. It touches you,
I think, most nearly. Tell me.[3]

and we see at once why Electra hates him. He is patently pleased with the news and hopes to hear it all soon for himself and to enjoy it. The prospect of seeing the ashes of Orestes gives him great pleasure (1456). At the same time he asserts his authority and orders the gates to be opened that any who set hopes on Orestes' return may be curbed before they are punished (1458 ff.). Yet this odious brute has a certain courage in his last moments. When he sees the dead body of Clytaemnestra he does not humble himself but makes some attempts to match Orestes in argument until he knows that he is lost and accepts his fate.

For Aristotle Aegisthus would no doubt have been an example of the incontinent man who pursues his pleasures and thinks that they are right.[4] But there is no need to classify him. We can see

---

[1] *Od.* iii. 259-61.   [2] *El.* 896-8, 1276-7.

[3] 1445-7   σέ τοι, σὲ κρίνω, ναὶ σέ, τὴν ἐν τῷ πάρος
χρόνῳ θρασεῖαν· ὡς μάλιστα σοὶ μέλειν
οἶμαι, μάλιστα δ' ἂν κατειδυῖαν φράσαι.

[4] *Nic. Eth.* 1150 a 30.

from what sources Sophocles derived him and what he meant us to see in him. Homer had called him 'cowardly',[1] and Electra does the same (301). So too did Aeschylus on the supposition that he stayed at home and made love to wives whose husbands were at the war.[2] Sophocles follows this with some care. His Aegisthus is not exactly woman-hearted but he is the typical paramour. His concern is not war or government but women. Like the Homeric Suitors, who are also 'cowardly',[3] his chief aim is to possess a woman. Such notable qualities as he possesses belong to him because Clytaemnestra depends absolutely on him and has done everything for him. Otherwise he is a miserable creature. His only claim is that he has caused her ruin. He is interesting for the light that he throws on her. It is for him that she has killed her husband and smothered her love for her children. Devotion to him has wrecked any nobility or decent feelings that she may have had. Aegisthus is the cause of her downfall and rightly shares her death. But in itself his death has no more significance than that of a common criminal. It is the final act of justice which frees Agamnemon's children from their miseries.

With this justice is done. Right is re-established; the dead Agamemnon and his protecting gods are appeased; Apollo has been obeyed. Yet an act so bloody and fearful as this can hardly lead at once to peace and satisfaction. The wound inflicted by it will take time to heal; some adjustment is necessary before Orestes and Electra can take their place in the company of other men. The anxieties through which they have passed, the exhausting effort, and the moral decision demanded of them, have left their mark. Sophocles might have ended his play on a note of joy, but actually he ends it with a full knowledge of what the matricide means. His method is subtle and has been misunderstood. But the clues that he provides show what he means.

First, the play closes with a few words from the Chorus. The examples in the *Ajax* and *Antigone* suggest that these are simply a summary or verdict. Yet they are not simple:

> O seed of Atreus, through what suffering,
> How hardly by this present enterprise
> Thy Destiny is consummated and thy Freedom won.[4]

The Chorus congratulate the House of Atreus on attaining freedom

---

[1] *Od.* iii. 310. [2] *Ag.* 1224; 1626–7. [3] *Od.* iv. 334.

[4] 1508–10 ὦ σπέρμ' Ἀτρέως, ὡς πολλὰ παθὸν
δι' ἐλευθερίας μόλις ἐξῆλθες
τῇ νῦν ὁρμῇ τελεωθέν.

after suffering. Their words seem a superficial comment on the horrors that have passed. They seem to say nothing of justice or vengeance, nothing of the heights of joy and depths of despair through which Electra, if not Orestes, has gone. They say simply that the House of Atreus is now free. It is easy to give a meaning to this. Electra has been all but a slave; Orestes has been kept out of his lawful inheritance. They have come into their own, and the usurpers are no more. But we may believe that Sophocles meant more than this, that the freedom of which the Chorus speak is something more important. We may recall how Aeschylus makes his Chorus pray to Apollo for the House of Atreus:

> May Freedom's bright light
> Look on it with friendly eyes
> From the veil of darkness.[1]

The freedom they desire is from the whole burden of sin and misery which the murder of Agamemnon has brought. And surely this is the kind of freedom to which Sophocles refers. The vengeance on the guilty has freed the innocent from the concatenation of evil from which they have suffered. The victory has been gained 'hardly', but it has been gained, and we may well feel a kind of relief, of deliverance. This is not to say that the play ends on a cheerful or even on a happy note. What has happened has been undeniably painful. But it had to be, and it is over. Orestes and Electra are now free.

Tradition did not end the story like this. The notion that Orestes was pursued by the Furies for killing his mother was as old as Stesichorus and played an extremely important part in Aeschylus' *Eumenides* and in Euripides' *Orestes*. May we assume that Sophocles ignored it? We know that he was not averse to such a notion, since his *Alcmeon* told of a man who was driven mad by the Furies for killing his mother. So in the *Electra* hints of such a fate have been found, and they must be treated with respect. The most important are the words of Aegisthus to Orestes:

> Is it ordained this house must see all woes
> Of Pelops' House, these now and those to come?[2]

Is this a hint of the troubles which await Orestes? Are the present woes those of Aegisthus and the woes to come those of Orestes?

---

[1] *Cho.* 809–11   καί νιν ἐλευθερίας φῶς
              λαμπρὸν ἰδεῖν φιλίοις
              ὄμμασιν ἐκ ᾽Δνοφερᾶς καλύπτρας.

[2] 1497–8   ἦ πᾶσ᾽ ἀνάγκη τήν᾽Δε τὴν στέγην ἰδεῖν
            τά τ᾽ ὄντα καὶ μέλλοντα Πελοπι᾽Δῶν κακά;

The answer must come from the context and from the next words
of Orestes:

> Yours it shall see. That I can prophesy.[1]

This shows that the evils to come are not Orestes' own but the
immediate death of Aegisthus. In that case those existing are what
have already taken place, and especially the death of Clytaemnestra. Aegisthus naturally mocks this answer of Orestes, but
makes no more threats. If he had any inkling of a future persecu-
tion of Orestes, he would be more explicit than this. We cannot
doubt that here at least there is no hint of future retribution.

We may still feel that Aegisthus speaks without knowing all
that he means and that through him the poet hints at woes to
come. On the stage this can be made most effective, and it is not
inconceivable. But on examination it breaks down. The persecu-
tion of Orestes by the Furies is due to the death not of Aegisthus
but of Clytaemnestra. The time for it to be foretold is in the last
moments of Clytaemnestra, and that is where Aeschylus places it.[2]
Sophocles' Clytaemnestra is silent about any woes to come. From
Aegisthus the threat, if it exists, comes with no authority. Nor
will the prospect of being pursued by the Furies deter Orestes
from killing Aegisthus. For it is not his death that they would
punish but Clytaemnestra's. Secondly, the last words of the Chorus
convey, as we have seen, a note of relief which would be out of
harmony if Sophocles really intended to forecast more sufferings
for Orestes. We may well contrast them with the last words of
Aeschylus' *Libation-bearers*:

> How shall it finish, how shall it cease,
> And fall asleep, the power of doom?[3]

It is true that Aeschylus' play is the second of a trilogy and can
afford to give a broad hint of what is to come next as the *Electra*
cannot. None the less there is a great difference of temper between
the note of relief and the note of anxious anticipation. The difference shows that Sophocles, who knew the play of Aeschylus and
could have followed its precedent, decided to do otherwise. The
natural conclusion is that he did not mean to forecast any further
sufferings for the House of Atreus.

Moreover, it looks as if Sophocles had considered the whole
question of the Furies and come to his own view of them. Electra

---

[1] 1499   τὰ γοῦν σ'· ἐγώ σοι μάντις εἰμὶ τῶνδ' ἄκρος.
[2] *Cho.* 924.
[3] *Cho.* 1075–6   ποῖ δῆτα κρανεῖ, ποῖ καταλήξει
                                     μετακοιμισθὲν μένος ἄτης;

is almost an avenging Fury herself, in her absolute conviction that blood must be paid for blood and her exultant merciless spirit. Orestes and Pylades are even more close to avenging spirits. When they enter the house to kill Clytaemnestra the Chorus comment:

> They have gone within,
> The implacable hounds, the pursuers of sin.[1]

The comparison to bloodhounds picks up Aeschylus' description of the Furies:

> Look out! beware your mother's angry hounds.[2]
> Truly these are my mother's angry hounds.[3]

So too in Euripides' *Electra* Castor warns Orestes to flee from the hounds who are the Furies.[4] It was familiar that the Furies were like bloodhounds, and when Sophocles uses the image for Orestes and Pylades, he suggests that they are like Furies come to punish the murderers. The Chorus amplify the idea when they say of Orestes:

> The crafty-footed avenger moveth on,
> He fights for the dead.[5]

He does what the Furies do, and Hermes helps him (1396). In effect Sophocles has changed the role of the Furies. They act not for Clytaemnestra but against her; they do not pursue Orestes but are embodied in him. And this is just what we might expect. For the play is concerned with a clear issue of justice. The divine powers of vengeance are on the side of the executioners.

Sophocles, then, dispenses with that part of the story in which Orestes is pursued by the Furies, and has good reason for doing so. The punishment of Clytaemnestra and Aegisthus is an act of justifiable homicide and would in Athens be tried before the court of the Delphinium. In fact Demosthenes says that trials of such cases were conducted there because Orestes' acquittal by the gods had shown that murder could be just, and such a case could hardly be tried before the Areopagus.[6] He even admits that in certain cases homicide was 'holy', and he quotes Orestes to his point.

---

[1] 1386–8   βεβᾶσιν ἄρτι Δωμάτων ὑπόστεγοι
                 μετάΔρομοι κακῶν πανουργημάτων
                 ἄφυκτοι κύνες.

[2] *Cho.* 924   ὅρα, φύλαξαι μητρὸς ἐγκότους κύνας.

[3] *Ib.* 1054   σαφῶς γὰρ αἵΔε μητρὸς ἔγκοτοι κύνες.

[4] *El.* 1342.

[5] 1391–2   παράγεται γὰρ ἐνέρων
                Δολιόπους ἀρωγὸς εἴσω στέγας.

[6] Dem. xxiii. 74.

This is the conclusion that we should draw from the *Electra*. The nearest parallel to Sophocles' treatment is Pindar's. Pindar too saw in the story a triumph of justice as ordered by the gods and understood some of the great issues involved. But with his wider scale Sophocles shows what this justice means in reality both to the killers and to the killed. He does not flinch from the truth. The actual killing of a mother is indeed ugly. That is why it affects Orestes and affects us. But once great wickedness prospers, ugly passions will grow, and the whole characterization of Electra shows how Clytaemnestra's crime breeds its own punishment in hatred and revenge. Except for the love of brother and sister there is no joy in the play. A stern task is carried out in a spirit of revenge and righteous wrath.

At the end it must be clear that in the *Electra* there is no conflict between what the gods command and what the human conscience feels. The gods order the death of Clytaemnestra; but it is none the less demanded by the justice of men. Murderers must pay for their crimes with their lives. What is important is that this punishment is a highly solemn act, a lesson to all wrongdoers, and a painful task to him who has to execute it. Yet once it is over, a new light shines for men. Justice and order are restored, and even in the welter of vengeance and hatred rises a new force of love. The lonely sister finds a substitute for her lost father in her brother. The long years of brooding end in a reality of affection at last. Once the destructive forces of evil are broken, normal life and order and trust are re-established. That is why the gods hate evil and demand its punishment.

VII

PHILOCTETES

ARISTOTLE recognizes a kind of tragedy in which the change of fortune is from bad to good,[1] but he is not much interested in it and says elsewhere that in the perfect plot the change should be from happiness to misery.[2] For him tragedy had already some of its modern associations, naturally enough since he is partly responsible for them. In his concentration on plays which end unhappily he neglected a large part of Greek tragedy. Aeschylus' *Oresteia* shows that a bloody and fearful catastrophe could end in joy and reconciliation. Plays of Euripides like the *Iphigeneia in Tauris* end, as Aristotle himself says,[3] in the characters being saved from disaster. Of the extant plays of Sophocles the three latest end with a change to good fortune. The *Electra* moves through powerful, even ugly, emotions, but justice is done and the humbled are exalted. In the *Philoctetes*, produced in 409 B.C., as in the *Oedipus at Colonus* produced after Sophocles' death, a despised and rejected man is brought beyond all likelihood to great glory. Yet despite their happy endings these plays are cast in so serious a spirit and deal with issues of such gravity that they have little in common with such a play as Euripides' *Helen*. If in the end they bring comfort and consolation, it is only after a riot of angry and even brutal passions. No less than the truly tragic plays they show the power of the gods to do what they will with men, the ignorance and the illusions in which men face their destinies, the final illumination which is forced on them even against their will. The dramatic action in the *Philoctetes* is a struggle between the will of the gods and the will of men just as it is in *King Oedipus*. The issues are hardly less momentous. On the one side are glory, decency, and honour, on the other deluding passion, moral weakness, and worldly ambition. The gods work more through the human beings than by external action on them, and in the end their will is done. The chief figure of Sophocles' play has spent ten years on Lemnos in solitude, squalor, and physical pain, but he is destined to be the captor of Troy, and his destiny is duly fulfilled. The play turns on the point where his fortunes change. It shows the accomplishment of the divine will as prophecy has foretold it. Too little is known about the *Philoctetes* of Aeschylus for us to say if he stressed this, but it is possible that Euripides did in his *Philoctetes*,

---

[1] *Poet.* 1451 a 14.   [2] Ib. 1453 a 14.   [3] Ib. 1455 b 12.

which appeared in 431 B.C., twenty-two years before the play of Sophocles. In it some character was sceptical about finding the gods' will from oracles:

> Why do you sit on seats of prophecy
> And swear you know well what the gods intend?
> In such words is no handicraft for men;
> For whoso boasts to know about the gods,
> Knows no more than to speak persuasively.[1]

The play surely mentioned an oracle in which some character did not believe. In any case the oracle was traditional to the story. It had its part in the *Little Iliad*,[2] and was known to Pindar. His Philoctetes is one

> Who broke down Priam's city and ended the Danaans' toil,
> His body weak as he went, yet it was to be.[3]

Despite his physical weakness Philoctetes was destined to take Troy where so many strong men had failed. The element of destiny, of the divine will, appealed no less to Sophocles. The reversal of fortune which he dramatized shows that the gods' will is done.

Sophocles, however, presents the working of the divine will in a highly unexpected way. It is of course accomplished. The play ends with the departure of Philoctetes for Troy and the sure promise of his success. But before this conclusion is reached, and it is only reached through the intervention of Heracles as *deus ex machina*, those who resist it are more attractive and more noble than those who claim that they work for it. Odysseus, who comes to fetch Philoctetes to his appointed task, may not be such a villain as in Euripides' play—Dio calls him 'much gentler and simpler'[4]—but he is not at all agreeable and can hardly fail to excite disapproval. Philoctetes himself, who proves to be the final obstacle to his own appointed destiny, is a noble and generous-hearted man who wins admiration by his heroic endurance and his candid simplicity. Neoptolemus, who bridges the gap between Odysseus and Philoctetes and changes from low cunning to coura-

---

[1] Fr. 795
τί δῆτα θάκοις μαντικοῖς ἐνήμενοι
σαφῶς Διόμνυσθ' εἰδέναι τὰ Δαιμόνων;
οὐ τῶνδε χειρώνακτες ἄνθρωποι λόγων·
ὅστις γὰρ αὐχεῖ θεῶν ἐπίστασθαι πέρι,
οὐδέν τι μᾶλλον οἶδεν ἢ πείθειν λέγων.

[2] Procl. *Chrest.*, p. 106. 24 Allen.

[3] *Pyth.* i. 54–5
ὃς Πριάμοιο πόλιν πέρσεν, τελεύτα-
σέν τε πόνους Δαναοῖς,
ἀσθενεῖ μὲν χρωτὶ βαίνων, ἀλλὰ μοιρίδιον ἦν.

[4] *Or.* lii. 16.

geous frankness, gains in moral stature with the change and with each step that he takes farther from what seems to be the gods' intention. So long as he tries to trick Philoctetes or to steal his bow from him, his behaviour is understandable, but we know that it is against his better feelings. But when he tells the truth, he is entirely admirable, and even when he consents to take Philoctetes home instead of to Troy, he acts on motives which do him credit as a man, though his decision is against what the gods desire. The play, we might think, enlists our dislike of those who do what the gods command and our liking for those who oppose it. The *Philoctetes* certainly produces this effect on most readers, and when it was first performed it must have had a similar effect on an Athenian audience. We can hardly believe that Sophocles intended our moral feelings to run counter to what is desired by the gods, and indeed an examination of the play suggests that he did not. His intention was more subtle and more complex.

In the *Philoctetes* Sophocles carries a step farther the notion that men do not know their own destinies. He had already done this in *King Oedipus* and shown how this ignorance leads to a tragic result. Now the method is elaborated. The victims of illusion are not a pair of characters closely connected together but a set of characters who work in different directions and with different motives. All the human characters of the *Philoctetes* are mistaken and deluded. The gods' plan is clear enough, but it meets with great difficulties, and in the end the gods have to find their own solution for it, so great are the entanglements and the obstacles which the human agents have created. Nor are these men the victims of the gods as Oedipus is. This time the conflict between reality and appearance, between knowledge and illusion, does not end in catastrophe. The play shows that men can be just as blind when the gods wish to glorify them as when they wish to humiliate them. And this blindness is both intellectual and moral. Because men judge things wrongly, they act wrongly, or rather their wrong judgements are inextricably connected with their faults of character. The *Philoctetes* does not display the nothingness of man before the gods as *King Oedipus* does, but it does display the confusion and chaos of his spirit. The gods' plan is extremely simple; yet it seems next to impossible to put it into effect, so strong are the passions and hallucinations which obstruct it. In hearing or reading the play we must throughout see it as a clash of deluded, headstrong souls, and we must, so far as we can, see the conflict of right and wrong which they display. Only so can we understand the play

in its full significance. Despite its happy ending and its web of
intrigue it is intensely serious and must be treated with complete
seriousness in return. The characters do not exist on an imaginary
plane where moral distinctions cease to count, but in a real world
of right and wrong which must be recognized for what they are.

The characters of the *Philoctetes* move in a mist of illusions and
mistakes, and the play conveys this atmosphere by concealing at
the start what its structure and central ideas are. In its excited
personal issues we may easily miss the divine plan which shapes the
action. And indeed Sophocles does not at once reveal this. It
comes out gradually, and just when the whole situation seems
hopelessly muddled, he begins to make the main plan clear. This
is his way of emphasizing the darkness in which men live and move.
The construction of the play corresponds to the obscure passions
of which it treats. With the advanced technique of his ripe old
age Sophocles makes the theme of his play determine its atmosphere. For a time the audience are almost as much in the dark
as the characters themselves are. In this condition we follow our
emotions, and are right to do so. So long as we really feel that
Neoptolemus is wrong to tell a lie and that Odysseus ought not
to persuade him to do so, we are doing what the poet expects.
This is his way of helping us to grope through an obscure situation
until in his own way and in his own good time he enlightens us.

The fundamental fact in the *Philoctetes* is that Philoctetes is
destined to take Troy. The audience are, no doubt, vaguely conscious of this before the play begins. Sophocles makes full use of
it. He embodies it in an oracle which is eventually fulfilled. The
precise terms of this are given by the assumed Merchant. He
says that Helenus gave it:

> Much else he prophesied to them, and said
> That they would never storm Troy's citadel,
> Unless with argument they win this man
> And bring him from the island where he dwells.[1]

In case we think that the Merchant is not entirely to be trusted,
we get unassailable confirmation of his story from Neoptolemus,
who tells Philoctetes that he will not be cured of his disease

> Till to Troy's plain you come of your own will
> And finding there Asclepius' sons with us

---

[1] 610-13   ὃς δὴ τά τ' ἄλλ' αὐτοῖσι πάντ' ἐθέσπισεν
                  καὶ τἀπὶ Τροίᾳ πέργαμ' ὡς οὐ μή ποτε
                  πέρσοιεν, εἰ μὴ τόνδε πείσαντες λόγῳ
                  ἄγοιντο νήσου τῆσδ' ἐφ' ἧς ναίει τὰ νῦν.

Be cured of this disease and find yourself
Troy's captor with these arrows and with me.[1]

The oracle looks, and is, clear; Troy cannot be taken until Philoctetes is persuaded to come there of his own free will. This is what
the gods through Helenus have told the Greeks. It is their plan
for the capture of Troy and the foundation of the play's action.
We do not learn it until the issues of the play have thoroughly
confused and perplexed us. When it comes, it is most important.
It is the first hint of what the gods really wish, and if we listen to
it carefully, it is clear that the plan by which Odysseus and Neoptolemus have tried to secure Philoctetes is not the gods' plan but
differs from it in essential points. Oracles are never easy to follow,
and when an oracle gives instructions which are misunderstood
or disobeyed, trouble is almost inevitable. The Merchant's words
give a hint which demands the greatest attention. Once we know
what the oracle is, we begin to understand the inner meaning of
the play.

The plot of the *Philoctetes* depends largely on the misinterpre-
tation of the oracle. The Greeks have been told that they will
take Troy if they can persuade Philoctetes to come there of his
own accord. There is no doubt about this. Both the Merchant
and Neoptolemus say so. This is not the same as to bring him by
force or to trick him into coming, nor is to bring him to Troy the
same as to bring his bow without him. Yet the oracle's instructions
are not followed closely, and failure follows. The case is of rather
a special kind, but we know the background of belief which explains it. In a poem to Cyrnus Theognis gives advice for a man
who makes inquiries at Delphi:

> Straighter than rule or square or line of compass,
>   Cyrnus, must that man be, keeping guard,
> To whom the Priestess gives a sign at Pytho
>   And declares god's voice from the rich shrine.
> For naught to help you shall you find by adding,
>   Nor be sinless if you take away.[2]

---

[1] 1332–5   πρὶν ἂν τὰ Τροίας πεδί᾽ ἑκὼν αὐτὸς μόλῃς,
        καὶ τοῖν παρ᾽ ἡμῖν ἐντυχὼν Ἀσκληπίδαιν
        νόσου μαλαχθῇς τῆσδε, καὶ τὰ πέργαμα
        ξὺν τοῖσδε τόξοις ξύν τ᾽ ἐμοὶ πέρσας φανῇς.

[2] 805–10   τόρνου καὶ στάθμης καὶ γνώμονος ἄνδρα θεωρὸν
        εὐθύτερον χρὴ ἔμεν, Κύρνε, φυλασσόμενον,
        ᾧτινί κ᾽ ἐν Πυθῶνι θεοῦ χρήσασ᾽ ἱέρεια
        ὀμφὴν σημήνῃ πίονος ἐξ ἀδύτου·
        οὔτε τι γὰρ προσθεὶς οὐδέν κ᾽ ἔτι φάρμακον εὕροις,
        οὐδ᾽ ἀφελὼν πρὸς θεῶν ἀμπλακίην προφύγοις.

The straightness required is strict attention to the oracle's text. A man must not assume that it means more or less than it says. The first will do no good, and there is an ironical understatement in the warning; the second is impiety in the eyes of the gods. The poem shows how important it is to do exactly what the god orders. It illustrates what Dio says when he attributes the apparent failure of oracles to the incompetence of those who receive them —'being unable to make use of the god, they then try something and blame not themselves but him'.[1] An oracle must be handled with scrupulous care, or disaster may follow.

Herodotus knew to what results a careless handling of oracles might lead. When Croesus assumed that an oracle from Delphi foretold good to him, and was disastrously defeated, his agents complained to the god and were told that if Croesus was in doubt he should have asked a second question; as it was, he had only himself to blame.[2] His case shows the general danger of assuming that one knew what an oracle meant. The Spartan Dorieus shows the special danger, foreseen by Theognis, of taking an oracle to mean more than it said. He was told by Delphi that he would take the place to which he was sent. This was duly fulfilled, but he went on to attack Sybaris and was killed. The moral was drawn that 'he acted contrary to the oracle and was destroyed'.[3] It was no less dangerous to assume that an oracle meant less than it said, and that part of it could with impunity be neglected. In exile Arcesilas of Cyrene consulted the Pythia about restoration to his kingdom. She told him to be gentle if restored. He forgot or disobeyed her instructions and treated his enemies harshly. The result was that they killed him, and Herodotus comments, 'Either willingly or unwillingly, he went wrong about the oracle, and fulfilled his destiny'.[4] He was punished for not carrying out exactly what the god ordered. It follows that if the oracle about Philoctetes was not correctly carried out, things would go badly with the Greeks.

Odysseus, who was present when Helenus gave the oracle, knew its contents (614). But he does not follow its instructions exactly. When he heard it, he promised that he would bring Philoctetes to the Achaeans:

[1] *Or.* x. 27 χρῆσθαι τῷ θεῷ ἀδύνατοι ὄντες, ἔπειτα ἐπιχειροῦντες, οὐχ αὑτούς ἀλλ' ἐκεῖνον αἰτιῶνται.

[2] Hdt. i. 91. 4.

[3] Id. v. 45. 1 παρὰ τὰ μεμαντευμένα ποιέων διεφθάρη.

[4] Id. iv. 164. 4 εἴτε ἑκὼν εἴτε ἀέκων ἁμαρτὼν τοῦ χρησμοῦ ἐξέπλησε μοῖραν τὴν ἑωυτοῦ.

Most like he'd bring him of his own accord;
If not, against his will. And if he failed,
He pledged that whoso would might have his head.[1]

Odysseus assumes that if Philoctetes does not come of his free
will, he can be forced to come against it. The assumption is
wrong, even impious; for the gods have said that he must come
'willingly'. Odysseus perverts the sacred text and adds to it. As
Theognis says, it will do him no good. In fact his efforts are frustrated. He is so sure that he is right that he offers his head if
he fails. This shows the arrogance and self-confidence in which
he acts. In such a mood he makes a big mistake. When the play
opens, we see how far his confidence has misled him and the corruption of spirit which it imposes on Neoptolemus. This should warn
us that something is wrong with the plan. We soon see that it
does not work, and later, that not only is it against the gods' orders
but fails for that reason; it involves deceit and violence of which
they disapprove. If a serious attempt had been made to persuade
Philoctetes to come, it might have succeeded. The alternative of
trying to get him or his bow by fraud or violence fails because he
is not a man to submit to such treatment. In his misinterpreta-
tion of the oracle Odysseus chooses means which are not suited
to the end which he desires.

Though he first said that he would try persuasion (617),
Odysseus never seriously tries it. He seems to think that the mere
sight of himself will enrage Philoctetes and make any solution impossible:

For if he knows me, while he has his bow,
I'm ruined, and my ruin will bring yours.[2]

He does not even believe that Neoptolemus can try persuasion
with any success but dismisses the idea as quite impracticable:

He will not listen.[3]

Still less does he contemplate subduing him by force. He is afraid
of the weapons in his possession:

Shafts inevitable that send forth death.[4]

---

[1] 617–19   οἴοιτο μὲν μάλισθ' ἑκούσιον λαβών,
                    εἰ μὴ θέλοι Δ', ἄκοντα· καὶ τούτων κάρα
                    τέμνειν ἐφεῖτο τῷ θέλοντι μὴ τυχών.

[2] 75–6   ὥστ' εἴ με τόξων ἐγκρατὴς αἰσθήσεται,
                    ὄλωλα καί σε προσδιαφθερῶ ξυνών.

[3] 103   οὐ μὴ πίθηται.

[4] 105   ἰοὺς ἀφύκτους καὶ προπέμποντας φόνον.

He has made up his mind that Philoctetes can be secured by
stratagem. It is in this that he himself excels, and his own incli-
nations prompt his decision. Yet when he gives his orders to
Neoptolemus, it is odd that they are not precise or clear. In his
first speech Odysseus clearly contemplates that Philoctetes can be
brought in person. He speaks of

> The trick by which I hope to capture him.[1]

The same notion underlies his emphatic command:

> I say, take Philoctetes by a trick,[2]

and Neoptolemus certainly understands him in this sense when he
asks:

> Why by a trick, not take him by persuasion?[3]

The plan seems to be a kind of abduction of Philoctetes. But
Odysseus varies this with another, the seizure of the bow without
its owner. He seems to think that this is equally good:

> For if we do not make his bow our prey,
> You cannot sack the realm of Dardanus.[4]

> But this must be your stratagem, to be
> The thief of his unconquerable arms.[5]

> These arrows, nothing else, will capture Troy.[6]

Odysseus is so convinced that guile will succeed that he does not
even take trouble to think out his plan carefully. His headstrong
confidence assumes success too easily. And both policies are
against the oracle and wrong. To seize Philoctetes by guile is not
to persuade him of his own free will; to get his bow is not to
bring him in person.

Odysseus does not consciously or deliberately disobey the oracle.
He is deluded by pride and too great trust in his own powers. In
his *Philoctetes* Euripides had made Odysseus conscious of this fault
and hope to avoid it. Sophocles makes full use of it. When Neoptolemus says of Odysseus:

[1] 14   σόφισμα τῷ νιν αὐτίχ' αἱρήσειν δοκῶ.

[2] 101   λέγω σ' ἐγὼ Δόλῳ Φιλοκτήτην λαβεῖν.

[3] 102   τί Δ' ἐν Δόλῳ Δεῖ μᾶλλον ἢ πείσαντ' ἄγειν;

[4] 68–9   εἰ γὰρ τὰ τοῦΔε τόξα μὴ ληφθήσεται,
              οὐκ ἔστι πέρσαι σοι τὸ Δαρδάνου πέΔον.

[5] 77–8   ἀλλ' αὐτὸ τοῦτο Δεῖ σοφισθῆναι, κλοπεὺς
              ὅπως γενήσῃ τῶν ἀνικήτων ὅπλων.

[6] 113   αἱρεῖ τὰ τόξα ταῦτα τὴν Τροίαν μόνα.

> He wrestles cleverly, but clever wits
> Are thwarted, Philoctetes, oft enough,[1]

he may not know the full import of his words but they are none
the less true. Odysseus is an example of a man who is too clever
and frustrates his own ends, the type which Pindar derides:

> Yet Lady Vixen was not so cunning for once.[2]

At a rather lower level Odysseus illustrates that excessive cleverness which Euripides' Bacchants deplore in Pentheus:

> The wisdom which is not wise.[3]

They go on to say that such a man will in his pursuit of great ends
miss what lies to hand, and that this is a kind of madness. In
Odysseus it is at least a deluding arrogance. He feels no qualms
about overriding Neoptolemus' honourable scruples against deceiving Philoctetes, and even tries to win him by saying that if
he succeeds he too will be called 'clever' (119). The dangers of
this kind of cleverness are familiar from Euripides. His Orestes
knows about it:

> Not without penalty
> Is cleverness for those who have too much,[4]

as do his Hippolytus,[5] his Phaedra,[6] and his Medea.[7] We therefore suspect that Odysseus' cleverness will frustrate his own ends
and lead to confusion.

Excess of cleverness was thought to be too often allied to moral
baseness. Pindar[8] and Bacchylides[9] both associate it with inordi-
nate desire for gain. Odysseus shows that he is not a man of fine
scruples. He has made up his mind that Neoptolemus must secure
Philoctetes or his bow by a trick, and sees nothing wrong in telling
lies for such a purpose, but he knows that Neoptolemus may object.
His argument is that the shame is small and the gain great. When
asked if such lying is not shameful he answers:

> If lying brings us safety, surely not.[10]

[1] 431–2   σοφὸς παλαιστὴς κεῖνος, ἀλλὰ χαὶ σοφαὶ
              γνῶμαι, Φιλοκτῆτ', ἐμποδίζονται θαμά.
[2] *Pyth.* ii. 78   κερδοῖ δὲ τί μάλα τοῦτο κερδαλέον τελέθει;
[3] *Bacch.* 395   τὸ σοφὸν δ' οὐ σοφία.
[4] *El.* 295–6   καὶ γὰρ οὐδ' ἀζήμιον
              γνώμην ἐνεῖναι τοῖς σοφοῖς λίαν σοφήν.
[5] *Hipp.* 640–4.   [6] Ib. 518.   [7] *Med.* 295–305.   [8] *Pyth.* iii. 54.   [9] Fr. 1.
[10] 109   οὔκ, εἰ τὸ σωθῆναί γε τὸ ψεῦδος φέρει.

and sees no reason for any hesitation:

> When gain's in question, it is wrong to shrink.[1]

His words should arouse distrust. The Greeks believed that in general it was wrong to lie. Not all would perhaps go so far as Plato, who says that to tell untruths is neither lawful nor holy,[2] or Aristotle, who praises the man who tells the truth always because he thinks that any falsehood is base.[3] But they would certainly approve of truth-telling and appreciate Herodotus' Persians who teach their young to regard any lie as 'most shameful'.[4] Of course they knew that sometimes a lie is necessary and justifiable as the lesser of two evils. Sophocles makes some character say:

> Unhandsome is the speaking of a lie;
> But when truth brings destruction to a man,
> What is not right may be forgiven him.[5]

Most of the audience would agree that if something really good was to be gained by it, it might be right for Neoptolemus to lie. But such a lie would require considerable justification.

Odysseus takes advantage of this belief when he says that the lie which Neoptolemus is to tell brings 'safety' (109). That sounds good, but this 'safety' soon turns out to be nothing but 'profit' (111). In Odysseus' view the deceit is justified not by any real gravity in the situation but by the glory which success will bring. There is a cynical tone in his exhortation to Neoptolemus:

> 'Tis sweet to win the prize of victory.
> Have courage. Time to come shall prove us right.[6]

We feel that he does not care whether a lie is wrong or not but is interested solely in getting what he wants. His sentiments are like those of the character in Sophocles' *Ethiopians* who says:

> To win you by persuasion, not by force,
> I say this. As the wise do, so should you
> Praise what is right but hold what profits most.[7]

---

[1] 111 ὅταν τι δρᾷς ἐς κέρδος, οὐκ ὀκνεῖν πρέπει.

[2] *Laws* ix. 861 d.   [3] *Nic. Eth.* 1127 b 4.   [4] Hdt. i. 136. 2; 138. 1.

[5] Fr. 352 καλὸν μὲν οὖν οὐκ ἔστι τὰ ψευδῆ λέγειν·
ὅτῳ δ' ὄλεθρον δεινὸν ἀλήθει' ἄγει,
συγγνωστὸν εἰπεῖν ἐστι καὶ τὸ μὴ καλόν.

[6] 81–2 ἀλλ' ἡδὺ γάρ τι κτῆμα τῆς νίκης λαβεῖν,
τόλμα· δίκαιοι δ' αὖθις ἐκφανούμεθα.

[7] Fr. 28 τοιαῦτά τοί σοι πρὸς χάριν τε κοὐ βίᾳ
λέγω· σὺ δ' αὐτὸς ὥσπερ οἱ σοφοὶ τὰ μὲν
δίκαι' ἐπαίνει, τοῦ δὲ κερδαίνειν ἔχου.

Odysseus is one of these 'wise', and intent on what will be of profit to him. He justifies his dishonesty by its results, like another Sophoclean character:

> 'Tis sweet to gain, e'en though it comes from lies.[1]

He plays on the young Neoptolemus and appeals not only to his ambition but to his natural sense of respect for an experienced soldier like himself. He wounds his self-respect when he insinuates that Neoptolemus' pretensions are grander than his performance:

> Son of a noble sire, I too was young
> And kept an idle tongue and active hand.
> But now when I put men to test, I find
> Not deeds but talk take lead in everything.[2]

He is sufficiently skilful in handling men to bring Neoptolemus round to his purpose, but in so doing he shows that he himself is not a man of high principles. He has the doubtful qualities of the clever.

Neoptolemus is the victim of a real moral struggle. On the one side is his natural decency which resists the idea of lying, on the other his desire to win the glory of taking Troy. He is the son of Achilles and fully conscious of it, but this pulls him in both directions. Odysseus knows this and prepares the way with some care:

> I know full well, you are not of such breed
> To say such things or plan what is not right[3]

and Neoptolemus himself declares:

> I am not one to act with cunning craft,
> Nor I, nor he, they say, whose son I am.[4]

He feels that lying is shameful:

> Do you not think it shameful to tell lies?[5]

On the other hand, his father was a great soldier, and he himself is avid of military glory. It is significant that Odysseus calls him 'Son of a noble sire' (96) when he half chides him for shirking

---

[1] Fr. 833   τὸ κέρδος ἡδύ, κἂν ἀπὸ ψευδῶν ἴῃ.

[2] 96–9   ἐσθλοῦ πατρὸς παῖ, καὐτὸς ὢν νέος ποτὲ
γλῶσσαν μὲν ἀργόν, χεῖρα δ' εἶχον ἐργάτιν·
νῦν δ' εἰς ἔλεγχον ἐξιὼν ὁρῶ βροτοῖς
τὴν γλῶσσαν, οὐχὶ τἄργα, πάνθ' ἡγουμένην.

[3] 79–80   ἔξοιδα, παῖ, φύσει σε μὴ πεφυκότα
τοιαῦτα φωνεῖν μηδὲ τεχνᾶσθαι κακά.

[4] 88–9   ἔφυν γὰρ οὐδὲν ἐκ τέχνης πράσσειν κακῆς,
οὔτ' αὐτὸς οὔθ', ὥς φασιν, οὑκφύσας ἐμέ.

[5] 108   οὐκ αἰσχρὸν ἡγῇ δῆτα τὰ ψευδῆ λέγειν;

his task. Odysseus appeals to his ambition and offers him the
honour of taking Troy (61, 69) and a reputation for being both
clever and noble (119). Neoptolemus is torn between shame and
ambition. The latter wins, when he consents:

> So be it. I consent and cast off shame.[1]

His better self has for the moment been vanquished. We understand his motives, but we need not approve of them. He recalls
the grave words of Thucydides on the corruption of political life,
'the cause of all these evils was the lust for power arising from ambition',[2] or Jocasta's words to Eteocles:

> Why do you love the worst of goddesses,
> Ambition? Do not so, son. She is wicked.[3]

It is ambition which has always moved Odysseus and now moves
Neoptolemus. In the fifth century a case of conscience like this
would have been well understood. In the sophistic *Double Arguments* it is argued that if it is right to deceive one's enemies—as
Odysseus might argue against Philoctetes—it is no less right to
deceive one's parents, a conclusion which shows that the premiss
is wrong.[4] So when Euthydemus says that a lie is justified against
enemies in war and that a general may lie to his own troops,
Socrates shows that this is to abandon any real distinction between
right and wrong.[5] Neoptolemus cannot even plead that Philoctetes
is his enemy, and he has no justification except his desire for glory.
Aristotle recognizes that a man may be incontinent with respect
to honour.[6] That is what Neoptolemus is. He makes his choice,
though he knows at the time that it is wrong.

Our feelings are justified. The whole plan to deceive Philoctetes is base. It is not what the gods ordered but what Odysseus
in his pride has conceived. We do not condemn the gods if we
condemn it. Moreover, it fails. Odysseus' cleverness frustrates
itself. Like other clever men, he does not always find the truth
which needs qualities of heart as well as of head for its discovery:

> A charitable and right-minded soul
> Finds out the truth before the subtlest wits.[7]

So Odysseus, who thinks that he understands the situation, gauges

---

[1] 120   ἴτω· ποήσω, πᾶσαν αἰσχύνην ἀφείς.
[2] iii. 82. 8 πάντων αὐτῶν αἴτιον ἀρχὴ ἡ διὰ πλεονεξίαν καὶ φιλοτιμίαν.
[3] Eur. *Phoen.* 531–2 τί τῆς κακίστης δαιμόνων ἐφίεσαι
                        Φιλοτιμίας, παῖ; μή σύ γ'· ἄδικος ἡ θεός.
[4] Δισσοὶ Λόγοι 3   [5] Xen. *Mem.* iv. 2. 14.   [6] *Nic. Eth.* 1147 b 33.
[7] Soph. fr. 101   ψυχὴ γὰρ εὔνους καὶ φρονοῦσα τοὔνδικον
                        κρείσσων σοφιστοῦ παντός ἐστιν εὑρετίς.

it wrongly. He assumes that Neoptolemus will either lure Philoctetes into coming to Troy or get hold of his bow. Both plans are
against the gods' orders. Obstacles, not foreseen by Odysseus,
arise, and in his over-subtlety he adds to them. His insight has
been faulty about the characters of the men concerned and his
scheme does not take account of the real facts. In the long passage
between the arrival of Philoctetes and the outbreak of his sickness Odysseus' plan is tried and found wanting.

Up to the unforeseen collapse of Philoctetes Neoptolemus pursues his task consistently. His aim is to establish friendly relations
with Philoctetes and so to get him on to the ship. Once aboard, he
seems to hope, Philoctetes can be brought to Troy. The plan at first
promises rapid success. The young man easily wins the confidence
of the castaway, who begs to be taken home (470 ff.). The Chorus
see that this is their chance, and in a highly disingenuous song
support the request (507 ff.). Neoptolemus consents in words
whose double meaning is imperceptible to Philoctetes:

> Let us then sail. Let him aboard with haste.
> The ship will take him; we shall not refuse.
> Only may heaven help us from this land
> And take us where our purpose is to sail.[1]

This is in accordance with Odysseus' general instructions. For
when his agent, the alleged Merchant, arrives, the tale that he tells
of men in pursuit of Neoptolemus is meant to hurry things up
by frightening Philoctetes, who now thinks that he is the victim
of a plot to pursue and capture him (628 ff.). Once again Neoptolemus agrees to sail, after some preliminary hesitations which
can only be intended to whet Philoctetes' desire (639–40). His
casual air of consent hides, as he believes, the success of his plan:

> If you will, let us go. Take from within
> Whatever most you need or most desire.[2]

Not only has he secured Philoctetes; he will also secure the famous
and indispensable bow. So far there has been no hitch, and all
has gone according to plan.

The plan is held up through what looks like an accident.
Philoctetes goes into his cave to fetch his possessions, and while he

[1] 526–9 ἀλλ' εἰ δοκεῖ, πλέωμεν, ὁρμάσθω ταχύς.
χἠ ναῦς γὰρ ἄξει κοὐκ ἀπαρνηθήσεται.
μόνον θεοὶ σῴζοιεν ἔκ τε τῆσδε γῆς
ἡμᾶς ὅποι τ' ἐνθένδε βουλοίμεσθα πλεῖν.

[2] 645–6 ἀλλ' εἰ δοκεῖ, χωρῶμεν, ἔνδοθεν λαβὼν
ὅτου σε χρεία καὶ πόθος μάλιστ' ἔχει.

is inside, the Chorus sing of his return to his home. When they have
finished, cries are heard. Philoctetes is in an agony of his disease.
By the time that it is over and the sick man has fallen into a healing sleep, Neoptolemus has changed his mind. He no longer
intends to abduct Philoctetes on false pretences. The actual onslaught is of course a chance, though it may be a chance sent by
the gods. But its importance is enormous. Odysseus has not foreseen anything of the kind or what effect it will have on his agent.
Once he sees the real misery of Philoctetes Neoptolemus is unable
to deceive him any longer. His desire for truth asserts itself. But
this change which reaches its crisis with the spectacle of the sick
man's suffering has been at work for some time in Neoptolemus.
Odysseus has not chosen his agent well; Neoptolemus is after all
too noble to put through a trick of this kind. Odysseus has also
miscalculated on the nature of Philoctetes. He seems to despise
him, to think that any lie will deceive him (64 ff.). But the lies
told by Neoptolemus have awoken the finest instincts in Philoctetes, and these in their turn have touched Neoptolemus and contributed to the change in him. All through the long and apparently
successful deception Neoptolemus' better nature is subject to
appeals which it finds hard to resist.

   Neoptolemus enters on his task with all the zeal and confidence
of youth in an exciting errand. He asserts boldly that he does not
know who Philoctetes is (250) and so safeguards himself from the
suspicion that he may be working for the Atridae and for Odysseus.
Despite a long and moving interruption from Philoctetes, he gets
back to his story and announces that he is the victim of the same
men (319–21). Finally he tells his false tale (343–90); the Chorus
testify to it with what is very like an oath (391–401), and Philoctetes' confidence and friendship are gained. All that remains to
do is to add some convincing details, and this Neoptolemus does
by attacking Odysseus (431–2) and pretending that he must be
off to Scyros (461 ff.). In all this he seems to act with remarkable
callousness, and we might feel that his sense of shame is quite lost
in his pleasure at doing his appointed task so well. He is in the
odious position of a false friend. Philoctetes has opened his heart
to him, and he takes advantage of it. He is like those men condemned by Theognis who say one thing with their lips and hide
another in their hearts.[1] His deceit is almost treachery. Moreover,
Philoctetes is in the position of a suppliant. His appeal is made in
such language:

[1] Theogn. 91–2.

Oh by your father and your mother, boy,
By everything that you hold dear at home,
I beg, beseech you, leave me not alone.[1]

Yet Neoptolemus is perfectly ready to take advantage of him. If he had really done so, he would have incurred the wrath of the gods, who do not permit suppliants to be deceived.[2] In his actions Neoptolemus has shown how base his present course is. It is worse than mere deception. It is the deception of a friend and a suppliant.

Yet with each step Neoptolemus encounters obstacles in his own decent feelings which are unexpectedly aroused by the simple sincerity and directness of the sick man. For instance, he is intimately touched in his regard for his dead father. We have seen that he greatly admires Achilles and wishes to be like him; we may assume that he felt sorrow at his death. So when he begins his tale to Philoctetes with the words,

When fate constrained Achilles to his death,[3]

he seems to be giving no more than a date, a mere preliminary to his story of maltreatment in the matter of his father's armour. He speaks with the glibness and lightness of heart that belong to his assumed part; the words have no real meaning to him. But Philoctetes, who knew and loved Achilles, does not take the words in that spirit:

Alas, tell me no more, till I have heard,
This first—say is the son of Peleus dead?[4]

He almost shakes Neoptolemus off his balance. The mention of his father's death as a real event which concerns human feelings is not what he expects. He gives a brief unemotional account of it (334–5), and manages to control his feelings, to continue his role. But again Philoctetes invades his pretences by praising the dead man and pitying Neoptolemus for his loss (336–7). Neoptolemus only keeps himself in hand by evading the point:

I think, unhappy friend, you have enough
Woes of your own not to lament your neighbours'.[5]

[1] 468–70   πρὸς νύν σε πατρός, πρός τε μητρός, ὦ τέκνον,
              πρός τ' εἴ τί σοι κατ' οἶκόν ἐστι προσφιλές,
              ἱκέτης ἱκνοῦμαι, μὴ λίπῃς μ' οὕτω μόνον.
[2] Theogn. 143–4.
[3] 331   ἐπεὶ γὰρ ἔσχε μοῖρ' Ἀχιλλέα θανεῖν
[4] 332–3   οἴμοι· φράσῃς μοι μὴ πέρα, πρὶν ἂν μάθω
              πρῶτον τόδ', εἰ τέθνηχ' ὁ Πηλέως γόνος;
[5] 339–40   οἴμαι μὲν ἀρκεῖν σοί γε καὶ τὰ σ', ὦ τάλας,
              ἀλγήμαθ', ὥστε μὴ τὰ τῶν πέλας στένειν.

After that he is able to embark on his story. But the incident
shows where the danger lies. The facts as Philoctetes knows them
are liable to introduce a note of truth and decency which may well
upset Neoptolemus' complacency and self-possession. The assault
which Philoctetes makes on his defences helps to awaken his real
self and his human feelings.

In contrast to his admiration for Achilles Philoctetes cherishes
a hatred for Odysseus. Odysseus knows this and warns Neoptolemus of it (64 ff.). It is soon clear that he is right. Philoctetes tells
how he was deserted by the Atridae and Odysseus and wishes a
like fate for them:

> This did the Atridae and violent Odysseus
> Do to me, boy, and may the Olympian gods
> Grant them to suffer like in recompense.[1]

Against this real hatred for Odysseus Neoptolemus puts up his
own simulated hatred because of an imaginary wrong (319–21).
He makes Odysseus the chief author of his humiliation (343 ff.)
and explains that he is sailing home:

> Robbed by him,
> Of a vile stock the vilest man, Odysseus.[2]

So far he is simply acting. He does not really feel any hatred, but
simulates it that Philoctetes may find a common bond with him.
He has actually a good reason to dislike Odysseus, who has made
him do a task that his conscience disapproves. So when he next
speaks of him and says that clever men of this kind often are frustrated (431–2), he is telling the truth. He thinks that he knows
what Philoctetes means when he asks about one who was 'crafty
and clever in speech' and suggests that it was Odysseus, though it
is really Thersites (439 ff.). Here, too, the results are not yet visible.
But when later in the play Neoptolemus has lost all respect for
Odysseus, we can hardly doubt that Philoctetes has contributed
to it. Odysseus has made Neoptolemus act against his conscience.
As his dormant nobility is awoken by references to his father,
his distrust of Odysseus grows. In this Philoctetes helps him back
to his true self.

Another way in which Neoptolemus' feeling of guilt deepens
and his conscience stirs may be seen when Philoctetes asks about

[1] 314–16   τοιαῦτ' Ἀτρεῖδαί μ' ἥ τ' Ὀδυσσέως βία,
                  ὦ παῖ, Δεδράκασ'· οἷς Ὀλύμπιοι θεοὶ
                  Δοῖέν ποτ' αὐτοῖς ἀντίποιν' ἐμοῦ παθεῖν.

[2] 383–4   τῶν ἐμῶν τητώμενος
                  πρὸς τοῦ κακίστου κἀκ κακῶν Ὀδυσσέως.

the Achaean warriors at Troy and shows a real admiration for
the great dead, for Antilochus (426–7), Patroclus (434), and Ajax
(410–11), and an equal contempt for the base spirits who survive,
for Odysseus (429) and Thersites (442–4). It is clear that Neoptolemus should admire not the ignoble living but the noble dead.
We may assume that to some extent he does, and that when he
says

> War does not love
> To take the base man but the best always,[1]

he speaks with sincerity. For it was in language like this that the
Greeks honoured the fallen in battle, as when Anacreon com-
memorates the dead Timocritus:

> Ares spares the good not, but the base.[2]

Aeschylus, Euripides, and Sophocles himself repeat the idea. It
was an accepted epitaph on the slain in war, and from Neoptolemus it comes with some degree of sincerity. So, too, when he says
that for the future he will keep a watch on the Atridae, he is
acting, but his reason looks honest and true to his real nature:

> Where the base man is stronger than the good
> And nobleness decays, and cowards rule,
> Such men as these I shall not ever love.[3]

This is what he would ordinarily think, even though it is dragged
in to support a false statement. Neoptolemus' lies involve assump-
tions of truth and decency. In his attempt to be persuasive he
cannot at times help saying what he really feels. He is no in-
veterate liar, and his fundamental decency obtrudes itself.

The Greeks would understand his position. They knew that
lies do not last, because they come into conflict with reality. When
Sophocles wrote in the *Acrisius*

> No falsehood lasts its course to time's decay,[4]

Theognis had said very much the same thing before him:

---

[1] 436–7   πόλεμος οὐδέν' ἄνδρ' ἑκὼν
            αἱρεῖ πονηρόν, ἀλλὰ τοὺς χρηστοὺς ἀεί.

[2] Fr. 101. 2   Ἄρης δ' οὐκ ἀγαθῶν φείδεται, ἀλλὰ κακῶν.
Cf. Aesch. fr. 100, Soph. fr. 724, Eur. fr. 728.

[3] 456–8   ὅπου θ' ὁ χείρων τἀγαθοῦ μεῖζον σθένει
            κἀποφθίνει τὰ χρηστὰ χὠ δειλὸς κρατεῖ,
            τούτους ἐγὼ τοὺς ἄνδρας οὐ στέρξω ποτέ.

[4] Fr. 62   ἀλλ' οὐδὲν ἕρπει ψεῦδος εἰς γῆρας χρόνου.

> There is small pleasure in a lie's beginning;
> At the end the gain is base and low.
> Nought 's good in him with whom a lie consorteth,
> From the moment that it 's past his lips.[1]

The trouble with lying is that in the end it makes the liar feel ashamed. This is what happens to Neoptolemus. As he tells his untruths against the forceful sincerity of Philoctetes, he feels uneasy and finds himself lapsing into truth about important matters of heart and conscience. In a special sense he illustrates the wisdom of Aristotle's words, 'With a true view all the data agree, but with a false the facts soon clash'.[2] There is a discord between what Neoptolemus says and what he really feels and knows to be right. This makes him uneasy and eventually changes his heart. For the moment he carries on with his task. His love of glory keeps him to it. But truth has come into conflict with untruth and is bound to win. Neoptolemus' decency is kept down by his ambition, but truth will out and force him to see that it is impossible for him to maintain his false position for long.

The strongest, most effective onslaught on Neoptolemus' deceit comes from the genuine pity which Philoctetes awakes in him. Later he reveals this:

> A strange compassion for this man has fallen
> Upon me, not now first but some while past.[3]

He has already shown signs of it when he first sees how Philoctetes lives:

> For this they say is the manner of life
> That is his, pursuing the beasts with his bow,
> With his arrows in flight, in pitiful wise,
> Nor is there at his side
> Any healer to tend his afflictions,[4]

---

[1] 607–10   ἀρχῇ ἔπι ψεύδεος μικρὰ χάρις· ἐς δὲ τελευτὴν
αἰσχρὸν δὴ κέρδος καὶ κακόν, ἀμφότερον,
γίνεται· οὐδέ τι καλόν, ὅτῳ ψεῦδος προσομαρτῇ
ἀνδρὶ καὶ ἐξέλθη πρῶτον ἀπὸ στόματος.

[2] *Nic. Eth.* 1098 b 11 τῷ μὲν γὰρ ἀληθεῖ πάντα συνᾴδει τὰ ὑπάρχοντα, τῷ δὲ ψευδεῖ ταχὺ διαφωνεῖ τἀληθές.

[3] 965–6   ἐμοὶ μὲν οἶκτος δεινὸς ἐμπέπτωκέ τις
τοῦδ' ἀνδρὸς οὐ νῦν πρῶτον, ἀλλὰ καὶ πάλαι.

[4] 164–8   ταύτην γὰρ ἔχειν βιοτῆς αὐτὸν
λόγος ἐστὶ φύσιν, θηροβολοῦντα
πτηνοῖς ἰοῖς σμυγερὸν σμυγερῶς,
οὐδέ τιν' αὐτῷ
παιῶνα κακῶν ἐπινωμᾶν.

and still more when he hears his miseries from Philoctetes' own
lips. Then Neoptolemus associates himself with the Chorus's
expression of pity, and we can believe that he speaks the truth
(319–21), though he soon adapts it to his own false policy. In a
similar mood he says that Philoctetes has enough sorrows of his
own not to worry about those of others (339–40). This pity is
kept well in control, and has only to make itself felt for Neoptolemus to dismiss it and resume his deceptions. But it is latent and
real, and once Neoptolemus sees Philoctetes in the agonies of his
sickness, his pity for him comes to the surface, and he says:

> Alas, alas, unhappy one,
> Unhappy, as I know, in all your woes.[1]

In this mood he promises not to leave him and for the moment
abandons his new plan of taking the bow from him while he is
helpless. While Philoctetes raves in delirium, Neoptolemus says:

> Long have I felt your woes and pitied them.[2]

He certainly speaks the truth. So, too, there is real compassion in
his words when he tells the Chorus to let the sick man stay quiet
until he recovers (825–6).

Neoptolemus has been moved by Philoctetes. He has managed
to keep up his assumed part and to tell his lies, but he is none the
less touched by the pitiful state of his victim and troubled in his
conscience by the appeals which Philoctetes makes to him as the
son of Achilles (242, 337–8, 364, 468). The result is that in the end
Neoptolemus' real nature, his kinship with his father, reasserts
itself. The Greeks believed firmly in such heredity. As Pindar says:

> Blood makes this noble temper
> Shine out from their fathers in the sons.[3]

Such hereditary nobility was almost biological. Aristotle says that
an animal is thoroughbred if it does not deflect from its racial
characteristics,[4] and the same doctrine could be applied to men. It
was thought easy to detect good breeding in a man, as Euripides
says:

> The excellence of noble men shines out
> In children.[5]

[1] 759–60   ἰὼ ἰὼ δύστηνε σύ,
              δύστηνε δῆτα διὰ πόνων πάντων φανείς.

[2] 806   ἀλγῶ πάλαι·δὴ τἀπὶ σοὶ στένων κακά.

[3] *Pyth.* viii. 44–5   φυᾷ τὸ γενναῖον ἐπιπρέπει
                ἐκ πατέρων παισὶ λῆμα.

[4] *H.A.* 488 b 19

[5] Fr. 232   ἐν τοῖς τέκνοις γὰρ ἀρετὴ τῶν εὐγενῶν
           ἔλαμψε.

Neoptolemus is true to his breeding. His inherited nobility shows itself in due course. He is not the son of Achilles for nothing. So Philoctetes thanks him for his kindness in his sickness:

> Noble your nature, and of noble breed,
> My son.[1]

It is this nobility which makes Neoptolemus weaken in his plan to deceive Philoctetes.

This nobility shows itself especially in the pity which Neoptolemus feels for the unfortunate castaway. This quality is itself hereditary. For just as Neoptolemus is moved to treat Philoctetes less dishonourably, so was his father moved by pity to give the body of Hector to Priam:

> In pity and reverence for his age and silvery-blancht head.[2]

In each case the younger man is moved by compassion for the older, and each is stirred by the thought of his own father. In effect what works in Neoptolemus is his sense of shame and of honour, his αἰδώς, the feeling which was due to the old,[3] the unfortunate,[4] and suppliants.[5] Philoctetes deserves it under all these headings. To show it was a mark of nobility[6] and of good training.[7] It has a special relevance to Neoptolemus because it was thought to be an enemy of dishonesty[8] and yet to succumb to ambition.[9] Common morality shows that it understood a case like that of Neoptolemus, whose decency is overcome by ambition and perverted into falsehood. But once a real appeal is made to it, it comes out in answer to the suffering Philoctetes. It is wider than mere compassion. It is the modest and decent frame of mind in which compassion has its place.

The crisis of the internal struggle in Neoptolemus is marked by Sophocles in a skilful and significant way while Philoctetes is asleep. The plan to take Philoctetes away has not succeeded, but there remains the alternative of taking his bow without him. Circumstances favour this. For the bow is already in the possession of Neoptolemus (762 ff.) and at the moment Philoctetes is unconscious and helpless. The Chorus urge that now is the time to act, and in dark words suggest to Neoptolemus that he should

---

[1] 874-5   ἀλλ' εὐγενὴς γὰρ ἡ φύσις κἀξ εὐγενῶν,
           ὦ τέκνον, ἡ σή.

[2] Trs. R. Bridges. *Il.* xxiv. 516 οἰκτίρων πολιόν τε κάρη πολιόν τε γένειον.

[3] *Od.* iii. 24, Eur. *Her.* 556, *Andr.* 918.

[4] Eur. *I.T.* 949, Plat. *Laws*, ix. 867 e.

[5] *Il.* xxii. 124, Aesch. *Supp.* 641, *Eum.* 475.   [6] Eur. *Alc.* 601.

[7] Eur. *Supp.* 911.   [8] Plat. *Laws*, xii. 943 e.   [9] Pind. *Nem.* ix. 33.

carry off the bow (849 ff.). But in the middle of their song Neoptolemus, who understands perfectly what they mean, interrupts
them:

Nothing at all does he hear, but I see that this booty is useless;
Useless to us is his bow that we have, if we take ship without him.
His is the crown of success, to fetch him the god us commanded.
Foul disgrace 'tis to boast of lies that have ended in failure.[1]

It is highly remarkable that a single character should speak like
this in dactylic hexameters. They may form part of a choral song,
but this is different. This is no song with a complex metrical
scheme. It comes unexpectedly with a shock. Its position between
the strophe and antistrophe of the Chorus draws attention to its
peculiar character. Neoptolemus speaks in hexameters because
they are the metre of oracles. He is speaking oracularly. It is
possible that they were used in the *Xantriae* of Aeschylus for some
such purpose,[2] but they are none the less unusual. Neoptolemus
has seen something of great importance concerned with the oracle
and is himself an interpreter and prophet. He sees what has so
far eluded his notice, that the bow is useless without its owner,
and that what the Chorus urge is against the god's command;
for the god told him to bring Philoctetes in person. Therefore to
boast of success is doubly foolish. The theft of the bow would be
dishonourable and would do no good. At this point Odysseus'
plan to secure the bow without Philoctetes is seen for its true
worth. Neoptolemus is begining to find his true self. He has still
a struggle ahead, but at least he knows that one method of attempting his task is useless. To this knowledge his own reawakened
decency has brought him.

This moment is of great importance because it marks the change
in Neoptolemus. Yet so many and so powerful are the forces at
work both in him and in Philoctetes that it brings no immediate
results. When Philoctetes recovers from his attack and awakes,
he returns at once to Neoptolemus' promise to take him home

[1] 839–42 ἀλλ' ὅδε μὲν κλύει οὐδέν, ἐγὼ Δ' ὁρῶ οὕνεκα θήραν
τήνΔ' ἁλίως ἔχομεν τόξων, Δίχα τοῦΔε πλέοντες·
τοῦΔε γὰρ ὁ στέφανος, τοῦτον θεὸς εἶπε κομίζειν.
κομπεῖν Δ' ἔστ' ἀτελῆ σὺν ψεύΔεσιν αἰσχρὸν ὄνειΔος.

[2] Fr. 168   ὀρεσσιγόνοισι
νύμφαις κρηνιάσιν κυΔραῖσι θεαῖσιν ἀγείρω
'Ινάχου 'Αργείου ποταμοῦ παισὶν βιοΔώροις.

The words are spoken by Hera, and she seems to have been transformed to look like a
priestess (Plat. *Rep.* ii. 381 d). A possible parallel is Eur. fr. 18 from the *Aeolus*
Δοξάσαι ἔστι, κόραι· τὸ Δ' ἐτήτυμον οὐκ ἔχω εἰπεῖν.

(891, 901). He is still the victim of deception. Neoptolemus, who has begun to see the truth, does not know what to do. At first he seems inclined to go on with his plan and says to Philoctetes:

> Now lift yourself up, or if you prefer,
> These men will carry you. They will not shrink
> From any task that you and I decide.[1]

Then, as his victim prepares to go with him, he feels qualms. Just as before he saw the futility and wrongfulness of taking the bow by itself, so now his natural decency works against taking Philoctetes on to the ship. For the moment he goes so far as he dares, and shows that he is in a quandary:

> Alas, what should I do next after this?[2]

He does not know what to say (897) and admits that he is in a difficulty (899); he has been untrue to his nature (902–3); he will be proved base (906); he cannot endure the prospect of degrading himself a second time with deceit and lies (908–9). At last he tells Philoctetes the truth:

> I will hide nothing. You must sail to Troy,
> To the Achaeans and the Atridae's host.[3]

The revelation overwhelms Philoctetes. He can hardly believe what he hears, feels betrayed and ruined. In his despair he asks Neoptolemus to give him back the bow. The confession of truth has failed. There seems no chance that Philoctetes will come willingly to Troy.

In this scene Neoptolemus has acted honourably and done what the gods require. We cannot but feel admiration for him as he steels himself to tell the truth and at last tells it. Yet he fails, and the reason is not far to seek. It is that his long attempt to deceive Philoctetes has succeeded only too well in awaking the injured man's suspicions and hatred of Odysseus. For this Odysseus is to blame. He told Neoptolemus to abuse him to Philoctetes, and Neoptolemus has done so. His impatient action in sending the assumed Merchant to hurry things has only added to Philoctetes' suspicions. The Merchant has made him fear that Odysseus is

---

[1] 886–8   νῦν δ' αἶρε σαυτόν· εἰ δέ σοι μᾶλλον φίλον,
οἴσουσί σ' οἶδε· τοῦ πόνου γὰρ οὐκ ὄκνος,
ἐπείπερ οὕτω σοί τ' ἔδοξ' ἐμοί τε δρᾶν.

[2] 895   παπαῖ· τί δῆτ' ἂν δρῷμ' ἐγὼ τοὐνθένδε γε;

[3] 915–16   οὐδέν σε κρύψω· δεῖ γὰρ ἐς Τροίαν σε πλεῖν
πρὸς τοὺς Ἀχαιοὺς καὶ τὸν Ἀτρειδῶν στόλον.

in pursuit of him, and just as he then refused to have anything to
do with him:

> No. Sooner would I listen to the snake
> My greatest enemy who lamed me thus,[1]

so now he is quite obdurate. He is panic-stricken:

> I am undone, alas, betrayed.[2]

He rightly sees that Neoptolemus took his bow from him under
false pretences, and almost his first thought is to ask for it, since
it is his only defence against his enemies. The whole elaborate
plot to get hold of him by stratagem ends in making him suspicious,
afraid, and obstinately determined not to go to Troy. The root
of the trouble is that deceit has been used. It is both wrong and
useless. The facts of the situation are more powerful than the
ingenious attempt to deceive Philoctetes.

Since Philoctetes refuses to listen to him, Neoptolemus has to
make a decision. For a moment he feels that he cannot give back
the bow; his ambition and his sense of military discipline prevent
him from doing so (925–6). But when Philoctetes bursts into a
long, harrowing speech and describes the misery which will be
his without his only means of subsistence, Neoptolemus weakens.
He is on the point of giving back the bow when Odysseus appears.
In what follows Neoptolemus is unimportant in comparison with
Philoctetes and Odysseus. He is torn between them. On the
one side are fame and obedience, on the other decency and truth
and compassion. He compromises and hopes that by leaving
Philoctetes alone he will give him a chance to find a better frame
of mind:

> And he meanwhile perhaps may find towards us
> A better wisdom.[3]

His position is hard because neither alternative is really satisfactory. Whether he keeps the bow or gives it back, Troy will
not be taken; for the bow is useless without its owner and its
owner is resolute in his refusal. Because the oracle has been
wrongly interpreted, the situation is chaotic. Neither fraud nor
frankness will bring Philoctetes to Troy. To sharpen the issue
Sophocles confronts Philoctetes with Odysseus and shows the

---

[1] 631–2   οὔ· θᾶσσον ἂν τῆς πλεῖστον ἐχθίστης ἐμοὶ
            κλύοιμ' ἐχίδνης, ἥ μ' ἔθηκεν ὧδ' ἄπουν.

[2] 923   ἀπόλωλα τλήμων, προδέδομαι.

[3] 1078–9   χοὗτος τάχ' ἂν φρόνησιν ἐν τούτῳ λάβοι
            λῴω τιν' ἡμῖν.

irreconcilable nature of the conflict. Each is sure that he is right and that the other is absolutely wrong. Any hope of a settlement is remote indeed.

A conflict of this kind is a moral conflict. We try to assess the right and wrong on either side. But there is a danger that we may do this too strictly and fail to see that each acts as he does because he is human and liable to err. Each in effect obstructs the divine plan, Odysseus by his wrong use of the oracle, Philoctetes by refusing to play his ordained part. The conflict is between two deluded men, each of whom fails to see what the gods really desire. In their ignorance they assume that they are right, but they judge with all the subjectivity and inconstancy of the human mind. They illustrate what the Hippocratic author says: 'What men determine never remains constant, whether right or wrong; but whatever the gods have determined, always remains right.'[1] The gods' purpose remains the same and is right; what the men think to be right is unstable. We may well, and with justice, feel more sympathy for Philoctetes than for Odysseus, but we must recognize that he is equally ignorant and deluded. Yet our preference for him is justified. The gods have chosen him for a great destiny, and they would not have done this if he were not in some way a superior being. In this too our feelings are a good guide. But they are not enough. There is more in the characters of the two men than superficial judgements allow.

Odysseus bears no resemblance to the Odysseus of the *Ajax*. Dio compares him favourably with his predecessor in Euripides' *Philoctetes*, but he is not altogether unlike Odysseus in the *Hecuba*. Both are moved by similar principles and both lack the warmer human feelings. Sophocles' Odysseus, as we have seen, conceives his plan in the over-confidence of the clever. He holds to it and feels no doubts about it even when it begins to fail. He honestly thinks that Neoptolemus will be guilty of a base act if he gives the bow back to Philoctetes instead of to himself:

> Villain, what are you doing?
> Get back, and give the bow to me again.[2]

He believes that he is carrying out the gods' will, and he is not to be suspected of hypocrisy when he says:

---

[1] *Diaet.* i. 11 τὰ μὲν οὖν ἄνθρωποι Διέθεσαν οὐΔέποτε κατὰ τωὐτὸ ἔχει οὔτε ὀρθῶς οὔτε μή· ὁκόσα Δὲ θεοὶ Διέθεσαν ἀεὶ ὀρθῶς ἔχει.

[2] 974-5   ὦ κάκιστ' ἀνΔρῶν, τί Δρᾷς;
         οὐκ εἶ μεθεὶς τὰ τόξα ταῦτ' ἐμοὶ πάλιν;

'Tis Zeus, I tell you, Zeus who rules this land,
Zeus who has ordered this, and I obey.[1]

His false belief has persuaded him that if the gods command it,
he may use force or fraud. So when Philoctetes answers him,

O hateful man, what do you find to say!
With gods as your excuse you make them false,[2]

he is right, though he does not understand the full meaning of
what he says. Odysseus assumes that the gods approve of treachery against a helpless victim. His whole plan is based on it; but
no ordinary man would agree with him, or fail to think the worse
of him for it. When he claims divine support for his dishonest
plan, Odysseus shows the illusion under which he labours.

A belief that the gods are good was by no means confined to a
few philosophic souls. Pindar emphatically dissociates the gods
from fraud and refuses to admit that they take any part in violence.[3]
He rejects the stories of Heracles' fights against them:

For to revile the gods
Is hateful wisdom, and to boast beyond measure
Plays to the tune of madness.[4]

Pindar follows Xenophanes and is followed by Plato when he refuses to attribute evil to the gods. Most pious men would have
agreed with him. So when Odysseus acts on the assumption that
the gods order craft and violence, he is unconsciously impious.
His wisdom is hateful and akin to madness. He is the victim of
an illusion not unlike that which Euripides' Iphigeneia attributes
to the barbarians of the Tauris:

Those here who offer human sacrifice
Put down, I think, their baseness to the goddess;
I cannot think that any god is bad.[5]

[1] 989–90 Ζεύς, ἔσθ', ἵν' ειἀῆς, Ζεύς, ὁ τῆσἀε γῆς κρατῶν,
Ζεύς, ᾧ ἀέἀοκται ταῦθ', ὑπηρετῶ ἀ' ἐγώ.

[2] 991–2 ὦ μῖσος, οἷα κἀξανευρίσκεις λέγειν·
θεοὺς προτείνων τοὺς θεοὺς ψευἀεῖς τίθης.

[3] Pyth. iii. 29, ix. 42.

[4] Ol. ix. 37–9 ἐπεὶ τό γε λοιἀορῆσαι θεοὺς
ἐχθρὰ σοφία, καὶ τὸ καυχᾶσθαι παρὰ καιρὸν
μανίαισιν ὑποκρέκει.

[5] Eur. I. T. 389–91
τοὺς ἀ' ἐνθάἀ', αὐτοὺς ὄντας ἀνθρωποκτόνους,
εἰς τὴν θεὸν τὸ φαῦλον ἀναφέρειν ἀοκῶ·
οὐἀένα γὰρ οἶμαι ἀαιμόνων εἶναι κακόν.

When men hold such beliefs, it merely shows their own evil fancies. Men should speak well of the gods,[1] and when Odysseus attributes evil designs to them, he is undeniably in the wrong.

Odysseus' particular boast is that he is a successful man of action. This is his answer to the long attack which Philoctetes delivers on him:

> When such are needed, such a man am I;
> But when the good and just are put to test,
> You'll find no man more reverent than I.
> Yet victory is always my desire.[2]

He believes above all in success, but he is prepared to be just and pious when such men are needed. But justice and piety are not absolute ends for him as success is. We can understand what impression this would make on an Athenian audience in 409 B.C. For the type was known to Thucydides. In his low estimate of honour Odysseus may not go so far as the Athenians of the Melian Dialogue who claim that 'expediency is accompanied by safety while justice and honour cannot be pursued without danger',[3] but in practice he believes that what counts is the advantage that comes to himself or to his own side. His mentality is close to that which Thucydides describes as the product of civil strife in Greece. His belief in violence and craft shows how values have been changed and 'frantic violence was accounted a man's part, cautious plotting a justifiable means of self-defence'.[4] His attitude to the gods, though by no means that of an atheist, is not far from that sketched in the same context—'neither side thought religiously, but they thought highly of fair phrases used to further guilty ends'. Like these men, Odysseus believes so much in success that he has to sacrifice many decencies and pieties to it.

Odysseus resembles other men produced and corrupted by war. His complete devotion to success is a natural result of ten years' fighting at Troy. He sees a chance of victory, takes full advantage of it, and throws himself into it. War, as Thucydides says, is a hard master 'and makes the moods of the many resemble their circumstances'.[5] That is what it has done to Odysseus. He applies to a divinely commanded task the qualities of cunning and violence which have hitherto served him well in war. His view that re-

---

[1] Pind. *Ol.* i. 35.

[2] 1049–52
> οὗ γὰρ τοιούτων δεῖ, τοιοῦτός εἰμ' ἐγώ·
> χὤπου Δικαίων κἀγαθῶν ἀνδρῶν κρίσις,
> οὐκ ἂν λάβοις μου μᾶλλον οὐδέν' εὐσεβῆ.
> νικᾶν γε μέντοι πανταχοῦ χρῄζων ἔφυν.

[3] Thuc. v. 107.   [4] Id. iii. 82, 4.   [5] Id. iii. 82, 2.

ligion is right enough in its own place but what really matters is success recalls the Old Man's words in Euripides' *Ion*:

> To honour reverence is well for those
> Who have good luck, but if you wish to harm
> Your enemies no law stands in the way.[1]

Odysseus is a type of the clever man as he was known in the last years of the fifth century. In the end his excessive cleverness spoils his character. It brings him into conflict with human decency. Neoptolemus makes this plain in a terse interchange with him:

> *Ne.* Wise though you are, nothing you say is wise.
> *Od.* Neither in speech or action are you wise.
> *Ne.* If these are just, 'tis better than your wisdom.[2]

The moral is obvious. Neoptolemus is right and Odysseus wrong. Once there is a conflict between wits and right, right should win. The wisdom of Odysseus is not real wisdom after all. Neoptolemus sees that it must yield to right. Of course such a conflict is not inevitable. It only comes into existence through Odysseus' perverse over-estimate of his own gifts.

Odysseus fails in his plan. He thinks that since Neoptolemus has the bow, all is well. So he says to Philoctetes:

> We have no need of you
> Now that we have this bow.[3]

He is still deluded by his own conceit, his false notion of what the oracle means. In brutal satisfaction that his task is done he leaves Philoctetes to his doom:

> What need of you? Walk Lemnos and farewell.[4]

He fails because he has miscalculated about Neoptolemus' character. This time honour triumphs over ambition, and Neoptolemus gives back the bow to its rightful owner. Odysseus at first fails to understand Neoptolemus' motives. When he sees what they are he resorts to threats; Neoptolemus shall pay for this (1241, 1243). He even threatens him with his sword (1254–5). But he is

---

[1] *Ion* 1045–7 τὴν 2' εὐσέβειαν εὐτυχοῦσι μὲν καλὸν
τιμᾶν· ὅταν 2ὲ πολεμίους 2ρᾶσαι κακῶς
θέλῃ τις, οὐ2εὶς ἐμπο2ὼν κεῖται νόμος.

[2] 1244–6 Νε. σοφὸς πεφυκὼς οὐ2ὲν ἐξαυ2ᾷς σοφόν.
Ο2. σὺ 2' οὔτε φωνεῖς οὔτε 2ρασείεις σοφά.
Νε. ἀλλ' εἰ 2ίκαια, τῶν σοφῶν κρείσσω τά2ε.

[3] 1055–6   οὐ2ὲ σοῦ προσχρῄзομεν,
τά γ' ὅπλ' ἔχοντες ταῦτ'.

[4] 1060 τί 2ῆτα σοῦ 2εῖ; χαῖρε τὴν Λῆμνον πατῶν.

answered with an equal threat and withdraws. Neoptolemus, now completely master of himself, passes judgement on him:

> You have learned sense. If you remain as wise
> Henceforth, your goings may be free of tears.[1]

He sees that Odysseus has been moved by pride and that it has brought him into trouble. He hopes that he has learned a lesson and will in the future avoid pride and the trouble that it brings. His hope is hardly fulfilled. For although Odysseus disappears at this point, he has not yet abandoned his ambitions and makes a final reappearance at the moment when Neoptolemus gives back the bow to Philoctetes. His protest is characteristic:

> And I forbid it. Be the gods my witness,
> For the Atridae and for all the host.[2]

He still thinks that the gods are on his side and that he acts for the Achaean army. He even goes on to say that he will send Philoctetes by force to Troy, no matter what Neoptolemus does (1296–7). He remains obdurate in his illusions to the end and believes that his plan is right and that, if craft fails, force can be used.

In the end Odysseus is foiled by the threat of force. When Philoctetes turns his bow on the hated enemy, with intent to kill, there is nothing for Odysseus to do but retire. For all his trust in cleverness he has to recognize the presence of superior force. There is no sign that he has learned any other lesson or realized his own errors. He remains an unsympathetic, almost a base character. His 'wisdom' deludes him and prevents him from seeing the situation as it really is. If he were not odious, he might have a certain pathos. For he illustrates the Greek belief that the 'wise' often fail to know their own interests.[3] His chief asset is his power of persuasive speech. It is this which first seduced Neoptolemus into accepting his plan. But now this is useless equally with Neoptolemus and with Philoctetes. He himself lays stress on the importance of deeds rather than of words (98–9), but he has put his trust in words and they have failed him. Euripides' Hecuba almost describes his case:

---

[1] 1259–60   ἐσωφρόνησας· κἄν τὰ λοίφ' οὕτω φρονῇς,
ἴσως ἄν ἐκτὸς κλαυμάτων ἔχοις πόδα.

[2] 1293–4   ἐγὼ δ' ἀπαυδῶ γ', ὡς θεοὶ ξυνίστορες,
ὑπέρ τ' Ἀτρειδῶν τοῦ τε σύμπαντος στρατοῦ.

[3] Eur. fr. 905   μισῶ σοφιστήν, ὅστις οὐχ αὑτῷ σοφός.

Oh they are strict professors of the art,
And they are wise; yet in the end of all,
Not wise enough. They perish. None escapes.[1]

When Odysseus leaves the stage, he shows himself for what he is,
a man who in his false cleverness fails to get what he wants and
continues to think that scruples are otiose when ambition is concerned. He may have courage and determination, but his failure
is complete. It is clear that the divine plan will not work through
agents like him. His own plan which he substitutes for it involves
means which the gods condemn, and fails for that reason.

Philoctetes is completely unlike Odysseus. He is cast in a different mould and seems to come from another, more heroic society.
He is in no sense clever. He is pre-eminently brave, truthful,
affectionate. He is a Greek, who welcomes the Greek dress of his
visitors (223-4) and the sound of a Greek voice:

O speech I love! O the delight to hear
The voice of such an one, unheard so long![2]

He has the pride of a great man and is pained that Neoptolemus
seems not to know who is he (254 ff.). He admires the noble and
detests the base. He warms in touching affection to the young
Neoptolemus because he is the son of Achilles and has, as he
believes, also been injured by Odysseus. Firm in his loyalties,
he is no less firm in his hates. He desires revenge on those who
have wronged him, especially on Odysseus and the Atridae (315-16).
In this he conforms to accepted standards of manhood. To punish
one's enemies was the right of any man. Archilochus claims that
he knows how to do it,[3] and Euripides gives expression to the
common sentiment:

'Tis a man's part to harm his enemies.[4]

To be loyal to friends and harsh to enemies was almost the traditional duty of a man.[5] In Philoctetes this double duty takes an
advanced form. The strength of his affections is matched by the
strength of his hates. He has, as he thinks, been abominably

[1] Eur. *Hec.* 1192-4

σοφοὶ μὲν οὖν εἰσ' οἱ τάδ' ἠκριβωκότες,
ἀλλ' οὐ δύνανται διὰ τέλους εἶναι σοφοί,
κακῶς δ' ἀπώλοντ'· οὔτις ἐξήλυξέ πω.

[2] 234-5   ὦ φίλτατον φώνημα· φεῦ τὸ καὶ λαβεῖν
πρόσφθεγμα τοιοῦδ' ἀνδρὸς ἐν χρόνῳ μακρῷ.

[3] Fr. 66, cf. Aesch. *Cho.* 123.

[4] Fr. 1092 ἐχθροὺς κακῶς δρᾶν ἀνδρὸς ἡγοῦμαι μέρος.

[5] Solon fr. 1. 5-6, Pind. *Pyth.* ii. 83-4, Eur. *Med.* 809, Plat. *Clit.* 410 a.

treated. For long he has brooded over his wrongs. It is only natural that he should demand amends.

In considering Philoctetes we must distinguish between his legitimate wrath against the Atridae and Odysseus and his illegitimate refusal to accept what the gods give him. The situation is complex. His foot, the source of his miseries, is a punishment for an offence committed, albeit unconsciously and unwillingly, against the gods. He walked in a forbidden place and was bitten by its guardian snake. Neoptolemus understands the reason of his sufferings:

> This sickness that torments you comes from heaven.
> You came to Chryse's guardian, the snake
> Who keeps with unseen watch her roofless shrine.[1]

Philoctetes erred inadvertently, but none the less he has to pay for violating the holy place of Chryse. Such a punishment is inevitable when men go where they should not. The Chorus indeed consider that Philoctetes' sufferings are undeserved (685), but Neoptolemus knows better and sees that they are sent by the gods (192, 196). Philoctetes has not sinned deliberately against the gods, but he has to suffer for breaking their rules. His punishment may seem disproportionate to his offence, but the gods will make amends to him by the glory which he will win and by his ultimate recovery from sickness. His final fame, coming after years of misery, is part of their plan for him. They have decided that he shall come to Troy of his own accord, and there is justice in this; for it will show that he bears no resentment at what has happened to him. But it is in this that the greatest difficulty lies. On the other hand, Philoctetes has legitimate cause for resentment against the human beings who have abandoned him on a desolate island. Odysseus makes no real attempt to justify this action. He shelves the responsibility on the grounds that he acted on orders from his generals (6), and his excuse is that Philoctetes' ill-omened cries made it impossible to keep him aboard ship (8 ff.). Something, no doubt, had to be done, but it was not necessary to treat Philoctetes with so callous a brutality. The Atridae and Odysseus were his colleagues in a great undertaking and should have shown consideration to him in his misfortune. They should have felt that sympathy,

[1] 1326-8 σὺ γὰρ νοσεῖς τόδ' ἄλγος ἐκ θείας τύχης,
Χρύσης πελασθεὶς φύλακος, ὃς τὸν ἀκαλυφῆ
σηκὸν φυλάσσει κρύφιος οἰκουρῶν ὄφις.

or αἰδώς, which is due between comrades. For a comrade

> Is bound by unforged chains of reverence.[1]

Soldiers particularly were expected to show such consideration to
one another.[2] In his misfortune Philoctetes had a real claim to
good treatment. He should certainly not have been abandoned
in his sleep on a desert island with only a few rags of clothing
and hardly any of the necessaries of life. His anger is quite
natural and up to a point justified. It asserts itself in a desire for
revenge.

So long as he knows nothing about the oracle and his destiny,
Philoctetes' wrath against his enemies is natural enough. In his
ignorance he cannot be accused of opposing the divine will.
But once he knows what this is, the situation is changed. He hears
of it from the Merchant, but refuses to believe in it because he
suspects Odysseus' hand in it. This is understandable after all he
has suffered. He fears that there may be a trap somewhere, that
Odysseus hopes to lure him with soft words (629). He knows
that there is no limit to which Odysseus will not go:

> There's nothing that he will not say or dare.[3]

So long as he believes that the oracle is part of a plot against
himself, he is incapable of understanding his destiny and what is
required of him. But there is less excuse for him when Neoptolemus
tells him the facts (919–20), and he simply refuses to listen. His
resentment and suspicion are so ingrained in him that he cannot
see beyond them. Even when Neoptolemus in tones of complete
friendliness and moderation has told him the whole position,
Philoctetes persists in his obstinate refusal. His passion blinds him
to the truth. He would rather die than have anything to do with
his enemies (1348–9). It is not so much rancour about the past
that counts as fear for the future:

> It is not grief afflicts me for the past,
> But what I yet must suffer at their hands,
> I think that I foresee. The heart that once
> Breeds evil, teaches evil to the end.[4]

---

[1] Eur. fr. 595 αἰδοῦς ἀχαλκεύτοισιν ἔζευκται πέδαις.

[2] Il. xv. 562, Xen. Symp. 8. 35.

[3] 633–4   ἀλλ' ἔστ' ἐκείνῳ πάντα λεκτά, πάντα δὲ
                    τολμητά.

[4] 1358–61   οὐ γάρ με τἄλγος τῶν παρελθόντων δάκνει,
                    ἀλλ' οἷα χρὴ παθεῖν με πρὸς τούτων ἔτι
                    δοκῶ προλεύσσειν. οἷς γὰρ ἡ γνώμη κακῶν
                    μήτηρ γένηται, πάντα παιδεύει κακούς.

His distrustfulness is the fruit of his sufferings. His words have an irony of which he is unconscious. It is his own error of judgement that leads him to refuse his destiny. He genuinely believes that he cannot go to Troy because he will be maltreated by his enemies. Neoptolemus answers him as a moderate man should:

> There's reason in your words, and yet I wish,
> That, trusting in the gods and my own words,
> You, with this man for friend, would sail from here.[1]

Philoctetes should trust in the gods and the friendship of Neoptolemus, but he refuses absolutely to do so.

Philoctetes refuses his destiny. Like Odysseus he is the victim of illusions, and in his case anger is the cause. His excuse of distrust is wrong and can only be deplored. The answer to him comes with decision and clarity from Neoptolemus, who is now in a position to speak with authority:

> The lot that the gods give
> To men, they cannot choose but bear it all.
> Those who persist in self-inflicted woes,
> As you do, such men merit no forgiveness,
> Nor is it right for us to pity them.[2]

Philoctetes is wrong to refuse what the gods send. Neoptolemus appeals to an ancient belief that men must accept this whether it be good or ill. Homer had made Paris say:

> Not to be cast away are the gods' most glorious presents,
> Whatsoever they give, tho' a man himself would not choose them,[3]

and Sophocles makes a character in a lost play say:

> This is a god's gift, and from what the gods
> Have given, you must never run away, my child.[4]

Naturally, when such a gift was ill, patience was required to

---

[1] 1373–5 λέγεις μὲν εἰκότ', ἀλλ' ὅμως σε βούλομαι
θεοῖς τε πιστεύσαντα τοῖς τ' ἐμοῖς λόγοις
φίλου μετ' ἀνδρὸς τοῦδε τῆσδ' ἐκπλεῖν χθονός.

[2] 1316–20 ἀνθρώποισι τὰς μὲν ἐκ θεῶν
τύχας δοθείσας ἔστ' ἀναγκαῖον φέρειν·
ὅσοι δ' ἑκουσίοισιν ἔγκεινται βλάβαις,
ὥσπερ σύ, τούτοις οὔτε συγγνώμην ἔχειν
δίκαιόν ἐστιν οὔτ' ἐποικτίρειν τινά.

[3] Il. iii. 65–6 οὔτοι ἀπόβλητ' ἐστὶ θεῶν ἐρικυδέα δῶρα,
ὅσσα κεν αὐτοὶ δῶσιν, ἑκὼν δ' οὐκ ἄν τις ἕλοιτο.

[4] Fr. 964 θεοῦ τὸ δῶρον τοῦτο· χρὴ δ' ὅσ' ἂν θεοὶ
διδῶσι, φεύγειν μηδέν, ὦ τέκνον, ποτέ.

endure it, but it might be pleasant and still refused.¹ Theognis
thinks it the mark of a bad character not to know how to accept
such gifts.² If the gods send evil, it must be endured; if good, it
must be accepted with gratitude. To Philoctetes they offer health
and glory, but he rejects the offer and prefers to live in misery
because he is full of resentment and suspicion. His choice is
doubly discreditable. It is irreverent to the gods, and it does him
discredit as a man to persist in grief and self-pity, which would be
more appropriate to a woman.³ The Chorus rightly deplore his
decision:

> When you might have had wisdom,
> Instead of a nobler fortune,
> You chose to accept the worse.⁴

Moreover, though Philoctetes might have claimed before that his
misfortunes were outside his own control, he cannot do so now.
Neoptolemus has told him the facts with such authority that he
cannot still disbelieve them. In so far as he acts of his own choice,
he is to be condemned. For while Greek morality was prepared
to bestow pity or pardon on involuntary actions, it knew that
voluntary call for praise or blame.⁵ Since Philoctetes now acts of
his own choice, he is beyond pity or pardon. He may rightly be
condemned, and Neoptolemus says so (1319–20).

To this argument Neoptolemus adds another:

> You have grown wild and hear no counsellor,
> And, though he speaks in love advising you,
> You hate him like a bitter enemy.⁶

In indulging his fury and in refusing the obligations of decency
Philoctetes behaves like a savage or a beast. He refuses to take
advice given in perfect friendliness and treats his friends as if they
were enemies. Like the beasts he obeys not his reason but his
passions,⁷ and what in beasts is pardonable is deplorable in a man.
It is the state of the Homeric Achilles when he prefers nursing
his wrath to helping his friends in their need.⁸ In such a savage
fury Philoctetes neglects both the gods and his friends. The strength

¹ Hom. Hymn ii. 147, Aesch. Pers. 293–4.   ² 443–6.   ³ Eur. Andr. 91 ff.
⁴ 1098–1100   εὖτέ γε παρὸν φρονῆσαι
                λῴονος ἐκ Δαίμονος εἵ-
                λου τὸ κάκιον αἰνεῖν.
⁵ Ant. v. 92, Aristot. Nic. Eth. 1109 b 31.
⁶ 1321–3   σὺ Δ' ἠγρίωσαι, κοὔτε σύμβουλον Δέχῃ,
            ἐάν τε νουθετῇ τις εὐνοίᾳ λέγων,
            στυγεῖς, πολέμιον Δυσμενῆ θ' ἡγούμενος.
⁷ Aristot. Pol. 1254 b 21.   ⁸ Il. ix. 629–30.

of his passion is seen when he turns his bow on Odysseus with intent to kill (1299), rather as Achilles thinks of killing Agamemnon.[1]
He is stopped only by Neoptolemus, who knows that such an
action is wrong (1300), but he is hardly convinced by him. For
the moment hatred dominates him completely.

In effect Philoctetes disregards the gods rather as Odysseus does,
but while Odysseus is moved by pride in his cleverness, Philoctetes is moved by suspicious anger. In him too there is a subtle
element of impiety. It takes the form of assuming that the gods
must support and approve any choice that he makes. So when
Neoptolemus asks him to come to Troy, he seems to be horrified
at the suggestion and asks:

> Have you no shame before the gods to say this?[2]

He feels that it must be against the gods' will for him to go, no
doubt because it will, as he believes, play into the hands of his
enemies. Neoptolemus' answer to him is quite right:

> How could a man feel shame if he is helped?[3]

Since the gods desire it, there can be nothing wrong in the benefit
which Philoctetes will receive if he goes. He sets his will against
the gods because he cannot see that their plan for him may be at
variance with his own feelings. This obstinacy has already shown
itself in another form. When he hears that Thersites is alive, he
bursts into a great denunciation:

> So would he be. Nought evil yet has died,
> But the gods deck it up in finery,
> And what is double-dyed in wickedness
> They joyfully turn back from death, but what
> Is just and good they always send away.
> What must I think, what praise, when in my praise
> Of things divine I find the gods are base?[4]

He finds it hard to believe that the gods are good when they reward the wicked—like Sisyphus—by bringing them back to life

---

[1] *Il.* i. 193 ff.
[2] 1382   καὶ ταῦτα λέξας οὐ καταισχύνῃ θεούς;
[3] 1383   πῶς γάρ τις αἰσχύνοιτ' ἂν ὠφελούμενος;
[4] 446–52   ἔμελλ'· ἐπεὶ οὐδέν πω κακόν γ' ἀπώλετο,
            ἀλλ' εὖ περιστέλλουσιν αὐτὰ δαίμονες,
            καί πως τὰ μὲν πανοῦργα καὶ παλιντριβῆ
            χαίρουσ' ἀναστρέφοντες ἐξ Ἅιδου, τὰ δὲ
            δίκαια καὶ τὰ χρήστ' ἀποστέλλουσ' ἀεί.
            ποῦ χρὴ τίθεσθαι ταῦτα, ποῦ δ' αἰνεῖν, ὅταν
            τὰ θεῖ' ἐπαινῶν τοὺς θεοὺς εὕρω κακούς;

and destroy all that is noble. The doubt is sincere and natural.
In Euripides' *Bellerophon* the unpunished outrages of the wicked are
used for an argument against the existence of the gods.[1] Philoctetes does not go so far, nor is his scepticism more than tentative.
But he is on the way to doubting the justice of the gods, like the
impious man condemned in the *Agamemnon*.[2] He is almost guilty
of one of the three forms of impiety noted by Plato, that the gods
exist but do not care for men.[3] Such was the belief of Diagoras of
Melos, who was sentenced to death for blasphemy.[4] The more
pious members of the audience would feel a shock of disapproval.

Philoctetes does not quite condemn the gods, but he is certainly
puzzled. His words recall those of Euripides' Creusa when she
remembers her treatment by Apollo and bursts out:

> In what court shall we seek justice
> If we must perish by our masters' crimes?[5]

Euripides intends to attack Apollo, and the parallel does not make
Philoctetes seem any more reverent. Yet his thought has a more
respectable example in a Theognidean poem which begins by
showing that the just are treated unjustly and continues:

> Who then would look on him and still feel honour
> For the gods, and what would be his heart,
> When someone wicked and unconscienced, paying
> No regard to wrath of men or gods,
> Wreaks insolence in pride of wealth, while good men
> Are worn down by grievous poverty?[6]

The doubt is honest and seems justified by the facts. But there is
an answer to it, not that the gods do not care for what men do
but that men cannot understand their ways. So Sophocles says:

> But since the gods conceal what is divine,
> You will not learn it, though you search it out.[7]

Aeschylus[8] and Pindar[9] would agree. Since the gods are inscrutable,

[1] Fr. 286.   [2] *Ag.* 369–73.   [3] *Laws*, x. 885 b.   [4] Cic. *N. D.* iii. 37.
[5] *Ion*, 253–4   ποῖ Δίκην ἀνοίσομεν,
εἰ τῶν κρατούντων ἀδικίαις ὀλούμεθα;
[6] 747–52   τίς κεν δὴ βροτὸς ἄλλος ὁρῶν πρὸς τοῦτον ἔπειτα
ἅζοιτ' ἀθανάτους καὶ τίνα θυμὸν ἔχων,
ὁππότ' ἀνὴρ ἄδικος καὶ ἀτάσθαλος οὔτε τευ ἀνδρὸς
οὔτε τευ ἀθανάτων μῆνιν ἀλευόμενος
ὑβρίζῃ πλούτῳ κεκορημένος, οἱ δὲ δίκαιοι
τρύχονται χαλεπῇ τειρόμενοι πενίῃ;
[7] Fr. 919   ἀλλ' οὐ γὰρ ἂν τὰ θεῖα κρυπτόντων θεῶν
μάθοις ἄν, οὐδ' εἰ πάντ' ἐπεξέλθοις σκοπῶν.
[8] Aesch. *Supp.* 93–5.   [9] Pind. Fr. 50. 4–5.

men should not criticize them but acquiesce in their will. In his *Epigoni* Sophocles makes this clear:

> How can a man, as I, fight heaven-sent doom,
> When hope helps nothing in calamity?[1]

We may almost apply the words to Philoctetes. He fights against the doom that the gods send, and his hope that he can continue in his hatred is useless against them. But he does not see this. He continues to struggle.

The words of Philoctetes, coming quite early in the play, show that he is not likely to accept the gods' will without question. When he hears what it is, he rejects it. At the same time he assumes that this cannot really be their will. His delusion arises out of his anger and fear. He supports the gods so long as they help him in what he wishes. He beseeches Neoptolemus by Zeus, the god of suppliants, to take him home (484) and by his father's gods to give him back the bow (992–3). He regards Odysseus as hated by the gods (1031), not without reason since Odysseus is in his own way impious, but here too his reasons are not impartial: he feels that the gods must hate Odysseus who wishes to take him to Troy. The irony of his error is that the gods are just and wish to do him a benefit. He does not see that they keep their word and are more to be trusted than men.[2] His blindness, which arises out of his anger, may be natural, but it is not right. Just as Odysseus obstructs the divine plan by his cleverness, so Philoctetes obstructs it by refusing to have anything to do with his enemies. At times it is right to hate enemies, but when the gods order something that overrides such hatred, they must be obeyed. For men err and the gods are always right.

Between these extremes is a Mean, and for a short period it is represented by Neoptolemus. From the moment when he decides to give back the bow to Philoctetes until he gives in to Philoctetes' desire to sail home, Neoptolemus is beyond criticism. He behaves as a man of decent feelings should, and his failure shows how wrong a turn events have taken. To reach this state of mind he has to pass through a considerable struggle. When he first feels shame about deceiving Philoctetes, he is not deterred from acting dishonourably. He keeps the bow because he is still moved by ambition and the claims of military duty as

[1] Fr. 196   πῶς οὖν μάχωμαι θνητὸς ὢν θείᾳ τύχῃ,
ὅπου τὸ δεινὸν ἐλπὶς οὐδὲν ὠφελεῖ;
Cf. also frs. 585, 680, 947, Eur. *Med.* 1018, *Phoen.* 382, *Heraclid.* 618.
[2] Soph. fr. 228.

Odysseus has presented them to him. But at least he finds this decision painful and is the victim of a real moral struggle. We can understand his feelings when he says:

> What shall I do? Would I had never left
> Scyros. So painful is my circumstance.[1]

He gives in unwillingly to Odysseus, with a last hope that Philoctetes may change his mind if the Chorus stay with him (1078–9). He trusts that after all things may turn out well, but for the moment he obeys his superior officer. He explains his reasons with youthful candour to Philoctetes when he refuses to surrender the bow:

> I cannot. To obey authority
> Right forces me, and my own interest.[2]

His motives are mixed. He still believes that the plan of Odysseus is to his own advantage and will bring him glory. Perhaps at the back of his mind he hopes that Philoctetes may yet see reason, but none the less he is still as misguided as Odysseus about the prospects of success by such means. Secondly, he feels that he must obey his superiors. As a young soldier he naturally feels this. Plato thought that a man must always look to his commanders even in the smallest matters and be ruled by them.[3] Perhaps he erred on the side of admiring Spartan discipline, and his views may not have been shared by all Athenians. Yet the Athenian belief in individual initiative cannot have excluded all respect for discipline, and Neoptolemus' regard for the higher command is natural in a subaltern. For, as Socrates saw, the chief requirements in an army are good order and good discipline.[4] So Neoptolemus feels the claims of military obedience, especially as he thinks them to be closely connected with his own prospects of glory.

Despite these powerful and persuasive impulses Neoptolemus changes his mind and goes back with the bow to Philoctetes. This time he has really changed his mind, and the change is dictated purely by reasons of conscience. He still does not fully understand the oracle and is moved simply by a feeling of shame. All his earlier course was shameful (1228, 1234, 1249). He refers

---

[1] 969–70   οἴμοι, τί δράσω; μή ποτ' ὤφελον λιπεῖν
τὴν Σκῦρον· οὕτω τοῖς παροῦσιν ἄχθομαι.

[2] 925–6   ἀλλ' οὐχ οἷόν τε· τῶν γὰρ ἐν τέλει κλύειν
τό τ' ἔνδικόν με καὶ τὸ συμφέρον ποεῖ.

Laws, xii. 942 b.   Xen. Mem. iii. 5. 21.

directly to the lies and the deceit which won him the bow. To undo this wrong he must give the bow back:

I shall undo the fault I made before.[1]

The 'fault' is his moral failure, and it is significant that Neoptolemus used the same word earlier in a different sense, when in resisting Odysseus' proposals he said

Sooner would I commit
A noble fault than win base victory.[2]

There the fault was military disobedience; now it is moral failure. The different use of the word shows the change in Neoptolemus. In the interval he has tried to carry out Odysseus' orders and has found that his failure is worse than if he had disobeyed from the start. At first he was concerned about disobeying his superior officer; now he is concerned about offending the gods. His experience with Philoctetes has cleared his mind for him. What before looked like a serious offence against his leader is now seen to be right; what was disobedience to Odysseus is obedience to the gods. In this frame of mind the duty of military discipline fades into unimportance. What matters is doing the right thing. By giving back the bow Neoptolemus intends to undo the harm that he has done.

Once rid of the bow and of his sense of guilt, Neoptolemus allows no obstacle to come between him and his duty. He is ready to defy Odysseus (1255–6), and no less to stop Philoctetes from killing his old enemy (1300). He is now truly the son of Achilles, as Philoctetes tells him (1310–13), and as he himself is glad to hear (1314–15). In the confidence of being right he tells the truth to Philoctetes with firmness and friendliness. He expects his words to carry weight and to persuade Philoctetes to come to Troy. His natural noble instincts have brought him to act as the oracle has throughout required. He believes in reason and persuasion and shows Philoctetes that if he comes to Troy he will carry out a divine duty (1338–9) and win great glory (1346–7). But Philoctetes answers with a passionate refusal. The right and honourable course adopted by Neoptolemus has failed. He sees that Philoctetes' obstinacy is the cause:

Friend, let not sorrow make you hard of heart.[3]

[1] 1224   λύσων ὅσ' ἐξήμαρτον ἐν τῷ πρὶν χρόνῳ.
[2] 94–5   βούλομαι δ', ἄναξ, καλῶς
       δρῶν ἐξαμαρτεῖν μᾶλλον ἢ νικᾶν κακῶς.
[3] 1387   ὦ τᾶν, διδάσκου μὴ θρασύνεσθαι κακοῖς.

But there is little that he can do against it. He admits defeat:

> What can I do, if any word I say
> Fails to persuade you about anything?
> 'Tis easiest for me to cease from words,
> For you to live, as now you live, unsaved.[1]

Even when the gods' plan is attempted as it ought to be, with persuasion and goodwill, it has no result.

To this deadlock all the different attempts to bring Philoctetes have contributed. He cannot be brought by fraud; his bow cannot be brought without him; he will not come of his own free will. The first two failures arise because they involve means which are against the gods' will. Odysseus' dishonest plan ends in the repentance of Neoptolemus, the exposure of the stratagem, and the return of the bow. Neoptolemus' plan, right though it is, fails because of the evil which has preceded it. The treachery practised on Philoctetes has aroused his suspicion, resentment, hatred, and fear. The last failure is the fruit of the first. Honesty is tried too late, when Philoctetes is on his guard and incapable of listening to reason. By yielding to Odysseus Neoptolemus has himself created a situation which cannot be remedied simply by his own change of heart or reversal of policy. Dark powers have been awoken which cannot lightly be set at rest. If from the first Philoctetes had been treated with candour, his generous nature might have responded to it, and he might have gone willingly to Troy. Now his passions have been so aroused that nothing will persuade him to go. The first error of misinterpreting the oracle and being cleverer than the gods has brought its harvest of ugly feelings and blank failure. The confident fantasy in which Odysseus formed his plan and Neoptolemus tried to put it into effect have been wrecked on stern facts. Philoctetes will not be cheated, and at last he will not be persuaded either.

Neoptolemus has behaved rightly, and failed. What is he to do? The best course is impossible; so he takes the second-best. Philoctetes asks him to take him to Malis, and Neoptolemus consents. He cannot leave the castaway on the island; pity and decency forbid. He cannot take him to Troy; for he will not go. In the circumstances he might as well take him to his home. This is at least human and charitable, and if the Achaeans take violent action about it, Neoptolemus will have Philoctetes to protect him

[1] 1393–6   τί δῆτ' ἂν ἡμεῖς δρῷμεν, εἰ σέ γ' ἐν λόγοις
πείθειν δυνησόμεσθα μηδὲν ὧν λέγω;
ὡς ῥᾷστ' ἐμοὶ μὲν τῶν λόγων λῆξαι, σὲ δὲ
ζῆν, ὥσπερ ἤδη ζῇς, ἄνευ σωτηρίας.

(1405–6). There are even other advantages. Neoptolemus has
found a true friend; Philoctetes is delivered from his miseries;
Odysseus, their common enemy, is discredited. But it is not what
the gods desire. Neoptolemus' action has its own nobility. It
means the end and sacrifice of his ambition for military glory;
it is a proper amends for his deceit. Our human feelings again
seem to run counter to the will of the gods. But that does not
prove the gods wrong. If men act against the gods, they may well
create a situation in which the second-best is the only possible
course, and even the finest feelings fail to secure the right end as
the gods require it. The moral process through which Neoptolemus passes, his passage from light-hearted deceit to brave honesty
and noble compassion, is at least a sign of his capacity to be his
true self, but in itself it is useless. It needs the co-operation of
Philoctetes to win a proper result, and that, because of the false
wisdom of Odysseus, is lacking.

Philoctetes was known to have gone to Troy, and the play could
not end on this note of defeat. Sophocles must still reverse his
situation and show how after all Philoctetes went. With great
daring he used Euripides' beloved device of the *deus ex machina*. He
seems to have used it also in some of the lost plays. In the *Feasters*
(Σύνδειπνοι) Thetis appeared, and is thought to have composed a
feud between Achilles and Odysseus. It is also conjectured that
Poseidon appeared in the *Tyro* and some god in the *Tereus*. But
it does not seem likely that Sophocles often ended a play with
a divine epiphany, and if he did in the *Philoctetes*, he must have had
good reasons. Just as Neoptolemus and Philoctetes are about to
depart for Malis, Heracles appears on high and stops them. He
tells them what the future will be, and at the end of his words
Philoctetes is entirely changed. His passion and obstinacy have
left him; he is humble and obedient. His few words show how
deeply he is touched, how completely he accepts Heracles' orders:

> O thou who hast sent the voice I desire,
> O face long unseen,
> I shall not disobey thy words.[1]

Neoptolemus naturally agrees with him. The whole situation has
in a few moments been reversed. Philoctetes will go of his own
accord to Troy, and Troy will be taken. From defeat and conflict
we are raised to harmony and a glad consciousness that the gods'

[1] 1445–7   ὦ φθέγμα ποθεινὸν ἐμοὶ πέμψας,
                  χρόνιός τε φανείς,
                  οὐκ ἀπιθήσω τοῖς σοῖς μύθοις.

will is after everything to be done. Though their plan has been misunderstood and mishandled, they themselves put it right. The whole hideous life on Lemnos is now seen in retrospect with a feeling that amounts almost to affection. Philoctetes says good-bye to the places where he has spent ten weary and desolate years, to his cave, to the sea-lashed promontories, the streams, and the mountains. At last the conflict between moral feelings and the gods' will is over. Neoptolemus' self-denial has not been in vain, and Philoctetes' essential nobility, warped by resentful anger in the past, is restored.

Though Sophocles may well have been influenced by Euripides in introducing his *deus ex machina*, his intervening god is not Euripidean. The gods and goddesses who close a play of Euripides serve a purpose by cutting the knot which the human actors have tied. Heracles of course does this, but in his own way. He does not merely tell Neoptolemus and Philoctetes what to do, nor merely prophesy what glory lies ahead for them. He does both these things, and to that degree resembles Apollo in the *Orestes* and Castor in the *Electra*. But he differs from these bright presences by appealing to fundamentally more devout feelings. Even when the Euripidean epiphanies are of real and powerful divinities, like Artemis in the *Hippolytus* or Dionysus in the *Bacchants*, what counts is not their intimate appeal to the human soul but their remoteness from it, the distance between them and suffering humanity. They display power, but they do not bring comfort or strength. Even Castor in the *Electra*, who certainly gives a kind of consolation, does not give it with the direct and inevitable intimacy that Heracles shows to Philoctetes. Such divinities hold out hope, but they do not heal stricken consciences by appealing to their noblest qualities. There is still something re-mote about their intervention. Not only does Heracles bring calm and reason to a disordered mind, but he appeals to the better and deeper instincts in Philoctetes. He enlightens his conscience, soothes his suspicions, brings him to himself. In his own way he propounds to Philoctetes the lesson of 'Know thyself', and restores him to modest sanity.

The immediate success of Heracles' words comes partly from the simple fact that in life he was Philoctetes' trusted friend. The play has more than once touched on this. Philoctetes tells Neop-tolemus that he possesses Heracles' bow (262); the Chorus sing how he comes from the place where Heracles passed to Olympus amid the lightnings of Zeus (727-9); his own thoughts in delirium

turn to the time when he received the bow for setting fire to
Heracles' pyre (801–3); he himself feels the more bitterly the loss of
the bow because it belonged to his friend (1131 ff.). In Heracles
Philoctetes places absolute trust. Whatever doubts he may have
had about the future, whatever desire for revenge on his enemies
or suspicions of Odysseus, are dissolved by the calm words of his
friend. When Heracles says

> For thy sake I have come from my dwelling-place
> In the sky above,
> To reveal to thee the counsels of Zeus,[1]

Philoctetes knows that he can trust him absolutely. He makes no
conditions, asks no questions. The gods' plan which excited his
angry suspicions is accepted now. Between Philoctetes and Heracles exists a friendship in which each places absolute trust in the
other. They are like those friends who, in Aristotle's words, 'wish
good things alike to each other, being good men, and are good in
themselves'.[2] Philoctetes knows that Heracles wishes him well,
and that is the basis of his trust in him.

This human relation is strengthened by something else. Heracles is now a god and speaks with divine authority. His appearance to Philoctetes recalls other occasions when a god appears to
a man and stops him from doing what is wrong, as when in the
Iliad Achilles is restrained from drawing his sword on Agamemnon
because Athene appears to him. Just as Athene seems almost a
personification of conscience or decency, or at least appeals to
such feelings, so Heracles stands in an intimate relation to Philoctetes' real and better self. Aristotle remarks that the friendship
of men for gods, like that of children for their parents, is 'as to
something good and superior',[3] for they have received the greatest
benefits from them. It is true that elsewhere he denies the possibility of such a relation, but he seems to recognize that if it exists
it must have a very special character. His own words that it is
'of the benefactor to the benefited, and in general of the natural
ruler to the natural subject'[4] show a noble and simple conception
which agrees with what Heracles feels for Philoctetes. Philoctetes

---

[1] 1413–16   τὴν σὴν δ' ἥκω χάριν οὐρανίας
                  ἕδρας προλιπών,
                  τὰ Διός τε φράσων βουλεύματά σοι.

[2] *Nic. Eth.* 1156 b 8 τἀγαθὰ ὁμοίως βούλονται ἀλλήλοις, ᾗ ἀγαθοί, ἀγαθοὶ δ'
εἰσὶ καθ' αὑτούς.

[3] Id. 1162 a 5.

[4] *Eud. Eth.* 1242 a 32 τοῦ εὖ ποιήσαντος πρὸς τὸν παθόντα καὶ ὅλως τοῦ φύσει
ἄρχοντος πρὸς τὸν φύσει ἀρχόμενον.

returns this with complete affection and trust. The words which
come with all the authority of a god and the claim of a friend,
are enough to clear his mind and to change his heart. Heracles
himself has in his own lifetime suffered no less than Philoctetes,
only to win great glory in the end. He speaks of this that Philoctetes may see how alike their cases are and makes it the basis of
his appeal:

> And first of my own fortunes I shall speak,
> The labours that I laboured and endured,
> And won immortal honour, as you see.
> This destiny, be sure, awaits you too,
> To change your labours for a glorious life.[1]

He knows from his own experience how the gods can treat
suffering men. In the face of such testimony coming from such
authority Philoctetes can no longer refuse to accept his destiny.

As Heracles says, the plan that Philoctetes shall take Troy comes
from Zeus (1415). Heracles acts as intermediary between him
and Philoctetes. Greek religious thought knew that Heracles could
act like this. Pindar addresses him as an intercessor whose
prayers are of much avail between men and the gods:

> 'Tis fit for thee to win Hera's master
> And the bright-eyed Maiden. Thou canst often give
> Succour to men in their pathless perplexities.[2]

Heracles is well qualified to act as messenger for Zeus and to
deliver Philoctetes from the hopeless quandary in which he is
placed. He was honoured as a succourer from evil,[3] and as such
he appears here. But he brings more than strength and power;
he brings friendship and truth. He comes less to relieve physical
sufferings than to heal a stricken heart. And with this healing he
brings victory, as is right for one who was a great victor. The
process of repentance and submission is also the acceptance of
a glorious destiny. The gods give freely by their own means.

Heracles promises 'immortal honour' to Philoctetes. But this

---

[1] 1418–22 καὶ πρῶτα μέν σοι τὰς ἐμὰς λέξω τύχας,
ὅσους πονήσας καὶ Διεξελθὼν πόνους
ἀθάνατον ἀρετὴν ἔσχον, ὡς πάρεσθ' ὁρᾶν.
καὶ σοί, σάφ' ἴσθι, τοῦτ' ὀφείλεται παθεῖν,
ἐκ τῶν πόνων τῶνΔ' εὐκλεᾶ θέσθαι βίον.

[2] *Nem.* vii. 95–6 τὶν Δ' ἐπέοικεν Ἥρας πόσιν πειθέμεν
κόραν τε γλαυκώπιδα· Δύνασαι Δὲ βροτοῖσιν ἀλκὰν
ἀμαχανιᾶν Δυσβάτων θαμὰ Διδόμεν.

[3] Luc. *Alex.* 4 ἀλεξίκακος.

is not his only message, nor the most important. He gives also a warning. When its captors take Troy they are to remember

Reverence the gods;
For Father Zeus holds all else less than that.
For reverence dies not with men, but if
They live or if they die, is not destroyed.[1]

This strong lesson on the duty of reverence is deserved by Philoctetes, who has allowed his anger to make him shirk what the gods have allotted to him, and by Neoptolemus, who in the early stages flung aside his respect for truth and decency. So the moral of the play is driven home. Men must reverence the gods. Too many mistakes and too much evil have arisen from the lack of reverence. This is more important than the glory which will be Philoctetes' reward. It lives for ever, like the Unwritten Laws, and its validity survives the individual life. It is noteworthy that Sophocles may have had in mind some lines of Euripides:

But glory, though a man dies, does not die,
But lives on when the body is no more;
With the base all dies and goes beneath the earth.[2]

But whether he had this passage in mind or not, his position is different. The younger poet believes in the importance of glory, the older in the greater importance of reverence. The gods may give glory, as they have to Heracles and will to Philoctetes, but men must find reverence themselves. In so far as he has resisted the divine will, Philoctetes has not been reverent. Now he has a chance to retrieve himself. Heracles speaks with the voice of conscience and divine authority no less than as a friend.

The intervention of Heracles frees Philoctetes of any tendency to irreverence. It has removed his anger which was its cause and destroyed his doubts. In particular it strengthens the affection which he has already formed for Neoptolemus and turns it to good. When Heracles tells the two:

But like two lions of one lair protect
Each other[3]

[1] 1441-4
εὐσεβεῖν τὰ πρὸς θεούς·
ὡς τἄλλα πάντα δεύτερ' ἡγεῖται πατὴρ
Ζεύς.   οὐ γὰρ ηὐσέβεια συνθνῄσκει βροτοῖς·
κἄν ζῶσι κἄν θάνωσιν, οὐκ ἀπόλλυται.

[2] Fr. 734
ἀρετὴ δέ, κἄν θάνῃ τις, οὐκ ἀπόλλυται,
ζῇ δ' οὐκέτ' ὄντος σώματος· κακοῖσι δὲ
ἅπαντα φροῦδα συνθανόνθ' ὑπὸ χθονός.

[3] 1436-7
ἀλλ' ὡς λέοντε συννόμω φυλάσσετον
οὗτος σὲ καὶ σὺ τόνδε.

he shows what their relations will be. The two men who are attracted to one another by natural nobility but have been placed in a false relation by wrong ambition and wrong pride will now be faithful friends and work for a common end. They will be like lions, for the lion is 'noble and courageous and high-bred',[1] and so are they. They are, moreover, soldiers, and their lion-like qualities will be needed, for the lion is 'ferocious to such as come in its way',[2] and Homeric similes show what qualities it shares with warriors. Nothing is said about Odysseus and the Atridae, but we may surely assume that since Philoctetes is ready without reservations to assume his task at Troy, he is ready also to forgo his hatred. The discords which have risen from the faults of the different characters are resolved. If the divine plan had been followed correctly from the beginning, no crisis or conflict would have arisen. But it has been hampered by human passions and weaknesses. In due course the gods themselves intervene and put everything right. Nor is this intervention entirely undeserved by the human actors. The chief characters, Philoctetes and Neoptolemus, are superior beings with noble qualities. But each has some obsessing fault which holds up the right conclusion. But these faults are not enough to make either unworthy of the destiny which the gods have assigned to him. Just as Ajax is a hero despite his treachery, so Neoptolemus and Philoctetes are sent in the end to a noble destiny because they deserve it. Just as Ajax rids himself of his madness and the pride which bred it, so these two are purged of their faults and made fit to be the gods' instruments in a high undertaking.

The end of the play shows the triumph of the gods' plan. Philoctetes recognizes this when he prays to be sent

> Where I am brought by powerful Fate,
> And the counsel of friends, and the Power
> All-conquering who has brought this to pass.[3]

All has happened and will happen as Fate rules. But this conclusion is not fatalistic. This Fate is not a power behind Zeus and superior to him but the 'fate of Zeus' as Homer knew it. It is the will of Zeus. Its instrument is the 'counsel of friends', the words of Heracles and even of Neoptolemus which have woken the true self in Philoctetes. Behind these is the 'all-conquering

---

[1] Aristot. *H.A.* 488 b 17.   [2] Ib. 571 b 28.

[3] 1466–8   ἔνθ' ἡ μεγάλη Μοῖρα κομίζει,
γνώμη τε φίλων χὠ πανδαμάτωρ
δαίμων, ὃς ταῦτ' ἐπέκρανεν.

Power' which is Zeus. He is last named because he matters most. The destiny is his will; the counsel of friends comes ultimately from him. Against these Philoctetes has fought. Now he accepts them gladly and goes willingly. The close of the play shows that Zeus' will is done. He does not wish Philoctetes to be ruined by his own faults, but helps him out of them and shows him what to do. Philoctetes' fine nature responds, and all is well. Harmony, joy, and obedience take the place of discord, misery, and distrust.

In retrospect the *Philoctetes* shows its underlying principles, its structure. A situation exists in which the faults of men have created mistrust and resentment. Men try to turn this situation to their own profit, but only make it worse. The mistrust and the resentment are increased; innocent beings are involved and add to the difficulties. The order of things which was violated when Philoctetes was abandoned on Lemnos is further violated when Odysseus tries to bring him to Troy by fraud or violence. The stratagem of Odysseus makes the position much worse. In the end a solution comes through the intervention of the gods. This works because Philoctetes is no ordinary man and is ready to listen to his old friend. The end is entirely satisfying. We feel that Philoctetes, despite his mistakes, deserves amends for his sufferings, that Neoptolemus' noble attempt to be honest should not end in failure, that Odysseus should not have the credit of bringing Philoctetes to Troy. The conclusion is just and merciful. It shows that, after all, our feelings about the characters are right. Odysseus fails because he goes against the will of the gods; Neoptolemus and Philoctetes succeed because in the end they work for it.

VIII

OEDIPUS AT COLONUS

IN 406–405 B.C. Sophocles died in his ninetieth year, and *Oedipus at Colonus* was produced by his grandson in 402. It has the peculiar interest that belongs to the last work of a great poet, especially since it was written in extreme old age and is in this respect comparable to the last dialogues of Plato or the last paintings of Titian. When Sophocles wrote it he must have known that the end was near, and it is only natural to assume that in it he took a kind of leave to his life and gave his conclusions on it, rather as Shakespeare is thought to have taken leave of the stage and dramatic poetry in *The Tempest*. It has in consequence often been treated as if it were a more personal and more intimate document than his other plays. Its episodes and emotions have been explained with reference to the poet's last years. The angry old man, Oedipus, who quarrels with his son, is compared with Sophocles who quarrelled with Iophon[1]; the lament of the Chorus on the miseries of old age is sometimes thought to have little dramatic relevance and to be the old poet's lamentation on his private sorrows[2]; even the heroization of Oedipus has been claimed to show prophetic insight into the destiny which awaited Sophocles after death.[3] But such views, even when based on sufficient evidence, reveal nothing about the actual play. They may help to explain why Sophocles wrote the play or wrote it as he did, but not what the play is or what it means. They belong, if anywhere, to the poet's biography, not to the study of his work. Nor do they help us to understand the play. It stands in its own strength and needs no reference to such external facts. It is written with remarkable power and shows no signs of flagging inspiration. It has a noble and simple design. And more than any other Greek play it touches the heart of Greek religion with its belief in the existence of two worlds, natural and supernatural, human and divine, separate yet often interpenetrating, and at times united.

The central theme is the transformation of Oedipus into a hero. As such he seems to have been honoured in Sophocles' own deme of Colonus,[4] and it is unlikely that Sophocles invented the whole story.[5] It was no doubt of little importance, but in the last years of

---

[1] K. Robert, *Oedipus*, i, pp. 470 ff.   [2] G. Perrotta, *Sofocle*, p. 602.
[3] A. v. Blumenthal, *Sophokles*, p. 237.   [4] Paus. i. 30. 4.
[5] Cf. K. Robert, op. cit., pp. 14–38.

the fifth century devout and patriotic Athenians must have turned their minds to all the supernatural helpers that they could find. In this case they may have felt that the hero had proved his worth. For near Colonus the Athenian cavalry had defeated a Theban force in 407 B.C.,[1] and some may have attributed the victory to the dead hero who was hidden near the battle-field. Since Sophocles was familiar from childhood with the neighbourhood and its memories he may have been impressed by the event and seen in it a sign of the care which the gods had for Attica. In any case the theme of a hero in Attic soil permeates the play. The power of such a tutelary being is assumed and indirectly dramatized. This hero is the same person whose hideous misfortunes Sophocles had already presented in *King Oedipus*. His *Oedipus at Colonus* is in some senses a sequel to the earlier play. It shows how a lifetime of sufferings closes in peace and power; it displays the power of the gods to exalt, as *King Oedipus* displayed their power to humble; it shows that they who have seemed cruel and relentless can grant rewards and make amends. It concentrates on the heroization of Oedipus, and in this it differs from the *Phoenician Women* of Euripides which also dealt with Oedipus' old age and foretold his end at Colonus but said nothing about his becoming a hero (1703–7). Whatever Sophocles may owe to the play of Euripides, he does not owe to it his central formative idea. What concerns him is precisely Oedipus' heroization. In his old age, in the darkening shadows of a hopeless war, he turned his thoughts to the landscape of his own home and to its indwelling power. Just as he won his first prize in 468 B.C. with *Triptolemus* on an Athenian legend and an Athenian cult, so in his last play he dramatized another legend and honoured another cult from his own place. At a time when his country needed every possible help, he thought of the unseen helper in Colonus and made his heroization the subject of a play.

In his *Ajax* and *Women of Trachis* Sophocles had presented the last hours of men who were honoured as heroes after death. But of this heroic state he gave only slight, easily negligible, hints.[2] Perhaps he believed that heroization was for Ajax and Heracles a reward for their great achievements and an amends for their sufferings, but he was much more concerned with the sufferings than with the amends. He does not explain why they became heroes; he does not even say that they did, and he says nothing about the process or meaning of such heroization. In *Oedipus*

[1] Xen. *Hell.* I. i. 33, *Mem.* III. v. 4; Diod. xiii. 72; Schol. *O.C.* 92.
[2] *Aj.* 1166–7, *Trach.* 1193–1202, 1270.

at Colonus his subject is the actual process, the passing of Oedipus
from a human to a heroic state. He bridges the gap between the
blind outcast who knows himself to be an incestuous parricide and
the potent spirit who lives in the earth at Colonus. He shows what
this transition means. No other Greek play treats of such a theme.
Euripides ends the *Hippolytus* and *Helen* with prophecies of heroization, but he does not attempt to show how it takes place or
what significance it has for the religious consciousness. To do
what Sophocles attempted in *Oedipus at Colonus* involved two great
difficulties. First, the supernatural process of heroization must be
real. The audience must be satisfied that it could and did happen
like this, that it is what religious experience would expect. Secondly, it must be dramatic. Yet it was no easy thing to show how
a man passes into a state akin to divinity and at the same time to
infuse into this passing the struggles and excitements of drama.

Sophocles might have confined his play to the passing of
Oedipus to the other world. No poet could have done this with
greater power or have shown better by what mysterious means the
gods guide the blind beggar to his predestined resting-place and
call him with signs and voices to a new existence in the earth. In
effect he has included such scenes in his play. At the beginning the
old outcast reaches Colonus and knows that his wanderings are
over; at the end a Messenger tells the manner of his disappearance.
In both there is a magical, even mystical, power, a compelling
sense that the gods are at work and that miracles are happening.
For the actual heroization these are perhaps the only indispensable scenes of the play. But they are not in themselves enough to
create drama. Perhaps if Aeschylus had chosen this subject he
might have contented himself with such material and have created
a lyrical play in which the sheer sweep of poetry would carry us to
the close. But for Sophocles such a subject was insufficient. It
would have too little action. There would be no real reversal of
fortune after Oedipus reaches Colonus and knows that it is his goal.
Thenceforward he is no longer an outcast. Divine powers work
for him; he knows that the end is near. So between this beginning
and this end Sophocles has set a series of violent and excited
episodes. He crowds the last earthly hours of Oedipus with crisis,
tumult, and anxiety. This makes the play much more dramatic,
makes it a real play. But it does something more. The scenes are
essential to the whole design. They illustrate some vital points in
the nature and state of a hero. Through them we see what the new
power of Oedipus should mean to the ordinary man.

The paradox of *Oedipus at Colonus* is the transformation of the polluted, blind, poverty-stricken Oedipus into something more than man. This is the dramatic stuff of which it is made. We know that Oedipus has been in conflict with the gods because he has broken their laws; we soon hear that he is still in conflict with men. These conflicts are resolved in a final reconciliation when the gods take him to their own and his transformation helps his friends and harms his enemies. Even his old conflict with himself, his sense of uncleanness and degradation, is overcome. He learns that the gods do not hate but love him, that they wish not to humble but to exalt him. The chaos of his life, pierced by shame and hatred and contempt, is reduced to order. And this reversal is of much more than fortune. The play displays the beginning and the end of it, shows first the abject poverty of Oedipus and then the special attentions which the gods pay to him. The change from one state to the other is not sudden or abrupt. It takes place through the play. Oedipus discovers not only that he is destined for this high end, but gradually, without himself knowing it, he feels in himself the qualities of a hero, a *daimôn*, a being more powerful than men. He grows in strength and stature until he is able, blind though he is, to find his way unguided and unhelped. The divine power is at work in him to prepare him for what he is to be. The process of his transformation is highly dramatic. He is subjected to searching tests, and in each he shows his new strength, his more than human character. At the end he has found his new nature in all its force. He is ready to join the gods.

The structure of *Oedipus at Colonus* owes much to a type of play which seems to have existed from early years of Greek tragedy. A suppliant comes to a strange place and asks for help against persecutors; those whom he asks grant his request and are thrown into difficulties by it. The earliest example of the type is the *Suppliant Women* of Aeschylus, which dates from the first years of the fifth century. Euripides revived it in his *Sons of Heracles* and his *Suppliant Women*. In both these plays he made Athens champion the oppressed and provide a refuge for them. In the second play Theseus is almost an incarnation of what Euripides thought that an Athenian ought to be. To both Sophocles may have owed something. The welcome and understanding which Oedipus finds in Attica, his gratitude for it, the dangers which it brings to his benefactors, have their parallels and precedents in Euripides. But when all the similarities have been acknowledged, there remains a great difference. For while Euripides was concerned

entirely with the question of helping suppliants and found in it
material enough for drama and ethical controversy, Sophocles
treats this as subordinate to something larger and more important,
the protection which the gods will give to Athens if it accepts the
body of Oedipus. What was for Euripides a matter of national
honour and international duty is for Sophocles a religious obligation. The fate of Oedipus concerns Athens because the gods wish
to help her and choose to combine this with amends to him for his
sufferings. His individual destiny is an example of their ultimate
justice to men, his help to Athens a sign that they reward the good.
And since Sophocles gives this new character to the old form, he is
able to make his drama turn on the relations of gods with men.
His Oedipus is more than the instrument of their designs and the
object of their justice. He is in some sense half-way between them
and mankind. Because he is going to be a hero, he is already more
than man. He shows human qualities, it is true, but they are those
which belong specially to a hero. He must be judged less as a man
than as a being more powerful and more formidable.

The *Oedipus at Colonus* has been criticized for its episodic construction. It certainly consists of a series of episodes and has not a
closely knit structure like that of *King Oedipus*. But this episodic
character is of a special kind and serves a special purpose. The
successive scenes are not disconnected, nor are they held together
merely by the presence of Oedipus or the ups and downs of his fortune. They show his last hours, the extremes of hope and anxiety
through which he passes, the forces of discord and of harmony
which surround him. But they have a more general function.
They illustrate the extremes of his character in love and hate, in
gratitude and vengefulness. And this makes the play what it is.
Through it we see a hero's nature. To make his design clearer
Sophocles constructs the play in what may be called three movements. In the first Oedipus comes to Athens and finds a welcome.
In this we see the devotion of his daughters and the generous
courtesy of Theseus. In return Oedipus shows fatherly affection
and warm-hearted gratitude. The section ends appropriately with
the great song in which the Chorus welcome Oedipus to Attica
and sing of its glories (668–719). The second section shows the
other side of the picture, the cruel calculating Creon and the
disloyal son Polynices. To them Oedipus shows all his harshness
and hardness, the stern side of his heroic nature, of his retributive
justice. The final section begins with the departure of Polynices
and the thunderclaps which announce the passing of Oedipus, and

ends with the lament of his daughters over him. We might say that the play is constructed as thesis, antithesis, and synthesis. The tender and harsh sides of Oedipus, the contrasted human beings who evoke these different qualities in him, are presented in strong opposition, only to be harmonized in his final state to which both sides of his character belong and in which his friends will be rewarded and his enemies punished. A design of this kind is not episodic in any derogatory sense. Indeed it is hard to think by what other means Sophocles could have shown the full range of Oedipus' character and what his heroic state means. His drama has a beginning, a middle, and an end. It has a single action, the transformation of Oedipus into a hero.

The action depends on the prophecy which long ago foretold his misfortunes to Oedipus. This also foretold that he would find a resting-place at Colonus, that he would be a bane to those who cast him out and a help to those who welcome him (88–95). As soon as the Stranger tells him that he is at Colonus, Oedipus knows that he has reached his goal (44–5). The oracle, remembered through long years of adversity, shows signs of fulfilment. Oedipus now knows that his end is near and that after it he will be in a very special position, powerful to benefit his friends and to injure his enemies. So he tells Theseus that he brings a unique gift and that in time to come, when present treaties of friendship are violated, it will help Athens against her foes:

> When my cold body, sleeping secretly,
> Shall drink the warm blood of my enemies,
> If Zeus is Zeus, and his son, Phoebus, true.[1]

He seems to forecast a time when the earth in which he lies will be soaked by the blood of his enemies. This will, we may be sure, be a satisfaction to him, a pleasant vengeance. He will enjoy what men sometimes pray for, notably Theognis:

> May I drink their black blood. May some good spirit
> Rise up and fulfil my need for me,[2]

or the subject population of Sparta who prayed 'to eat their lords raw'.[3] But behind this wish we may detect a secondary meaning of which Oedipus himself is unconscious, a hint that, like other

---

[1] 621–3   ἵν' οὑμὸς εὕδων καὶ κεκρυμμένος νέκυς
ψυχρός ποτ' αὐτῶν θερμὸν αἷμα πίεται,
εἰ Ζεὺς ἔτι Ζεὺς χὠ Διὸς Φοῖβος σαφής.

[2] 349–50   τῶν εἴη μέλαν αἷμα πιεῖν· ἐπὶ Δ' ἐσθλὸς ὄροιτο
Δαίμων, ὃς κατ' ἐμὸν νοῦν τελέσειε τάδε.

[3] Xen. Hell. iii. 3. 6.

heroes, he will receive blood-offerings, as Pelops did at Olympia[1] or the fallen at Plataea.[2] Oedipus prophetically foresees that he himself will receive the kind of offering that is made to heroes.[3] He knows that he will be in a special position, that his body will watch over Athens and protect it from its enemies. So, as he tells Theseus, his body is worth keeping:

> That it may always give you succour, worth
> Far more than many shields or foreign spears.[4]

Of the manner of his passing and the nature of his after-life he seems to know next to nothing, but he knows at least that the possession of his body will mean much to Athens and that he is reserved for a peculiar destiny.

The belief that Oedipus' body will protect Athens would not seem unduly strange to an Athenian audience. When Aeschylus makes his Amphiaraus say:

> I shall bring richness to this land of yours,
> A hidden seer come from an enemy land[5]

he follows the belief that Amphiaraus is hidden in the earth at Thebes[6] and is its helper. His Orestes, too, foresees a somewhat similar destiny for himself and says that he will be an enemy to Argos if she attacks Athens, but that, if she remains friendly, he will aid her.[7] Euripides makes Eurystheus prophesy a future for himself which is very like that which Sophocles gives to Oedipus: he will be a friend to Athens and an enemy to her enemies.[8] In each of these cases the body lies in a foreign country, Amphiaraus in Thebes, Orestes and Eurystheus in Athens, and will protect it from its enemies, even though they come from the dead man's own home. So Oedipus will lie in Attica and guard it especially from the attacks of his own Thebes. In Orestes and Oedipus this protection is a form of gratitude for services given, in Eurystheus and Amphiaraus it is amends for hostile actions done. In any case the presence of a hero's body might be a great help to a country.

That the gods should appoint Oedipus to such a destiny may well excite surprise. He is not only defiled and polluted, but poverty-stricken, blind, and homeless. The degree of his

---

[1] Pind. *Ol.* i. 90.   [2] Plut. *Aristid.* 21.

[3] Thuc. v. 11; Plut. *Sol.* 9; Paus. x. 4. 7; Eur. *Tro.* 381, *El.* 92.

[4] 1524-5   ὡς σοι πρὸ πολλῶν ἀσπίΔων ἀλκὴν ὅΔε
                Δορός τ' ἐπακτοῦ γειτόνων ἀεὶ τιθῇ.

[5] Aesch. *Sept.* 587-8 ἔγωγε μὲν Δὴ τήνΔε πιανῶ χθόνα
                μάντις κεκευθὼς πολεμίας ὑπὸ χθονός.

[6] Hdt. i. 46, viii. 134.   [7] Aesch. *Eum.* 763 ff.   [8] Eur. *Heracl.* 1032-4.

humiliation is shown at the beginning of the play when he says to
Antigone:

> Who will receive the wandering Oedipus
> To-day with scanty pittance? For I ask
> For little, and yet even less than that
> Do I receive, but it suffices me.[1]

Yet it is this old beggar whom the gods have chosen to be almost
of their company, to receive special honours and to have superhuman powers. The paradox is plain, and Sophocles does not
neglect it. The Chorus, who in this play represent ordinary
uninstructed opinion, shrink in horror from him when they know
who he is, unable to utter anything but cries of stupefied amazement (220 ff.). Even when Oedipus says that he brings them help
(288 ff.), they are still afraid (292 ff.), and leave the decision to
their king. Of course they do not understand what Oedipus
means, and some time later they still dwell with horrified curiosity
on his past (510 ff.). These interchanges between them and
Oedipus emphasize the paradox of his destiny. He who excites
such consternation among ordinary men is fated to receive peculiar
honour and power. The Chorus fail at first to grasp the full
significance of what is in store for him. Even Theseus has some
difficulty in grasping it. In men's eyes Oedipus is hated by the
gods because he has broken their laws, and it is difficult to
believe that they have chosen him for a hero. Yet they have, and
this must be set beyond all doubt. For such an act the gods have
their reasons, and these Sophocles; in due course, conveys.

The heroization of Oedipus is an amends for his past sufferings.
The Chorus eventually see this and say:

> Though many woes came to him
> To no purpose once,
> Yet God in just requital will exalt him.[2]

Though the gods have inflicted many sorrows on Oedipus, they
will now exalt him because they are just. Oedipus himself says
nothing of this, but these words come at so important a place that
we are bound to pay attention to them and accept them as at
least a partial explanation of what happens. And this recompense

[1] 3–6   τίς τὸν πλανήτην Οἰδίπουν καθ' ἡμέραν
τὴν νῦν σπανιστοῖς δέξεται δωρήμασιν,
σμικρὸν μὲν ἐξαιτοῦντα, τοῦ σμικροῦ δ' ἔτι
μεῖον φέροντα, καὶ τόδ' ἐξαρκοῦν ἐμοί;

[2] 1565–7   πολλῶν γὰρ ἂν καὶ μάταν
πημάτων ἱκνουμένων
πάλιν σφε δαίμων δίκαιος αὔξοι.

is not uncharacteristic of the gods. Pindar regards the apotheosis of Heracles as a reward for his labours,[1] and though these are not like the woes of Oedipus, his destiny shows that the gods reward those who have been subjected to heavy trials. Even Euripides recognizes that the gods make amends for suffering, when his Artemis says to the dying Hippolytus:

> To you, unhappy one, for all these woes
> High honours I shall give in Troezen town,[2]

and tells of the cult that shall be his after death. Oedipus differs from Heracles and Hippolytus in that his sufferings entail pollution and the hatred of the gods. But even in such cases they might show mercy and grant amends. Tlepolemus killed Licymnius in a fit of rage, fled to Rhodes, and there eventually received divine honours as a

> Sweet amends for pitiful misfortune.[3]

His case shows that the pollution of bloodshed was no obstacle to heroization. So, too, the athlete Cleomedes of Astypalaea, who killed his man in a boxing-match, went mad, and destroyed a school with sixty children in it, was none the less honoured as a god.[4] The audience would understand that the gods make amends to Oedipus and accept heroization as his due. But it is not the whole explanation. Not all who suffer become heroes. To win such a reward there must be something else in Oedipus which deserves special treatment from the gods, something in his nature which qualifies him to be a hero.

What distinguishes a hero from ordinary men is his superior power. This may be displayed in many ways, commonly of course in battle or government, but also in athletics or healing or prophecy or song. If anyone displays a really superior eminence in one of these, he may show that he is above other men, that he is that strange being 'which is neither man nor god and is both',[5] a hero. Oedipus is such. In the past he was a great deliverer and a great king. In his years of wandering he has endured his privations with more than common patience (7–8). Above all, there is something about him which inspires respect and awe. Despite his sightless

---

[1] *Nem.* i. 70.
[2] *Hipp.* 1423–5 σοὶ δ', ὦ ταλαίπωρ', ἀντὶ τῶνδε τῶν κακῶν
          τιμὰς μεγίστας ἐν πόλει Τροζηνίᾳ
          δώσω.
[3] Pind. *Ol.* vii. 77 λύτρον συμφορᾶς οἰκτρᾶς γλυκύ.   [4] Paus. vi. 9.
[5] Luc. *Dial. Mort.* 3. 2 ὃ μήτε ἄνθρωπός ἐστι μήτε θεὸς καὶ συναμφότερόν ἐστιν.

eyes and his beggar's garb, his essential nobility is immediately manifest. The Stranger says that he is

> Noble to look on, save in destiny.[1]

He himself has already told how his nobility has helped him to endure his vagrant life (8). There is also something formidable in him,

> Dread his appearance, dread is his voice.[2]

As each crisis arises he deals with it in a spirit of firm decision and high authority. He demands of the Chorus that he shall meet their king (302). When Theseus comes, he treats him as an equal and is recognized as such by him. His daughters are devoted to him and serve him with reverent loyalty; even his rebellious son Polynices is first terrified by his silence, then overwhelmed and broken by his curse. When the signs from heaven call him, he acts with immediate resolve. He is still the old Oedipus, high-tempered and passionate, though he calls himself 'a miserable phantom' (110). Like Ajax or Heracles, he has those superior qualities which win respect and awe. Because of them he is entitled to become a hero.

Some might find it strange that a man who killed his father and married his mother, who has been 'godless', can yet become a kind of divine being. Yet in practice the Greeks seem to have felt little difficulty in this. The blood-guilty Tlepolemus and Cleomedes were still worshipped; the impious Bellerophon had a cult at Corinth,[3] and the impious Ajax Oileus at Opus,[4] though both were destroyed by the gods. Acts of bloodshed or of impiety did not prevent a man from becoming a hero if he had sufficient power and the right kind of pre-eminence. Yet Sophocles saw that the difficulty might be felt and took pains to establish the real innocence of Oedipus. The first hint comes from Antigone, who tells the men of Colonus that her father's acts were involuntary (240). When they still hesitate about welcoming him, Oedipus himself explains that he is not to blame:

> My deeds have been
> More what was done to me than what I did,[5]

and that he is not 'base by nature' (270). He dwells on the same point in his lyrical interchange with them (530 ff.) and makes an

---

[1] 76   γενναῖος, ὡς ἰδόντι, πλὴν τοῦ Δαίμονος.
[2] 141   Δεινὸς μὲν ὁρᾶν, Δεινὸς Δὲ κλύειν.
[3] Paus. ii. 2. 4.   [4] Pind. Ol. ix. 112.
[5] 266–7   τά γ' ἔργα μου
πεπονθότ' ἐστὶ μᾶλλον ἢ Δεδρακότα.

even more comprehensive defence to Creon (962–94). So far
from admitting any responsibility for his misfortunes, he now
places the whole blame on the gods:

> For so the gods ordained,
> Perhaps from some old wrath against my race.[1]

He himself acted in ignorance (983) and unwillingly (987).
The audience, familiar with Athenian law, would recognize his
claim to be innocent in law and morals. Sophocles seems to
have thought that some might still misunderstand the nature of
Oedipus' pollution and think him a criminal. He takes care to
clear their minds.

In *King Oedipus* the essential moral innocence of Oedipus is also
assumed, though with far less emphasis. But he is a polluted
being, a creature defiled and hateful to the gods. It makes no
difference that he acted in ignorance; the pollution is on him, and
he must rid himself of it. So in *Oedipus at Colonus* Sophocles must
transcend this breach between Oedipus and the gods. He does so
quietly but emphatically. When Oedipus comes to Colonus, he
tells the Chorus:

> Holy and reverent I come.[2]

We can only guess what he means. He does not say that he has
been purified as Attic law demanded that homicides should be.[3]
These rites were performed when the polluted person came home
after a period of exile, and we might think that since Oedipus
cannot return to Thebes, he cannot perform them. In that case
his exile is enough. But such an explanation is too artificial for the
text. Sophocles solves the problem in a more dexterous and more
radical way. Though Oedipus still feels himself in some sense
polluted when he tells Theseus that he is one

> In whom what stain of sin
> Has not its dwelling?[4]

that is no more than a natural feeling, a memory of the hideous
sense of uncleanness which once was his and still, naturally enough,
haunts him. What matters is that Oedipus, who was at enmity
with Apollo and the Erinyes, is now at peace with them. Apollo

[1] 964–5   θεοῖς γὰρ ἦν οὕτω φίλον,
τάχ' ἄν τι μηνίουσιν ἐς γένος πάλαι.
[2] 287   ἥκω γὰρ ἱερὸς εὐσεβής τε.
[3] Dem. xxiii. 72–3.
[4] 1133–4   ᾧ τίς οὐκ ἔνι
κηλὶς κακῶν ξύνοικος;

has ordained his end and brought him to Colonus (86, 102); the
Erinyes rule in the grove where he knows that Apollo's prophecy
will be fulfilled. When Oedipus hears that the grove is theirs, he
prays that they will receive him graciously (44). Then he asks
them not to be hard-hearted to him (86); he knows that some
omen has guided him to them (97); he begs them to help his end
(101–3). Then he closes with a final prayer:

> Hear, you sweet daughters of primeval night.
> Hear, city called by mighty Pallas' name,
> Athens most honoured of all towns that are,
> Have pity on this poor wraith of Oedipus;
> 'Tis not the body that I had of old.[1]

When he associates the Erinyes with Athens, he honours them as
the Eumenides. They are now not ministers of vengeance but
succourers of the oppressed, not enemies but 'sweet'. Since
Oedipus comes by Apollo's design, the Erinyes welcome him and
make their peace with him. It is fitting that his end should come
in the holy place of the dread powers who once harried and pursued him. It is a sign that his pollution is cleansed, his enmity
with divine powers turned to friendship. And the physical em-
blem of this change is his own aged and wasted body. The old
polluted flesh has gone, and its defilement with it.

The peace which Oedipus makes with the Dread Goddesses is
marked by a ritual act. At the suggestion of the Chorus (466),
Ismene carries out rites to appease the Goddesses for trespassing in
their holy place. Its effect is to seal the reconciliation between
them and Oedipus, and that is no doubt why Sophocles describes
each stage in it so carefully. First, water must be fetched in clean
hands from a running spring (469–70). Water was 'undefiled'[2]
and commonly used for purification.[3] Next, the ritual bowls must
be crowned with the freshly shorn wool of a lamb (472–5); for the
wool takes into itself the harmful pollution. Then Ismene must
face the East and make libation (477); for the East is the source of
light and purity, and all who purified themselves faced it,[4] just
as those who cursed turned to the West.[5] The first two libations are
of water, the third of water and honey but no wine (481); for the

---

[1] 106–10   ἴτ’, ὦ γλυκεῖαι παῖδες ἀρχαίου Σκότου,
             ἴτ’, ὦ μεγίστης Παλλάδος καλούμεναι
             πασῶν Ἀθῆναι τιμιωτάτη πόλις,
             οἰκτίρατ’ ἀνδρὸς Οἰδίπου τόδ’ ἄθλιον
             εἴδωλον· οὐ γὰρ δὴ τό γ’ ἀρχαῖον δέμας.

[2] Aesch. Pers. 578.   [3] Empedocl. fr. 143.
[4] Cratin. fr. 232.   [5] 'Lys.' vi. 51.

Erinyes do not drink wine,[1] but honey is the proper offering to the dead.[2] Finally sprays of olive must be spread on the ground (483-4); for the olive, too, cleanses from pollution and is sacred to the gods of the Underworld.[3] The elaborate ceremony concludes with a prayer to the Eumenides;

> With friendly hearts
> Receive the suppliant and keep him safe.[4]

More is asked than that the Goddesses should not be angry for trespass on their ground. They are asked to welcome and protect Oedipus because he is a suppliant. The rite shows that he makes his peace with them in the correct form and that they will accept him.

Oedipus' body will protect Athens which receives it, reward his helpers and friends in their time of need, and harm those who have cast him out, notably the Thebans. But the situation is complicated by another oracle, reported by Ismene, which says that if Oedipus lies in Thebes he will help it as otherwise he would help Athens:

> Some day its habitants will search for you,
> Dead or alive, to bring deliverance.[5]

What counts is the presence and possession of the body; whoever has it will benefit by it. In this Sophocles touches on a belief not unfamiliar to his time. The Greeks, like the men of the Middle Ages, attached great importance to the possession of certain relics. For this reason Creon is eager to secure Oedipus dead or alive and attempts to do so by fraud. Herodotus' account of the discovery of the bones of Orestes in the sixth century shows how important such a body might be. For he explains that before the discovery Sparta was unsuccessful in her wars against Tegea, but after it all went well.[6] When Cimon discovered the bones of Theseus on Scyros, they were thought to be a great addition to the national strength, and their arrival in Athens was celebrated by the dedication of a special temple for them.[7] Since their discovery was followed by the subjugation of Scyros, it is natural to assume that their loss was as great to Scyros as their gain was to Athens. When the Athenians went to Amphipolis, they were advised by an oracle to secure the bones of Rhesus from the Troad if they wished to succeed.[8] What

---

[1] Aesch. *Eum.* 107.　　　　[2] *Il.* xxiii. 170.　　　　[3] Artemid. iv. 57.

[4] 486-7　　　　　　　ἐξ εὐμενῶν
στέρνων δέχεσθαι τὸν ἱκέτην σωτηρίους.

[5] 389-90　　　σὲ τοῖς ἐκεῖ ζητητὸν ἀνθρώποις ποτὲ
θανόντ' ἔσεσθαι ζῶντά τ' εὐσοίας χάριν.

[6] Hdt. i. 68-9.　　　[7] Plut. *Cim.* 8, *Thes.* 36.　　　[8] Polyaen. vi. 53.

mattered with such relics was the possession of them. The dead man need not have had any previous connexion with the city to which he was brought nor even to have been its friend. It was natural that Thebes should, after the oracle, wish to get Oedipus within its boundaries. His presence would be a protection and prevent hostile Athens from being strengthened by a superhuman ally.

The fate in store for Oedipus is that of a protecting hero or *daimôn*. Xenophon believed that when Greece fought 'all the barbarians in the world', it was through her heroes that she triumphed.[1] A hero was remarkable for his loyalty to the land which he guarded. He was a faithful friend and a relentless enemy, in private as in public matters. He illustrated in a vivid form the Greek view that a man should spare nothing to help his friends and to harm his enemies. With rare exceptions this was a fundamental tenet of Greek ethics. Virtue was sometimes thought to consist of 'surpassing in doing good to friends and evil to enemies',[2] and the devotion which such an ideal aroused may be seen in 'Theognis'' prayer that the skies may fall on him

> If I should fail to succour those that love me
> Or to trouble and confound my foes.[3]

To the correct Isocrates it was equally disgraceful 'to be surpassed by enemies in ill-doing and by friends in good'.[4] Conversely, if a man failed to act like this, it was held to his great discredit, so that 'Lysias' condemns Andocides because 'this is his way, to do no evil to his enemies but whatever evil he can to his friends'.[5] What an ordinary man was expected to do, a hero did with superior force and power. The saga of the Persian Wars abounded with cases of heroes at Athens or Delphi or Aegina who had helped to inflict disaster on the enemy. Athens will have such a hero in Oedipus.

This capacity for loyalty and for enmity was no less clear in private matters. Heroes were brutal to those who opposed or offended them. Such violence might be expended on a whole country, as when Minos sent a pestilence to Crete because his death was not avenged,[6] or it might be confined to a small area, as at

---

[1] *Cyn.* i. 17.

[2] Xen. *Mem.* ii. 6. 35 νικᾶν τοὺς μὲν φίλους εὖ ποιοῦντα, τοὺς δὲ ἐχθροὺς κακῶς.

[3] Theogn. 871–2 εἰ μὴ ἐγὼ τοῖσιν μὲν ἐπαρκέσω οἵ με φιλεῦσιν
τοῖς δ' ἐχθροῖς ἀνίη καὶ μέγα πῆμ' ἔσομαι.

[4] Isocr. i. 26 τῶν ἐχθρῶν νικᾶσθαι κακοποιίαις καὶ τῶν φίλων ἡττᾶσθαι ταῖς εὐεργεσίαις.

[5] 'Lys.' vi. 7 τέχνην ταύτην ἔχει, τοὺς μὲν ἐχθροὺς μηδὲν ποιεῖν κακόν, τοὺς δὲ φίλους ὅτι ἂν δύνηται κακόν. [6] Hdt. vii. 169–71.

Tanagra Eunostus, who had lost his life through a woman, would allow no woman to come near his grove and grave.[1] The power of heroes to do harm was so well known that the proverb 'I am not one of those heroes'[2] was used by a man who wished to declare his goodwill. So it is with Oedipus. He knows that with his body he brings a gift to Athens that will help it and hurt Thebes which has driven him out:

> I come to dwell, with profit to my hosts
> And bane to those who drove me from my home[3]

and tells the Chorus that if they welcome him:

> For this city you shall win
> A mighty saviour, and troubles for my foes.[4]

He wishes to benefit Athens and to harm Thebes. But his motives for both are personal. Athens has received him, Thebes has driven him out. A whole country must suffer benefit or harm because of what some individuals have done. Oedipus will punish Thebes because he cherishes resentment against his sons and Creon; he will help Athens because Theseus welcomes him. When their pride is insulted, gods are no respecters of persons, as Pindar knew when he told how Apollo and Artemis destroyed Coronis for being unfaithful and with her many other, doubtless innocent, people:

> Much is the timber on the hillside
> That fire destroys, leaping from a single seed.[5]

Such is the destruction which an evil act may bring. For as Hesiod says,

> Often a whole city reaps the recompense of a sinner.[6]

So Oedipus will not confine his help to Theseus nor his punishment to his sons and Creon. Athens will gain from his presence and Thebes be harmed. His motives, like his actions, are those of an authentic hero.

The presence of Oedipus at Colonus shows the signs of a great event. He himself is prepared for it; the gods have guided him to the destined place. But the actual process, so strange to ordinary experience, must be convincing and real. Sophocles presents it

---

[1] Plut. *Qu. Gr.* 40.   [2] Zenob. v. 60.

[3] 92–3   κέρδη μὲν οἰκήσαντα τοῖς δεδεγμένοις,
           ἄτην δὲ τοῖς πέμψασιν οἵ μ' ἀπήλασαν.

[4] 459–60   τῇδε τῇ πόλει μέγαν
       σωτῆρ' ἀρεῖσθε, τοῖς δ' ἐμοῖς ἐχθροῖς πόνους.

[5] Pind. *Pyth.* iii. 36–7   πολλὰν δ' ὄρει πῦρ ἐξ ἑνὸς
       σπέρματος ἐνθορὸν ἀΐστωσεν ὕλαν.

[6] *Op.* 240 πολλάκι καὶ ξύμπασα πόλις κακοῦ ἀνδρὸς ἐπαυρεῖ.

both directly and indirectly. The Messenger describes the passing of Oedipus in a speech unequalled even by Sophocles for mystery and grandeur, but the whole play illuminates what a hero is. The scenes between Oedipus' arrival at Colonus and his passing illustrate a hero's character. In them he seems to find his new powers and to show them, sometimes in an extreme form. His relations with his daughters and with his son, with Creon and with Theseus, show the powerful extremes of his nature in love and hatred, in repugnance and gratitude. He bears the marks of his new state. He is not the man we knew in *King Oedipus*, though he is not entirely different from him. We can believe that his sufferings, the passage of years, his new sense of power, have changed him. But what matters is not his likeness nor his unlikeness to his former self, but what he is now. From the moment when he knows that he has reached the place of his passing he is filled with strength and confidence. The divine will sustains him and makes him exercise his new power. In the play we must look on him as one who, without fully understanding his destiny, yet shows that he is already on the way to a half-divine state and is moved by potent impulses such as belong to a hero.

This new strength may be seen in Oedipus' relations with his daughters and with his son. The contrast between his love for the first and his hatred for the second is absolute. He shows the limits of his nature in his devotion to those who have tended and accompanied him in his troubles and in his destructive outburst against the son who has driven him out of Thebes. He is in effect the domestic hero, the presiding spirit of the family. His task is to protect his own and to be merciless to those who break domestic ties or introduce strife into the home. Oedipus, who is becoming a hero, stands in a special relation to his children. He is closely connected with the gods of kinship and comradeship.[1] It was the special duty of the males in a family to honour these gods,[2] and in some families the head might come to be honoured as a hero.[3] So Oedipus, as father and almost as protecting hero, has a special concern with his family. His domestic duties do not conflict with his national; for the fathers' gods are part of the national heritage and must be protected with it.[4] Oedipus is such a guardian. He watches over his family and is relentless against those who attempt to destroy its unity.

Oedipus' ties with his daughters are peculiarly intimate; for

---

[1] Xen. *Hell.* ii. 4. 21.   [2] Eur. fr. 318.

[3] Paus. i. 26. 6; schol. *O.C.* 489.   [4] Aesch. *Pers.* 400 ff.

they have shared his sufferings with him. When the daughters of Scedasus were assailed by Spartans, their father killed himself on their grave and cherished wrath against the assailers and their descendants, so that when Epaminondas was at Leuctra, where their tomb was, he offered prayers and offerings in the belief that they would help him against Sparta.[1] This close intimacy in suffering between father and daughters resembles that between Oedipus and Antigone and Ismene. Nothing in the play is so touching as the old man's love for his daughters. We see it as he enters supported by Antigone, and it lasts to the lament which she and Ismene make for him at the end of the play. This love has been strengthened by the sacrifices made by each daughter, Antigone in accompanying Oedipus in his wanderings:

> In the savage wood
> Wandering often, starving and unshod,
> By many showers of rain and scorching suns
> Sore troubled;[2]

and Ismene in the risks which she takes in riding from Thebes to tell of the plot against him (353–6). No wonder that he stresses their unlikeness to other women and compares them to Egyptian women who work for a living while the men sit indoors (337–45). This neat piece of anthropology comes from Herodotus,[3] but it is not a mere titbit of picturesque information. It shows how unwomanly Antigone and Ismene are if judged by Greek standards; it emphasizes the peculiar way of life to which their devotion has brought them; it is a tribute to their loyalty and affection, to the bonds which unite father and daughters. The hero, true to his own type, knows their full worth and is deeply grateful to them.

Oedipus repays his daughters with a love no less than theirs for him. His delight on seeing Ismene, his anguish when she and Antigone are carried off, show the strength of his affection. He speaks with touching gratitude of what they have done for him and compares them more than favourably with their brothers:

> Now these protect me, these look after me,
> No women they, but men, who share my toils.[4]

[1] Plut. *Pelop.* 20; Paus. ix. 13. 5.

[2] 348–51
> πολλὰ μὲν κατ' ἀγρίαν
> ὕλην ἄσιτος νήλιπός τ' ἀλωμένη,
> πολλοῖσι δ' ὄμβροις ἡλίου τε καύμασι
> μοχθοῦσα.

[3] Hdt. ii. 35.

[4] 1367–8
> νῦν δ' αἵδε μ' ἐκσῴζουσιν, αἵδ' ἐμαὶ τροφοί,
> αἵδ' ἄνδρες, οὐ γυναῖκες, ἐς τὸ συμπονεῖν.

He sums up his affection for them when he takes his farewell:

> One thing alone,
> A single word redeems this suffering.
> For never have you had such love as you
> Have had from me. Now robbed of it
> You shall live out your lives' remaining days.[1]

The love that he has had for them in the past must make up for
his loss. It is not a very great consolation, but it is true to life and
to the heart. Such a memory is a possession which cannot be
taken away. To Ismene the loss of Oedipus is almost beyond
consolation. She wishes to die:

> May Hades the Destroyer
> Take me and join me in death
> To my old father,
> Such grief is mine.[2]

But Antigone shows greater wisdom and implicitly corrects her.
She will be content to love and remember Oedipus, though he has
been taken:

> Though below earth night for ever encompass you,
> Though far away, yet you never shall lack
> My love and hers.[3]

The affection between Oedipus and his daughters will continue
after death.

In vivid contrast to Oedipus' love for his daughters is his anger,
even hatred, against his sons. The epic told that they grossly insulted him and he cursed them,[4] and that this curse led to their
deaths at one another's hands. It is possible that the *Thebaid* made
Oedipus act in a mad fury as Aeschylus did,[5] but by Greek
standards he was right. His sons had seized his power, and to this
injury they added the insult of offering him rotten pieces of sacri-
ficial meat.[6] The curse belonged to the saga, but Sophocles gives

---

[1] 1615–19   ἀλλ' ἐν γὰρ μόνον
τὰ πάντα λύει ταῦτ' ἔπος μοχθήματα.
τὸ γὰρ φιλεῖν οὐκ ἔστιν ἐξ ὅτου πλέον
ἢ τοῦδε τἀνδρὸς ἔσχεθ', οὗ τητώμεναι
τὸν λοιπὸν ἤδη τοῦ βίου διάξετον.

[2] 1689–92   κατά με φόνιος
'Αΐδας ἕλοι πατρὶ
ξυνθανεῖν γεραιῷ
τάλαιναν.

[3] 1701–3   ὦ τὸν ἀεὶ κατὰ γᾶς σκότον εἱμένος,
οὐδέ γ' ἀπὼν ἀφίλητος ἐμοί ποτε
καὶ τᾷδε μὴ κυρήσῃς.

[4] *Thebais*, fr. 2 Allen.   [5] *Sept.* 781 ff.   [6] *Thebais*, fr. 3.

it a new shape. He says nothing about the insult; he postpones the curse to the end of Oedipus' life and transfers it from Thebes to Colonus; he makes its cause the expulsion of Oedipus by his sons from Thebes. In the epic the curse preceded and caused the brothers' strife; Sophocles assumes that this has already begun. Ismene tells how the sons have shown their evil natures some time before their father's wrath turns on them:

> Now from some god and sinful soul has come
> An evil strife on those thrice hapless ones,
> To seize the government and kingly rule.[1]

When Oedipus pronounces his curse, it prevents this strife from having a peaceful issue. The sons have had their chance and missed it. They have shown their wickedness and are not to be pitied when they find their doom. Sophocles' postponement of the curse makes it more just and more terrible. The hostility which Oedipus feels for his sons is the reverse side of his heroic nature, the capacity for hate which balances his capacity for love. In this, too, he is the domestic hero, the avenger of wrongs done to the family which he rules. His sternness may appear harsh, but it is true to his daemonic destiny.

The angry father curses Polynices. Yet Polynices may not seem to deserve all that he gets. He comes humbly as a suppliant. He feels sorrow for his father's hapless and squalid plight (1254–61). He has some claim against his brother who is younger than he is and has driven him out of his kingdom (1295–7). He has an air of right when he asks Oedipus for help in punishing Eteocles and regaining his throne (1326–30). There is no reason to suspect his sincerity when he says that if Eteocles is defeated he will re-establish Oedipus in his own home (1342). He seems even to be sorry for his harsh treatment of Oedipus in the past and to be willing to make amends. Such at least is the natural meaning of his words:

> But on the throne of Zeus beside him sits
> Mercy in all he does, and, father, let
> Her stand by you. 'Tis possible to heal
> Old faults of mine; I cannot make them worse.[2]

[1] 371–3   νῦν δ' ἐκ θεῶν του κἀλιτηρίου φρενὸς
εἰσῆλθε τοῖν τρὶς ἀθλίοιν ἔρις κακή,
ἀρχῆς λαβέσθαι καὶ κράτους τυραννικοῦ.

[2] 1267–70   ἀλλ' ἔστι γὰρ καὶ Ζηνὶ σύνθακος θρόνων
Αἰδὼς ἐπ' ἔργοις πᾶσι, καὶ πρὸς σοί, πάτερ,
παρασταθήτω. τῶν γὰρ ἡμαρτημένων
ἄκη μέν ἐστι, προσφορὰ δ' οὐκ ἔστ' ἔτι.

He hopes that his father will show mercy to him, and so heal his faults. It would have been easy for Sophocles to put Polynices entirely in the wrong, to make him the wanton provoker of Eteocles and the vengeful enemy of his own city. But he has not done this—on purpose, as he shows by making Polynices the elder brother (1295)[1] and rightful king (1294). He gives him a good case that Oedipus' anger may be all the more striking.

Before Polynices appears, before it is known that he is coming, Oedipus has made up his mind about him. When Ismene tells him of the second prophecy and of his son's knowledge of it, he says:

> May the gods never quench this fated strife
> Of theirs, and may it fall to me to make
> Decision in this battle which their hands
> Are clutching after with uplifted spears.[2]

He means to doom both his sons with a father's curse, and soon we know why—because they did not help him when he was driven out from Thebes (427–30). He thinks that if they had uttered a word on his behalf he would not have been sent into exile (443–4). But they did nothing. They have sacrificed their father to their own lust for power:

> Instead of me, their father, they chose thrones,
> The sceptre's sway and monarchy of lands.[3]

For this reason Oedipus will never consent to help them. The same spirit moves him when he rejects Creon's demand that he should go to Thebes. He wishes to punish Thebes and with it his sons:

> My sons shall have enough of my own land
> For an inheritance in which to die.[4]

So, when he hears that Polynices has come as a suppliant to Athens, he is still full of hatred for him:

> My hated son, o king, whose words would vex
> My ears as words could from no other man.[5]

---

[1] Aeschylus seems to make the brothers twins (*Sept.* 576, 890, 933 ff.), and Euripides makes Polynices the younger (*Phoen.* 71). Cf. Apollod. iii. 6. 1.

[2] 421–4 ἀλλ' οἱ θεοί σφιν μήτε τὴν πεπρωμένην
ἔριν κατασβέσειαν, ἐν ᾿ ἐμοὶ τέλος
αὐτοῖν γένοιτο τῆσ᾿ε τῆς μάχης πέρι,
ἧς νῦν ἔχονται κἀπαναίρονται ᾿όρυ.

[3] 448–9 τὼ ᾿ ἀντὶ τοῦ φύσαντος εἱλέσθην θρόνους
καὶ σκῆπτρα κραίνειν καὶ τυραννεύειν χθονός.

[4] 789–90 ἔστιν ᾿ὲ παισὶ τοῖς ἐμοῖσι τῆς ἐμῆς
χθονὸς λαχεῖν τοσοῦτον, ἐνθανεῖν μόνον.

[5] 1173–4 παῖς οὑμός, ὦναξ, στυγνός, οὗ λόγων ἐγὼ
ἄλγιστ' ἂν ἀν᾿ρῶν ἐξανασχοίμην κλύων.

We are well prepared for what will happen when father and son meet.

Polynices entreats his father with a moving tale of misfortune, but Oedipus is grimly and stonily silent. The long silence of Aeschylus' Niobe, which so impressed Aristophanes, or of Achilles in the *Phrygians*,[1] cannot have been more agonizing than the fierce determined silence of Oedipus. Polynices, wild to the point of despair, stakes all on his father's help. With short panic-stricken sentences he tries to get him to speak. When he fails, he asks his sisters if they cannot move

The obdurate and unrelenting lips[2]

of the old man. But Antigone's gentle intercession fails (1280-3). Then Polynices tells his long, dismal tale and begs his father for help. At the end of it, after a word of commendation from the Chorus, Oedipus speaks. He would not have spoken if Theseus had not sent Polynices to him, but since he has, he will speak (1348-51). What follows is not what might be expected after such an opening. The burden of it is that since Polynices drove his father out of Thebes, he cannot expect any help from him. And this blank refusal is delivered with an appalling violence. Oedipus calls his son 'most evil' (1354), his murderer (1361), no son of his (1369). Then he lays his curse on him, saying what he has already said to others. He sends him away:

And you, abhorred, unfathered, get you gone,
Vilest of vile, and take with you this curse
That I call on you.[3]

He shall never see his home again but be overwhelmed by the Furies and by Ares, the god of destruction, and his brother shall share his ruin (1391-6). Oedipus' curse on the murderer of Laius is less violent than this fearful destructive outburst. No wonder that at the end of it the Chorus tell Polynices that there is nothing for him to do but go away in his misery.

To understand why Oedipus shows this unforgiving and unrelenting anger against Polynices we must consider what the Greeks thought about a son's duty to a father. It was an Unwritten Law that a son should honour his parents, and this took a concrete form

---

[1] *Ran.* 912 cum scholl.
[2] 1277   τὸ δυσπρόσοιστον κἀπροσήγορον στόμα.
[3] 1383-5   σὺ δ' ἔρρ' ἀπόπτυστός τε κἀπάτωρ ἐμοῦ,
κακῶν κάκιστε, τάσδε συλλαβὼν ἀρὰς
ἅς σοι καλοῦμαι.

in the laws of Athens. Solon is said to have legislated about wrongs done to parents,[1] and among his headings was failure to look after,[2] or to provide lodging for,[3] a parent. It penalized the deprivation of parents of what was due to them,[3] and a son who was convicted of maltreating his parents lost his personal rights as a citizen.[4] Plato seems to have thought that the law erred on the side of laxity and wished to make the punishment harder, to banish the offender from the country for assault[5] and to have him flogged for neglect.[6] It is clear that Polynices has failed in his duty of looking after his father. He himself admits as much when he says:

> I witness that I come the worst of men
> In care I should have given you.[7]

Though he now claims to be repentant, his motives are dubious, and his sincerity suspicious, since he wishes to secure Oedipus' help for his own political ambitions. To the impartial observer he is a bad son, condemned by the moral feeling which prompted and sustained Solon's law. Indeed his ingratitude is of a specially heinous kind. For, as Xenophon's Socrates shows, this is the only kind of ingratitude which the State punishes, and a man guilty of it is unlikely to do anything right or honourable.[8] So despite his pathos and his persuasive case Polynices is indisputably and deplorably in the wrong. His misfortunes do not obliterate his crime against his father. In fact, since ambition has moved him to treat Oedipus so callously, his misfortunes may be regarded as its direct result. On grounds of ordinary morality Oedipus has the right to condemn Polynices.

It is not the legal aspect of Polynices' behaviour that concerns Oedipus, nor strictly the moral, but the religious. Polynices has sinned against the gods. Plato says that even those who fail to rescue their parents from maltreatment by their sons are liable to the curse of Zeus who looks after kinship.[5] His view is not far removed from that of Oedipus, who supports his imprecations with appeals to higher powers. The first is

> She, revealed of old,
> Justice who sits with Zeus in ancient rule.[9]

---

[1] Dem. xxiv. 103; Aeschin. i. 28.   [2] Lys. xiii. 91.   [3] Id. xxxi. 21.
[4] Andoc. i. 74.   [5] Laws ix. 881 d.   [6] Ib. xi. 932 d.
[7] 1265–6   καὶ μαρτυρῶ κάκιστος ἀνθρώπων τροφαῖς
τᾶις σαῖσιν ἥκειν.
[8] Mem. ii. 2. 13.
[9] 1381–2   ἡ παλαίφατος
Δίκη ξύνεδρος Ζηνὸς ἀρχαίοις νόμοις.

This is the power whom Antigone invokes as her authority for burying her brother, the protective deity of right and affection in the family. Polynices has offended against her, and will be punished for it. She is the associate of Zeus in all such matters, and Oedipus' curse is like Plato's. But from this appeal to the powers of the family Oedipus advances to something stranger and more forbidding:

> May the hideous dark
> Of father Tartarus give you a home.[1]

This darkness of Tartarus, the Father, is the Chaos which preceded the making of the world, the primeval disorder of things. Oedipus sends his son to it that he may be cut off from his home and his family, from the protection which he has found in them and from the loyalties which he has violated. It is fittingly associated with the Furies, daughters of Night everlasting, and with Ares the Destroyer (1391). Oedipus condemns Polynices to uttermost destruction, to severance from the ordered life of the world, to a place in primal chaos and pain. Polynices deserves his doom because he has himself invoked the powers of destruction (1392). The hatred which he and his brother feel for one another will be their undoing. The family ties which Polynices has broken contribute to his fall. He despises his father, and is cursed by him; he hates his brother, and will die at his hand.

When Oedipus associates himself with the powers of the nether world and calls on Tartarus to carry out his curse, his authority is more than a father's. It is that of a chthonic *daimôn*. Just as heroes are sometimes born from the earth and as they return to it in death, so from this seat of the dead and darkness they draw mysterious powers. On these Oedipus, as is his right, calls. He can invoke them because he will soon be with them and because the nether powers are the special guardians of domestic sanctities. They protect the dead and the hearth. They include the Furies whom the Ghost of Clytaemnestra summons to vengeance. In this case there is no doubt, as there is with Orestes, about Polynices' deserts. Like the Chorus of the *Eumenides* who claim that they are still powerful in the sunless gloom under the earth, the curse of Oedipus is powerful because it has behind it all the power that belongs to a chthonic *daimôn*. The gods, as Plato says, listen to the curses of parents, 'for a parent lays a curse on his kin with more justice than anyone on anyone else'.[2] His instances are Oedipus,

---

[1] 1389–90 τὸ Ταρτάρου
στυγνὸν πατρῷον ἔρεβος, ὥς σ' ἀποικίσῃ.

[2] *Laws* xi. 931 c.

Amyntor, and Theseus, and though he may refer to the epic version
of Oedipus' curse, there is no doubt that he would approve of its
use and form here. Polynices deserves what he gets because his
offence against the divine laws of the family allows no excuse and
no appeal. He has on him the curse of a father who is becoming a
daimôn, and he will soon feel its appalling force.

On the other hand, neither Theseus nor Antigone shows any
hostility to Polynices. We might expect Theseus to condemn him
for his treatment of his father, and Antigone to express sorrow at
his quarrel with Eteocles. But Theseus treats Polynices with
courtesy, Antigone with affection. Their moderation throws into
harsh relief the implacable temper of Oedipus and sheds some
light on the rights and wrongs of the situation. In their own way
Theseus and Antigone act rightly. Theseus, as king of Athens, extends courtesy to a suppliant and furthers his requests; he feels that
Polynices deserves the same consideration that he has shown to
Oedipus and for the same reason (1179–80). Antigone acts as a
loving sister who wishes to save her brother from misfortune and
to heal the breach between him and his father. There is nothing
wrong in the behaviour of either. But whereas they move in a
human world and observe human rules, Oedipus moves in a different world and exercises the powers of a *daimôn*. It is for him to
punish the wrongdoer, for them to show mercy and consideration.
Heroes differed from men in being like the gods, even if their
power was less.[1] Oedipus' curse on Polynices is an exhibition of
heroic wrath against wickedness. As such it overrules any authority that might be given to the more charitable but merely human
Theseus and Antigone.

The contrast between the superhuman view of Polynices' offence
and the human view is specially marked in the difference between
Oedipus and Antigone. Like Theseus, she presses Polynices' rights
as a suppliant (1189–91). But she goes beyond this. She asks
Oedipus to abandon his wrath against his son and even thinks
that it is wrong:

> Turn your gaze from the present to the past,
> Think of your father's and your mother's wrong,
> And, seeing them, I know, you will confess
> That evil anger has an evil end.[2]

[1] Artemidor. *On.* iv. 78.

[2] 1195–8   σὺ δ' εἰς ἐκεῖνα, μὴ τὰ νῦν, ἀποσκόπει
πατρῷα καὶ μητρῷα πήμαθ' ἅπαθες,
κἂν κεῖνα λεύσσῃς, οἶδ' ἐγώ, γνώσῃ κακοῦ
θυμοῦ τελευτὴν ὡς κακὴ προσγίγνεται.

She would have him remember that in the past wrath has brought
harm to his family and to him. For the moment she seems to hope
that Oedipus may even forgive his son and cease to hate him.
When Polynices comes in tears and humility, she encourages him to
speak (1280–3). So far she acts as a woman and a sister. It is not
her business to interfere in high affairs. But when there is strife
between father and son, she tries to heal it. As in the *Antigone*, her
nature is to join not in hate but in love.[1] She does what is right in
her own eyes and in her station. But her gentle feelings are over-
ridden by the higher authority of Oedipus. Once she knows what
he thinks, she accepts the position and makes no further attempt to
persuade him. But as a sister she still has her feelings and does her
best to make Polynices turn his army back from Thebes (1416–17).
Her request is right. If Polynices does this, he will save his city
and his own life. But from pride he refuses (1418–19). He
justifies Oedipus' wrath against him, and surely the curse has
begun to work in him, to drive him to a fratricidal death. But
Antigone still does not condemn him. She still tries to use persuasion, until she sees that her efforts are hopeless and gives them
up. Though she knows that he is in the wrong, she does not cease
to care for him. She is moved by purely human emotions, but in
her state these are right. She has not the authority or the vision of
Oedipus and does not see the truth in its right perspective. On the
essential issue between Polynices and the gods Oedipus has spoken
the final word.

Just as his daughters and his son bring out the extremes of
Oedipus' character in what concerns the family, so Theseus and
Creon do in what concerns the state. Oedipus is to be a national
hero, the protector of Athens against her enemies, especially
against Thebes. The play therefore shows how he treats friends
and enemies and how they treat him. Its method is to present
Oedipus in close contact with two very different personalities.
Neither Theseus nor Creon is a lay figure. Each acts on understandable motives and is sufficiently characterized to be real, but
each also stands for something else and is a symbol or a type. Both
belong to politics; both are rulers; both are confronted with the
plight of a blind suppliant who carries a promise of great succour
to them if he stays in their land. The likeness of their circumstances is matched by the unlikeness of their characters. Like
Odysseus in the *Ajax*, Theseus is wholly admirable, a model of
courtesy and courage, who appeals at once by his obvious nobility

[1] *Ant.* 523.

and generosity; Creon, despite his years and experience, is far removed from his old self in *King Oedipus*, and is little less than a heartless, scheming villain. The complete difference in Oedipus' feelings about the two is justified by their natures and their actions.

Theseus shows his essential nobility in his greeting to Oedipus (551–68). As yet he knows nothing of any benefit that Oedipus may bring but only of his misfortunes. He welcomes him without hesitation, because he has himself known what misfortune is; therefore he will not shrink from helping a stranger:

> Now therefore from a stranger, as you are,
> I cannot turn aside, refusing help.[1]

He adds his reason; he knows that a similar fate may at any moment be his own:

> I know I am a man and that my share
> In any morrow is no more than yours.[2]

This is the language and the spirit of true modesty, but it has a special application. It is Theseus' own reason for showing courtesy to a suppliant. Suppliants were under the protection of Zeus,[3] and Theseus would anyhow show Oedipus the consideration that is due. Theseus reveals himself as a good king, like Croesus who accepted Adrastus, though he was polluted with bloodshed, and gave him his friendship. But while Croesus acted in princely generosity, Theseus acts in modesty and even in humility. He feels that he himself may some day need such a kindness. It is the principle on which Theognis advises that no man be reproached with poverty because the reproacher himself may one day be poor,[4] or Isocrates tells Demonicus 'Chide no man with his misfortune; for fortune is common to all, and the future is invisible.'[5] In Theseus this moderation is a principle of behaviour. It is based on the notion that all human life is uncertain and that the morrow may bring disaster. The old rule is given an active, practical turn. We see what modesty means when found in a noble nature and applied to a definite problem.

Theseus' welcome to Oedipus may be contrasted with the first words of the men of Colonus in the Chorus. They are appalled at Oedipus being who he is (224 ff.) and at his trespassing in the

---

[1] 565–6   ὥστε ξένον γ' ἂν οὐδέν' ὄνθ', ὥσπερ σὺ νῦν,
                ὑπεκτραποίμην μὴ οὐ συνεκσῴζειν.

[2] 567–8   ἔξοιδ' ἀνὴρ ὢν χὤτι τῆς ἐς αὔριον
                οὐδὲν πλέον μοι σοῦ μέτεστιν ἡμέρας.

[3] *Od.* ix. 270–1.   [4] Theogn. 157–8.

[5] i. 29 μηδενὶ συμφορὰν ὀνειδίσῃς· κοινὴ γὰρ ἡ τύχη καὶ τὸ μέλλον ἀόρατον.

sacred grove. They wish to drive him out of the country (264), and
Oedipus complains that Athens does not deserve her reputation
for being god-fearing (258-62); for their action in repelling him is
godless. That is why he threatens them with divine punishment:

> Remember this:
> That the gods look upon the godly man,
> And look on the ungodly; no escape
> Has yet befallen to the impious.[1]

He so impresses them that they consent to leave the decision to
Theseus (292-5). But the effect has been made. We see why some
men are unwilling to take Oedipus within their boundaries. In
their attachment to certain religious rules, their horror of parricide,
and their devotion to their own holy place, the Chorus do not see
that other religious considerations are more important, and that the
claims of a suppliant cannot be refused. Theseus knows where his
duty lies and does not trouble even to argue against doubts and
objections. He speaks for Athens, and in his unqualified welcome
to Oedipus we may perhaps catch an echo of the old Athenian
pride in welcoming strangers, when Pericles claimed that his city
observed especially those laws which protect the injured and was
open to all men,[2] or Socrates said to him that the older generations
of Athenians provided a haven when 'many injured by those
stronger than themselves took refuge with them'.[3] This spirit
informs the welcome given to suppliants in Euripides' *Sons of
Heracles* and *Suppliant Women*. Theseus acts in the traditional
spirit of Athens.

Theseus is rewarded by hearing that Oedipus brings the unique
gift of his body. At first he does not grasp the full significance of
this and thinks that Oedipus is simply asking for a burial-place.
This he grants (586), but his misunderstanding sets him on a false
trail. He does not see why Oedipus refuses to be buried in Thebes
and blames him for it:

> Fool, in misfortune anger is not meet.[4]

---

[1] 278-81   ἡγεῖσθε Δὲ
βλέπειν μὲν αὐτοὺς πρὸς τὸν εὐσεβῆ βροτῶν,
βλέπειν Δὲ πρὸς τοὺς Δυσσεβεῖς, φυγὴν Δέ του
μήπω γενέσθαι φωτὸς ἀνοσίου βροτῶν.

[2] Thuc. ii. 37. 3 and 39. 1.

[3] Xen. *Mem.* iii. 5. 12 πολλοὶ ὑπὸ κρειττόνων ὑβριζόμενοι κατέφυγον πρὸς
ἐκείνους. Cf. *Hell.* vi. 5. 45; Isocr. iv. 41 and 52, ii. 22.

[4] 592   ὦ μῶρε, θυμὸς ἐν κακοῖς οὐ ξύμφορον.

Even when he hears that the Thebans need Oedipus' presence to help them in war against Athens, he is still dubious:

> Whence should come enmity 'twixt me and them?[1]

His hesitation comes from his noble character. As king of Athens he is eager to be at peace with his neighbours and unwilling to think of a future in which Thebes shall be an enemy. Theseus has nothing in common with the restless Athenian imperialists of the fifth century. He stands for that peace of mind which the enemies of Athens, such as the Corinthians, said that the Athenians neither desired for themselves nor allowed to others.[2] He is far from Pericles, who thought that such moderation was contemptible idleness.[3] On this vexed question of Athenian politics Sophocles seems through Theseus to indicate his own position. It is that it is right for a man like Theseus to suspect no evil of his neighbours and to be at peace with them; what the gods send is another matter, Theseus will soon be corrected by Oedipus. But for the moment Theseus' moderation is right in his circumstances. He is as modest in foreign politics as any critic of Athens could desire. But his wish to remain at peace, admirable as it is, prevents him from seeing the importance of what Oedipus offers.

Oedipus answers Theseus' doubts with words of such power and beauty that they seem to pass far beyond the particular issue of the moment and to be little less than a whole view of life:

> Dear son of Aegeus, to the gods alone
> Belongs immunity from death and age:
> All else doth all-controlling time confound.
> Earth's strength decays, the body's strength decays,
> Faith dies, and faithlessness bursts into flower,
> And never does the same wind blow for long
> Steadfast from friend to friend, from town to town.[4]

Because there is a law of universal change, Thebes will turn from friendship with Athens to enmity, and then Oedipus' body will be

---

[1] 606   καὶ πῶς γένοιτ' ἂν τἀμὰ κἀκείνων πικρά;

[2] Thuc. i. 70. 9.

[3] Id. ii. 63. Cf. J. E. Finley, *Harvard Studies*, xlix (1937), pp. 45–6, and H. T. Wade-Gery, *J.H.S.* lii (1932), pp. 224–5.

[4] 607–13   ὦ φίλτατ' Αἰγέως παῖ, μόνοις οὐ γίγνεται
θεοῖσι γῆρας οὐδὲ κατθανεῖν ποτε,
τὰ δ' ἄλλα συγχεῖ πάνθ' ὁ παγκρατὴς χρόνος·
φθίνει μὲν ἰσχὺς γῆς, φθίνει δὲ σώματος,
θνῄσκει δὲ πίστις, βλαστάνει δ' ἀπιστία,
καὶ πνεῦμα ταὐτὸν οὔποτ' οὔτ' ἐν ἀνδράσιν
φίλοις βέβηκεν οὔτε πρὸς πόλιν πόλει.

of great use. The impressive cosmic argument has its special relevance. In essence it is the old Pythagorean view of the 'circle of necessity',[1] that fortune goes round like a wheel. This view has its significance for morality. It might be used as a warning against over-confidence. So Herodotus' Croesus warns Cyrus against attempting too much and appeals to 'the circle of human affairs'[2] which does not allow men to prosper for long. Pindar makes variations on the theme to Theron,[3] and in a lost play Sophocles makes some character speak of his or her fate in this way:

> But my fate circles on the shifting wheel
> Of God's reversal, and still suffers change,

and concludes that fortune changes like the moon's orb:

> And once at her bright fairest—then forthwith
> Lapses and fades, and comes to nothingness.[4]

Oedipus enriches this idea with the high poetry of its full significance, and answers Theseus' optimism with it. Theseus, being a man, is buoyed up by false hopes; Oedipus, from the height of his new powers and insight, counters him with the statement that though the gods live in undeviating order, free from old age and death, all that belongs to the world, whether physical or moral, personal or social, decays. Therefore we must not indulge in over-confidence. Oedipus sets his superhuman wisdom against Theseus' limited human vision and wins. Once Theseus hears the truth he welcomes Oedipus to Attica as a protector (631–5).

Theseus is the good king of a good city, its leader and its representative. As such he treats Oedipus well and wisely, and Oedipus is grateful. The future protecting *daimôn* feels affection for Athens which is to be his everlasting home and for the Athenian king who welcomes and promises to look after him. In polar contrast to Theseus is Creon, king of that Thebes which is the potential enemy of Athens and has driven Oedipus out. Creon differs from the self-deceived tyrant of the *Antigone* and still more from the decent citizen of *King Oedipus*. Of all Sophocles' characters he is the least attractive, the hardest of heart and the coldest of blood.

---

[1] Diog. Laert. viii. 14. The matter is fully discussed by W. Headlam in *J. Ph.* xxx, pp. 291 ff.

[2] Hdt. i. 207. 2. [3] *Ol.* ii. 21–2. Cf. *Ol.* xii. 6, *Pyth.* ii. 89, *Isthm.* iii. 18.

[4] Trs. W. Headlam.

Fr. 871. 1–2 ἀλλ' οὑμὸς ἀεὶ πότμος ἐν πυκνῷ θεοῦ
τροχῷ κυκλεῖται καὶ μεταλλάσσει φύσιν.

7–8 χὥτανπερ αὐτῆς εὐπρεπεστάτη φανῇ,
πάλιν διαρρεῖ κἀπὶ μηδὲν ἔρχεται.

Yet he is not driven by an unmotived passion for evil. He acts not for himself but for his city. His pretence of sympathy for Oedipus, his equally dishonest plea to Theseus that Athens cannot receive a parricide (943–50), his attempt to kidnap Ismene and Antigone, all reveal a base unscrupulous nature. When lies fail he resorts to violence. Yet he is not moved by self-interest or by any obvious passion of hate, revenge, or resentment. He acts in what he believes to be the best interests of Thebes of which he is king, and he even claims that he obeys orders (850–1). He, too, stands for a political idea, for the antithesis of the moderation incarnate in Athens. His attempt to secure Oedipus is dictated by the national interest of Thebes. Ismene has said this (396 ff.), and Creon's action must be judged in the light of her words. Unlike Theseus, he assumes that there will be war between Athens and Thebes, and he is ready to go to any length for his country.

Creon resembles Odysseus in the *Philoctetes* in his conviction that where public success is in question moral scruples are out of place. But while Odysseus acts for his own glory, Creon acts for the State. His point of view was naturally familiar enough in the fifth century, especially in the Peloponnesian War. Euripides dramatized it in the first version of his *Hippolytus* where such passages as

> I say you should not reverence the law
> More than necessity in times of risk,[1]

and

> Men's fortunes do not go by reverence;
> But by bold acts and hands that grasp too much
> Are all things hunted and made prisoner.[2]

show how much in the air these ideas were. But the best background for Creon's political opportunism is in Thucydides' picture of Cleon. In the Mitylenean debate Cleon expounds the nature of power, says that pity has no place in imperial matters,[3] and urges the Athenians not to yield to three things most disadvantageous to empire—pity, sentiment, and reasonableness.[4] Creon acts in this spirit. In his desire to secure Oedipus for Thebes he has no considerations of pity and decency. He acts, as the Athenians act to the Melians, on the principle that 'the strong do

[1] Eur. fr. 433　　ἔγωγέ φημι καὶ νόμον γε μὴ σέβειν
　　　　　　　　　ἐν τοῖσι Δεινοῖς τῶν ἀναγκαίων πλέον.

[2] Eur. fr. 434　　οὐ γὰρ κατ᾽ εὐσέβειαν αἱ θνητῶν τύχαι,
　　　　　　　　　τολμήμασιν Δὲ καὶ χερῶν ὑπερβολαῖς
　　　　　　　　　ἁλίσκεταί τε πάντα καὶ θηρεύεται.

[3] Thuc. iii. 37. 2.　　　　　[4] Ib. 40. 2.

what they can and the weak acquiesce'.[1] Even when he fails he
does not admit that he has been wrong, but leaves with a threat
of more evil to come (1037).

Creon can be answered both as an individual and as his
country's agent. Oedipus deals with him under the first heading,
Theseus under the second. It is significant that the coming hero
answers him on what look like purely personal grounds. Gods and
heroes take acts of wickedness as personal affronts, and Oedipus
treats Creon with the angry contempt that a divine being may
show to a man who has first insulted and then tried to deceive him.
Creon's first speech sounds generous and friendly. He claims that
Oedipus should return to Thebes which is his home, that he is
sorry for the plight of the old man and his daughters, that all
Thebans share his feelings. It is bold and deliberate deceit. But
it fails completely to deceive Oedipus. He knows that Creon is
lying:

> You come with many counterfeited words,
> A sharp edge on your tongue;[2]

that he has no intention of allowing him to live in Thebes (784-6);
that he offers

> Things fair in word, but in their substance base.[3]

He knows this partly from knowledge of Creon in the past when he
advocated that Oedipus should be expelled from Thebes (770-1),
but also by the special insight of his new powers. The god of
Delphi knew at once that Glaucus was trying to deceive him,[4] and
heroes, like gods, were often gifted with prophetic clairvoyance.
The special knowledge which Teiresias has among the shades is
typical.[5] So Oedipus knows that Creon's generosity is a mask, a
cover to make use of him. Therefore he deserves wrath. Oedipus
curses him (787 ff.) and prophesies evil to the country whose emis-
sary he is. He speaks with a special knowledge which comes from
the gods:

> Am I not wiser about Thebes than you?
> Wiser indeed, by truer teachers taught,
> By Phoebus and by Zeus himself, his sire.[6]

---

[1] Thuc. v. 89 δυνατὰ οἱ προύχοντες πράσσουσι καὶ οἱ ἀσθενεῖς ξυγχωροῦσιν.

[2] 794-5   τὸ σὸν δ᾽ ἀφῖκται δεῦρ᾽ ὑπόβλητον στόμα,
πολλὴν ἔχον στόμωσιν.

[3] 782   λόγῳ μὲν ἐσθλά, τοῖσι δ᾽ ἔργοισιν κακά.

[4] Hdt. vi. 86.   [5] *Od.* x. 495.

[6] 791-3   ἆρ᾽ οὐκ ἄμεινον ἢ σὺ τἀν Θήβαις φρονῶ;
πολλῷ γ᾽, ὅσῳπερ καὶ σαφεστέρων κλύω,
Φοίβου τε καὐτοῦ Ζηνός, ὃς κείνου πατήρ.

This, too, was a privilege of heroes. Foreknowledge of the future belongs to Oedipus because he is already more than man.

The personal character of the dispute between Oedipus and Creon may be seen especially when Creon tells Theseus that Athens will never welcome a parricide. To this Oedipus answers with a long defence of his innocence. He adds that there is no more god-fearing land than Athens (1006–7) and calls to his aid her tutelary deities (1010–13). He rebuts the charges against himself and against the land which has received him as if they were mere insults. He breaks out in anger, as a hero may whose honour has been assailed, and he knows that the gods are on his side, that they will help him and Athens:

> Wherefore I call now on these goddesses,
> I supplicate them and beseech with prayer,
> To rescue me and help me in my fight
> That you may know what men protect this town.[1]

He has a right to assume that the gods are closer to him than to Creon. For he will soon stand in a special relation to them. Not only were heroes a subordinate kind of divinity, but they were able, by intercession or some other influence, to make the gods act on their behalf and on behalf of those whom they protected. On Ceos the hero Aristaeus secured the help of Zeus in stopping a long drought,[2] and on Aegina Aeacus used his position to a similar purpose.[3] Oedipus knows that when he prays to the gods they will answer his prayer. To Creon's taunts he replies with a declaration of his own superior power. Only a hero can do this with assurance. If men pray, they have no confidence that their prayers will be granted.

Oedipus treats Creon as a hero may. But Theseus is a man and may not use the same methods or see the issues in so personal a light. He meets Creon on grounds of political and international morality. As king of Athens, he is master in his own land and gives prompt decisive orders for the recovery of Ismene and Antigone (897–903). Then he turns to Creon, and his judgement on him is highly significant; he shall be treated by his own rules and not allowed to leave Athens until his prisoners are restored (909–10). This is corrective justice on the old principle of Simonides, 'to pay

---

[1] 1010–13   ἀνθ' ὧν ἐγὼ νῦν τάσδε τὰς θεὰς ἐμοὶ
καλῶν ἱκνοῦμαι καὶ κατασκήπτω λιταῖς
ἐλθεῖν ἀρωγοὺς ξυμμάχους θ' ἵν' ἐκμάθης
οἵων ὑπ' ἀνδρῶν ἥδε φρουρεῖται πόλις.

[2] Ap. Rhod. ii. 524 ff.   [3] Isocr. ix. 14.

to each his due',[1] but it is singularly free from any thought of revenge. Theseus is content that the wrong should be righted. He realizes that Creon has insulted both him and Athens by trying to force his will on them:

> Did you believe this city had no men,
> Or was a slave, or me a nobody?[2]

This is the spirit in which Demophon in Euripides' *Sons of Heracles* refuses to yield up the suppliant who has appealed to him:

> If I allow this altar to be spoiled
> With violence by a stranger, no free land
> Shall men think mine.[3]

A king who yields to threats from a foreign power is not worthy of his name or responsibilities. But Theseus sees deeper than Demophon and strengthens his case with a general argument of some moment. He tells Creon that he has acted unworthily of himself and of his country:

> You come into a justice-loving land
> Where all is done by law, then set at naught
> This country's ordinances, loot and grab
> All that you please and lay strong hands on it.[4]

Theseus himself would never have acted in this way to Thebes, even with the best reasons in the world (924-8). What moves him is respect for the rights and laws of another city and the conviction that Athens deserves as much consideration from Thebes as she herself would show. He wishes to live and let live. He sees the cities of Greece as living 'on equal and like terms, settling justice according to their traditions',[5] and anticipates that view of an Hellenic concord and mutual respect which Isocrates displayed in his *Panegyric*, when he claimed that Athens has respected the laws

---

[1] Plat. *Rep.* i. 331 e τὸ τὰ ὀφειλόμενα ἑκάστῳ ἀποδιδόναι.

[2] 917–18   καί μοι πόλιν κένανδρον ἢ δούλην τινὰ
            ἔδοξας εἶναι, κἄμ' ἴσον τῷ μηδενί;

[3] Eur. *Heracl.* 243–5 εἰ γὰρ παρήσω τόνδε συλᾶσθαι βίᾳ
                ξένου πρὸς ἀνδρὸς βωμόν, οὐκ ἐλευθέραν
                οἰκεῖν δοκήσω γαῖαν.

[4] 913–16   ὅστις δίκαι' ἀσκοῦσαν εἰσελθὼν πόλιν
            κἄνευ νόμου κραίνουσαν οὐδέν, εἶτ' ἀφεὶς
            τὰ τῆσδε τῆς γῆς κύρι' ὧδ' ἐπεσπεσὼν
            ἄγεις θ' ἃ χρῄζεις καὶ παρίστασαι βίᾳ.

[5] Thuc. v. 79. 1. Cf. Hdt. ix. 7.

and rights of other cities, 'thinking it right to abide by agreements as if they were necessities'.[1] Theseus assumes that cities must respect each other's laws and that Creon is wrong to use violence on Attic territory.

By these different means Oedipus is revealed in his heroic power. In his love and his anger, in his gratitude for kindness and his resentment at injuries, in his power to help and to harm, in his knowledge of what will happen and of what is right, he is superior to the human beings who are in contact or conflict with him. This superiority is of force, of power. His emotions are stronger, his insight keener, his capacity to deal weal and woe more assured, than may be found in ordinary men. He deserves and demands respect. He fits Hesychius' definition of a hero as 'powerful, strong, noble, august'.[2] Through the different stresses which afflict or exalt him Oedipus shows his unusual, his daemonic stature. It grows in contrast to his former sufferings and outcast state. The insistence on his innocence, the fury which greets any doubt of it, the implicit paradox that a blind beggar is more than a fit companion for kings and the honoured guest of a great city, all underline the lesson that the gods know true nobility when it exists and reward it with its proper due. We may even fancy that Sophocles turns Oedipus' old faults to his advantage. His high temper, which before contributed to his undoing, is now an instrument of strength when he deals with Polynices and Creon. His violence in action, which led to the death of Laius, is now the militant force which will protect Athens. The forbidden and fatal tenderness for Jocasta has become an unbreakable bond with his daughters, children of incestuous wedlock. The passions, which before worked, despite themselves, against the gods, are now used by the gods for their own ends. The old disorder and conflict are replaced by a new harmony and a new strength.

With the departure of Polynices Oedipus' earthly troubles end. Creon has been frustrated, the kidnapped daughters recovered, the rebellious son sent to his doom, the hostile home of Thebes condemned. Sophocles has shown the range of Oedipus' daemonic powers; he has now to essay the even more formidable task of presenting the actual passing and end of Oedipus. When peals of thunder announce the end, Oedipus knows at once what they mean and that he must obey. The Chorus, too, know that something dread is at hand:

[1] Isocr. *Pan.* 81.
[2] Hesych. s.v. ἥρως· Δύνατος, ἰσχυρός, γενναῖος, σεμνός.

I am afraid. Never in vain
Does it crash forth, nor without dread hap.
O mighty Heaven, o Zeus![1]

The insistent thunder makes Oedipus eager to obey the divine summons at once. He delays only because he needs Theseus, and Theseus is away (1475–6, 1486–7). He feels that he cannot go without him, because he, and no one else, must know the place of passing (1522–3). When Theseus dies, he will reveal the secret to his heir, and so on in succession (1530–2). Where Oedipus lies will be known only to the hereditary rulers of Athens. If the secret comes out, the body may be removed and Athens robbed of its protector. Not even Antigone and Ismene may know where the body lies The circumstances and their consequences are unusual. A hero's grave was usually known and was the place where he was honoured. It might even be empty like that of Achilles at Elis[2] or of Teiresias at Thebes.[3] At Troezen, it is true, local authorities felt some doubt about showing the grave of Hippolytus,[4] but that was because he had been translated to the skies and hardly needed an earthly grave. The case of Oedipus is different. He is to have a resting-place, but only the king must know where it is, as at Thebes only the rulers knew where was the grave of Dirce.[5] Oedipus is primarily a national hero, and his daughters are shut out from the secret.

Oedipus' passing is no apotheosis. It is not accompanied by storms and thunderbolts. The Messenger is explicit at least about what does not happen:

No fiery-flashing thunderbolt of God
Encompassed his destruction, and no wind
Came whirling from the ocean in that hour,
But either the gods took him, or the earth
In good will opened up its lightless caves.[6]

Oedipus has not, like Amphiaraus, been swallowed up in the earth by a thunderbolt,[7] nor, like Heracles, been carried off to heaven in

---

[1] 1469–71 Δέδια τόδ᾿· οὐ γὰρ ἅλιον
ἀφορμᾷ ποτ᾿ οὐδ᾿ ἄνευ ξυμφορᾶς.
ὦ μέγας αἰθήρ, ὦ Ζεῦ.

[2] Paus. vi. 23. 3.   [3] Id. ix. 18. 4.   [4] Id. ii. 32. 1.   [5] Plut. *Gen. Soc.* 5.

[6] 1658–62 οὐ γάρ τις αὐτὸν οὔτε πυρφόρος θεοῦ
κεραυνὸς ἐξέπραξεν οὔτε ποντία
θύελλα κινηθεῖσα τῷ τότ᾿ ἐν χρόνῳ,
ἀλλ᾿ ἤ τις ἐκ θεῶν πομπός, ἢ τὸ νερτέρων
εὔνουν Διαστὰν γῆς ἀλάμπετον βάθρον.

[7] Pind. *Nem.* ix. 24–5.

a storm.[1] He has gone below, and some god has accompanied him or the earth has opened to receive him. The Chorus have rightly foreseen his end:

> Down to the all-concealing
> Plain of the dead and the Stygian dwelling.[2]

The actual passing is mysterious, and what follows is no less. The poet is studiously vague and makes no clear statement about either. On the one hand, Oedipus seems to think that he will die since he speaks of his corpse (621), Antigone assumes that he has died (1706, 1714), and even the Messenger refers to him as having perished (1656). On the other hand, Theseus never says that Oedipus dies, and the Messenger hints that he has passed alive into earth (1661) and says that he simply disappeared:

> We saw
> Oedipus nowhere in the neighbourhood.[3]

The Chorus take up the idea:

> The unseen places took him,
> Carried off in a sightless doom.[4]

His disappearance is in fact 'marvellous' (1665), and nothing is known of its details except to Theseus, who will say nothing. There is a mystery without an answer. What matters is that Oedipus, whether dead or alive, is now powerful in the Underworld. His passing is a miracle. Theseus, who is the only living being to have seen it, is found shrouding his eyes after it:

> As if some awful thing
> Had happened that no eyes could look upon.[5]

Such an event is not for human sight or understanding.

This mysterious climax is preceded by other wonders. Once Oedipus hears the thunder and knows that the end is near, he overcomes his blindness. He knows that now he can find his own way:

---

[1] Apollod. *Bibl.* ii. 7. 7.

[2] 1564–5
  τὰν παγκευθῆ κάτω
  νεκύων πλάκα καὶ Στύγιον Δόμον.

[3] 1648–9
  ἐξαπείδομεν
  τὸν ἄνδρα τὸν μὲν οὐδαμοῦ παρόντ' ἔτι.

[4] 1681–2
  ἄσκοποι δὲ πλάκες ἔμαρψαν
  ἐν ἀφανεῖ τινι μόρῳ φερόμενον.

[5] 1651–2
  ὡς δεινοῦ τινος
  φόβου φανέντος οὐδ' ἀνασχετοῦ βλέπειν.

Myself shall be the guide now to the place
With none to lead or hold me[1]

and soon after we hear how he went:

He had no friend to guide his steps
But was himself the guide to all of us.[2]

The sightless vision which guides Oedipus is not merely a special privilege, a means to accomplish his destined end. It is an amends for his years of blindness and a forecast of the new vision which is to be his. When he moves without a guide, we cannot but recall how when he still had his sight he was led on as if by a guide to find his dead wife.[3] Again, now he says farewell to the lightless world of his blindness which he has known for so long:

O lightless daylight, mine you once have been;
For the last time my limbs have sense of you.[4]

Before, when he found the full measure of his humiliation, he took a farewell to the real light of day.[5] In his passing he reverses the process. He who was led though seeing now leads others though he is sightless; he who deprived himself of the light of day now takes leave of his own blindness. Just as his fall was furthered by some supernatural power, so his glorification is no less the work of the gods who are now beneficent.

This marvel is followed by another which shows how near the gods are. After the touching farewells between Oedipus and his daughters there is a great silence, and a voice is heard from heaven:

There was a silence. Suddenly a voice
Came summoning him, and straightway all in fear
Were shaken, and their hair stood up on end.
The god was calling him and called again:
'Oedipus, Oedipus, why do we delay
To go? Too long have you been lingering'.[6]

---

[1] 1520-1   χῶρον μὲν αὐτὸς αὐτίκ' ἐξηγήσομαι
              ἄθικτος ἡγητῆρος.

[2] 1588-9   ὑφηγητῆρος οὐδενὸς φίλων,
              ἀλλ' αὐτὸς ἡμῖν πᾶσιν ἐξηγούμενος.

[3] O.T. 1260.

[4] 1549-50   ὦ φῶς ἀφεγγές, πρόσθε πού ποτ' ἦσθ' ἐμόν,
              νῦν δ' ἔσχατόν σου τοὐμὸν ἅπτεται δέμας.

[5] O.T. 1183.

[6] 1623-8   ἦν μὲν σιωπή, φθέγμα δ' ἐξαίφνης τινὸς
              θώϋξεν αὐτόν, ὥστε πάντας ὀρθίας
              στῆσαι φόβῳ δείσαντας ἐξαίφνης τρίχας.
              καλεῖ γὰρ αὐτὸν πολλὰ πολλαχῇ θεός·
              ὦ οὗτος οὗτος, Οἰδίπους, τί μέλλομεν
              χωρεῖν; πάλαι δὴ τἀπὸ σοῦ βραδύνεται.

This recalls another famous scene of Greek tragedy. In Euripides' *Bacchants*, when the worshippers of the god gather on Cithaeron and with them is the pitiful Pentheus disguised as a woman, there is a like silence:

> Silent the sky, silent the wooded vale
> In all its leaves; no wild beast's cry was heard,[1]

and a similar divine voice from the sky:

> Out of the sky a voice, and you may guess
> 'Twas Dionysus, cried aloud.[2]

Such a silence and such voices show that the gods are displaying their power to men. They are like the noonday silence on the mountain in which Teiresias saw Pallas naked and heard her pronounce doom on him.[3] But the silence which portends doom to Pentheus or Teiresias portends glory and deliverance to Oedipus. The god who summons him regards him as a companion and wishes him to come with him on their common errand. Oedipus is not only at peace with the gods; he is almost of their company.

The passing of Oedipus is mysterious and fully intelligible only to those who are admitted, like Theseus, to the secrets of the gods. For some of the human beings who are affected by it it has a different meaning. Before it comes they are apprehensive; when it comes they are still anxious. Through the Chorus and Oedipus' daughters Sophocles shows how an event like this may appear to the ignorant or imperfectly illumined minds of those concerned. Its full significance can only be seen when all the facts are known and rightly interpreted. So when Oedipus has left the stage and his end is not yet known, the Chorus reveal their fears for him. In solemn tones they invoke the gods of death and the underworld to make his passing easy. Their opening shows with what shyness and awe they enter on their supplications:

> If it is right to invoke the Unseen Goddess
> And thee with supplications,
> Lord of the hosts of Night,
> Aïdoneus, Aïdoneus.[4]

---

[1] Eur. *Bacch.* 1084–5 σίγησε δ᾽ αἰθήρ, σῖγα δ᾽ ὕλιμος νάπη
φύλλ᾽ εἶχε, θηρῶν δ᾽ οὐκ ἂν ἤκουσας βοήν.

[2] Ib. 1078–9 ἐκ δ᾽ αἰθέρος φωνή τις, ὡς μὲν εἰκάσαι
Διόνυσος, ἀνεβόησεν.

[3] Call. *Hymn.* v. 74 ff.

[4] 1556–9   εἰ θέμις ἐστί μοι τὰν ἀφανῆ θεὸν
καὶ σὲ λιταῖς σεβίζειν,
ἐννυχίων ἄναξ,
᾽Αϊδωνεῦ ᾽Αϊδωνεῦ.

We can understand why they are so hesitant about praying to Hades. Of all the gods he alone does not listen to prayers, is inexorable[1] and unmoved by persuasion,[2] and confers neither kindness nor favour.[3] The Chorus subdue this doubt and call on him, on Persephone, on the powers of the underworld (1568), who must be the Erinyes, and on Cerberus, 'the untamable watcher' (1572), to make Oedipus' passing easy. They fear that in death something terrible may still await him. Death is full of unknown mysteries, and as Heraclitus says 'there awaits men when they die such things as they look not for nor dream of'.[4] Perhaps they wonder whether a parricide can escape vengeance in Hades. What they wish for Oedipus is peace and rest. Therefore they call on Death,

On thee I call, giver of sleep unending,[5]

as if the best that could be desired for Oedipus were everlasting sleep. They do not yet know the truth of his translation, nor see that it is the entry into a new life.

For Antigone and Ismene their father's passing is a matter for deep sorrow. They weep when they accompany him on his last journey (1603-9) and when they say good-bye to him (1647). When they have heard the Messenger's tale they lament Oedipus in a kind of dirge. Their first feeling is of their own irreparable loss. They are deserted and wish to join their father in death; they have not even the satisfaction of performing the last rites for him (1714). The Chorus try to comfort them, but their gentle words are not the real or the right answer to these doubts:

Since he has found an end to life
Happily, friends, give over grief;
For none is not caught in sorrow.[6]

This is the well-worn consolation that Oedipus has died happily and that his children must endure the common fate of the bereaved. Both the daughters and the Chorus see Oedipus' passing with a limited human perspective. Its divine significance eludes them. The loss which the girls weep, the sleep which the Chorus asks, are of small importance in comparison with the new life, the

[1] *Il.* ix. 158.   [2] Aesch. fr. 161.   [3] Soph. fr. 770.
[4] Trs. J. Burnet fr. 27 ἀνθρώπους μένει ἀποθανόντας ἅσσα οὐκ ἔλπονται οὐδὲ δοκέουσιν.
[5] 1578   σέ τοι κικλήσκω τὸν αἰένυπνον.
[6] 1720-3   ἀλλ' ἐπεὶ ὀλβίως γ' ἔλυ-
σεν τὸ τέλος, ὦ φίλαι, βίου,
λήγετε τοῦδ' ἄχους· κακῶν
γὰρ Δυσάλωτος οὐδείς.

victory which Oedipus has won. He has been taken from his human ties. Reference to them now is irrelevant. What counts is that he is a *daimôn*.

Theseus has a clearer insight into the truth and shows it in the comfort which he offers to Antigone and Ismene:

> Cease your lamenting, maidens. When
> Night below earth is a gift to him,
> It is wrong to weep. The gods forbid.[1]

Oedipus' new habitation in the earth is a gift from the gods. To mourn this is to set oneself against the divine will. Theseus seems to remember what Oedipus said to him at the start of his last journey:

> Dearest friend,
> May you, your country, and these men of yours
> Be blest, and in good times remember me
> Who die, and be for ever fortunate.[2]

Oedipus knows that his death is a good fortune to himself and to Athens; therefore he must be remembered with joy. What this means all have known since he revealed that his body will protect Athens. So in comforting the bereaved daughters Theseus speaks with a quiet confidence, knowing that what they mourn is really an occasion for joy. He reminds them of what their father's body will do for Athens:

> He said that if I obeyed him aright
> My land would be ever untroubled.[3]

Antigone accepts his word and his refusal to let her know where her father went. She turns from the dead and the past to the insistent present and asks that she may be sent to Thebes to save her brothers (1764–5). For her, as we know, troubles are not over. But the future that awaits her is not our present concern. What matters is the passing of Oedipus, the divine act which is a recompense for past sufferings and a promise of protection to Athens and which shows that the gods are just.

That the gods should so favour Athens needed no argument.

---

[1] 1751–3
> παύετε θρῆνον, παῖδες· ἐν οἷς γὰρ
> χάρις ἡ χθονία νὺξ ἀπόκειται
> πενθεῖν οὐ χρή· νέμεσις γάρ.

[2] 1552–5
> ἀλλά, φίλτατε ξένων,
> αὐτός τε χώρα θ' ἥδε πρόσπολοί τε σοὶ
> εὐδαίμονες γένοισθε, κἀπ' εὐπραξίᾳ
> μέμνησθέ μου θανόντος εὐτυχεῖς ἀεί.

[3] 1764–5
> καὶ ταῦτά μ' ἔφη πράσσοντα καλῶς
> χώραν ἕξειν αἰὲν ἄλυπον.

Yet into this last play Sophocles has flung his unwithered love of
his country. By hints and touches, by marvellous song and description, he shows what Athens is, why it deserves and wins the
favour of the gods. It is, in the first place, a town with a landscape.
When Antigone first sees its towers and looks about her, she says:

> But this is holy ground, as I can see,
> Clustered with olive, bay, and vine; close-winged
> Within it sing the tuneful nightingales.[1]

The same familiar features, olive and vine and nightingale, appear
again in the song with which the Chorus, freed of their misgivings,
welcome Oedipus. To these delights they add others, the narcissus
and the crocus, the waters of Cephisus and the lands that it feeds.
Behind these glories of the eye are the deities who sustain them, the
god Colonus, Dionysus and the Nymphs, Demeter and flower-
crowned Korê, Aphrodite and the Muses. The powers of fertility
and joy are honoured with the landscape. The song may be compared with that of Euripides' *Medea* 824–45 which also celebrates the waters of Attica, the Muses, and Aphrodite. That song
was written just before the outbreak of the Peloponnesian War and
comes as the last voice of the days of peace. It differs from the
Sophoclean song in being less religious. It celebrates the achievements of human wisdom as Sophocles does not. The difference is
due no doubt mainly to the difference of temperament in the two
poets, but difference of date may also account for something.
What matters for Sophocles is the place with its divine powers.
Towards the end of a long destructive war, when vines and olives
had been destroyed and the gods had lost much of their old re-
nown, he sang boldly and blithely of their presence.

Attica is also a land of soldiers. Creon, liar though he is, says
the right thing to the Chorus:

> I know that I have come
> To the city that is strongest in all Greece.[2]

The Chorus have already included symbols of war in their praise
of Attica, such as the olive-wood,

> To the enemy spears' dismay,[3]

---

[1] 16–18   χῶρος δ' ὅδ' ἱρός, ὡς σάφ' εἰκάσαι, βρύων
             δάφνης, ἐλαίας, ἀμπέλου· πυκνόπτεροι δ'
             εἴσω κατ' αὐτὸν εὐστομοῦσ' ἀηδόνες.

[2] 733–4   πρὸς πόλιν δ' ἐπίσταμαι
             σθένουσαν ἥκων, εἴ τιν' Ἑλλάδος, μέγα.

[3] 699   ἐγχέων φόβημα δαΐων.

the curb first discovered there (712–15), and the oar which leaps through the waves

> Following Nereus' daughters
> In the dance of the hundred feet.[1]

Through these three symbols of spear and bit and oar Sophocles praises his country in its infantry, cavalry, and fleet. Each is under the patronage of a god. The olive-tree belongs to Zeus and Athene (705–6), the bridle and the oar to Poseidon (713). A similar tribute to Attic strength and courage is paid in the song which the Chorus sing when, old men though they are, they wish to be present in the battle against Creon's soldiers. They would like to see the fight:

> There, there would I be
> Where the foemen are wheeling round
> To join in the War God's brazen din
> Where the Pythian temple stands
> Or on the glittering beach.[2]

Here, too, the display of force has the support of the gods. The Chorus are confident that the Athenians will win; for Athene and Poseidon, the champions celebrated in the earlier song, are with them (1070–3), and Zeus and Apollo will aid them (1086 ff.). Sophocles proclaims his belief in his land and its inhabitants. He feels that they derive their strength from the divine powers who watch over them.

The gods love Attica because its men are just and devout. Theseus makes the proud boast that in it justice is done and nothing is done without law (913–14); Creon pays service to the wise councils of the Areopagus (947); Oedipus knows that Athens is the special city of Athene (107–8) and is 'most god-fearing', though the men of Colonus seem for the moment to belie its reputation (260). When the end is near, he speaks to Theseus of Attic reverence for the gods:

> If any land honours the gods,
> With reverent knowledge, this surpasses all;[3]

---

[1] 718–19   τῶν ἑκατομπόδων
Νηρήδων ἀκόλουθος.

[2] 1044–9   εἴην ὅθι δαΐων
ἀνδρῶν τάχ' ἐπιστροφαὶ
τὸν χαλκοβόαν Ἄρη
μείξουσιν, ἢ πρὸς Πυθίαις,
ἢ λαμπάσιν ἀκταῖς.

[3] 1006–7   εἴ τις γῇ θεοὺς ἐπίσταται
τιμαῖς σεβίζειν, ἥδε τῷδ' ὑπερφέρει.

and before his passing he prays to the gods to show their goodwill
to Athens:

> For reverence
> In you, alone of all men, have I found,
> And gentleness, and no lies on your lips.[1]

The insistence on the god-fearing character of Athens explains
why the gods love it and why it has received the privilege of
Oedipus' protection. The gods are not after all undecipherable;
they reward the just. At the end of *Oedipus at Colonus* no unresolved
discords remain, no mysteries call for an answer. Even Antigone
and Ismene have the comfort that their father has made his peace
with the gods. The bad son is punished; the good friends are rewarded. This moral of ultimate justice was stated with authority by
Oedipus to the Chorus (278–81) and in his warning to Theseus
that Athens may still have enemies he returns to it:

> Full well, tho' late, the gods observe a man
> Who leaves their service for his own mad whim.[2]

Men may take advantage of the gods' slowness to punish wickedness, but in the end the punishment comes. The gods are just to
punish as to reward.

Behind the anxieties and passions of the play lies a firm trust
in the gods. The peace which Oedipus finds under the earth is
matched by the peace of mind which the audience should find in
the proofs of divine justice. To emphasize this Sophocles moves
through angry and tormented scenes, displays the basest as well as
the noblest elements in the human soul, touches extremes of darkness and light. Peace and trust are his solution for the troubles of
humankind. This is of course his own conclusion, and to this
extent the play is his testament. This trust is different from the
modesty inculcated by the earlier plays. The justice of the gods is
no longer revealed in a half-light as something not wholly explic-
able but to be accepted without murmur; its workings are shown
and its rightness emphasized. Such a conclusion cannot be called
pessimistic. It is true that the fierce minatory Oedipus is no
power of mercy and forgiveness, but he confines his curses to the
wicked and rewards the good. The impenetrable darkness which
surrounds the gods' ways has been pierced. Their goodness and

[1] 1125–7
   ἐπεὶ τό γ᾿ εὐσεβὲς
  μόνοις παρ᾿ ὑμῖν ηὗρον ἀνθρώπων ἐγὼ
  καὶ τοὐπιεικὲς καὶ τὸ μὴ ψευδοστομεῖν.

[2] 1536–7
   θεοὶ γὰρ εὖ μέν, ὀψὲ δ᾿ εἰσορῶσ᾿, ὅταν
  τὰ θεῖ᾿ ἀφείς τις ἐς τὸ μαίνεσθαι τραπῇ.

justice are not after all so different from their human counterparts.
Even in the ebb and flow of fortune we see that good comes with
evil and that there is a rhythmical law of change. With this reflection we may welcome the good that comes after so much evil
and yet be prepared for further evil in the future.

Yet in one place Sophocles seems to contradict this message and
to give a peculiarly personal reflection which is far removed from
acceptance or trust. Not without reason have many regarded the
choric song of 1211–48 as the poet's own judgement on the last
days of life. The Chorus are not in themselves sufficiently characterized to be allowed so passionate a display of feeling about their
own troubles. Nor are their words perfectly applicable to Oedipus;
for he will pass not into nothingness but to power. It is therefore
natural to think that in this incomparable song Sophocles reveals
his own feelings. We can imagine that wearied with his ninety
years and oppressed by his country's disasters he felt a desire for
release and rest, that in the world about him he saw

> Envy, sedition, discord, strife,
> Murder too,[1]

that in this mood he longed for death, the impartial deliverer:

> When Hades' doom is revealed,
> Without bridal song, lyre, or dance,
> Death that comes at the last.[2]

Even the lines on the passing of youth and its airy follies (1229–30)
come appropriately from the poet who wrote with such tenderness
of childhood and its freedom from care.[3] It is, however, strange
that Sophocles should include a personal document in a play without making it relevant to his main structure. We may well
believe that these feelings were in some sense his own, but we
expect them to be adapted to his artistic design. And it is still more
strange that this song should be at variance with the chief conclusion of his play. The doctrine that not to be born is best conflicts
with the stress laid on the nobler human qualities and on the care
which the gods have for men. In the play Sophocles presents a
clear and cogent message about what gives value to life; in the

---

[1] 1234–5   φθόνος, στάσεις, ἔρις, μάχαι,
              καὶ φόνοι.

[2] 1221–3   Ἄιδος ὅτε μοῖρ' ἀνυμέναιος
              ἄλυρος ἄχορος ἀναπέφηνε,
              θάνατος ἐς τελευτάν.

[3] Aj. 553 ff.; Trach. 144–7; fr. 583.

song he seems to contradict it and to praise nihilism and annihilation. The common view cannot be right.

The song is sung when, after all his other troubles, Oedipus hears that Polynices wishes to see him. The Chorus, composed of old men, are sorry for Oedipus, in whose miseries they see a mirror of their own. Their pity moves them to denounce the horrors of old age and the worthlessness of life. But their message is not the poet's. They are human beings who do not see the whole significance of what happens and are hampered by not knowing what awaits Oedipus. Their commentary is not final. For those who know the truth Oedipus' sufferings teach a very different lesson. Nor indeed do the Chorus speak decisively. The Strophe, Antistrophe, and Epode each advance a different point. The first is concerned with the misery of old age, the second with a wider and more general pessimism, the third with praise for Oedipus' endurance. Like the third Stasimon of the *Antigone* (944–87) the song presents different views of the situation. It moves from pity to pessimism and from pessimism to admiration, much as we may ourselves have moved through the scenes of the play. It is a human commentary on what has happened, and is therefore uncertain, indecisive, and incompletely informed. It judges the events by common standards, and to some extent shows their inadequacy. They are contradicted by the truth. Its function is to set out ordinary beliefs in an extraordinary situation and to show that they do not fit. The meditations of the Chorus are based on common ideas, on traditional wisdom. Some of the audience would accept them, but even to these truisms there were answers hardly less accepted, of which others might be conscious.

The Strophe displays the miseries of old age in contrast to the joys of youth and says that the end of them is death. The theme is as old as Mimnermus,[1] and was elsewhere treated by Sophocles:

> There is no misery like length of days,[2]

and

> All evils are ingrained in long old age,
> Wits vanished, useless actions, empty thought.[3]

Of all this Menander[4] and Euripides[5] were no less conscious, and indeed the theme is almost common form. But to it there was a

---

[1] Frs. 1–5.
[2] Fr. 556   οὐδὲν γὰρ ἄλγος οἷον ἡ πολλὴ ζόη.
[3] Fr. 949   πάντ᾿ ἐμπέφυκε τῷ μακρῷ γήρᾳ κακά,
             νοῦς φροῦδος, ἔργ᾿ ἀχρεῖα, φροντίδες κεναί.

[4] *Mon.* 745.   [5] *Her.* 637–9.

common answer, that the horrors of old age were compensated by its superior wisdom and experience. So Sophocles himself says:

> The wise never grow old; their mind is nursed
> To company with the holy light of day;
> For foresight's a great benefit to men.[1]

He elsewhere stresses the knowledge of the old,[2] and with him Euripides[3] and Menander[4] again agree. Such experience belongs to Oedipus. His long life of suffering has taught him the all-important lesson of contentment with his lot:

> Contentment have I learned from suffering
> And my long years and from nobility.[5]

His actions show that he is no longer his old self, liable to illusions and wrong judgements, but an old man who can distinguish truth from falsehood and knows that he can trust the gods. Therefore he endures what comes. This, too, was approved by common thought. In his *Epigoni* Sophocles made someone say:

> Keep the good spirit that befits old age,[6]

and the position is well stated by his friend Cephalus when he says that old age is not burdensome if men are self-controlled and contented, while, if they are not, youth, too, is difficult for them.[7] The view of the Chorus would not meet with universal acceptance. The wiser members of the audience would know that there was an answer to it and that perhaps Sophocles had one ready.

The Antistrophe advances a different point, that all life is a sorrow. This appears as a variation on a traditional theme:

> Not to be born surpasses all,
> But, if a man has seen the light,
> Thither should he return again
> Straightway whence he arose at first.[8]

Behind this lies an ancient adage, a remark which Silenus is said to

---

[1] Fr. 950   οὐκ ἔστι γῆρας τῶν σοφῶν· ἐν οἷς ὁ νοῦς
                     θείᾳ ξύνεστιν ἡμέρᾳ τεθραμμένος·
                     προμηθία γὰρ κέρδος ἀνθρώποις μέγα.

[2] Frs. 260 and 664.   [3] *Phoen.* 528–30; fr. 619.   [4] Fr. 676.

[5] 7–8   στέργειν γὰρ αἱ πάθαι με χὼ χρόνος ξυνὼν
               μακρὸς διδάσκει καὶ τὸ γενναῖον τρίτον.

[6] Fr. 193   γήρᾳ προσῆκον σῷζε τὴν εὐθυμίαν.

[7] Plat. *Rep.* i. 329 d.

[8] 1224–8   μὴ φῦναι τὸν ἅπαντα νι-
                     κᾷ λόγον· τὸ δ᾽, ἐπεὶ φανῇ,
                     βῆναι κεῖσ᾽ ὁπόθεν περ ἥ-
                     κει πολὺ δεύτερον ὡς τάχιστα.

have made to Midas, that it is best for a man not to be born and failing that, to die as soon as possible.[1] This may perhaps have been told in some fable. In any case it was well known and used in different forms by 'Theognis',[2] Bacchylides,[3] Euripides,[4] and Alexis.[5] The theme crystallizes dark thoughts which the Greeks felt from time to time about the misery of existence, but it has no apocalyptic authority. It could be, and was, disputed. Epicurus quoted the Theognidean verses and commented, 'If he really believes this, why does he not depart from life?'[6], and Aristotle expresses a somewhat similar view when he says: 'It is softness to fly from evil, and such a man endures death not because it is noble but to fly from evil.'[7] In his sufferings Oedipus has not sought death, though now that the gods send it he welcomes it. It does not come of his own seeking, and he has no thought of hastening it. If the Chorus's words were to be translated into action, Oedipus would kill himself. But that is against the gods' special purpose for him. He knows better than the Chorus what his sufferings mean and what awaits him. The Chorus are limited by their human state and their infirmities. Their word is not final.

In the Epode they show this. It corrects what has been said in the Strophe and Antistrophe and gives a new and truer view. Oedipus may be assailed by miseries, but he endures them heroically like a rocky promontory which waves wash and winds beat from every quarter of the horizon:

> So on him without respite
> Dread; like great billows breaking,
> Shocks fall upon him and shake him,
> Some from the side where the sun sinks,
> Some from its orient dawning,
> Some by the midday glow,
> Some from the Arctic night.[8]

The Chorus have changed their emphasis from the misery of Oedipus' life to his endurance and steadfastness. Behind their

---

[1] Aristot. fr. 44 Rose; Cic. *Tusc. Disp.* i. 48. 114.   [2] 425–8.
[3] v. 160–2.   [4] Fr. 449.   [5] Fr. 141. 14–16.   [6] Diog. Laert. x. 127.
[7] *Nic. Eth.* 1116 a 12 ff.

[8] 1242–8   ὡς καὶ τόνδε κατ' ἄκρας
            2εινα`ι κυματοαγεῖς
            ἆται κλονέουσιν ἀεὶ ξυνοῦσαι,
            αἱ μὲν ἀπ' ἀελίου 2υσμᾶν,
            αἱ 2' ἀνατέλλοντος,
            αἱ 2' ἀνὰ μέσσαν ἀκτῖν',
            αἱ 2' ἐννυχιᾶν ἀπὸ 'Ριπᾶν.

words we may detect a Homeric simile which describes the Achaean resistance to Hector:

Like to a tow'r they held, firm fasten'd, just as a great rock,
Rising high in the air, at the side of the silvery-grey sea,
Waits and endures the attacks of the winds that whistle against it
And of the full-bellied waves that break into foam all about it.[1]

Just as these heroes resisted what looked like an overwhelming onslaught, so Oedipus resists onslaughts on his peace and happiness. His endurance is no less heroic than theirs and no less worthy of admiration. The comparison is much nearer to the truth than the preceding lamentations. The Chorus, who have been, as it were, thinking aloud, begin to see things as they are and to realize the paradox that the miseries of life may call out greatness in him who resists them. Oedipus' nobility in suffering is another sign of his worthiness to be a hero. The old man who does not falter is made of more than mortal stuff. His superior power is at last apparent to the Chorus, even though they do not yet understand its full meaning. By a devious journey, through doubts and hesitations, they have come to the right conclusion. Their song with its shifting sentiments is a human comment on the events of the play.

Oedipus' endurance in adversity entitles him to honour and ultimately to heroization. He shows his daemonic power at a time of life when most men are incapable of prolonged fortitude. He overrides the encumbrances of advanced years and the troubles which gather round him from his family and country. This superior strength is recognized and rewarded by the gods who prolong it in the grave and make it a means to protect Athens. We do not know precisely what his state will be, but we can be sure that he will be conscious and active, rather as Protesilaus was believed to be able to punish the wrongdoer from the grave because the gods gave him special power.[2] Oedipus will watch over Athens and protect her from her enemies. Nor is this protection beyond comprehension. It is based on a kind of intimacy between the living and the dead, on the love which Oedipus has for Athens, and on the honour in which Athens holds him. It is a real relation. Oedipus belongs to the company of the 'Stronger',

---

[1] *Il.* xv. 618–22 Ἴσχον γὰρ πυργηδὸν ἀρηρότες, ἠύτε πέτρη
ἠλίβατος μεγάλη, πολιῆς ἁλὸς ἐγγὺς ἐοῦσα,
ἥ τε μένει λιγέων ἀνέμων λαιψηρὰ κέλευθα,
κύματά τε τροφόεντα, τά τε προσερεύγεται αὐτήν.

[2] Hdt. ix. 120. 2.

who must be treated with respect and have nothing ill said of
them.[1] The dead not only give life, nourishment, and increase,[2]
but, if rightly entreated, they can send other and less tangible
blessings.[3] This power to send good or evil in return for care or
neglect shows that heroes, like the other dead, stood in a special
relation to their cities and families. If such honoured them, they
prospered. And in a deeper sense the dead were believed to partake in the life of the living, the living to owe a peculiar regard to
the dead. The two were closer than common language would
suggest. When Heraclitus says, 'Mortals are immortals and immortals are mortals, living the others' death and dying the others'
life',[4] he may have intended a special reference now lost, but he
bases himself on something familiar to the Greek consciousness.
When Oedipus is below earth with the dead, he will still live in the
life of the living, while the living, in their communion with him,
will partake of his state and of the power that comes from the
dead.

   Oedipus at Colonus is full of extremes of hatred and devotion, of
passion and patience, of misery and power. The extremes in the
human soul are matched by the contrast between the sunlit land
of Attica and the sunless realm of the dead. These contrasts are
the tragic material, the discords which must be harmonized, the
disorder which must be reduced to order. Harmony and order
come because the gods will it so and because Oedipus accepts
their will. The play ends in a sublime reconciliation not merely between Oedipus and the gods but between all the warring elements
in the situation. All is seen to be as it ought. The close is not in
humble acquiescence but in strength and power and knowledge.
The justice of the gods is vindicated in their treatment of Oedipus
and of Attica. At the end of his long life Sophocles comforted his
war-worn people with his vision of a heroic being who sustains
Attica by his presence, and showed what men and women may
gain by loyalty to the superhuman powers who live around and
beneath them looking after their lives and lands.

---

[1] Aristot. fr. 44.   [2] Hippocr. *Diaet.* iv. 92.
[3] Aesch. *Pers.* 222; Aristoph. fr. 488.

[4] Fr. 62 ἀθάνατοι θνητοί, θνητοὶ ἀθάνατοι, ζῶντες τὸν ἐκείνων θάνατον, τὸν
δὲ ἐκείνων βίον τεθνεῶτες.

IX

SOME CONCLUSIONS

THE seven surviving plays of Sophocles form so small a propor-
tion of what he wrote that it is rash to generalize from them
about the nature of his art. Some of the lost plays, over a hundred
in number,[1] may have been constructed on principles quite different
from those that survive. In the circumstances we can only hope
that the surviving selection is somehow representative. It is at
least a real selection.[2] Whenever it was made, it was made with
an educational purpose and must represent the choice of educated
men who believed that it gave a fair or useful notion of Sophoclean
tragedy. Moreover, despite great uncertainty about dates, this
selection covers some forty years of Sophocles' life. The *Ajax* seems
to be earlier than the *Antigone*, which was produced about 442 B.C.,
the *Philoctetes* was produced in 409 B.C., and the *Oedipus at Colonus*
must have been composed in the poet's last years. The other three
plays cannot be dated except perhaps relatively, and even about
this there is much dispute, though no one has suggested that any
of them is much earlier than the *Ajax*. The seven plays cover
a wide extent of time and differ much in construction, temper,
and formative idea. Nor with Sophocles are we handicapped as
with Aeschylus by possessing single plays of trilogies whose full
import could be seen only if we had all the members of a complex whole. Each of the seven plays is at least complete in itself.
Widely different as they are, it should be possible to discover
what principles underlie them, what evidence they give about
Sophocles' tragic art.

At the outset it may be well to consider a view which has won
more respect than it deserves and is still not quite discredited. It
has often been said that Sophocles is in some sense a 'purer' artist
than Aeschylus or Euripides, that he was not concerned with the
wider implications of the events which he dramatized or to draw
conclusions from them, that he was not deeply interested in the
problems, religious or ethical or metaphysical, which his plots
might sugggest, and that he had no answer for them. In so far as
Sophocles, unlike Aeschylus or Euripides, hardly refers to contemporary events, there is truth in these claims. It is also true that

---

[1] A. C. Pearson, *The Fragments of Sophocles*, i, pp. xiv–xxii.
[2] U. v. Wilamowitz, *Einleitung*, pp. 196 ff.

in comparison with Euripides he was not impressed by the more ingenious intellectual activities of his time or charmed by the agile acrobatics of the Sophists. But analysis of the plays has shown that each involves serious considerations about the nature of gods and of men and gives a clue to what verdict should be passed on the events dramatized. Sophocles is not a mere playwright, not a 'pure' dramatist in the sense of one who is interested in nothing but plot and character, whose only aim is to arouse excited anticipation about what will happen next or enjoyment in the presentation of vivid actions. Still less does his profound, searching, and sympathetic knowledge of the human soul justify us in thinking of him as remote and detached. A man does not write like this unless he has been deeply moved by the vagaries and passions which cast men up and down. His detachment may indeed be godlike in its width of vision and its power to create, but such a god feels for his creatures and is deeply concerned about their destinies. The notion of the impartial dispassionate Sophocles is so wrong that it needs a word of comment.

It is based on two kinds of material, both interesting in their own way but neither relevant to the conclusion which they are supposed to prove. The first consists of some ancient comments on Sophocles. It happens that some literary critics of the Graeco-Roman age praise the beauty of his poetry and say nothing about his tragic vision or view of life. Even Dio Chrysostom, who was much interested in the ethical aspects of tragedy, praises him chiefly as a poet and quotes with approval two lines of Aristophanes:

> He used to lick the lips of Sophocles
> Smear'd o'er with sweetness like a honey-jar.[1]

Dionysius praises the harmony of his composition,[2] and the author of *On the Sublime*, who fully admires the majesty of his work,[3] says nothing about its religious side. These critics admired his poetry, but that does not prove that they failed to see what lay behind it. Their judgements should not be extended to matters which they did not discuss. The theological background of Sophocles' work happened not to be their subject. Secondly, a few scraps of evidence about Sophocles' appearance and manners have been taken to be evidence about his art. The famous statue in the Lateran

---

[1] Fr. 581. Trs. J. D. Denniston.

ὁ δ' αὖ Σοφοκλέους τοῦ μέλιτι κεχρισμένου
ὥσπερ καδίσκου περιέλειχε τὸ στόμα.

[2] *De Comp.* 24. [3] *De Subl.* 15. 23. 33.

may be of him and may reveal a man who looks calm and dispassionate, but his looks do not always betray a poet's inmost
thoughts. When Ion of Chios said of Sophocles, 'in state business
he was neither clever or energetic but like one of the Athenian
nobles',[1] he tells us something about the poet's public life, which
has little to do with his art, and something about his manners,
which have nothing. When Aristophanes, soon after the death of
Sophocles, characterised him as

> He, who was happy here, is happy there,[2]

he described the man whom he had known, with a hint at his
heroization after death, but he says nothing about his work. Phrynichus summed up his life in a similar spirit:

> How blessed Sophocles, who, dying old,
> Was old in happiness and skill of hand.
> Beautiful were his Tragedies, and many;
> And beautiful his end, who lived untroubled;[3]

and his words get some support from Cephalus' account of the old
Sophocles who has found peace of mind in his freedom from the
passions of youth. These are the personal judgements of friends
on a friend. They tell nothing of the experiences through which
Sophocles passed in creating his tragic world and nothing of what
he meant by his art. They add no more to our knowledge of
his work than the contemporary description of Shakespeare as
'a handsome well shaped man, very good company, and of very
ready and pleasant smooth wit' does to our knowledge of *Hamlet*
and *King Lear*. For Sophocles, as for Shakespeare, what matter are
the plays.

Another error is more likely than this to impose on good judges
just because they feel the force of Sophocles' art and know what
poetry is. It is the belief, partly due to a verbal confusion, that in
the last resort Sophoclean and Shakespearian tragedy are both
variants of a single form. It seems only right that Greek *tragoedia*
should be similar to Elizabethan Tragedy. The words suggest it.

---

[1] Trs. T. B. L. Webster. Ion fr. 8 v. Blumenthal τὰ μέντοι πολιτικὰ οὔτε σοφὸς
οὔτε ῥεκτήριος ἦν, ἀλλ' ὡς ἄν τις εἶς τῶν χρηστῶν 'Αθηναίων.

[2] *Ran.* 82   ὁ Δ' εὔκολος μὲν ἐνθάδ', εὔκολος Δ' ἐκεῖ.

The word εὔκολος is probably used with deliberate ambiguity in reference to the
heroization.

[3] Trs. T. F. Higham.

Fr. 31   μάκαρ Σοφοκλέης, ὃς πολὺν χρόνον βιοὺς
ἀπέθανεν, εὐδαίμων ἀνὴρ καὶ δέξιος,
πολλὰς ποιήσας καὶ καλὰς τραγῳδίας·
καλῶς δ' ἐτελεύτησ' οὐδὲν ὑπομείνας κακόν.

Moreover, the two are like each other in many important respects. Both display abrupt and unforeseen changes of fortune which engage profound interest and sympathy; both display the hazards of the mortal state and the depths, no less than the heights, which human nature can touch; both are concerned with the great not merely in station but in natural endowments and force of character; both involve, sooner or later, speculations about the powers that govern the universe, about their justice or injustice, their solicitude or indifference to suffering men; both lead through crisis, agony, and disaster to an end which somehow, despite all the horror, provides peace. The similarities between Sophoclean and Shakespearian tragedy justify comparison and suggest speculations. But there are also differences, and to neglect these may lead to misunderstanding and false analogies. Sophoclean *tragoedia* is not Shakespearian Tragedy. Narrower in some respects, it is wider in others, and the differences show a real difference of conception.

The first, most obvious, distinction between the two kinds is that while Shakespeare's tragedies end in the death of the chief character or characters, only one of Sophocles' surviving plays, the *Women of Trachis*, so ends. To this we may well add the *Antigone*, in which Creon loses all that makes life worth living, and *King Oedipus*, in which Oedipus' fall is a kind of obliteration, a severance from his own past life and from the lives of other men. But of the other four plays not one has even an unhappy ending. The *Ajax* does indeed show the hero's death, but it ends with the satisfaction of honour and amends paid to him. The last three plays end in glory and triumph, however tempered such may be by the agony and shame through which they are reached. It is true that the Shakespearian Folio classes *Troilus and Cressida* and *Cymbeline* as tragedies, but this has been regarded as an eccentric foible and is not commonly accepted. It is not on these plays that critics base their views of Shakespeare's tragic art. It is also true that certain plays of Shakespeare, such as *A Winter's Tale* and even *The Tempest*, have something in common with the last plays of Sophocles in so far as their movement is through ugly passions and even gruesome situations to a quiet end. But in these plays there is an element of unreality, of remoteness from ordinary life, of magic and marvel, which is alien to Sophocles. It seems to soften the harshness of what happens, to throw a romantic light over it, even to detract from its importance. A similar art may well be observed in such plays of Euripides as the *Helen* and *Iphigeneia in Tauris* which are rightly compared to romantic comedies. But such plays have no real tragic conflict; they display no really serious issue. Therefore they are unlike those plays of Sophocles which end happily. For these are profoundly serious and arouse tragic emotions. In them Sophocles reveals a conception of tragedy to which Shakespeare provides no real parallel. It is therefore wrong to assume that his tragic art is the same as Shakespeare's.

A second difference is more fundamental. In every play of Sophocles the gods take an active, even a decisive, part. Their will is done, even though men resist it. It may work on or through the characters, but it works. The gods may participate directly in the action like Athene or Heracles, or indirectly as through Teiresias in the *Antigone* or through oracles which are invariably fulfilled. In Shakespeare, too, superhuman powers are at work. The Witches in *Macbeth* and the Ghost in *Hamlet* affect the action, but only a part of it, and that only because they appeal to something latent in those human beings to whom they appear, to the hidden ambition of Macbeth and the lurking suspicions of Hamlet. Even the malign coincidence which blasts fortunes in *King Lear* and *Othello* is not nearly so potent or so present as the divine powers which Sophocles sets to work. The evil that wrecks Lear and Othello is not in their stars but in the corrupt souls of men. Shakespeare is so untheological a poet that we do not know what his religious beliefs were, whereas it is impossible to appreciate Sophocles without seeing him against the background of the Olympian gods as the fifth century knew them. His plays are religious in a sense that Shakespeare's are not. They display directly the relations between gods and men. The field of their action is not political or national or even domestic; it is the single reality to which both gods and men belong. Nor is this accidental. The plays were performed at a religious festival. Precedent, as we know it in Aeschylus, shows that at an earlier stage tragedy was concerned with essentially religious issues. Sophocles followed precedent and propriety when he made plays about the relations of gods and men.

If this modern analogy is in some ways deceptive, we might still hope to learn something from the ancients, especially from Aristotle's discussion of tragedy in his *Poetics*. He knew and admired the work of Sophocles; much of his theory is based on *King Oedipus*; he was born some twenty years after the death of Sophocles and was well qualified to understand the plays as their author intended them to be understood. No critic, ancient or modern, compares with him for authority. He had at his disposal the author's complete works; he could approach them with his omnivorous curiosity and incomparable memory; he must have seen many of them acted and learned how Athenian actors thought that the parts should be interpreted. It is therefore no matter for surprise that his analysis of Greek tragedy dominated poetical thought for generations and gave to its study many standards and conceptions which are still current. Yet wonderfully acute and true though much of his criticism is, Aristotle does not entirely satisfy when he deals with the nature of tragedy, at least as we know it in the practice of Sophocles. At times in his desire to find a comprehensive formula he seems to neglect important factors; at other times he finds a formula which is indeed true so far as it goes, but he fails to see how much there is in it. Of course he generalizes from so vast a mass of particular cases that no formula can suit every one of them. Nor was he concerned so much with tragedy as it is as with what in his opinion it ought to be. Yet he does define tragedy and analyse its essential characteristics. We are therefore justified in applying his doctrine to the surviving plays of Sophocles.

When Aristotle says that tragedy is 'an imitation of an action that is serious'[1] in the sense that it deals with material that is not paltry or ridiculous, there can be no quarrel with him. His definition covers the plays of Sophocles, though it may not be so apt for all the plays of Euripides. Whatever the conclusion of a Sophoclean tragedy may be, it is reached only when issues of great importance have been fought out on the stage. The mood in which these are presented, the characters who display them, the language of speech and song, all contribute to an extremely serious result. This is no pastime, but the imaginative vision of a poet who makes his art a means to present important issues with great intensity and concentration. Moreover, when Aristotle goes on to say that tragedy produces its effect through pity and fear, he may not say everything that might be said but his words are applicable to Sophocles. Pity for the characters in their illusions and their helplessness induces a mood of humility closely allied to fear, not merely when the characters come to a tragic end, like Creon, Heracles, and Oedipus, but when, like Neoptolemus and Philoctetes, they pass through great moral dangers before finding success. It is true even of Electra, in whose ultimate triumph there is still an element of horror not far from fear, and of the old Oedipus, whose end, fraught with anxieties and mysteries, awakes both pity for him

---

[1] *Poet.* 1449 b 24 μίμησις πράξεως σπουδαίας.

and awe before the incalculable justice of the gods. And these feelings, despite the horrors that arouse them, lead to a final sense of
relief and harmony even in the *Women of Trachis* and *King Oedipus*,
an acceptance of the divine will and a mood of resignation, of
'calm of mind, all passion spent'. This process may well have been
what Aristotle meant by 'purification'. So far his analysis is pene-
trating and right. It is when he advances to more detailed matters
that he suggests certain corrections.

Aristotle attaches special importance to two elements in the plot,
Reversal and Discovery. So far as dramatic action is concerned,
he is right. No play is really conceivable without something of
each. For while Reversal means that the situation of the chief
characters changes, Discovery means that something unknown is
made known. Without these two elements a play would lack
development and dramatic interest. They are present in all plays
of Sophocles, but their significance is greater than Aristotle seems
to have seen, certainly greater than he said. He defines both
too carefully. First, Reversal. This he defines as 'the change
from one state of things in the play to its opposite',[1] and he
means change of fortune whether from good to bad or from bad
to good.[2] It is true that the chief characters of Sophocles endure
some such Reversal. While Creon, Heracles, and Oedipus pass
from prosperity to misery, Electra, Philoctetes, and the old Oedipus pass from misery to something that might be called prosperity,
and Ajax illustrates both changes in his fall from honour to death
and in his rehabilitation after death. But Aristotle's formula does
not convey the wide variety of which such changes are capable.
He seems to regard them as a matter of good or bad luck. This is
inadequate in two ways. First, by stressing the element of luck he
omits the parts played by the characters themselves and by the gods.
He seems to suggest that external circumstance, coincidence or
the like, is more important than motivated action. This is untrue.
Luck plays almost no part in the careers of Sophoclean heroes and
heroines. Secondly, even if we do not press his words too closely,
it is clear that the actual changes are by no means confined to mere
good and bad fortune, to the happiness and misery of the characters. Deianira is unhappy even before her disasters begin; Electra's
triumph is hardly matter for true joy even to her. It is true that
Creon passes from self-satisfied contentment to utter misery and
Philoctetes from obstinate misery to glory. But in most cases the

---

[1] *Poet.* 1452 a 23 εἰς τὸ ἐναντίον τῶν πραττομένων μεταβολή.
[2] Ib. 1451 a 13.

reversal is something different. The question of happiness or unhappiness seems irrelevant to what really happens. When Ajax
changes from mad arrogance to humble sanity, Deianira from rash
hope to suicidal despair, Oedipus from confident illusion to self-
abasing knowledge, Electra from hate to love, the old Oedipus from
human to superhuman life, the changes are so various that no
single word covers them. Most of them indeed are less of fortune
than of heart, and even if they are not so much as this, what counts
is not the reversal in the hero's position but the change in himself.

A similar narrowness may be found in Aristotle's treatment of
Discovery. He defines it carefully as 'a change from ignorance to
knowledge, and thus to either love or hate, in the personages
marked for good or evil fortune'.[1] The only Discovery he recognizes is that of one person by another, and his example of Orestes
and Iphigeneia in the *Iphigeneia in Tauris* shows what he means.
In Sophocles the only Discovery of this kind is between Electra and
Orestes. It conforms to Aristotle's description. Brother and sister
discover each other, find a new love and a new strength, and
through these a change for the better in their fortunes. But in the
other plays the Discoveries are not like this. It is true that Aristotle mentions Oedipus in this connexion[2] and must refer to the
scene where the Messenger recognizes Oedipus as the child whose
life he saved years before on Cithaeron. But in the context this is
important not because the Messenger recognizes Oedipus but
because Oedipus discovers who he himself is. It is the self-dis-
covery that matters. Because of it Oedipus blinds himself. And
in most of the other plays the Discoveries are not of other persons
by the chief characters but of themselves. Ajax finds that he has
been the victim of insane delusions, Creon that he has acted with
gross injustice, Heracles that the gods have kept him not for peace
but for a hideous death, Philoctetes that he has been obstructing
the divine will, the old Oedipus that he, a beggar and an outcast,
has the powers of a hero. Even Electra in her discovery of her
brother finds something about herself, her need for love after
hatred, and the satisfaction which it brings. In each case the chief
character finds something about himself, and this discovery determines the course of the play.

It seems then that Aristotle is right to attach importance to
Reversal and Discovery, but that his analysis unduly limits them.

[1] Trs. I. Bywater. *Poet.* 1452 a 30 ἐξ ἀγνοίας εἰς γνῶσιν μεταβολή, ἢ εἰς φιλίαν
ἢ εἰς ἔχθραν, τῶν πρὸς εὐτυχίαν ἢ δυστυχίαν ὡρισμένων.
[2] Id. 1452 a 33.

If we look more closely, we see how essential both are for Sophoclean tragedy, how closely related to each other in its most crucial moments. This, too, within his limits, Aristotle saw when he said that the best form of Discovery was that attended by Reversals.[1] The truth is that the two are intimately, even inevitably, connected, and that this connexion is fundamental to Sophocles' effects. We might even say that if Sophoclean Discovery is the discovery by a character of some vital truth about himself, Sophoclean Reversal is the reversal in his condition, both inner and outer, which attends this. Aristotle praises this combination in *King Oedipus*, and rightly, though there is more in it than he says. For when Oedipus finds out who he is, his fall is complete. The mere fact of discovery is his humiliation. Ajax' decision to kill himself arises directly from his recognition of what he has done in his madness and from the shame that he feels at it; Creon's final annihilation owes much to his discovery that he has acted like a fool; Deianira's life is ruined with her realization of her hideous mistake. So, too, in the plays that end happily Discovery promotes the end. Orestes and Electra find enough strength from their recognition of one another to proceed at once to vengeance; Philoctetes accepts his glorious destiny when he finds his true self through Heracles' intervention; the old Oedipus is ready for his passing when he has found the range of his daemonic powers and knows that he has settled his earthly claims. In each case the character's discovery of an important truth is the dramatic climax. Compared with this result Aristotle's insistence on the change to 'either hate or love' is secondary even when it occurs.

The discovery of such a truth is a severe test of those who make it. Pindar says

> Trial is the test of men,[2]

and his words may be applied to Sophoclean Discovery. Only when they know the real facts about themselves do the characters show what they really are. All of them live in some kind of illusion or ignorance until the gods force the truth on them. In their reception of it they show their worth. At the bottom of the scale are those who are so ruined by vice or brutality that they fail altogether to learn anything. Clytaemnestra neglects the dream by which the gods warn her; Creon in *Oedipus at Colonus* profits nothing by the salutary lesson which Theseus gives him. Such invincible ignorance betrays its victims as beyond hope or redemption.

---

[1] *Poet.* 1452 a 33.
[2] *Ol.* iv. 22 Διάπειρά τοι βροτῶν ἔλεγχος.

The others learn at least something of what happens to them. Creon in the *Antigone* realizes at least his own insignificance, and better men than he learn more and profit more. Women like Deianira and Jocasta kill themselves rather than face the consequences of their discoveries, but before they die they at least show their true selves, Deianira in her love for her home and Jocasta in her decision that her right place is with her dead husband. The men are more impressive. They suffer more, and the first shock of the truth may be, as it is for Ajax, almost annihilating. But Ajax recovers and humbles himself; Heracles accepts his hideous end with heroic fortitude; Oedipus assists the gods in their plan to humiliate him. Blows which might have broken lesser men bring out noble modesty and courage. So, too, in a different way, those for whom the discovery of the truth means a change to better times reveal their hidden strength and new forces of character. Electra, Philoctetes, and the old Oedipus show unexpected powers when at last they know what their destinies are.

The knowledge acquired by the characters is about themselves, but primarily about themselves in relation to the gods. For Sophocles this is the essential and fundamental knowledge. A man does not know himself or his place until he knows how he stands with the gods. This is obvious with Ajax, Creon, Oedipus, and Philoctetes. They are taught directly who they are and what they must do. When at last they understand the divine will, they have no more illusions and accept their condition. It is also true of Heracles, who forgets his sufferings and his hatred of Deianira when he knows that his death is ordained by the gods; of Electra, whose doubts and hesitations and despairs are resolved by the confidence that the gods are acting for her; of the old Oedipus, who sees on arriving at Colonus that his end is near and, when the thunder sounds, knows that he must go. This acceptance of the truth is a kind of submission, of obedience, even when it brings hope to Electra or a promise of power to the old Oedipus. The characters have learned that they must do what the gods demand, and illustrate what the Platonic Socrates means when he says that the commands 'Know thyself' and 'Be modest' are the same.[1] They find modesty because they have learned to know themselves. So the central idea of a Sophoclean tragedy is that through suffering a man learns to be modest before the gods. Each leading character is taught by the gods the lesson which Pindar preaches to Hieron:

O find, and be, yourself![2]

[1] Plat. *Charm.* 164 e.   [2] *Pyth.* ii. 72 γένοι' οἷος ἐσσὶ μαθών.

Each learns his real state and accepts it by abandoning his illusions. To the audience the plays convey such a lesson. The characters whom they see humbled or exalted are types of men who, through ignorance or blindness of soul, have resisted their destinies. When they are finally forced to see the truth, we know that the gods have prevailed and that men must accept their own insignificance. It is this feeling which brings a sense of relief at the end of a Sophoclean tragedy. Despite all the suffering and horror we feel not indignation but relief, because in spite of everything the human characters have made their peace with the gods.

The lesson is taught through suffering. Those who learn it must pay heavily for it, even if it is to bring them happiness in the end. Behind this lies the old adage that learning comes through suffering.[1] The older poets who preached this were not always concerned with knowledge of the gods, but Sophocles was. He applies the lesson in a special way. The wisdom that man learns through suffering is that he is nothing before the gods and must conform to their will. The plays show the process and the means by which this is learned. Therefore the conflict in them is not so much between men and men as between men and gods. This is of course clear in the *Women of Trachis*, where Heracles and Deianira both struggle for ends which the gods deny to them. It is also clear in *King Oedipus*, where the conflict is between Oedipus' beliefs and the truth as it is presented by Teiresias and the Messenger. In other plays the human beings are involved in human conflicts, but even so the gods take part. Ajax resists them, and we know their will from Athene; the Atridae refuse burial, and the gods' point of view is given by Odysseus; Antigone throughout acts for the gods, and in resisting her Creon resists them and pays for it; Electra fights for the gods even at the cost of much spiritual damage to herself; in *Oedipus at Colonus* both Creon and Polynices oppose the divine will which Oedipus represents and Theseus assists; the whole trouble in the *Philoctetes* is that all the characters in their separate ways oppose the divine plan for the capture of Troy. The conflict in Sophoclean tragedy is mainly between divine and human purposes. It may, and usually does, involve conflicts between human beings, but in the last resort it arises from the differences between gods and men, from men's ignorance of their own state, or refusal to do what the gods demand.

Such a conflict has a peculiar poignancy because men must in the end lose. Since they act in ignorance, they are entitled to com-

---

[1] *Il.* xvii. 32; Hes. *Op.* 218; Aesch. *Ag.* 177; Hdt. i. 207. 1.

passion, understanding, even forgiveness. But we must beware of thinking them noble simply because they resist the gods. The gods are always right and should not be opposed. When Hyllus or Philoctetes denounces the government of the universe, he is deluded by his passions and shows his pathetic ignorance. With Euripides it is different. His gods are of so questionable worth that those who fight against them have a kind of nobility because they resist powers who seem, and may indeed be, malign. There is real dignity when Hippolytus strives against Aphrodite or Creusa against Apollo. These gods are powerful, but their justice is dubious. Sophocles allows no doubts, no criticism of the gods. Sometimes indeed they are hard to understand, but none the less men must assume that all is as it ought to be. If divine ways seem wrong, human ignorance is to blame. In the end the gods will be proved right. The lowest kind of human being is he who is impervious to such enlightenment as the gods give. In their different ways Clytaemnestra, Odysseus in the *Philoctetes*, and Creon in *Oedipus at Colonus* show how certain passions can so harden the heart and delude the mind that generous or decent feelings die. Yet these degraded beings are still human. They are moved by familiar motives of sexual passion, ambition, and public advantage. No Sophoclean character, except perhaps Aegisthus, is so unmixedly evil as Lycus in Euripides' *Heracles*. There is no struggle in Sophocles between good and bad men except in a very limited sense. There is sometimes a struggle between the good and bad in a single man, but most commonly it is between men and the gods or those who represent their will. In this respect Sophocles presents a contrast to Shakespeare, who finds his tragic conflict between men who despite their faults are essentially noble and others who embody an active principle of wickedness. Iago, Lady Macbeth, and Goneril act on motives so devilish and destructive that there is no apology for them. They belong to the evil powers of the world, and it is against them that Othello, Macbeth, and Lear fight and fail. Sophocles' characters cannot be so divided into good and bad. They come from one mould and suffer in different degrees from the same defects.

We might explain this absence of evil characters by saying that Sophocles lacked the Christian sense of sin, or at least the sense of evil which was prominent in the Renaissance. There might be truth in this, but it is hardly relevant. Euripides could create types of unmitigated evil, and we have no right to assume that the Greeks were duller to the potentialities of wickedness than we are.

Sophocles recognized a bad man when he saw one and at times produced such on the stage. But what counted with him was not the division of men into good and bad, which must always be arbitrary, but the differing degrees of illusion which obsess men. His characters might almost be graded in such a scale. At the top are Odysseus in the *Ajax*, Antigone, and Theseus. They are enlightened and wise in that they know the will of the gods or at least accept it as soon as it is shown to them. But all the other characters, except the old Oedipus, are in some way deluded. One delusion may be greater and worse than another. Oedipus' belief in his innocence is plainly less odious than Odysseus' belief in his cleverness. Yet both are false, and both lead to harm. These delusions are manifested in several ways. The kingly temper of Oedipus, the possessive love of Deianira, the obstinate resentment of Philoctetes, are all equally misguided. Such delusions become wrong when their victims are so blinded by them that they cannot or will not see the truth. Then they work a fearful havoc in the human soul, as they do in Clytaemnestra. She is no triumphant murderess, but a creature of passion who is unable to resist her desires or to forgo her gains. She is made of 'frail clay, nay but foul clay', but she is not an incarnate devil. We excuse her as we do not excuse Goneril, though we know that her punishment is right. In fact the evil characters of Sophocles are surely nearer to actual life than those of Shakespeare, whose Iago is almost a symbol of the evil which every man may find in himself. They belong to the same stock as the other characters. What differentiates them is their deafness to what the gods teach.

Since most of Sophocles' characters are built on this plan it is not easy to see what is meant by saying, as is commonly said, that they are 'ideal'. Such an adjective may be deserved by the early Odysseus, by Antigone, by Theseus, and by the old Oedipus. For these act as the gods will. But the word 'ideal' suggests a lack of individuality and life, and is more appropriate to types than to individuals. None of these are types or lack recognizable characteristics. Still less are most of the other characters 'ideal' in any ethical sense. They have great qualities, but these are often marred by faults. The alleged 'ideal' characters of Sophocles may owe something to the idealizing Hellenism of the eighteenth century, but the belief has a more reputable base in his own words, as Aristotle reports them, 'I make men as they should be, Euripides as they are'.[1] Yet this surely means no more than that Sophocles claimed

---

[1] *Poet.* 1460 b 34 αὐτὸς μὲν οἵους δεῖ ποιεῖν, Εὐριπίδην δὲ οἷοι εἰσίν.

to make characters as they should be in a play, while Euripides copied life. This seems to have been what Aristotle understood him to mean. For in the section where he quotes the remark he uses it as an argument that what is not true may none the less be what it ought to be in a play, and postpones till later his discussion whether actions in a play are really good and bad, as if this were a separate consideration. The 'ideal' characters of Sophocles seem to be a mirage. At least they do not exist in his plays.

At the other extreme is the view that so far from creating 'ideal' characters Sophocles did not create characters at all, that his personages do not speak and act in accordance with any principle of personality but simply because such speech and such action are demanded by the plot.[1] Two examples will show how this method works. Ajax, it is claimed, lies when he says that he has made his peace with gods and men. There is no reason for this lying except that the poet wishes to get him away from the Chorus and Tecmessa that he may die alone. Again, when Deianira claims that she will endure Heracles' love for Iole, she is acting dishonestly because the poet wishes to prepare the way for sending the robe. It is clear that if this theory is accepted, it is quite wrong to speak of characterization in Sophocles: for what interested him was plot, and he sacrificed characterization to this. As in many exaggerations, there is perhaps a very small grain of truth in this, though its exponent did not know it. In all great tragic poetry there comes a moment when characters cease to be individuals and become almost types of suffering humanity. In the first onrush of despair one character may speak very much like another. It is conceivable that what Lear says at the height of his tragedy might be said by Macbeth at the height of his; what Heracles says when he knows his doom is not unlike what Tecmessa says when she knows hers.[2] But this is not what the advocate of the theory means. He maintains that there is no real characterization in Sophocles but only actions and statements that are out of situations.

It is perhaps no fatal objection to this view that it was not held by Sophocles himself. He recognized a stage in his own development when he changed his style to 'what is most expressive of character and best'.[3] He evidently believed that he created characters and tried to make them speak in a suitable way. So most of his readers have also believed. Nor can such a belief be

---

[1] T. v. Wilamowitz, *Die dramatische Technik des Sophokles*.
[2] *Trach.* 1143–4; *Aj.* 896.
[3] Plut. *De Prof. in Virt.* 7 ὅπερ ἐστὶν ἠθικώτατον καὶ βέλτιστον.

abandoned without good reason. If the characters can be interpreted as consistent and real, they have a right to be. Nor on
close examination are the so-called inconsistencies of any importance. The alleged deceptions practised by Ajax and Deianira are
illusory. The lack of clarity in Odysseus' plan to get hold of
Philoctetes is not due to a lack of characterization but to his being
characterized in a special way as the clever man who frustrates his
own ends. The appearance of Teiresias in *King Oedipus* certainly
has a wonderful dramatic value, but that does not mean that the
old seer is unintelligible. He is sinister, remote, and forbidding,
but that is what we might expect him to be. The theory assumes
inconsistencies so gross as to make the characters absurd. But what
are called inconsistencies are usually based on a misunderstanding
of the text and afford small basis for so devastating a conclusion.
Secondly, it is possible to imagine a drama in which character
plays a small or negligible part, but Sophoclean drama is not of
this kind. His characters come to their ends because they are what
they are. They almost illustrate Heraclitus' words that 'character
is destiny',[1] though there is more in their destinies than character.
Still, if they were not intelligible as men and women of this or that
kind, their fates would have little significance and the dramatic
scheme would be without interest. It is because Ajax is proud that
he falls, because Philoctetes is fundamentally noble that he is at last
rewarded, because the old Oedipus is superior to other men that
the gods make him a *daimôn*. Their main characteristics are never
out of our minds because we know that these help to determine
their destinies and to explain them. Indeed it is hard to believe
that the Greeks did not have so keen a sense of character as we like
to claim for ourselves. The contemporaries of Herodotus and
Aristophanes would look for human beings in Sophocles, and the
fact that they admired him so much as they did indicates that they
found them.

The world created by Sophocles has its own individuality, as have
all worlds created by great artists. It is impossible to define it, but
we may note some of its outstanding qualities. His personages of
course belong to the great ones of the earth, kings and queens, commanders and rulers. That is natural enough; for most characters
of Greek tragedy come from this class. Euripides may sometimes
break its bounds and introduce his humbly born but noble-hearted
Farmer into the *Electra*, but that is only another example of his
tendency to break the traditional rules. There may well be a real

[1] Fr. 119 ἦθος ἀνθρώπῳ δαίμων.

tragedy of the humble, of men and women whose narrow com-
pass makes their fall or failure seem no less cosmic than the fall
of the great. But this was not what the Greeks practised. They
were concerned with the great in station, with the heroic world
which was the source of their plots and stories. Such persons were
especially likely to be the victims of divine displeasure; their lofty
position made their fall all the greater when it came; they could
have that strength or force of character which belongs to the
mighty and is of peculiar interest to the dramatist. Whatever their
reasons, poets dealt with the great, and so did Sophocles. But his
great have something more than birth or position. They have
a real nobility of character, a natural superiority or *aretê* which
displays itself in word and action. Each of his great princes, Ajax,
Heracles, Oedipus, Philoctetes, is superior to other men in power
to command or ability to endure or simple greatness of heart.
Their superiority comes out in contrast with the qualities of men
less gifted than themselves. Ajax' full stature is revealed when the
Atridae, men of far baser mould, try to denigrate him. The stern
masculinity of Heracles, severe and forbidding though it is, belongs
to a grander order of being than the desperate uncertainty of
Deianira. The kingly pride of Oedipus, ready to face emergencies
and to take every responsibility, is more adventurous than the self-
effacing modesty of Creon. The impressive, passionate Philoctetes
shows his true worth in contrast to the cold-blooded calculating
Odysseus. These heroes are alike in their *aretê*. We can understand why they hold great positions and win respect, why they face
their sufferings with such endurance and their humiliations with
a high sense of their own honour, why they count their reputation
before everything else. They are superior beings, gifted above
other men.

More surprising than Sophocles' men are his women. He certainly understood the conventional ideal of womanhood as it was
held in Periclean Athens. His Tecmessa shows what poetry he
found in the type, and what pathos. But she is hardly a tragic
heroine. His great women are not like her and are more calculated
to shock Athenian opinion than to conform to it. Antigone and
Electra know that they act in the face of respectable opinion and
that they are right to do so. Their resistance demands a heavy
price, but nothing undermines their determination. The superiority
which they display is not a woman's but a man's in its unflinching
purpose and refusal to compromise. But they are driven not by
desire for honour but by affection and loyalty to the dead who have

been injured and to the sacred ties of their families. They break the limits proper to womanhood because the gods require it. The truly tragic heroines, Deianira and Jocasta, also break these limits, but for wrong reasons and to their own great harm. Yet in them too affection is the driving force. Deianira's love for Heracles drives her to her desperate decision to secure him by magic; Jocasta's love for Oedipus makes her shun the truth and then kill herself. The women of Sophocles have this in common, that affection moves them both to good and to ill. Even Clytaemnestra is driven to crime by love for Aegisthus. And the women who fail to be great, the typically modest Chrysothemis and to a lesser extent Ismene, fail because their affections are feeble. In their desire for a quiet life they are prepared to take no risks, even though they know that such are demanded of them by their loved ones.

The climax of Sophoclean tragedy comes when these superior beings pass through a change for better or for worse. When Theophrastus defined tragedy as 'a revolution in heroic fortune',[1] his words are relevant to Sophocles. For these characters are heroic both in the ancient and in the modern sense; they belong to the high company of the epic world, and they have the endurance and noble spirit which we call heroic. Sophocles peopled his tragic world with superior beings, men of great power and character, women of deep and tender affections. When such fall, their fall is great. The men lose power, reputation, honour, respect, happiness, all that they have desired and enjoyed with their strong, tenacious natures; the women lose home, love, contentment, ease, all that has made them happy. In their fall both men and women may be the objects of scorn, misunderstanding, and hatred. The deaths of Ajax, Antigone, Jocasta, and Deianira are all accompanied by one or other of these undeserved wrongs. The wound is the sharper because it is inflicted at the very centre of honour or affection. It is the most noble qualities which are misunderstood, the courage of Ajax, the loyalty of Antigone, the love of Deianira and of Jocasta. The reversal is in more than their fortunes; it is in their lives and what makes life worth living. So, too, in the plays which end happily, the suffering or frustrated characters find the one thing that they most need, the satisfaction of their most hungry instinct. Electra's hatred for her mother turns into a new love for Orestes; the resentful and lonely Philoctetes is restored in honour to the company of living men; the despised and polluted Oedipus is raised to power and glory. The change through which the

---

[1] Diomed. iii. 8. 1 ἡρωϊκῆς τύχης περίστασις.

Sophoclean characters pass is not external or accidental. It concerns their innermost natures, their essential qualities.

The suffering which is part of the tragic destiny usually arises from some element in the souls of those who are destined to it. Most often this is a passion which dominates the character, confounds the judgement, and leads to a disastrous conflict. It makes men assert their will at the expense of truth and overpowers their sense of reality. This passion takes different forms. In Ajax it is an uncompromising sense of his own worth, his pride, his heroic honour; in Deianira a desperate confidence that she can, despite all propriety and likelihood, keep her husband to herself; in Oedipus a kingly pride and high spirit which prevents him from seeing the truth; in Philoctetes a strength both in love and in hate which blinds him to his glorious destiny. In each the passion is strongly self-assertive and makes its possessor feel that he is right and that almost everyone else is wrong. It produces a special delusion which contains the beginnings of ruin. Passions like these are the portion of great characters. Plato regards the self-assertive element as fundamental to human nature and thinks that it normally works for good. Sophocles created characters in whom it may normally work for good but at times works for ill. The qualities which have raised Ajax and Heracles and Oedipus to glory are the cause of their undoing. Nor can we really say that their mistakes come from a perversion or misuse of their great qualities. The quality which makes Ajax a great soldier makes him incur the anger of the gods by his self-confidence; the passionate intensity which carries Heracles through his life of labours informs his love for Iole and drives him to the destruction of Oechalia; the temper of Oedipus has made him king of Thebes, but prevents him from seeing the truth and makes him feel his humiliation all the more when at last he knows it. In this respect the heroes of Sophocles differ from Shakespeare's. Hamlet, Lear, Othello, and Macbeth fall because of some fault in an otherwise noble nature, a fault which grows until it dominates their characters and encompasses their ruin. This fault is a real flaw, at variance with their true selves. The great men of Sophocles fall because they are what they are, because their great gifts may in the wrong circumstances be turned against them, because the gods choose to humble them by the same means which once exalted them. Even when all is well in the end, the same process is at work and great qualities create great dangers. Electra's love for her father almost ruins her nature with hate for his murderers; the generous emotional Philoctetes nearly

wrecks himself by following his emotions too far. In this there is
a kind of justice which is lacking in Shakespeare. If Shakespeare
creates tragedy out of human weakness, out of small faults which
spread and work havoc, Sophocles creates his out of human
strength. The qualities which exalt a man above his fellows are
those which sooner or later bring him into conflict with them and
with the gods. At the worst pride may turn into madness as it
does with Ajax, but even if it does not, the danger is always present
and the gods may send suffering to its actual or potential victim.
In Shakespeare the tragic scheme is different. The theological
background is absent. He is concerned with the fall of the great,
and attributes it to some weakness in them on which powers of
evil play until they work destruction.

Since the conflict is with the gods, it is natural that men should
be humiliated by violent and unconquerable forces. These need
not be supernatural, though the madness of Ajax, the shirt of
Nessus, the *daimôn* who guides Oedipus, are. But it happens that
Sophocles sometimes depicts kinds of suffering from which modern
sensibility shrinks. The great Heracles, racked and rotted by the
Hydra's poison, Oedipus with his bleeding and blinded eyes,
Philoctetes with his festering and stinking foot, are gruesome and
almost unbearable. Nor did the ancients feel differently about
them. At least Aristotle thought that horrors were more properly
narrated than acted,[1] and Horace followed him.[2] Neither Aeschylus nor Euripides presents such physical horrors on the stage. Nor
is it an accident that Sophocles' surviving plays have such. They
could have been found in plays now lost, in the hideous catastrophes of the *Tereus* or the destruction of children on the stage in
the *Niobe*.[3] The element of physical horror was used by Sophocles
to secure tragic effect. We can only guess why. It is possible that
he was moved by his great sense of the difference between gods and
men. The gods are immortal and ageless, free from suffering and
disease, as Pindar says:

> For they are without eld and sickness,
> Without knowledge of sorrow, and have escaped
> The loud cries of Acheron's flood.[4]

But men are easily assailed through their bodies. In these lies
their strength, and when they are destroyed through them, it is

---

[1] *Poet.* 1453 b 7.   [2] *Ars Poet.* 185–7.   [3] Plut. *Amat.* 17.

[4] Fr. 131   κεῖνοι γάρ τ' ἄνοσοι καὶ ἀγήραοι
πόνων τ' ἄπειροι, βαρυβόαν
πορθμὸν πεφευγότες 'Αχέροντος.

a sign that their strength is gone. When Ajax kills himself with the sword that slew the cattle, when Heracles perishes through the Hydra's poison, they show that the very source of their power is the means of their destruction. When Oedipus, the great king, appears blind with blood on his face or Philoctetes is flung into senseless delirium, we see how helpless even these strong men are. It is another sign of their inferiority to the gods.

The collapse or destruction of physical strength is often accompanied by a spiritual state of great tragic import. The sufferer finds himself isolated from his kind. He may have his devoted friends and adherents, as Ajax has Tecmessa and his sailors, Electra the Chorus, the old Oedipus his daughters. But somehow these confidants stand at a distance and do not quite enter into the lives of those whom they attend. Heracles, Antigone, Electra, Philoctetes live by themselves, almost for themselves, and this isolation is all the greater when the crisis comes. At the end Heracles has no one but Hyllus; Antigone bewails her utter desolation; Philoctetes makes his last decision in solitude. Even Ajax goes out alone to die, and Electra's darkest hour is when she believes that her brother is dead and decides to exact vengeance without him. This isolation is right. These great personalities are not made for easy companionship. They demand too much, their standards are too high, for them to enter into the compromises of ordinary life. Even the old Oedipus has a forbidding majesty which keeps him apart and instils awe and fear into the men of Colonus. Such·beings are alone because they are unlike others, because they are superior. When they act in defiance of ordinary rules, their isolation is accentuated still more when disaster comes. Even after death Ajax is severed from the other dead when burial is denied to him; in her rocky prison Antigone belongs neither to the living nor to the dead; when Deianira goes round her house for the last time, she feels that she is no longer a wife or a mother; Oedipus blinds himself that he may be severed from all human contacts; Philoctetes accepts the gibe of Odysseus that he must walk Lemnos alone. But after the tragic crisis and the isolation which it brings, the sufferers are restored to a kind of communion with their kind. Ajax is buried, and his spirit joins the company of honoured dead; Antigone kills herself and finds her brother in Hades; Deianira is forgiven by her son; Oedipus accepts his destiny and assists it; Philoctetes finds a new friend in Neoptolemus and then makes his peace with the Achaeans. The tragic conflict forces its victims out of the framework of organized harmonious life, but once the crisis is over, and the price has been paid, the sufferers return to some kind of order, even of union with their kind whether living or dead.

Sophoclean tragedy turns on a conflict between gods and men. For this conflict the gods have a reason. They wish to teach a lesson, to make men learn their mortal limitations and accept them. It is the lesson which Pindar draws from the story of Asclepius:

> We must ask from the Gods things suited to hearts that shall die,
> Knowing the path we are in, the nature of our doom.[1]

This is what Sophocles' characters learn, but it is applied on a much wider scale than in Pindar's instance. When Asclepius revived a man from the dead, he broke the gods' laws and had to pay for it. His punishment is deserved. But with the exception of Creon hardly one of Sophocles' characters is in a position to avert his doom. They are so blinded by their illusions, so much the victims of their own natures and passions, that they have little freedom of choice. The sudden rush of confidence in Deianira, the growing obstinacy of Philoctetes, are beyond rational control. In Heracles and in Oedipus the doom which the gods have ordained allows no escape. No matter what they do, they will be forced to learn their lesson. Human suffering may come through men themselves, but the primal cause of it lies with the gods. Sophocles was for most purposes anticipated by Theognis,[2] who tells Cyrnus that no man is responsible for his own weal or woe or knows what will happen: all mortal calculations are useless, for the gods carry out everything according to their own designs. Such a theology covers cases so different as Deianira and Philoctetes, Electra and the old Oedipus. It recognizes the ignorance in which men live and the power of the gods to do what they will with them.

When the gods treat men in this way, it is natural to ask if they are just. The same question occurred to Euripides, who more than once puts Apollo in the wrong and makes even real powers like Aphrodite and Dionysus destructive and heartless. There is undeniably a kind of tragedy in which man fights a futile battle against merciless superhuman powers who seek his destruction. It has its own grandeur and is the only kind of tragedy possible in an age which has ceased to believe that the gods are beneficent or rational. But such tragedies were not written by Sophocles.

[1] *Pyth.* iii. 59–60   χρὴ τὰ ἐοικότα πὰρ Δαιμόνων μα-
στευέμεν θναταῖς φρασίν
γνόντα τὸ πὰρ ποδός, οἵας εἰμὲν αἴσας.

[2] 133–42.

Philoctetes and Hyllus may cry out against divine injustice, Jocasta ascribe everything to chance, but their decisions are not final and are reversed by facts. Sophocles accepts the ultimate justice and wisdom of the gods. He would agree with Theognis that they act according to their own plans, and he would add that these plans are just. He does not always make their reasons clear, but he assumes that they have reasons, and he hints that once the divine will has been done men are better for it. This theological background does not make the plays less tragic. The sufferings may be by human standards undeserved, but they still arouse pity and fear. The gods are always right, but their victims are entitled to compassion and understanding.[1]

Sophocles might well have stopped at the assumption that whatever the gods do is right and have made no further attempt to explain their ways. But in each case he suggests or gives an explanation for what they do. It is hard to reduce these explanations to a single belief, and perhaps it is foolish to attempt it. For Sophocles may have changed his ideas with the years. But we may in fact recognize three stages in his theology which are not absolutely different but certainly distinguishable. In the first stage, in the *Ajax* and *Antigone*, the scheme is simple and almost traditional. Ajax is punished for pride to Athene; Creon is the victim of a pride which breeds destructive infatuation. The notions are familiar from Aeschylus and need no comment. But this scheme which works well with the guilty does not suit cases where guilt is less clear and the apparently innocent or unconsciously guilty suffer. In the *Women of Trachis* and *King Oedipus* the gods act as they do simply to teach a lesson. It is salutary but not a punishment; it is even in its dark way a benefit. In the third stage, in the plays which end 'happily', the gods are with some care shown to be just. In the *Electra* they further the punishment of the wicked; in the *Philoctetes* a much injured man is raised to health and honour; in *Oedipus at Colonus* the gods make amends to one who has suffered greatly at their hands. There is certainly a difference between the confident trust of the last plays and the dark hints of the middle plays. In the last three the ways of the gods are presented in a way that satisfies the human conscience. Their participation in men's lives is shown to be governed by such rules as men set up for themselves; they display right and justice in the human sense of the

---

[1] In fr. 107 from the *Aletes* Sophocles makes some character denounce the justice of the gods in a way that recalls Euripides fr. 293, but nothing is known of the context, and there is no need to assume that the lines represent Sophocles' own opinion.

words. At the end of his life Sophocles seems to have wished to demonstrate the justice no less than the power of the gods.

This apparent divergence of outlook may possibly indicate a real development in Sophocles' opinions. He may have passed from an Aeschylean theology to something less definite and from that to a position in which he vindicated the justice of the gods by human standards. But in the absence of so much of his work and in the uncertain state of his chronology it is dangerous to trust such a conclusion. For the different views displayed in his trage-dies could after all be held by the same man without any gross inconsistency. In all three stages we might discern a general-view that the gods are ultimately just both in punishment and in reward but that sometimes their reasons are not easy to discern. In fact all three positions seem to have been held by Herodotus. His Cambyses and Xerxes are examples of the presumption which the gods punish through its own infatuation; his Croesus is a good king who is humbled to learn modesty; his Cyrus is a noble but unknown man who is raised to great glory in accordance with a divine plan revealed in dreams. Greek theology had no single theory to account for the changes and chances of mortal life, and explained diverse events in diverse ways. It was possible for Sophocles, as it was for Herodotus, to use now this explanation, now that. Yet though his different views may be harmonized, we must still feel that in the last three plays Sophocles makes the power of the gods less external and more intimate than in the first four. In *Ajax* and *Antigone* the gods interfere almost from without by direct action. Ajax is driven mad by Athene; Creon is forced to repent by the evil omens and unburned sacrifices. In the *Women of Trachis* and *King Oedipus* oracles are fulfilled because they must be, but their fulfilment does not follow any plan of good in con-flict with evil. The fight against them is not really wrong so long as it is ignorant. But in the last plays the gods are emphatically on the side of right against wrong. They further the just punish-ment of Clytaemnestra and Aegisthus, refuse to allow their plan for the capture of Troy to succeed through the unprincipled methods of Odysseus, and sustain Oedipus in his battle against dark powers of political opportunism and filial neglect. Sophocles may not have changed the main structure of his beliefs, but he seems to have deepened their meaning, to have come to see more clearly how closely the power of the gods was interwoven with human life.

In this respect Sophocles was a true successor of Aeschylus, whose trilogies were equally concerned with the relations of gods and men. It is true that Aeschylus used themes like that of an hereditary doom, which Sophocles avoided, and that he is more obviously didactic. But there is a greater difference between him and Sophocles than this, a difference in the kind of solution found to the tragic conflict. For Sophocles, as we have seen, the end is a resigned, reverent state of mind in the characters and through them in the audience. In Aeschylus the solution is more varied and more complex. In the *Oresteia* the dark issue of matricidal vengeance is solved by a new order of law and civic morality; the institution of the Areopagus embodies the conclusion that Orestes has acted rightly and been rightly acquitted, since murder must be punished. Aeschylus sees the question as one less for the private conscience than for society. In the trilogy which ends with the *Seven against Thebes* the hereditary doom which began with the impiety of Laius ends with the mutual slaughter of his two grandsons. In this there is certainly a warning against the far-reaching results of impiety, but the warning does not save Eteocles or Polynices. It concerns only the audience. And the curse, which they are forced to notice, belongs not to an individual but to a whole family for three generations. From this all too scanty evidence it is at least clear that Aeschylus followed different plans in his trilogies and did not make their conclusions conform to a single pattern. It is also probable that the ends which he found concerned the State and society more than individuals. What interested him in a tragic conflict was its effect on the world, not on a single soul. With this wide vision he could find conclusions which differed as much in temper as in content. If the *Oresteia* closes on a note of confident patriotic joy, the *Seven against Thebes* closes with a display of unfaltering doom. Sophocles works differently. His plays show what misfortune or good fortune do for the single soul and especially the modesty and acceptance which it learns. It looks as if Sophocles invented his own kind of tragedy and made it different from that of Aeschylus.

It is no less different from that of Euripides, in whose truly tragic plays there is often a note not of resignation but of disquiet, even of revolt. The gods' will is done and must be accepted, but with a sense that it is wrong. Such is certainly the feeling aroused by the *Trojan Women*, even to some extent by the *Hippolytus*. In the *Bacchants* Dionysus has much right on his side, but he seems to assert himself too savagely, and his final speech is neither satisfying nor comforting. In other plays a mood of acceptance is indicated, but it comes because of some divine intervention which overrules what has happened. The peace which concludes the *Electra* or the *Ion* comes almost in defiance of what has been done in the play. In the *Heracles* the conclusion is due to the nobility of man and comes in spite of the destructive gods. Euripides found no such formula as Sophocles found, even when he dramatized without irony or scepticism the power of gods over men. He may well have accepted this power as a fact and made his characters accept it, but this acceptance brings no peace of mind, no relief or satisfaction after torments of the soul, no comfort in modesty and reverence. Euripides is nearer to the modern world than Sophocles because his characters move us simply by the horror of their fates and because this horror serves no end but to inspire pity for them. That is perhaps why Aristotle's judgement that Euripides is 'the most tragic of the poets'[1] has been endorsed by so many. There is a finality about his disasters which contains no consolation and seems almost to be symbolical of the tragic condition of human life. Such things happen, as we all know, and it may be useless to inquire too much about them, or to expect to see them as parts in a harmonious whole. But such is not Sophocles' way. He is not content merely to portray evil, whether crime or waste or failure. He must relate it to what he believes to be the scheme of things and show that it comes from men's resistance to the gods.

For Sophocles the tragic issue arises in some breach in the divine order of the world. No matter how the play ends, the conflict which it shows comes because someone has gone too far and upset the ordered harmony of life. In the *Ajax* and *Antigone* Ajax and Creon transgress the Mean, are driven to brutal acts, and create destruction in themselves and in others. In the *Women of Trachis* Deianira's immodest decision to win back Heracles by magic leads to her own and to his doom, and, more subtly, Heracles' own past violence falls on his own head. In *King Oedipus* the great man's violation of the divine laws is no less a breach of harmony than the more conscious sins of Ajax and Creon. It brings disaster first to Thebes, then to himself. In the later plays, where all ends well, the tragic situation is caused by similar breaches of the divine order. The crime of Clytaemnestra and Aegisthus creates a situation so evil that is can be cured only by bloodshed; the original injustice done to Philoctetes is responsible for the collapse of the attempt to bring him to Troy; the earlier history of Oedipus, his pollution and his expulsion from Thebes, create a situation in which he curses his sons and shows all his terrible ferocity. In Sophocles

[1] *Poet.* 1453 a 30.

the tragic situation is always some breach in the order of things, a violent discord which promotes angry passions and clouds the judgement. It does not matter whether it is made deliberately or not. The evil caused by the innocent Oedipus is little less than that caused by Clytaemnestra. What matters is that disorder is created. The essence of the tragic situation as Sophocles saw it may be symbolized in some words of his own, though no doubt they dealt with some specific and quite different situation:

> Not order but disorder, luckless one,
> It seems to be, and madness in your heart.[1]

Some act of man destroys an existing order and substitutes disorder and madness for it. In different shapes this is the fundamental pattern of all Sophocles' surviving plays.

The tragic situation leads to a crisis which is usually violent. Then a conclusion comes either in destruction and loss or in some positive gain. In the later plays Sophocles happens to stress the gain, though there is no warrant for assuming that in old age he shrank from truly tragic catastrophes. In such cases we may well speak of reconciliation. The characters who have been at war with others or with circumstances or with themselves find peace and a new hope. Such a reconciliation is also to be felt at the end of the *Ajax*. Ajax has been at war with the gods and with men, but he has made his peace, and his burial shows that all is well. In the *Antigone* the reconciliation is sterner but hardly less satisfying. The amends which Creon pays for his work of destruction is right. He deserves what he gets; justice is done and right vindicated. His humiliation is a necessary preliminary to the re-establishment of justice in the world. In the *Women of Trachis* and in *King Oedipus* we may perhaps feel that, when all is said, there is still an unresolved discord, that such sufferings are heavier than they should be and that their cruelty is unexplained. Yet even here grave breaches are made in the divine order, and at the end they are healed. Heracles accepts his doom with heroic resignation; Oedipus takes upon himself the task of making amends. Both have broken the bounds set to men, and both end by subjecting themselves to the gods in consciousness of their own utter weakness. In each play the conflict is resolved in reconciliation. The disorder created by some untoward or violent act is ended, and harmony is restored.

---

[1] Fr. 846   οὐ κόσμος, οὔκ, ὦ τλῆμον, ἀλλ' ἀκοσμία
      φαίνοιτ' ἂν εἶναι σῶν τε μαργότης φρενῶν.

INDEX

Achmes, 225.
Adultery, 239.
Aegisthus, 253 ff.
Aelian, 177, 223.
Aeschylus, 10, 11, 64, 75, 87, 102, 106,
  133, 162, 163, 182, 212, 213, 215, 221,
  222, 224, 228, 231, 233, 236, 237, 252,
  256, 257, 259, 261, 295, 310, 313, 324.
αἰδώς, 280.
Ajax, construction of, 18 ff.; problem
  treated, and its sources, 16 ff.; the
  tragic issue, 27; second part, 50 ff.
Ajax, in epic, 17, in Pindar, 17–18; his
  character, 20 ff.; cause of fall, 26; his
  anger and pride, 28; his madness, 31;
  suicide, 44 ff.; his alleged treachery, 48.
Alcmaeon of Croton, 201.
Ambition, 272.
Anger, as dramatic motive, 28, 54, 76,
  192.
Antigone, date, 63; subject, 64; moral, 66;
  contrast of chief characters, 68; element
  of irony, 114.
Antigone, in *Antigone*, Ch. III *passim*.
  in *Oedipus at Colonus*, 322 ff., 330, 346 ff.
Antiphon, 219, 221, 222, 227.
Archers, 53, 54.
Aristarchus, 212.
'Aristocratic thought', 3.
Aristophanes, 357, 358.
Aristotle, 6, 26, 69, 95, 99, 135, 148, 166,
  172, 188, 232, 234, 255, 261, 270, 278,
  279, 302, 353, 360, 361.
Artemidorus, 225.
Athene, 27, 29, 33, 34, 35.
Athens, 338, 339, 347.

Bacchylides, 117, 146, 148.
Blood-offerings, 313.
Brothers and sisters, 94 ff.
Burial, duty of, 48, 64, 65, 70, 92, 255.

Casuistical element in Greek tragedy, 8.
Childhood, 119 ff.
Chorus, in *Ajax*, 20 ff.
  in *Antigone*, 84 ff.
  in *Electra*, 215, 226, 257.
  in *King Oedipus*, 165, 179, 180, 199, 200.
  in *Oedipus at Colonus*, 344, 347 ff., 349 ff.
  in *Philoctetes*, 273, 280.
  in *Women of Trachis*, 84 ff.
Chrysothemis, 244, 245.
Cleverness, excess of, 269, 288.
Clytaemnestra, 212 ff., 218 ff., 223 ff.,
  231 ff., 250 ff.
Colonus, 308.
Concubines, position of, 22, 127.
Courage, 79.
Cremation, 37.

Creon, in *Antigone*, Ch. III *passim*.
  in *King Oedipus*, 165, 180, 184, 185, 188,
    190, 192, 194, 195.
  in *Oedipus at Colonus*, 311, 319, 321, 322,
    326, 335 ff.
Curse, hereditary, 87 ff., 163.
Curses, 173 ff., 325 ff.

Daimon, 179 ff.
Death, 155 ff., 344, 345.
Deianira, Ch. III *passim*.
Democritus, 191, 198, 210.
Demosthenes, 68, 259.
Deus ex machina, 11, 262, 300, 301.
Diagoras of Melos, 295.
Dio Chrysostom, 214, 262, 284, 357.
Diogenes of Apollonia, 42.
'Discovery' in Tragedy, 362 ff.
Dreams, 223 ff.

Empedocles, 100.
Enemies, treatment of, 41.
Electra, other versions of story, 212 ff.;
  modern views, 215 ff.; the main problem, 219 ff.; moral and religious aspects,
  223 ff.; part of Electra, 241 ff.; contrast
  with Orestes, 247 ff.; conclusion, 256.
Electra, Ch. VI *passim*.
Envy, 26.
Error, tragic, 166 ff.
Euripides, 7, 10, 35, 71, 73, 91, 101, 108,
  127, 130, 162, 175, 184, 194, 208, 212,
  213, 214, 215, 220, 255, 257, 259, 261,
  268, 269, 272, 284, 285, 287, 288, 295,
  308, 310, 313, 332, 336, 339, 344, 347.

Fate, 305.
Friendship, 25.
Furies (Erinyes), 230, 237, 259, 318, 329.

Generals, Athenian conception of, 20, 21.
Gods, are not deceived, 337.
  are just, 349.
  cannot be evil, 285.
  decisions irrevocable, 168.
  embodiments of power, 35, 136.
  friendship with men, 301.
  gifts must not be refused, 292.
  humble the great, 154.
  look after their children, 157.
  punish the guilty, 113.
  punish the proud, 30 ff.
  purposes unknowable, 72.
Gorgias, 99.

Haemon, 102 ff.
Hegel, G. W. F., 65–6.
Heracles, in *Philoctetes*, 300 ff.
  in *Women of Trachis*, Ch. IV *passim*.

Heraclitus, 97, 194, 203, 209, 345, 355.
Hero, powers of, 315, 316, 319 ff., 329, 337, 338, 340, 341.
Herodotus, 93, 153, 158, 173, 175, 182, 186, 188, 216, 220, 224, 266, 270, 319, 323, 335.
Heroization, 309.
Hesiod, 171, 321.
Hippocrates, 240, 284.
Homer, 19, 20, 64, 106, 135, 169, 191, 193, 218, 255, 256, 292, 354.
Homicide, 174.
Honour, respect for, 26.
Hope, Greek view of, 128 ff., 199.
Hyllus, 140 ff.

Incest, 169 ff.
Innocent, suffering of, 113, 321.
International justice, 339, 340.
Ion of Chios, 358.
Irony, 73, 114, 254.
Ismene, in *Antigone*, 79 ff.
 in *Oedipus at Colonus*, 318, 323, 324, 325, 326, 338, 345.
Isocrates, 320, 332, 339.

Jocasta, 163, 167, 168, 178, 179, 188, 191 ff., 195, 196, 197, 199, 202, 204 ff., 209.

King Oedipus, popularity of theme, 162; various explanations, 163 ff.; activity of gods, 167 ff.; Oedipus' pollution, 169 ff.; his fall, 175 ff.; his blinding, 177 ff.; his character, 186 ff.; the tragic conflict, 199.
Kingship, 78, 186, 188, 193.

Laws, nature of, 79, 83, 85, 97, 229.
Laws, Unwritten, 98 ff., 169, 327.
Love, Greek views of, 134 ff., 155.
Love-charms, 127 ff.
Luck, 197, 207.
Lysias, 181, 184, 320.

Magic, 127, 147, 148.
Marriage, 191, 234.
Matricide, 219 ff.
Mean, the, 166.
Menander, 180, 229.
Military discipline, 297, 298.

Neoptolemus, Ch. VII *passim*.
Niobe, 243.

Odysseus in *Ajax*, 26, 36, 37, 57 ff.
 in *Philoctetes*, 262, 264, 265, 266 ff., 276, 282, 283 ff., 290, 291, 292, 294, 297, 299, 300.
Oedipus, in *King Oedipus*, Ch. V *passim*; in *Oedipus at Colonus*, Ch. VIII *passim*.
Oedipus at Colonus, date, 307; construction, 309 ff.; subject, 312 ff.; Oedipus as hero,
315 ff.; his passing, 340 ff.; praise of Athens, 347; alleged pessimism, 350.
Old Age, 350 ff.
Oracles, 149 ff., 167, 197, 206, 214, 264, 281, 312.
Orestes, 212 ff., 219 ff., 226 ff., 230 ff., 233, 234, 239, 240, 245 ff., 257 ff.

Parents and children, 74, 220 ff., 232, 234, 328.
Parmenides, 201, 202.
Patriotism, 68.
Pericles, 63, 68, 85, 97, 100, 129, 137.
Philoctetes, date, 261; essential elements in tradition, 261; importance of oracles, 265 ff.; Odysseus' plan, 267; part of Neoptolemus, 271 ff.; his failure, 275 ff.; nature of conflict, 284; solution, 300.
Phrynichus, 358.
Pindar, 5, 17, 18, 131, 136, 137, 157, 162, 181, 186, 188, 189, 201, 214, 236, 237, 238, 239, 262, 269, 279, 285, 303, 315, 321, 335.
Plato, 76, 99, 128, 169, 180, 192, 219, 220, 221, 229, 270, 285, 295, 328, 329.
Pollution, 170 ff.
Polynices, in *Antigone*, 64.
 in *Oedipus at Colonus*, 324 ff.
Pride, 28, 31, 71.
Protagoras, 84 ff.
Public opinion, 102.
Purification, 317, 318.

Racine, 13.
'Reversal' in tragedy, 362 ff.

Scapegoat, 183.
Shakespeare, 6, 7, 8, 13, 27, 358 ff.
Socrates, 186, 297, 328.
Solon, 106, 175, 328.
Sparta, 52.
State, Athenian conceptions of, 58 ff., 336.
Stesichorus, 214, 257.
Stoning, 49, 76.
Suicide, 46.
Suppliants, 330, 332, 339.

Tecmessa, 21 ff.
Teiresias, in *Antigone*, 105 ff.
 in *King Oedipus*, 165, 190, 194, 195, 202 ff.
Temper (θυμός), 192.
Teucer, 25, 43, 49, 50 ff.
Themistocles, 49, 50.
Theognis, 200, 265, 278, 295, 312, 320.
Theseus, 311, 312, 313, 316, 317, 321, 322, 327, 330, 331 ff., 338 ff., 341, 346, 349.
Thucydides, 63, 171, 272, 286, 336.
'Too late', dramatic device of, 102 ff.
Treachery, 48, 49, 64.

Tyranny, 75, 97.

Tyrants, character of, 72, 74, 77, 165.

Untruthfulness, 268 ff.

Vengeance, duty of, 219 ff.

War, 277.

'Warner', dramatic device of, 106 ff.

Wheel of things, 154 ff., 334 ff.

Women, Athenian view of, 21, 22, 23, 24, 323.

Women of Trachis, nature of conflict, 117 ff.; character of Deianira, 118 ff.; her fatal decision, 125; her death, 129; character of Heracles, 131 ff.; Hyllus 144; oracles, 149 ff.

PRINTED IN GREAT BRITAIN AT THE UNIVERSITY PRESS, OXFORD
BY VIVIAN RIDLER, PRINTER TO THE UNIVERSITY

324